MATH NATION - How It Works

Welcome to Math Nation! Our goal is to help you and all other students across Michigan master Geometry. Geometry is essential for success in future math and science courses, on standardized tests, and in your future career (whatever it may be)!

WHAT IS MATH NATION?

1. **Videos and Workbook**: Choose your Study Expert and watch them break down each topic as you follow along and mark up this workbook.
2. **Digital Practice:** Check your mastery of each topic online with the "Check Your Understanding" practice tool, and test your knowledge at the end of each section with the "Test Yourself!" practice tool.
3. **Geometry Wall**: Have questions? Want to chat about math with other students across Michigan in a safe, moderated, online environment? Go to the statewide Geometry Wall, where you can ask questions and receive help from other students, teachers, and our Study Experts. Study Experts will award Karma Points for helping other students. Top Karma Points earners will win prizes. Go to the Geometry Wall to learn more!
4. **Teacher Area**: Teachers can view data for their classes in the Teacher Area, access extra resources, and collaborate with colleagues through the Teacher Wall.
5. **On-Ramp Review Tool:** Assess your understanding of pre-algebra using the On-Ramp to Algebra 1 review.

Jump on Math Nation (by going to MathNation.com or downloading the free Math Nation app from your phone or tablet's app store) and get started!

Ideas, questions, comments, or suggestions?
Just email help@MathNation.com or call 1-888-608-MATH. We would love to hear from you!

TABLE OF CONTENTS

Full Instructional Coverage of Honors Standards Available at www.MathNation.com

Section 1: Introduction to Geometry - Points, Lines, and Planes

Topic 1: Basics of Geometry – Part 1 3
Standards Covered: G-CO.1
- ☐ I can define and represent points, lines, line segments, planes, rays, and angles.

Topic 2: Basics of Geometry – Part 2 5
Standards Covered: G-CO.1
- ☐ I can define and represent points, lines, line segments, planes, rays, and angles.

Topic 3: Introduction to Proofs 7
Standards Covered: This topic covers introductory material
- ☐ I can write and solve two-column proofs, flow proofs, and paragraph proofs.

Topic 4: Midpoint and Distance in the Coordinate Plane – Part 1 11
Standards Covered: G-GPE.6
- ☐ I can find midpoint coordinates, endpoint coordinates, or the length of segments.

Topic 5: Midpoint and Distance in the Coordinate Plane – Part 2 15
Standards Covered: G-GPE.7
- ☐ I can find the length of a segment or distance on a coordinate plane in real-world context.

Topic 6: Partitioning a Line Segment – Part 1 17
Standards Covered: G-GPE.6
- ☐ I can find a point of a line segment between two points that partitions the segment into a given ratio.

Topic 7: Partitioning a Line Segment – Part 2 19
Standards Covered: G-GPE.6
- ☐ I can find a point of a line segment between two points that partitions the segment into a given ratio.

Topic 8: Parallel and Perpendicular Lines – Part 1 21
Standards Covered: G-GPE.5
- ☐ I can identify parallel and perpendicular lines.
- ☐ I can write equations of lines parallel or perpendicular to another line.

Topic 9: Parallel and Perpendicular Lines – Part 2 23
Standards Covered: G-GPE.5
- ☐ I can identify parallel and perpendicular lines.
- ☐ I can write equations of lines parallel or perpendicular to another line.

Topic 10: Introduction to Coordinate Geometry 25
Standards Covered: G-GPE.4, G-GPE.7
- ☐ I can find perimeter, slope, and area of polygons on the coordinate plane using the distance formula, slope formula, and midpoint formula.

Topic 11: Basic Constructions – Part 1 27
Standards Covered: G-CO.12
- ☐ I can use a compass and a straightedge to construct congruent line segments.

Visit MathNation.com or search "Math Nation" in your phone or tablet's app store to watch the videos that go along with this workbook!

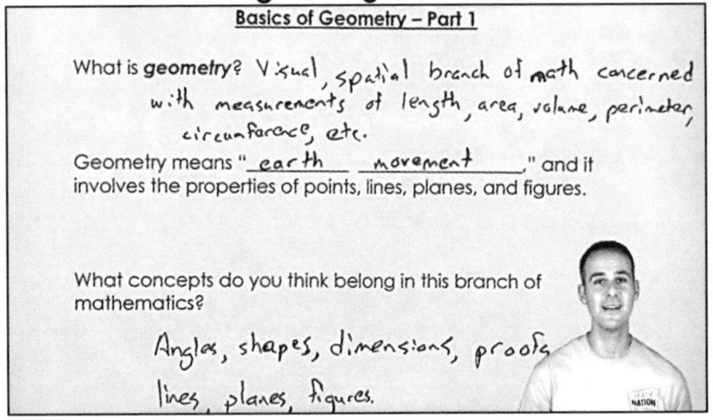
Basics of Geometry – Part 1
What is geometry? Visual, spatial branch of math concerned with measurements of length, area, volume, perimeter, circumference, etc.
Geometry means "earth movement," and it involves the properties of points, lines, planes, and figures.
What concepts do you think belong in this branch of mathematics?
Angles, shapes, dimensions, proofs
lines, planes, figures.

The following Michigan Mathematics Standards will be covered in this section:
G-CO.1 - Know precise definitions of angle, circle, perpendicular line, parallel line, and line segment, based on the undefined notions of point, line, distance along a line, and distance around a circular arc.
G-CO.9 - Prove theorems about lines and angles; use theorems about lines and angles to solve problems. *Theorems include: vertical angles are congruent; when a transversal crosses parallel lines, alternate interior angles are congruent and corresponding angles are congruent; points on a perpendicular bisector of a line segment are exactly those equidistant from the segment's endpoints.*
G-CO.12 - Make formal geometric constructions with a variety of tools and methods. *Copying a segment; copying an angle; bisecting a segment; bisecting an angle; constructing perpendicular lines, including the perpendicular bisector of a line segment; and constructing a line parallel to a given line through a point not on the line.*
G-GPE.4 - Use coordinates to prove simple geometric theorems algebraically.
G-GPE.5 - Prove the slope criteria for parallel and perpendicular lines and use them to solve geometric problems.
G-GPE.6 - Find the point on a directed line segment between two given points that partitions the segment in a given ratio.
G-GPE.7 - Use coordinates to compute the perimeter of polygons and areas of triangles and rectangles.

Section 1: Introduction to Geometry
Section 1 – Topic 1
Basics of Geometry – Part 1

What is ***geometry***?

Geometry means "__________ _________________," and it involves the properties of points, lines, planes and figures.

What concepts do you think belong in this branch of mathematics?

Why does geometry matter? When is geometry used in the real world?

Points, lines, and planes are the building blocks of geometry.

Draw a representation for each of the following and fill in the appropriate notation on the chart below.

Description	Representation	Notation
A ***point*** is a precise location or place on a plane. It is usually represented by a dot.		
A ***line*** is a straight path that continues in both directions forever. Lines are one-dimensional.		
A ***plane*** is a flat, two-dimensional object. It has no thickness and extends forever.		
A ***line segment*** is a portion of a line located between two points.		
A ***ray*** is a piece of a line that starts at one point and extends infinitely in one direction.		

Definition	Representation	Notation
An ***angle*** is formed by two rays with the same endpoint.		
The point where the rays meet is called the ***vertex***.		
Parallel lines are two lines on the same plane that do not intersect.		
Perpendicular lines are two intersecting lines that form a 90° angle.		

What can you say about multiple points on a line segment?

TAKE NOTE! *Postulates & Theorems*

Segment Addition Postulate

If three points, A, B, and C, are collinear and B is between A and C, then $AB + BC = AC$.

Let's Practice!

1. Consider the diagram below with parallel planes $\mathcal{P}$ and $\mathcal{M}$.

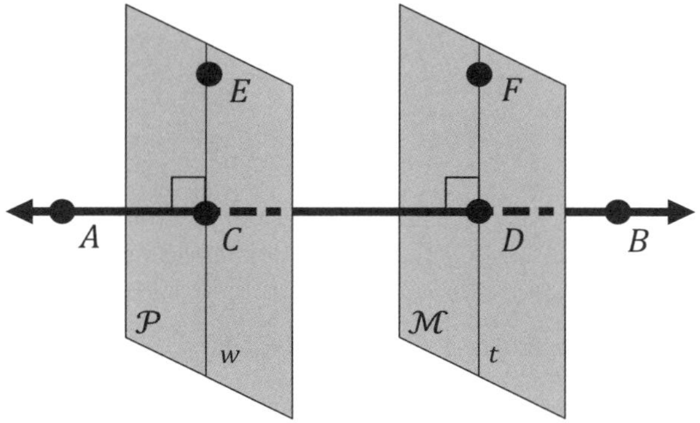

a. Give at most 3 names that represents the figure in the diagram above.

Figure	Name(s) denoted in diagram
Point	
Line	
Line Segment	
Plane	
Ray	
Angle	
Parallel Lines	
Perpendicular Lines	
Segment Addition Postulate	

b. Point C lies between points A and D. If $AC = 7$ inches and $CD = 13$ inches, what is the measure of $\overline{AD}$?

2. Point D lies between points P and Q. $PD = 3x + 6$. $DQ = 2x + 4$. $PQ = 30$. What is the measure of $\overline{PD}$?

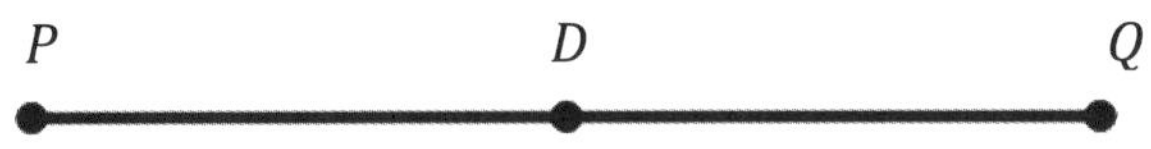

Try It!

3. Consider the diagram below.

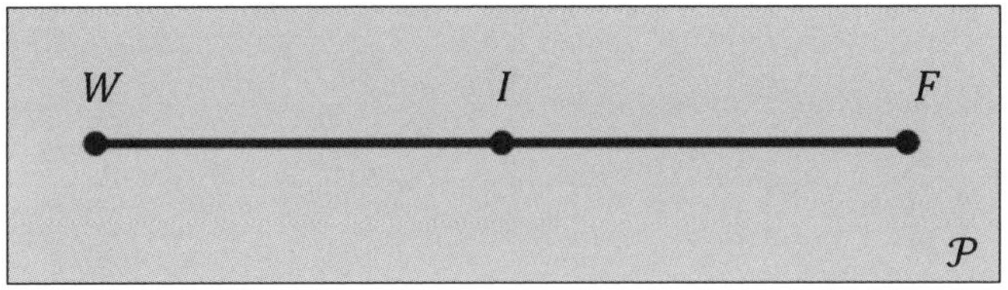

a. Determine if the following statements are true or false.

_______ Points W and F define a ray.
_______ $WI = WF$ by the Segment Addition Postulate.
_______ Points W, I, and F are collinear.
_______ Points W, I, and F are coplanar.

b. Point I lies between points W and F. $WI = 7x - 3$. $IF = 2x + 4$. $WF = 15x - 21$. What is the measure of $\overline{WF}$?

Section 1 – Topic 2
Basics of Geometry – Part 2

Let's Practice!

1. Consider the figure below.

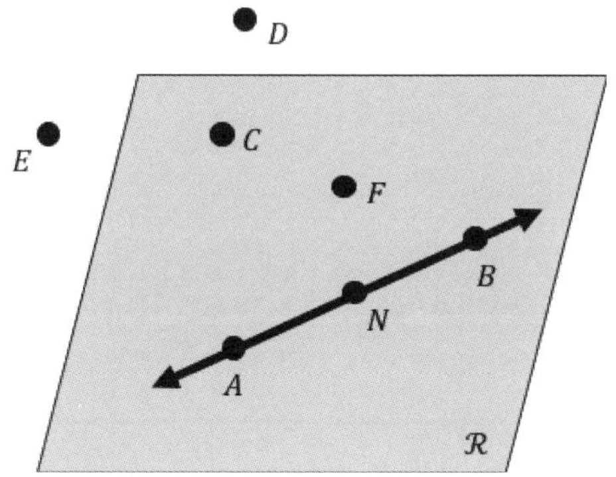

Select all the statements that apply to this figure.

- ☐ A, B, C, and D are coplanar in $\mathcal{R}$.
- ☐ A, B, C, and F are collinear.
- ☐ A, B, and N are collinear and coplanar in $\mathcal{R}$.
- ☐ B lies on $\overleftrightarrow{AN}$.
- ☐ A, C and F are coplanar in $\mathcal{R}$.
- ☐ C, D, E and F lie on $\mathcal{R}$.
- ☐ $AN + NB = AB$

Try It!

2. Plane $\mathcal{Q}$ contains $\overline{AB}$ and $\overrightarrow{BC}$, and it also intersects $\overleftrightarrow{PR}$ only at point M. Use the space below to sketch plane $\mathcal{Q}$.

For points, lines, and planes, you need to know certain postulates.

> **STUDY EDGE TIP**
>
> A ***postulate*** is a statement that we take to be automatically true. We do not need to prove that a postulate is true because it is something we assume to be true.

Let's examine the following postulates A through F.

A. Through any two points there is exactly one line.

B. Through any three non-collinear points there is exactly one plane.

C. If two points lie in a plane, then the line containing those points will also lie in the plane.

D. If two lines intersect, they intersect in exactly one point.

E. If two planes intersect, they intersect in exactly one line.

F. Given a point on a plane, there is one and only one line perpendicular to the plane through that point.

Let's Practice!

3. Use postulates A through F to match each visual representation with the correct postulate.

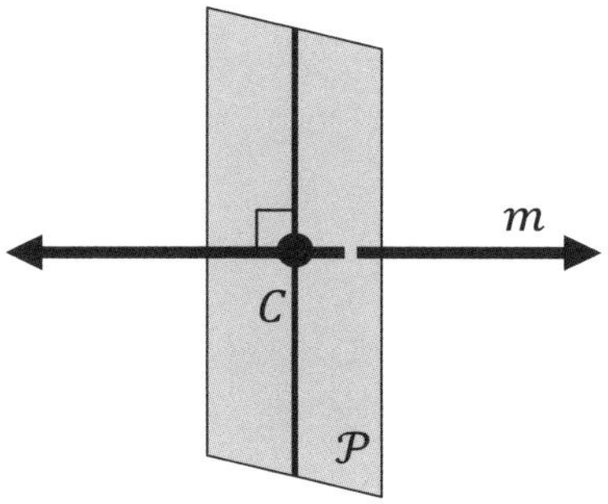

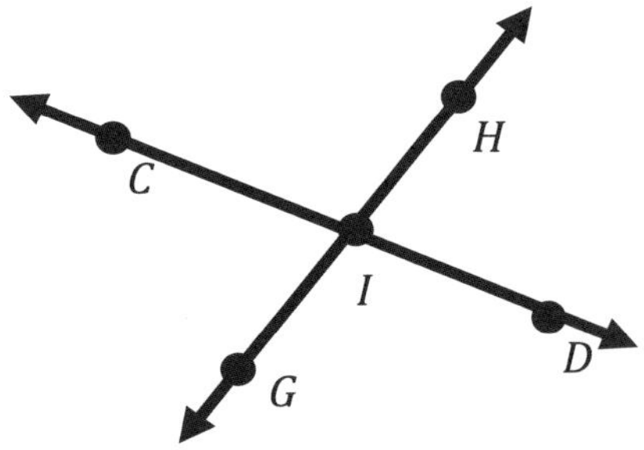

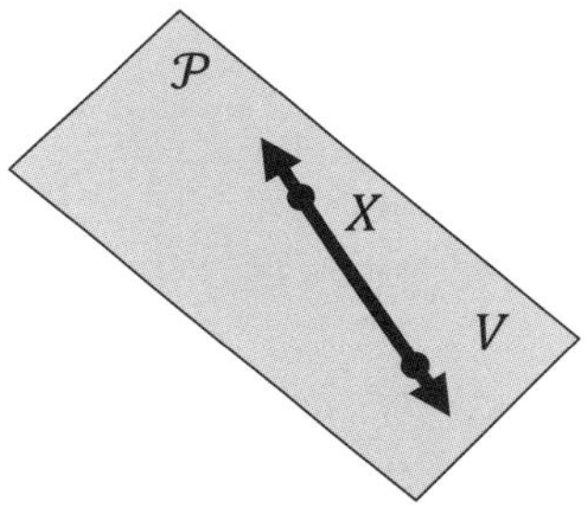

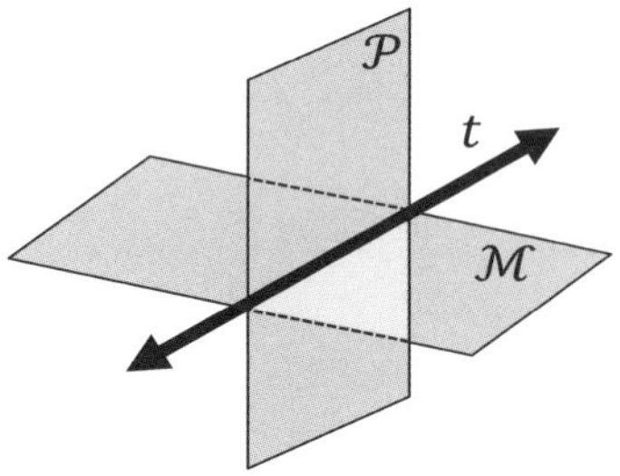

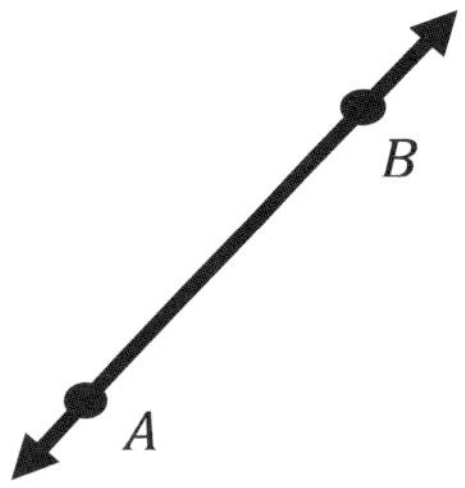

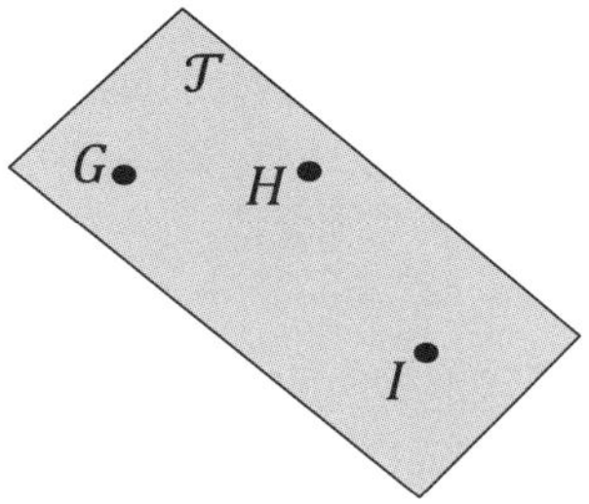

BEAT THE TEST!

1. Consider the following figure.

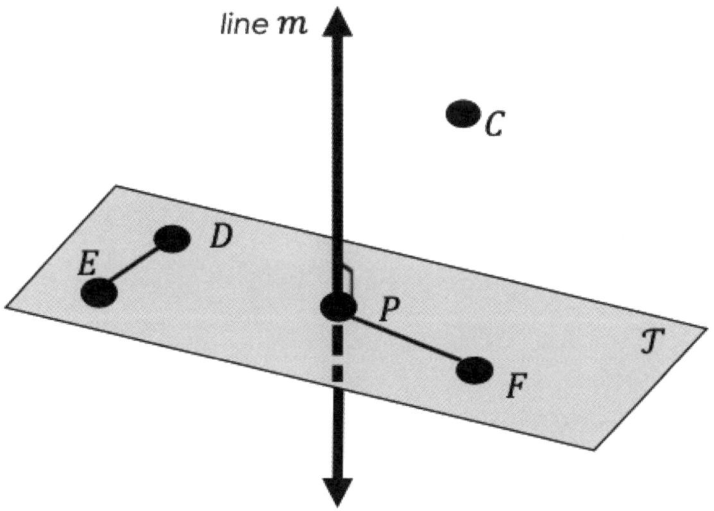

Select all the statements that apply to this figure.

- ☐ m is perpendicular through P to $\mathcal{T}$.
- ☐ C, D, E, and F are coplanar in $\mathcal{T}$.
- ☐ D, P, and F are collinear.
- ☐ $\overline{FC}$ is longer than $\overline{DF}$.
- ☐ $\overline{DE}$ and $\overline{PF}$ are coplanar in $\mathcal{T}$.

Section 1 – Topic 3
Introduction to Proofs

What are the next two terms in the following sequence?

$5, 7, 11, 17, 25, \ldots$

If the following pattern continues, how many dots will the fifth figure have?

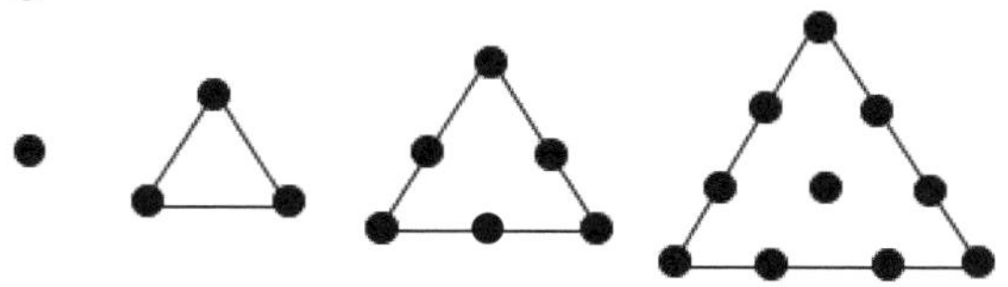

____________ reasoning is a type of reasoning that reaches conclusions based on a pattern.

A ____________ is a statement that is based on inductive reasoning but has not yet been shown to be true.

Make a conjecture: Based on the table, how many llamas would you expect the farm to have in year 7?

Year	Number of llamas at Sunny Day Farm
1	6
2	14
3	22
4	30

Conjecture: ____

____

STUDY EDGE TIP

To show that a conjecture is true, prove it is true for all cases, not just a few.

A _____________ is an example that shows a statement or conjecture is false.

What is a counterexample that shows the statement, "*If a number is a prime number, then the number is an odd number,*" is false?

Read the following statement. What can you logically conclude?

If $m\angle A$ is less than $90°$, then $\angle A$ is an acute angle.
$m\angle A = 85°$.

_____________ reasoning is a type of reasoning using given and previously known facts to reach a logical conclusion.

In this course, we will use deductive reasoning to prove statements. There are three different types of proofs:

Type of Proof	Definition
	uses a table and explicitly places the statements in the first column and the reasoning in the second column
	the statements and their reasoning are written together in a logical order in paragraph form
	a concept map where statements are placed in the boxes and the reason for each statement are placed under the box

Let's Practice!

1. Complete the two-column proof to prove that $x = 5$.

   Given: $LM = 3x + 1$
   $MN = x + 2$
   $LN = 23$
   Prove: $x = 5$

   L———————M——N

Statements	Reasons
1. $LM = 3x + 1$ $MN = x + 2$ $LN = 23$	1.
2.	2. Segment Addition Postulate
3.	3. Equivalent Equation
4.	4. Addition Property of Equality
5. $4x = 20$	5.
6.	6. Multiplication Property of Equality
7.	7.

   What will the *first* row of a two-column proof always be?

   What will the *last* row of a two-column proof always be?

2. The given figure is a square. The expression represents the area of the square. Use a paragraph proof to show that the length of one side of the square is $(2x + 3)$.

   Area: $4x^2 + 12x + 9$

   Given: _____

   Prove: _____

3. Use the word bank to prove the conditional using a flow chart proof.

   If $\frac{3x}{x+5} = 2$, then $x = 10$.

Given	Subtraction Property	$\frac{3x}{x+5} = 2$
$3x = 2(x + 5)$		Distributive Property
	$x = 10$	
Multiplication Property		$3x = 2x + 10$

   START → ☐ → ☐ → ☐ → ☐ → END

   ____ ____ ____ ____

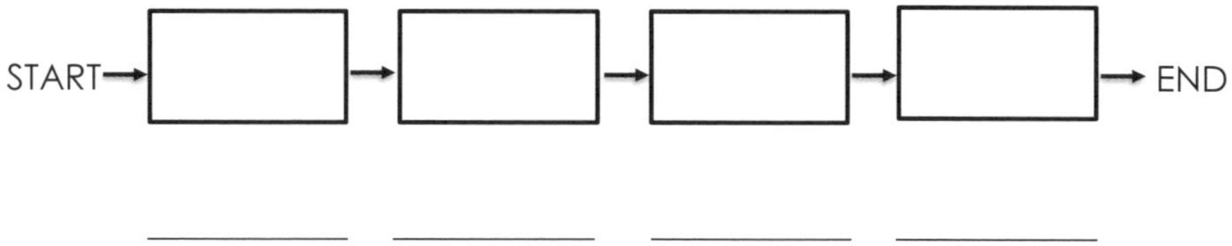

Try It!

4. When a natural number is added to three and the sum is divided by two, the quotient will be an even number.

   Which of the following is a counterexample to the statement above?

   Ⓐ $\frac{13+3}{2} = 8$, which is an even number.
   Ⓑ $\frac{12}{2} + 3 = 9$, which is not an even number.
   Ⓒ $\frac{3+4}{2} = \frac{7}{2}$, which is not an even number.
   Ⓓ The statement is correct. There is no counterexample.

BEAT THE TEST!

1. Consider the diagram below and finish the two-column proof to show $AC = BD$.

   Given: $AB = CD$
   Prove: $AC = BD$

Statements	Reasons
1. $AB = CD$	1.
2.	2. Reflexive Property
3. $AB + BC = BC + CD$	3.
4. $AB + BC = AC$ $BC + CD = BD$	4.
5.	5. Substitution

Section 1 – Topic 4
Midpoint and Distance in the Coordinate Plane – Part 1

Consider the line segment displayed below.

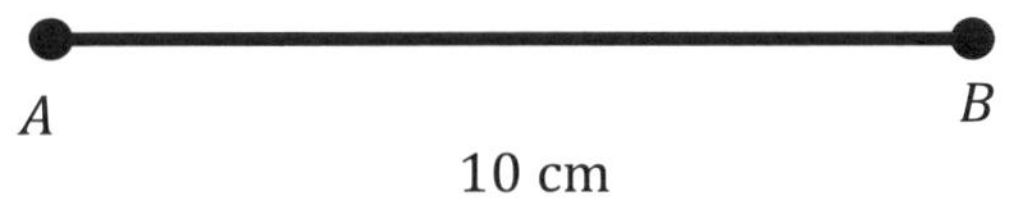

The length of $\overline{AB}$ is _____ centimeters.

- ______________________ is an amount of space (in certain units) between two points on a ______________________.

Draw a point halfway between point A and point B. Label this point C.

What is the length of $\overline{AC}$?

What is the length of $\overline{CB}$?

Point C is called the ___________________ of $\overline{AB}$.

Why do you think it's called the midpoint?

Let's Practice!

1. Consider $\overline{XY}$ with midpoint R.

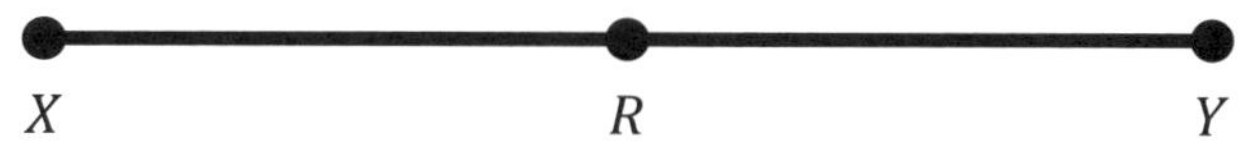

   a. What can be said of $\overline{XR}$ and $\overline{RY}$?

   b. If $\overline{XR}$ is $(2x + 5)$ inches long and $\overline{RY}$ is 22 inches long, what is the value of x?

2. Consider the line segment below.

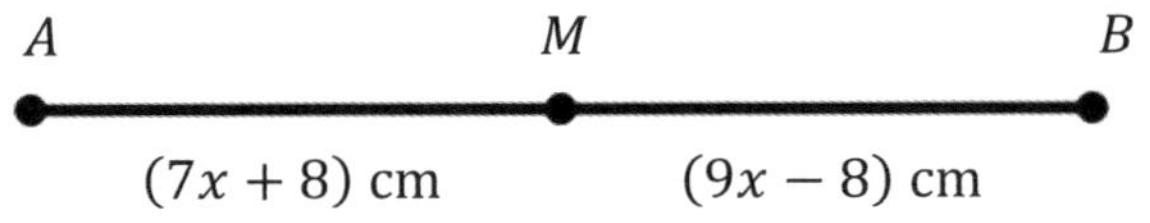

a. If $\overline{AB}$ is 128 centimeters long, what is x?

b. What is the length of $\overline{AM}$?

c. What is the length of $\overline{BM}$?

d. Is point M the midpoint of $\overline{AB}$? Justify your answer.

Try It!

3. Diego and Anya live 72 miles apart. They both meet at their favorite restaurant, which is $(16x-3)$ miles from Diego's house and $(5x+2)$ miles from Anya's house.

   Diego argues that in a straight line distance, the restaurant is halfway between his house and Anya's house. Is Diego right? Justify your reasoning.

Midpoint and ***distance*** can also be calculated on a coordinate plane.

The coordinate plane is a plane that is divided into ________ regions (called quadrants) by a horizontal line (______________) and a vertical line (______________).

- The location, or coordinates, of a point are given by an ordered pair, __________.

Consider the following graph.

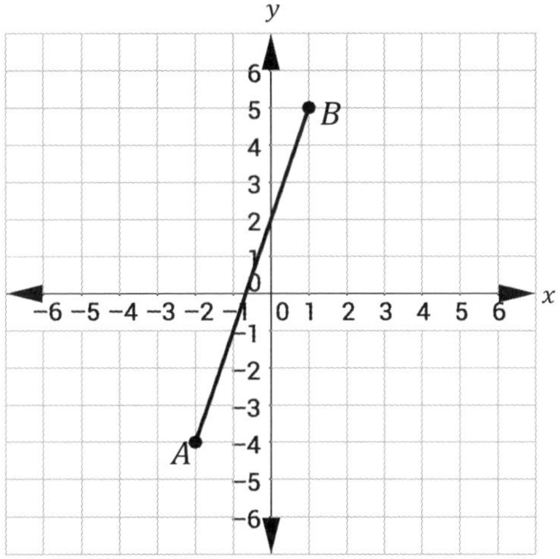

Name the ordered pair that represents point A.

Name the ordered pair that represents point B.

How can we find the midpoint of this line segment?

The midpoint of $\overline{AB}$ is (______ , ______).

Let's consider points X and Y on the coordinate plane below.

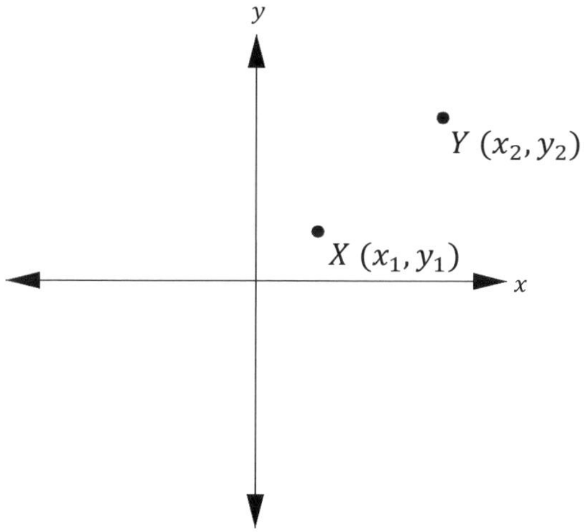

Write a formula that can be used to find the midpoint of any two given points.

Let's Practice!

4. Consider the line segment in the graph below.

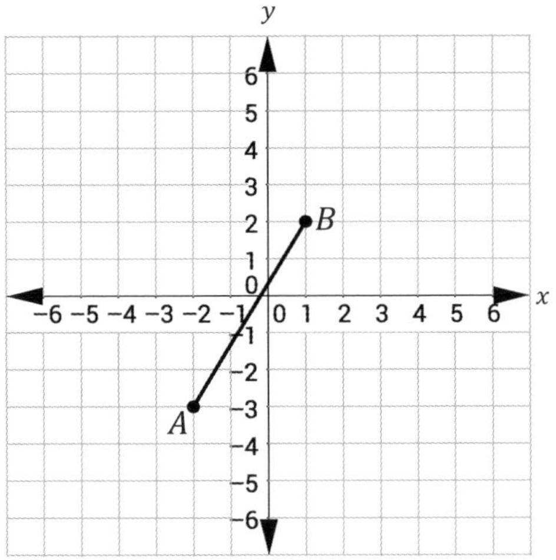

Find the midpoint of $\overline{AB}$.

5. M is the midpoint of $\overline{CD}$. C has coordinates $(-1,-1)$ and M has coordinates $(3,5)$. Find the coordinates of D.

Try It!

6. P has coordinates $(2,4)$. Q has coordinates $(-10,12)$. Find the midpoint of $\overline{PQ}$.

7. *Café 103* is collinear with and equidistant from the *Metrics School* and the *Angles Lab*. The *Metrics School* is located at point $(4,6)$ on a coordinate plane, and *Café 103* is at point $(7,2)$. Find the coordinates of the *Angles Lab*.

Section 1 – Topic 5
Midpoint and Distance in the Coordinate Plane – Part 2

Consider $\overline{AB}$ below.

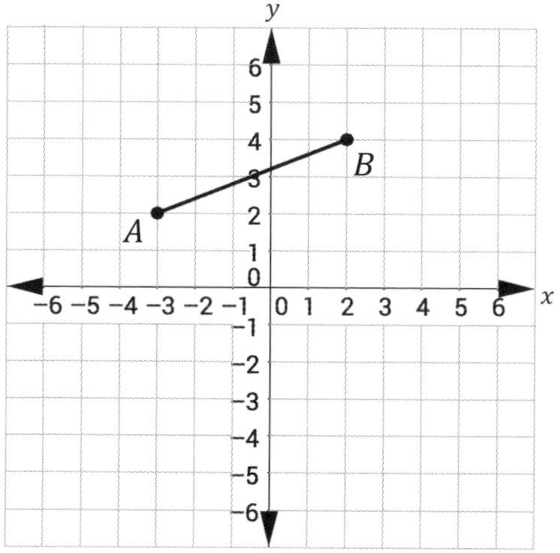

Draw point C on the above graph at $(2,2)$.

What is the length of $\overline{AC}$?

What is the length of $\overline{BC}$?

Triangle ABC is a right triangle. Use the Pythagorean Theorem to find the length of $\overline{AB}$.

Let's consider the figure below.

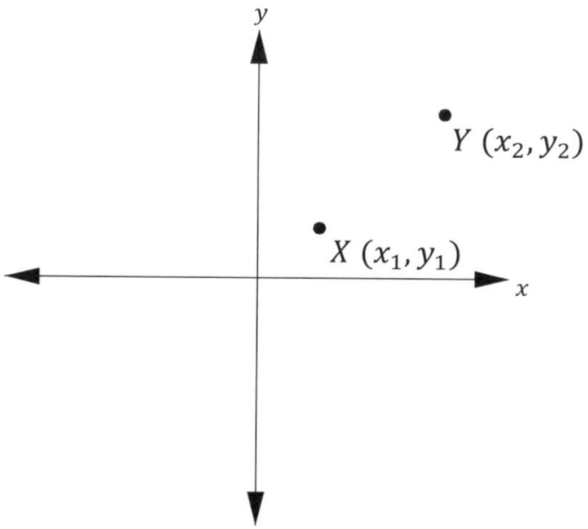

Write a formula to determine the distance of any line segment.

Let's Practice!

1. Find the length of $\overline{EF}$.

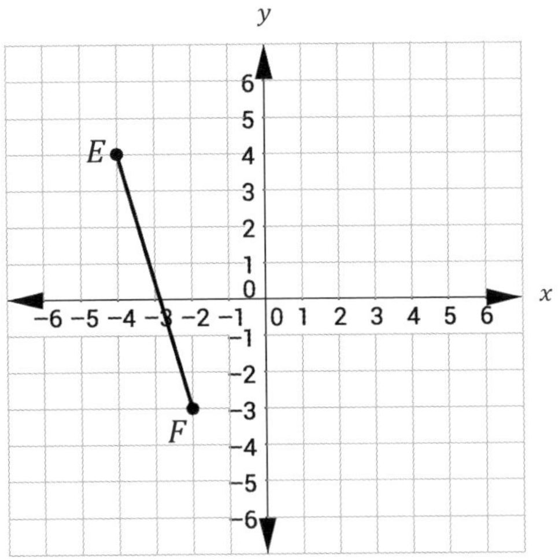

Try It!

2. Consider triangle ABC graphed on the coordinate plane.

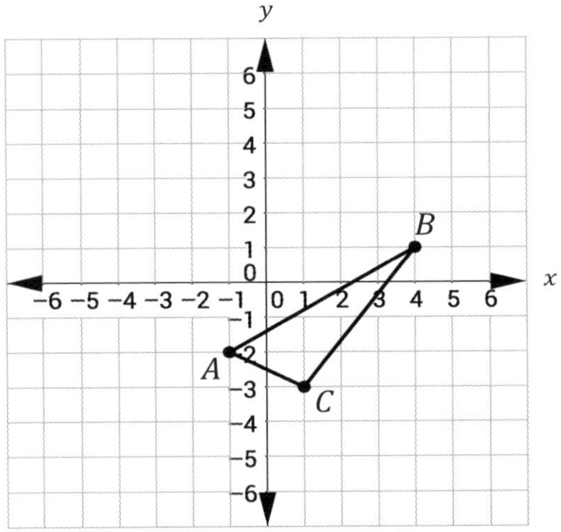

Find the perimeter of triangle ABC.

BEAT THE TEST!

1. Consider the following figure.

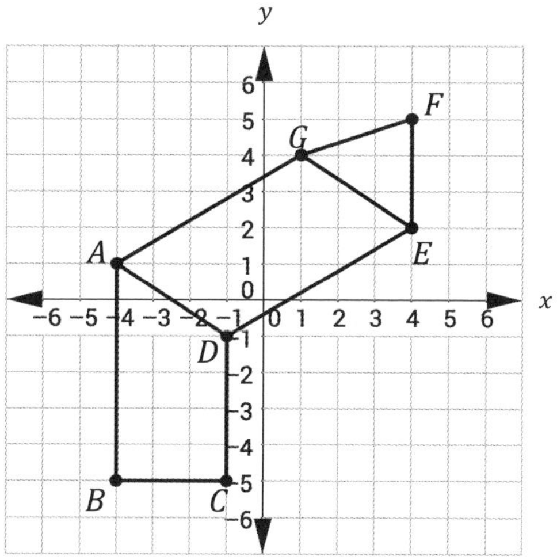

Which of the following statements are true? Select all that apply.

- ☐ The midpoint of $\overline{AG}$ has coordinates $\left(-\frac{3}{2}, \frac{5}{2}\right)$.
- ☐ $\overline{DE}$ is exactly 5 units long.
- ☐ $\overline{AD}$ is exactly 3 units long.
- ☐ $\overline{FG}$ is longer than $\overline{EF}$.
- ☐ The perimeter of quadrilateral $ABCD$ is about 16.6 units.
- ☐ The perimeter of quadrilateral $ADEG$ is about 18.8 units.
- ☐ The perimeter of triangle EFG is 9 units.

Section 1 – Topic 6
Partitioning a Line Segment – Part 1

What do you think it means to ***partition***?

How can a line segment be partitioned?

In the previous section, we worked with the__________, which partitions a segment into a $1:1$ ratio.

STUDY EDGE TIP

A ***ratio*** compares two numbers. A $1:1$ ratio is stated as, or can also be written as, "1 to 1".

Why does the midpoint partition a segment into a $1:1$ ratio?

How can $\overline{AB}$ be divided into a $1:3$ ratio?

Consider the following line segment where point P partitions the segment into a $1:4$ ratio.

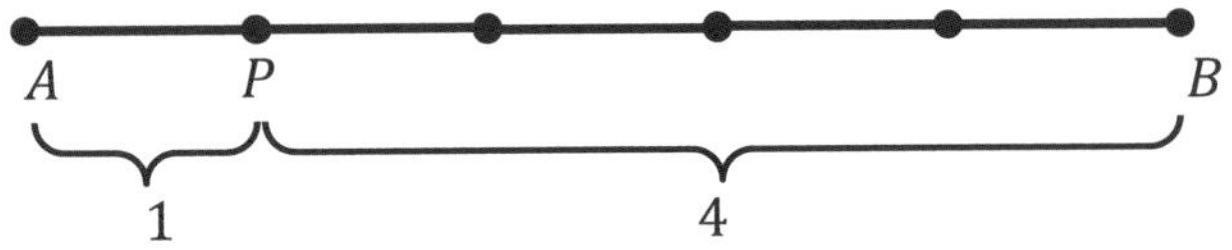

How many sections are between points A and P?

How many sections are between points P and B?

How many sections are between points A and B?

In relation to $\overline{AB}$, how long is $\overline{AP}$?

In relation to $\overline{AB}$, how long is $\overline{PB}$?

Let's call these ratios, k, a fraction that compares a part to a whole.

If partitioning a directed line segment into two segments, when would your ratio k be the same for each segment? When would it differ?

The following formula can be used to find the coordinates of a given point that partitions a line segment into ratio k.

$$(x, y) = \left(x_1 + k(x_2 - x_1), y_1 + k(y_2 - y_1)\right)$$

Let's Practice!

1. What is the value of k used to find the coordinates of a point that partitions a segment into a ratio of $4:3$?

2. Determine the value of k if partitioning a segment into a ratio of $1:5$.

Try It!

3. Point A has coordinates $(2,4)$. Point B has coordinates $(10,12)$. Find the coordinates of point P that partitions $\overline{AB}$ in the ratio $3:2$.

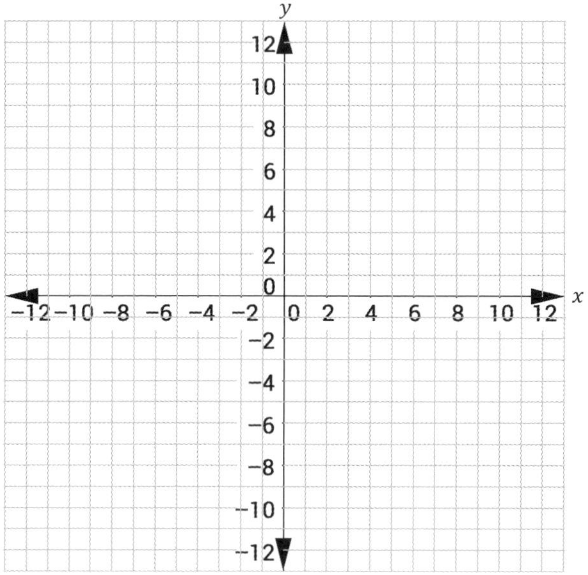

4. Points C, D, and E are collinear on $\overline{CE}$, and $CD:DE = \frac{3}{5}$. C is located at $(1,8)$, D is located at $(4,5)$, and E is located at (x,y). What are the values of x and y?

Section 1 – Topic 7
Partitioning a Line Segment – Part 2

Consider M, N, and P, collinear points on $\overline{MP}$.

What is the difference between the ratio $MN:NP$ and the ratio $MN:MP$?

What should you do if one of the parts of a ratio is actually the whole line instead of a ratio of two smaller parts or segments?

Let's Practice!

1. Points P, Q, and R are collinear on $\overline{PR}$, and $PQ:PR = \frac{2}{3}$. P is located at the origin, Q is located at (x,y), and R is located at $(-12,0)$. What are the values of x and y?

2. Consider the line segment in the graph below.

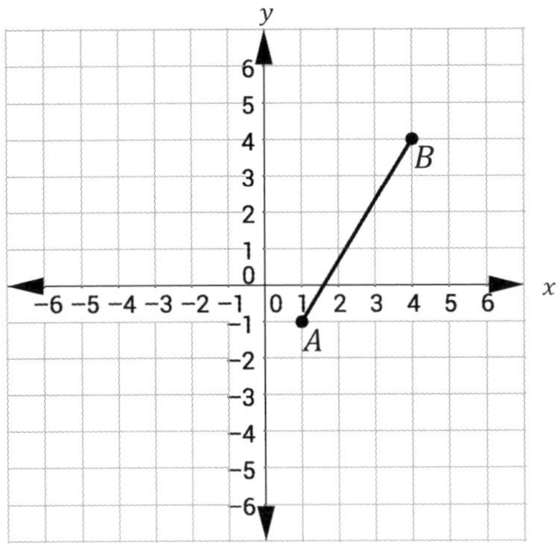

a. Find the coordinates of point P that partition $\overline{AB}$ in the ratio $1:4$.

b. Suppose A, R, and B are collinear on $\overline{AB}$, and $AR:AB = \frac{1}{4}$. What are the coordinates of R?

Try It!

3. $\overline{JK}$ in the coordinate plane has endpoints with coordinates $(-4, 11)$ and $(8, -1)$.

a. Graph $\overline{JK}$ and find two possible locations for point M, so M divides $\overline{JK}$ into two parts with lengths in a ratio of $1:3$.

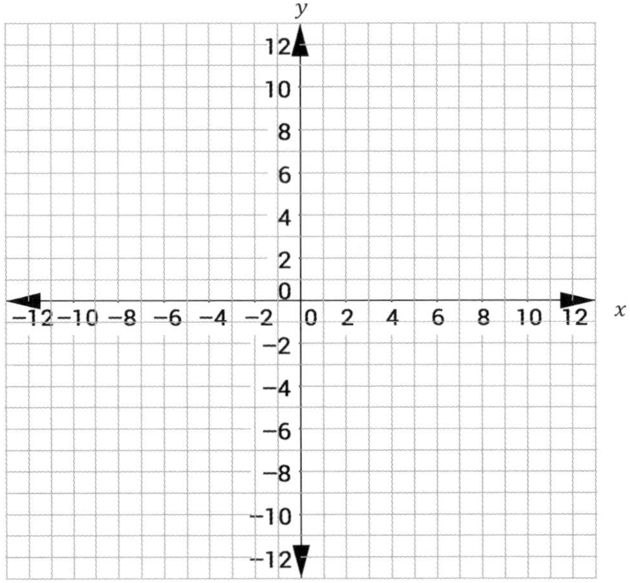

b. Suppose J, P, and K are collinear on $\overline{JK}$, and $JP:JK = \frac{1}{3}$. What are the coordinates of P?

BEAT THE TEST!

1. Consider the directed line segment from $A(-3, 1)$ to $Z(3, 4)$. Points $L, M,$ and N are on $\overline{AZ}$.

$L(-1, 2)$	$M\left(0, \frac{5}{2}\right)$	$N(1, 3)$

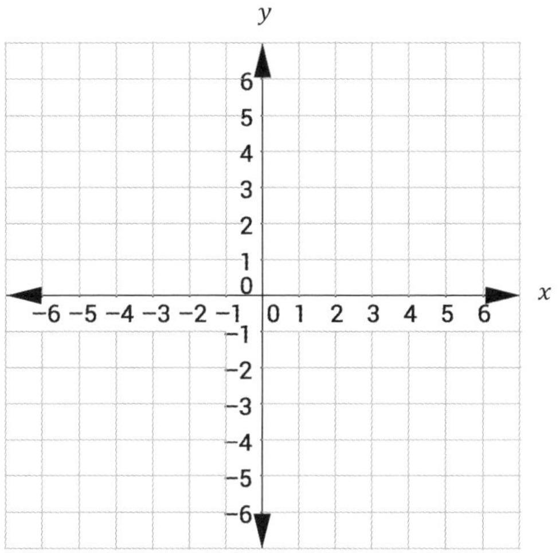

Complete the statements below.

The point _______ partitions $\overline{AZ}$ in a $1:1$ ratio.

The point _______ partitions $\overline{AZ}$ in a $1:2$ ratio.

The point _______ partitions $\overline{AZ}$ in a $2:1$ ratio.

The ratio $AL: AZ =$ __________.

Section 1 – Topic 8
Parallel and Perpendicular Lines – Part 1

Graph A

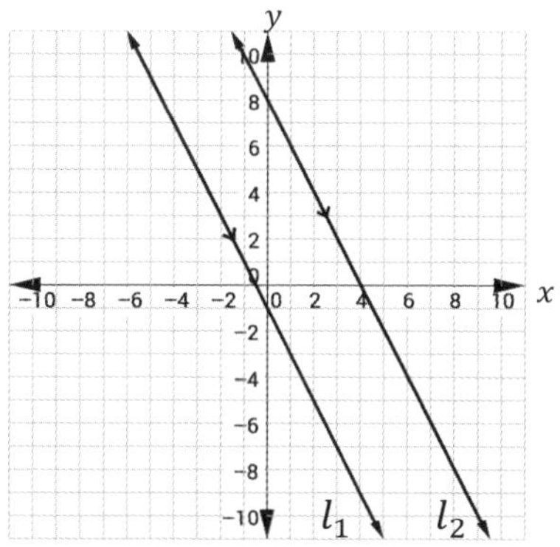

These lines are _________________.

The symbol used to indicate ***parallel*** lines is ______.

Graph B

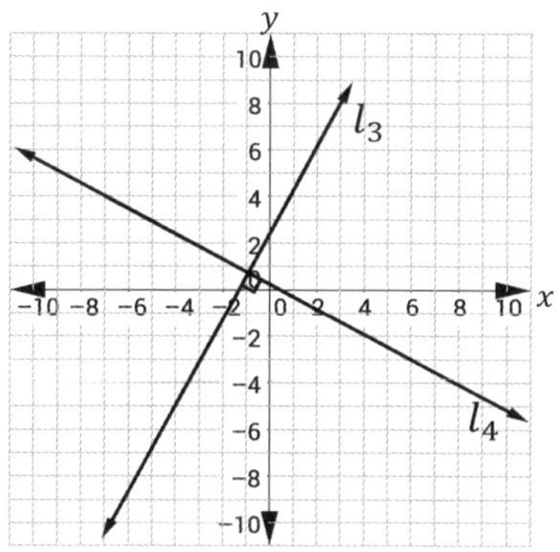

These lines are _________________.

The symbol used to indicate ***perpendicular*** lines is ______.

Choose two points on each graph and use the slope formula, $\frac{y_2-y_1}{x_2-x_1}$, to verify your answers.

What do you notice about the slopes of the parallel lines?

What do you notice about the slopes of the perpendicular lines?

What happens if the lines are given in equation form instead of on a graph?

Let's Practice!

1. Indicate whether the lines are parallel, perpendicular, or neither. Justify your answer.

   a. $y = 2x$ and $6x = 3y + 5$

   b. $2x - 5y = 10$ and $10x + 4y = 20$

   c. $4x + 3y = 63$ and $12x - 9y = 27$

   d. $x = 4$ and $y = -2$

Try It!

2. Write the letter of the appropriate equation in the column beside each item.

A. $x = -5$	**B.** $y = -\frac{1}{4}x + 1$	**C.** $3x - 5y = -30$	**D.** $x - 2y = -2$

	A line parallel to $y = \frac{3}{5}x + 2$
	A line perpendicular to $y = 4$
	A line perpendicular to $4x + 2y = 12$
	A line parallel to $2x + 8y = 7$

Parallel and Perpendicular Lines – Part 2

Let's Practice!

1. Write the equation of the line passing through $(-1, 4)$ and perpendicular to $x + 2y = 11$.

Try It!

2. Suppose the equation for line A is given by $y = -\frac{3}{4}x - 2$. If line A and line B are perpendicular and the point $(-4, 1)$ lies on line B, then write an equation for line B.

3. Consider the graph below.

   a. Name a set of lines that are parallel. Justify your answer.

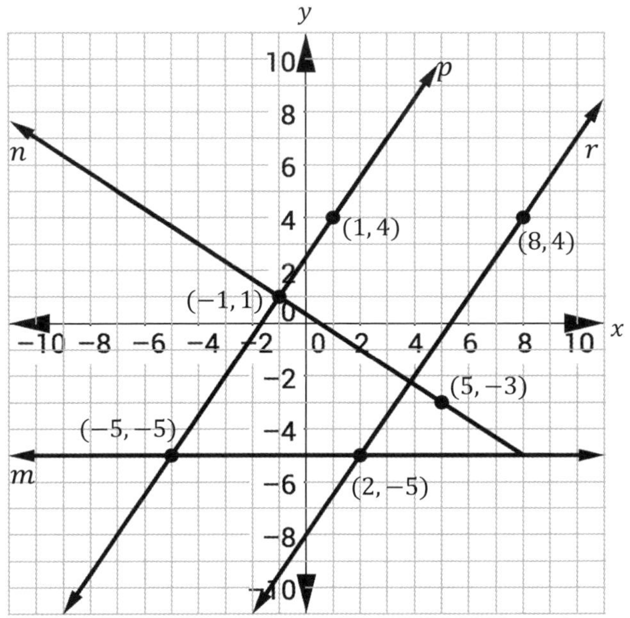

   b. Name a set of lines that are perpendicular. Justify your answer.

BEAT THE TEST!

1. The equation for line A is given by $y = -\frac{3}{4}x - 2$. Suppose line A is parallel to line B, and line T is perpendicular to line A. Point $(0, 5)$ lies on both line B and line T.

Part A: Write an equation for line B.

Part B: Write an equation for line T.

2. A parallelogram is a four-sided figure whose opposite sides are parallel and equal in length. Alex is drawing parallelogram $ABCD$ on a coordinate plane. The parallelogram has the coordinates $A(4, 2)$, $B(0, -2)$, and $D(8, -1)$.

Which of the following coordinates should Alex use for point C?

- Ⓐ $(6, -3)$
- Ⓑ $(4, -5)$
- Ⓒ $(10, -3)$
- Ⓓ $(4, 3)$

Section 1 – Topic 10
Introduction to Coordinate Geometry

____________ ____________ involves placing geometric figures in a coordinate plane.

So far in this course, we have used coordinates in the following ways:

	Formula	Description
Midpoint Formula		
Distance Formula		
Slope Formula		

Let's Practice!

1. Given $A(-4,8), D(-7,4)$, and $H(-3,1)$, plot the points, and trace the triangle.

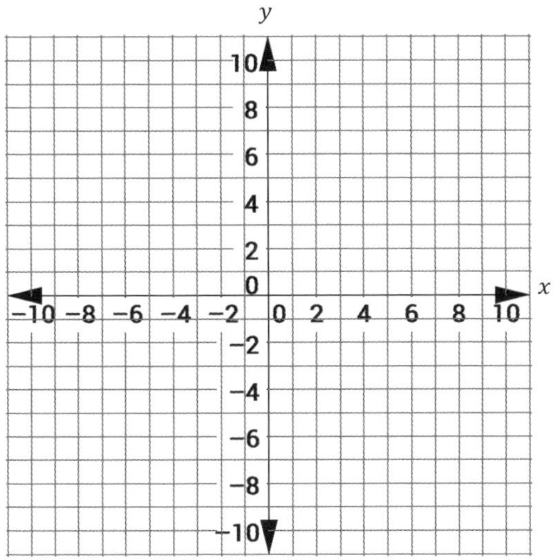

a. What is the perimeter of the triangle? Round to the nearest hundredth.

b. Prove that $m\angle ADH = 90°$ using the slopes of $\overline{AD}$ and $\overline{DH}$.

c. Find the area of the triangle. Round to the nearest hundredth.

2. Consider trapezoid $BADC$ in the figure below.

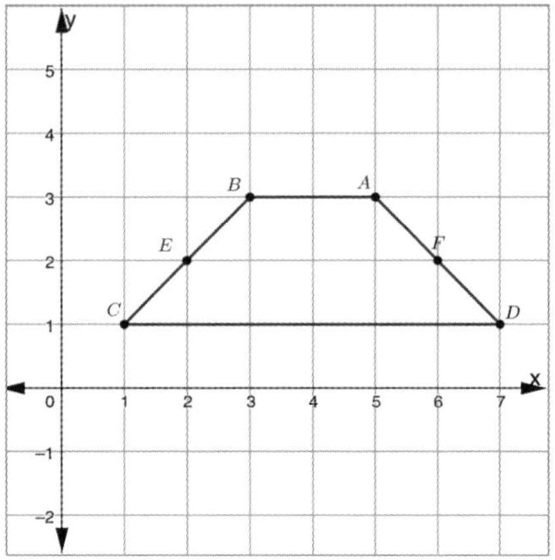

Given that E is the midpoint of $\overline{CB}$ and F is the midpoint of $\overline{AD}$, show that $\overline{BA} \parallel \overline{EF} \parallel \overline{CD}$ using a paragraph proof.

Given: E is the midpoint of $\overline{CB}$.
F is the midpoint of $\overline{AD}$.
$\mathrm{B}\ (3,3), \mathrm{A}\ (5,3), \mathrm{D}\ (7,1)$, and $C\ (1,1)$

Prove: $\overline{BA} \parallel \overline{EF} \parallel \overline{CD}$

Try it!

3. Cherise is planting a vegetable garden in the shape of a triangle. She plans to plant tomatoes on the left side and peppers on the right side of the partition that is perpendicular to $\overline{ON}$.

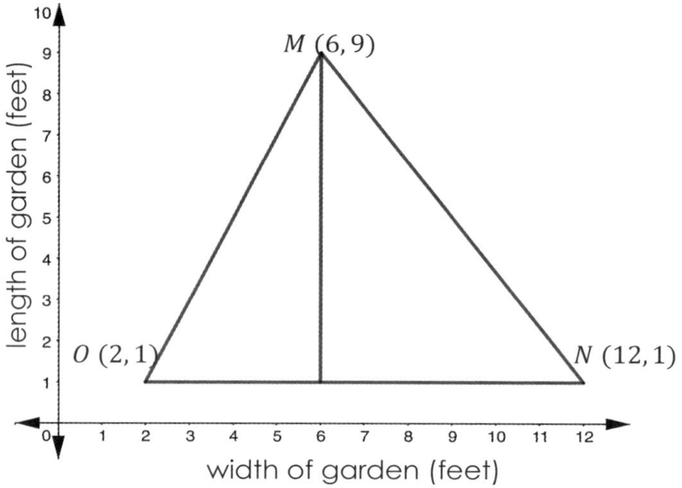

a. If Cherise has 35 feet of fencing, does she have enough to fence in the entire garden and add the partition? Round your answer to the nearest hundredth.

b. Each pepper plant will need at least 4 square feet of space to produce the most peppers. What is the maximum number of pepper plants she can plant in the right side of her garden?

BEAT THE TEST!

1. Jerome and Erik start their hike at point A and follow the trail in the counter clockwise direction. They stop at point W to eat lunch.

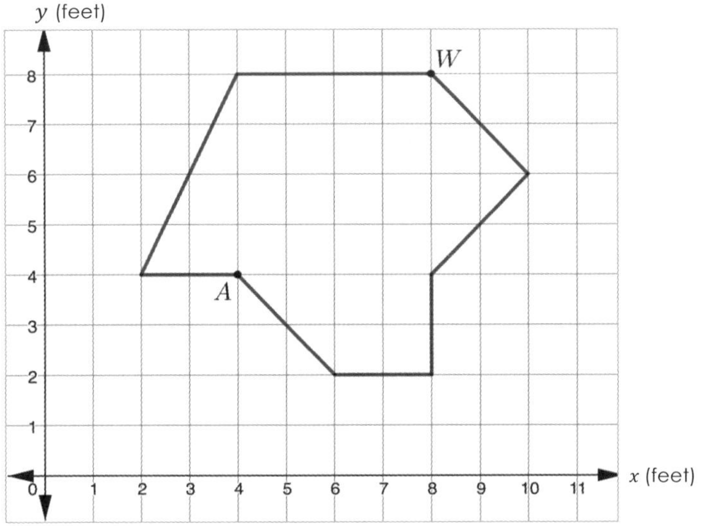

How many total miles have Jerome and Erik hiked when they stop for lunch? Round your answer to the nearest tenth of a mile.

Section 1 – Topic 11
Basic Constructions – Part 1

What do you think the term ***geometric constructions*** implies?

The following tools are used in geometric constructions.

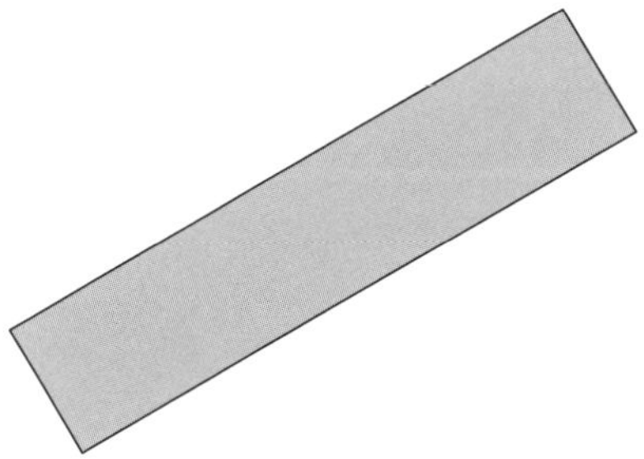

Straightedge

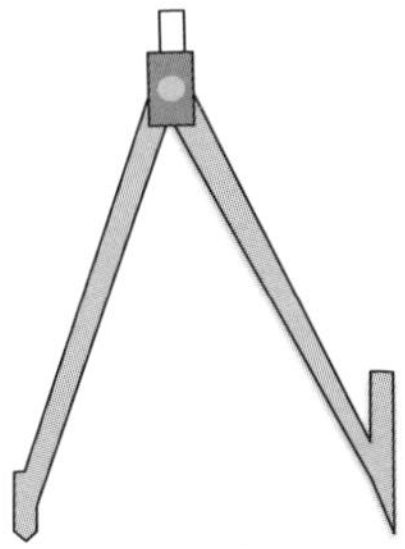

Compass

Which of the tools can help you draw a line segment?

Which of the tools can help you draw a circle?

Constructions also involve labeling points where lines or arcs intersect.

An ***arc*** is a section of the ________________ of a circle, or any curve.

Consider the following figure where $\overline{EF}$ was constructed perpendicular to $\overline{BC}$.

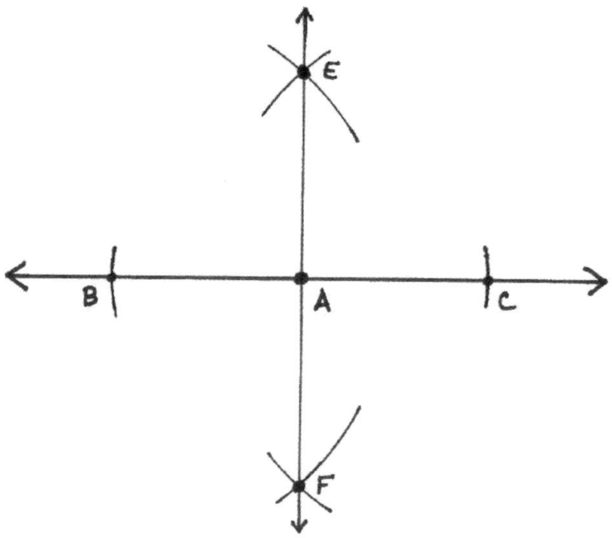

Label each part of the figure that shows evidence of the use of a straightedge with the letters SE.

Label each part of the figure that shows evidence of the use of a compass with the letter C.

Let's Practice!

1. Follow the instructions below for copying $\overline{AB}$.

Step 1. Mark a point M that will be one endpoint of the new line segment.

Step 2. Set the point of the compass on point A of the line segment to be copied.

Step 3. Adjust the width of the compass to point B. The width of the compass is now equal to the length of $\overline{AB}$.

Step 4. Without changing the width of the compass, place the compass point on M. Keeping the same compass width, draw an arc approximately where the other endpoint will be created.

Step 5. Pick a point N on the arc that will be the other endpoint of the new line segment.

Step 6. Use the straightedge to draw a line segment from M to N.

Try It!

2. Construct $\overline{RS}$, a copy of $\overline{PQ}$. Write down the steps you followed for your construction.

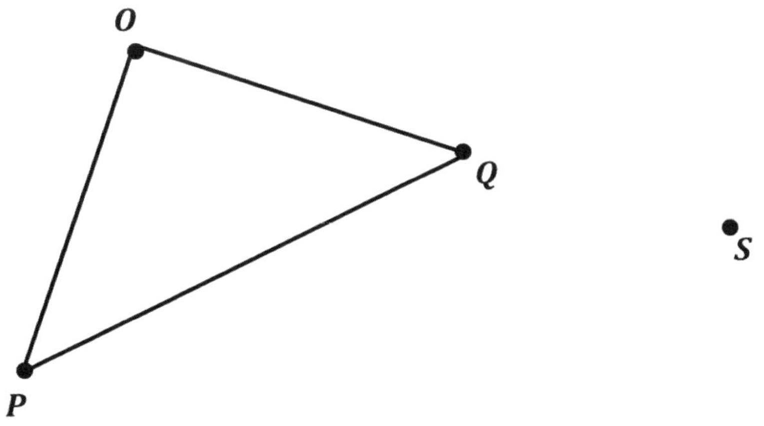

Section 1 – Topic 12
Basic Constructions – Part 2

In the constructions of line segments, we can do more than just copy segments. We can construct lines that are parallel or perpendicular to a given line or line segment.

Let's Practice!

1. Following the steps below, construct a line through P that is perpendicular to the given line segment $\overline{AB}$.

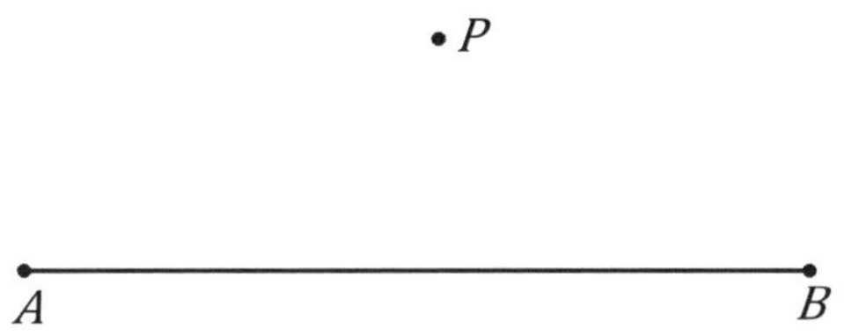

Step 1. Place the point of the compass on point P, and draw an arc that crosses $\overline{AB}$ twice. Label the two points of intersection C and D.

Step 2. Place the compass on point C and make an arc above $\overline{AB}$ that goes through P, and a similar arc below $\overline{AB}$.

Step 3. Keeping the compass at the same width as in step 2, place the compass on point D, and repeat step 2.

Step 4. Draw a point where the arcs drawn in Step 2 and Step 3 intersect. Label that point R.

Step 5. Draw a line segment through points P and R, making $\overline{PR}$ perpendicular to $\overline{AB}$.

Try It!

2. Following the steps below, construct a line segment through P that is parallel to the given line segment $\overline{AB}$.

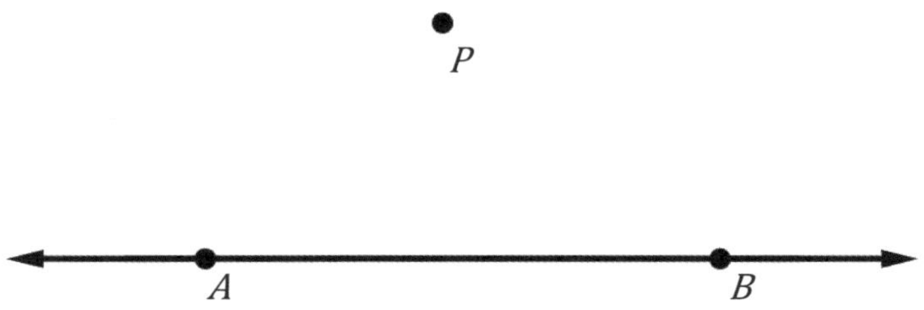

Step 1. Draw line r through point P that intersects $\overline{AB}$.

Step 2. Label the intersection of line r and $\overline{AB}$ point Q.

Step 3. Place your compass on point Q, set the width of the compass to point P, and construct an arc that intersects $\overline{AB}$. Label that point of intersection point C.

Step 4. Using the same setting, place the compass on point P, and construct an arc above $\overline{AB}$.

Step 5. Using the same setting, place the compass on point C, and construct an arc above $\overline{AB}$ that intersects the arc drawn in step 4. Label this intersection point D.

Step 6. Draw $\overline{PD}$.

STUDY EDGE TIP

This construction is for parallel lines using the rhombus method. Later on, we will learn about the properties of rhombi. The construction of parallel lines is also the construction of a rhombus.

BEAT THE TEST!

1. Consider the figure below.

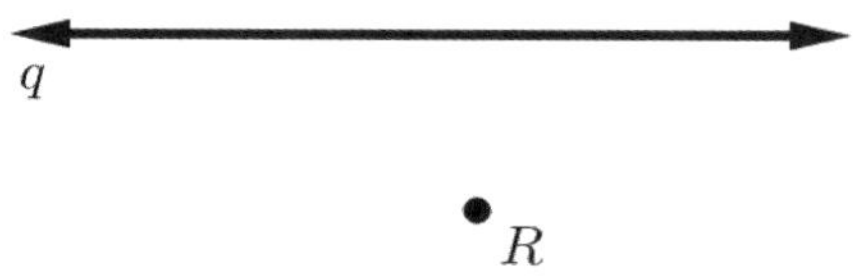

Celine attempted to construct a line through point R that is perpendicular to line q. In her first step, she placed the point of the compass on point R, and drew an arc that crossed line q twice. She labeled the two points of intersection A and B. Then, Celine placed the compass on point A and made an arc above line q that went through R; repeating the same process from point B. Finally, she drew a line from R crossing line q.

Part A: Celine's teacher pointed out that the construction is missing a very crucial step. Determine what the missing step is and why it is so crucial for this construction.

Part B: Another student in the classroom, Lori, suggested that Celine can construct a line parallel to q through R by drawing a horizontal line. The teacher also pointed out that Lori's claim was incorrect. Explain why.

2. Consider the diagram shown below.

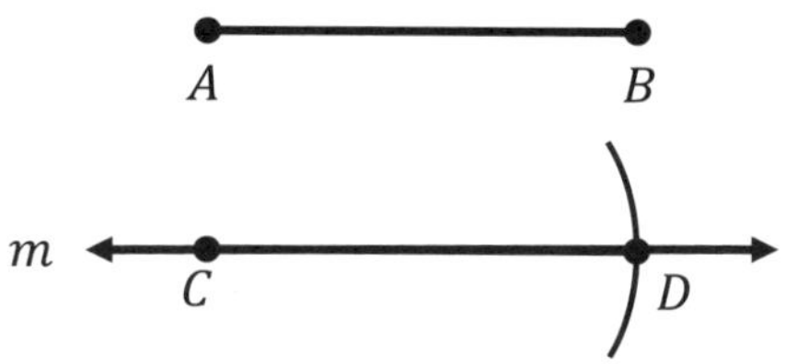

Which of the following statements best describes the construction in the diagram?

Ⓐ $\overline{AB} \parallel \overline{CD}$.
Ⓑ $\overline{AB} \cong \overline{CD}$.
Ⓒ C is the midpoint of m.
Ⓓ D is the midpoint of m.

Section 1 – Topic 13
Constructing Perpendicular Bisectors

Consider $\overline{JK}$ with midpoint M.

Draw a line through point M and label it r.

Line r is the segment ______________ of $\overline{JK}$.

A ***bisector*** divides lines, angles, and shapes into two equal parts.

A ***segment bisector*** is a line, segment, or ray that passes through another segment and cuts it into two congruent parts.

Consider $\overline{JK}$ and line t.

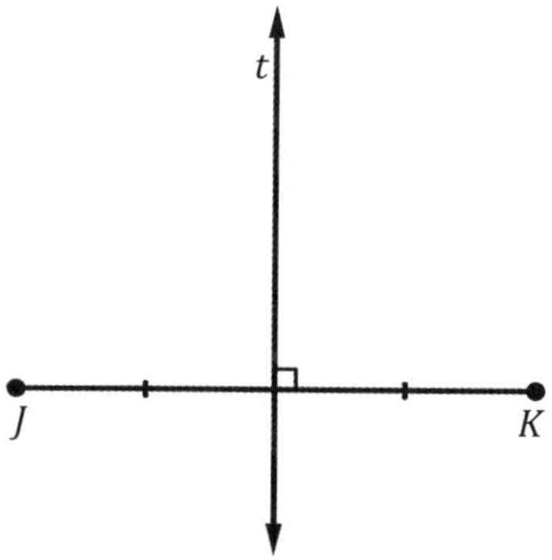

Line t is the ***perpendicular bisector*** of $\overline{JK}$. Make a conjecture as to why line t is called the perpendicular bisector of $\overline{JK}$.

> **STUDY EDGE TIP**
>
> When you make a ***conjecture***, you make an educated guess based on what you know or observe.

Let's Practice!

1. Follow the instructions below for constructing the perpendicular bisector of $\overline{AB}$.

Step 1. Start with $\overline{AB}$.

Step 2. Place your compass point on A, and stretch the compass more than halfway to point B.

Step 3. Draw large arcs both above and below the midpoint of $\overline{AB}$.

Step 4. Without changing the width of the compass, place the compass point on B. Draw two arcs so that they intersect the arcs you drew in step 3.

Step 5. With your straightedge, connect the two points where the arcs intersect.

Try It!

2. Consider $\overline{PQ}$.

a. Construct the perpendicular bisector of $\overline{PQ}$ shown above.

b. Consider $\overline{AB}$, which is parallel to $\overline{PQ}$. Is the perpendicular bisector of $\overline{PQ}$ also the perpendicular bisector of $\overline{AB}$? Justify your answer.

3. Consider the diagram below. What do you need to check to validate the construction of a perpendicular bisector?

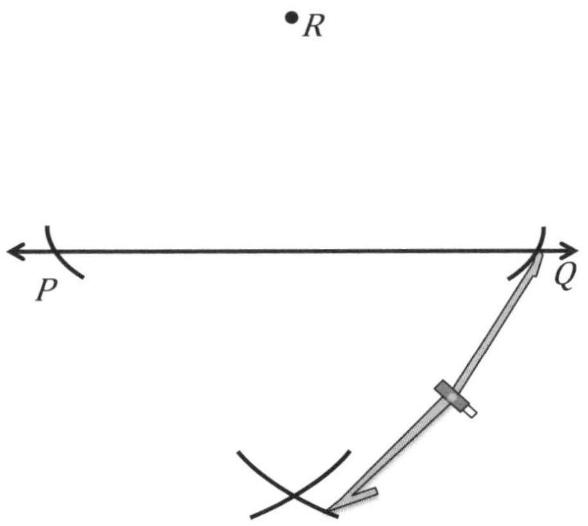

BEAT THE TEST!

1. Fernando was constructing a perpendicular line at point K on the line below.

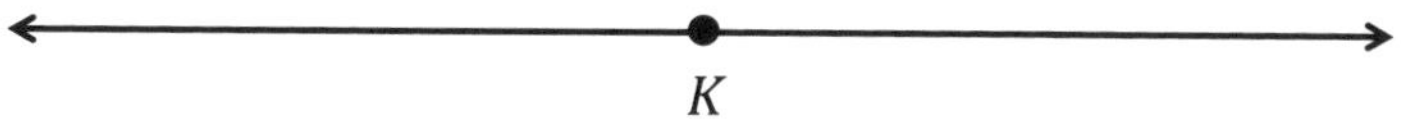

The figure below represents a depiction of the partial construction Fernando made.

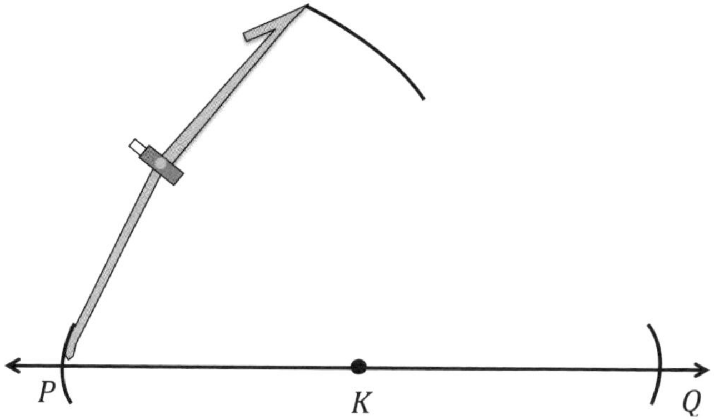

What should the next step be?

Ⓐ Increase the compass to almost double the width to create another line.
Ⓑ From P, draw a line that crosses the arc above K.
Ⓒ Without changing the width of the compass, repeat the drawing process from point Q, making the two arcs cross each other at a new point called R.
Ⓓ Close the compass and use the straight edge to draw a line from the midpoint of the arc to point K.

Section 1 – Topic 14
Proving the Perpendicular Bisector Theorem Using Constructions

Consider $\overline{JK}$ and line t again.

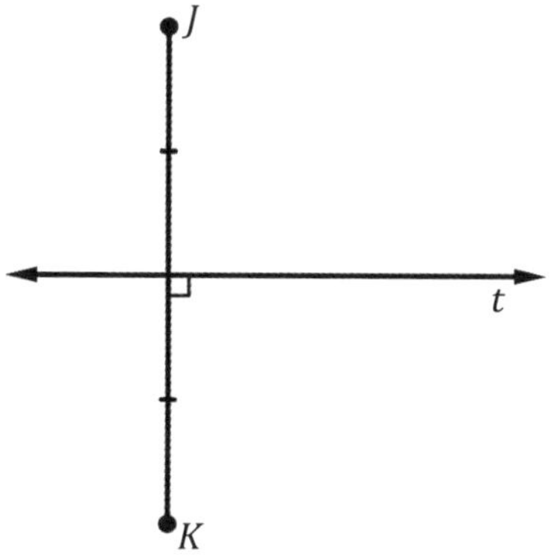

What is the intersection between line t and $\overline{JK}$ called?

Let's Practice!

1. Using the above diagram where line t is the perpendicular bisector of $\overline{JK}$, let M be the point where line t and $\overline{JK}$ intersect, and let P be any point on line t.

   a. Suppose that P lies on $\overline{JK}$. What conclusions can you draw about the relationship between $\overline{JP}$ and $\overline{KP}$? Explain.

   b. Suppose that P does not lie on $\overline{JK}$. What conclusions can you draw now about the relationship between $\overline{JP}$ and $\overline{KP}$? Explain.

Try It!

2. Suppose that C and D are two distinct points in the plane and a student drew line r to be the perpendicular bisector of $\overline{CD}$ as shown in the diagram below.

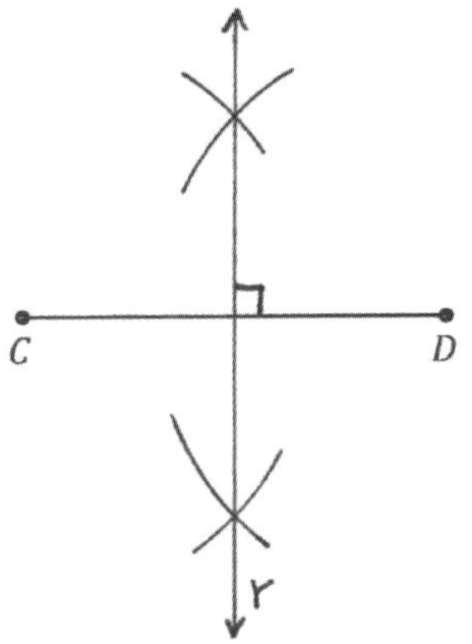

   a. If G is a point on r, show that G is equidistant from C and D.

   b. Conversely, use a counterexample to show that if Q is a point which is equidistant from C and D, then Q is a point on r.

   c. Determine if the following statement is true.

   The perpendicular bisector of $\overline{CD}$ is exactly the set of points which are equidistant from C and D.

Perpendicular Bisector Theorem

If a point is on the perpendicular bisector of a segment, then it is equidistant from the endpoints of the segment. The **converse** of this theorem is also true.

BEAT THE TEST!

1. Consider the following diagram. A and B are two distinct points in the plane and line l is the perpendicular bisector of $\overline{AB}$.

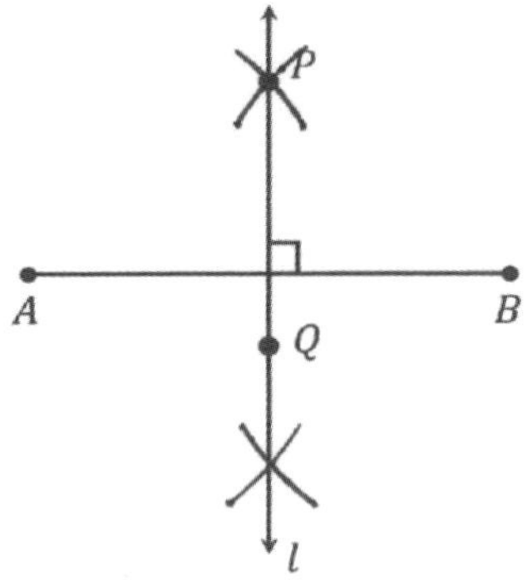

Yozef and Teresa were debating whether P and Q are both on l. Circle the correct response. Justify your answer.

Yozef's work	Teresa's work
I measured the distance between A and P, and B and P, and the width of the compass was the same for both. Same happened between A and Q, and B and Q. Therefore, P is equidistant from A and B, and Q is equidistant from A and B. P and Q are both on line l justified by the Converse of the Perpendicular Bisector Theorem.	P is on the intersection of the arcs drawn in the construction process above segment AB, so the width of the compass is the same from A to P and from B to P. However, Q is not on the intersection of the arcs drawn below the segment, so it is not equidistant from A and B. In conclusion, P is on the perpendicular bisector l but Q is not on it.

Test Yourself! Practice Tool

Great job! You have reached the end of this section. Now it's time to try the "Test Yourself! Practice Tool," where you can practice all the skills and concepts you learned in this section. Log in to Math Nation and try out the "Test Yourself! Practice Tool" so you can see how well you know these topics!

Section 2: Angles

Topic 1: Introduction to Angles – Part 1 37
Standards Covered: G-CO.9
- ☐ I can measure and classify angles.

Topic 2: Introduction to Angles – Part 2 40
Standards Covered: G-CO.9
- ☐ I can measure and classify angles.

Topic 3: Angle Pairs – Part 1 43
Standards Covered: G-CO.9
- ☐ I can apply knowledge of angle pairs to find the measure of a missing angle.

Topic 4: Angle Pairs – Part 2 46
Standards Covered: G-CO.9
- ☐ I can use the Congruent Complements and Supplements theorems to determine the measure of a missing angle.

Topic 5: Special Types of Angle Pairs Formed by Transversals and Non-Parallel Lines 50
Standards Covered: G-CO.9
- ☐ I can apply line relationships to determine an angle relationship.

Topic 6: Special Types of Angle Pairs Formed by Transversals and Parallel Lines – Part 1 55
Standards Covered: G-CO.9
- ☐ I can use patterns to determine an angle relationship when angles are formed by a transversal.

Topic 7: Special Types of Angle Pairs Formed by Transversals and Parallel Lines – Part 2 58
Standards Covered: G-CO.9
- ☐ I can prove theorems about angles formed by a transversal.

Topic 8: Perpendicular Transversals 61
Standards Covered: G-CO.9
- ☐ I can use angles created by a transversal to prove that lines are parallel to one another and perpendicular to the transversal.

Topic 9: Proving Angle Relationships in Transversals and Parallel Lines 63
Standards Covered: G-CO.9
- ☐ I can complete a proof for congruence of alternate interior angles and corresponding angles.
- ☐ I can complete a proof for points on the perpendicular bisector of a line segment that are equidistant from the segment's endpoints.

Topic 10: Copying Angles and Constructing Angle Bisectors 65
Standards Covered: G-CO.12
- ☐ I can construct an angle bisector.

Topic 11: Introduction to Polygons 67
Standards Covered: This topic covers introductory materials
- ☐ I can measure and classify an angle to determine if a figure is a polygon.

Topic 12: Angles of Polygons 70
Standards Covered: This topic covers introductory materials
- ☐ I can measure the interior and exterior angles or a regular and irregular polygon.

Topic 13: Angles of Other Polygons 73
Standards Covered: G-CO.1, G-CO.10
- ☐ I can calculate the base angles, interior angles, and exterior angles of a regular polygon with more than four sides.

Visit MathNation.com or search "Math Nation" in your phone or tablet's app store to watch the videos that go along with this workbook!

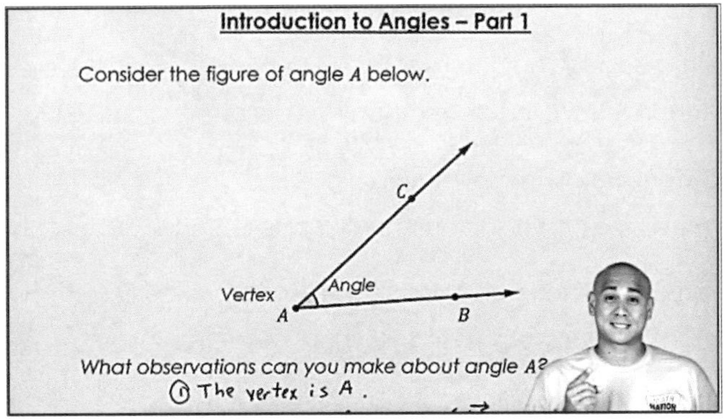

The following Michigan Mathematics Standards will be covered in this section:
G-CO.1 - Know precise definitions of angle, circle, perpendicular line, parallel line, and line segment, based on the undefined notions of point, line, distance along a line, and distance around a circular arc.
G-CO.9 - Prove theorems about lines and angles; use theorems about lines and angles to solve problems.
G-CO.10 - Prove theorems about triangles. Use theorems about triangles to solve problems: measures of interior angles of a triangle sum to 180.
G-CO.12 - Make formal geometric constructions with a variety of tools and methods. *Copying a segment; copying an angle; bisecting a segment; bisecting an angle; constructing perpendicular lines, including the perpendicular bisector of a line segment; and constructing a line parallel to a given line through a point not on the line.*

Section 2: Angles
Section 2 – Topic 1
Introduction to Angles – Part 1

Consider the figure of angle A below.

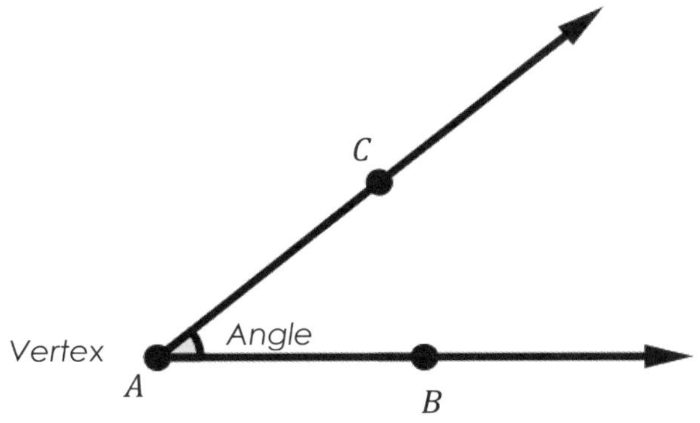

What observations can you make about angle A?

How else do you think we can name angle A?

Why do you think we draw an arc to show angle A?

Like circles, angles are measured in ______________ since they measure the amount of rotation around the center.

Use the figure to answer the following questions.

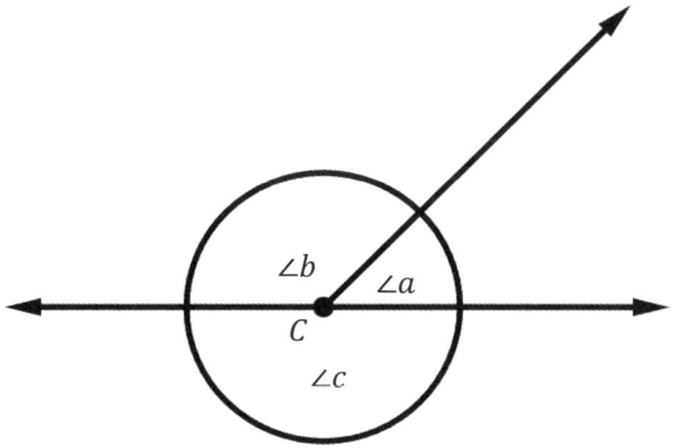

How many degrees are in circle C?

What is the measure of $\angle a + \angle b + \angle c$?

How many degrees are in half of a circle?

What is the measure of $\angle a + \angle b$?

Two positive angles that form a straight line together are called __________________ angles.

- When added together, the measures of these angles total ______________ degrees, forming a ___________ pair.

Draw an example of ***supplementary angles*** that form a ***linear pair***.

A quarter-circle is a(n) ______________ angle.

How many degrees are in a right angle?

Two positive angles that together form a right angle are called __________________ angles.

Draw an example of ***complementary angles***.

Let's Practice!

1. In the figure below, $m\angle a = 7x + 5$ and $m\angle b = 28x$. The angles are supplementary.

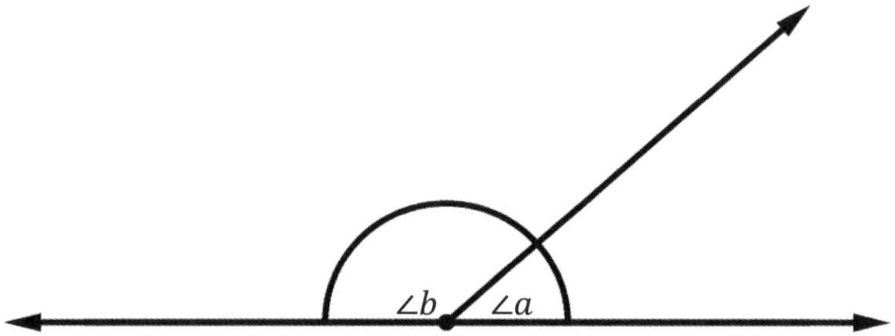

Find the value of x and the measure of $\angle a$ and $\angle b$ in degrees.

STUDY EDGE TIP

When we refer to an angle as $\angle ABC$, we mean the actual angle object. If we want to talk about the size or the measure of the angle in degrees, we often write it as $m\angle ABC$.

2. In the figure below, $m\angle c = 9x - 3$ and $m\angle d = 8x + 9$.

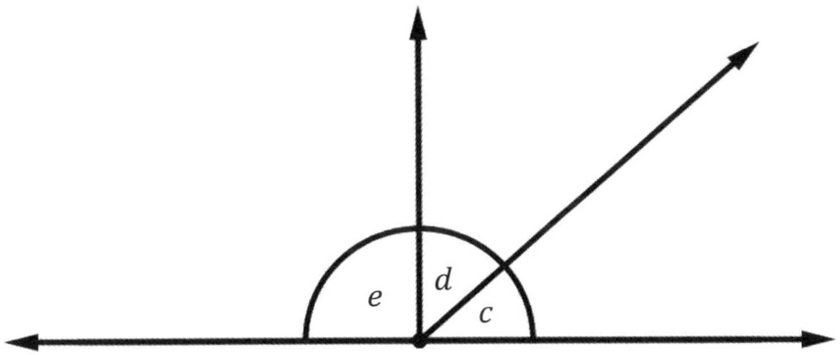

a. If $x = 5$, are $\angle c$ and $\angle d$ complementary? Justify your answer.

b. If $\angle c$, $\angle d$, and $\angle e$ form half a circle, then what is the measure of $\angle e$ in degrees?

Try It!

3. Angle A is $20°$ larger than angle B. If A and B are complementary, what is the measure of angle A?

4. Consider the figure below.

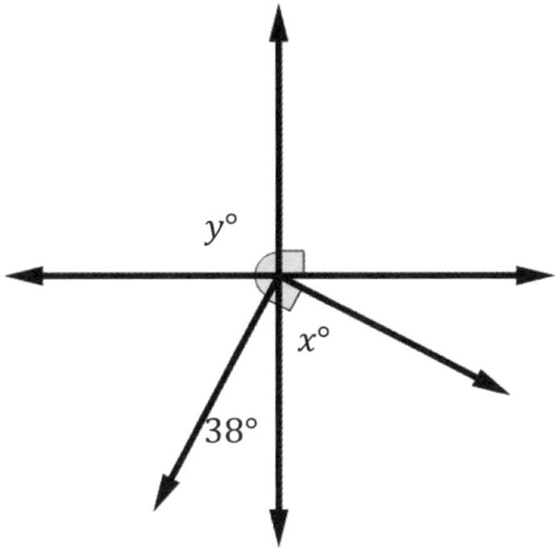

If the angle with value of $y°$ stretches from the positive y-axis to the ray that makes the $38°$ angle, set up and solve an appropriate equation for x and y.

Section 2 – Topic 2
Introduction to Angles – Part 2

Measuring and classifying angles:

- We often use a _______________ to measure angles.

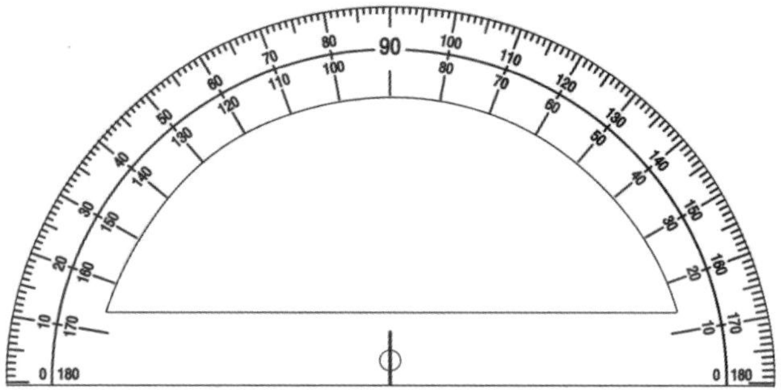

To measure an angle, we line up the central mark on the base of the ***protractor*** with the vertex of the angle we want to measure.

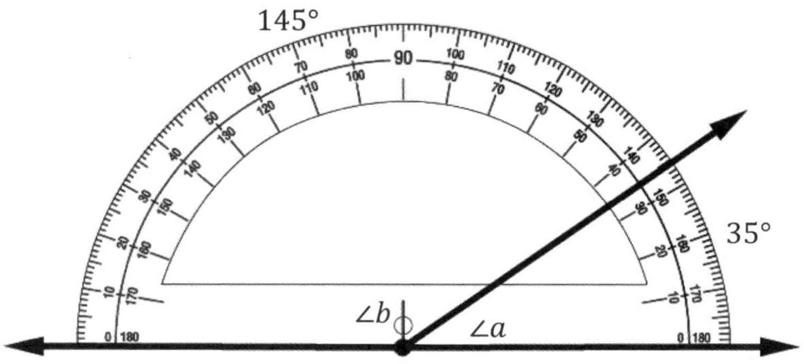

TAKE NOTE! *Postulates & Theorems*

The Protractor Postulate

The measure of an angle is the absolute value of the difference of the real numbers paired with the sides of the angle, because the parts of angles formed by rays between the sides of a linear pair add to the whole, $180°$.

Label and measure the angles in the following figure.

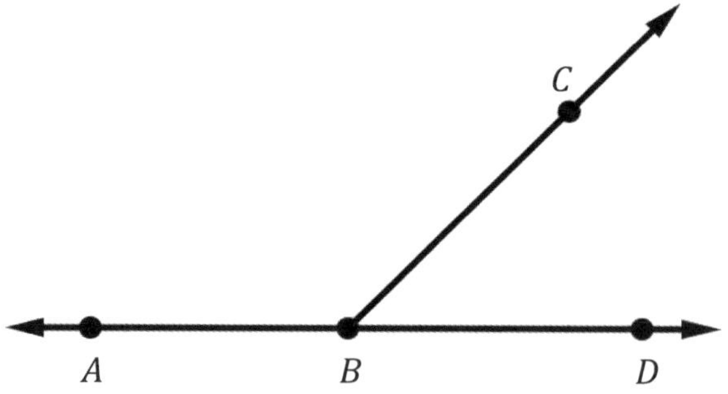

Match each of the following words to the most appropriate figure below. Write your answer in the space provided below each figure.

Acute	Obtuse	Right	Straight	Reflex

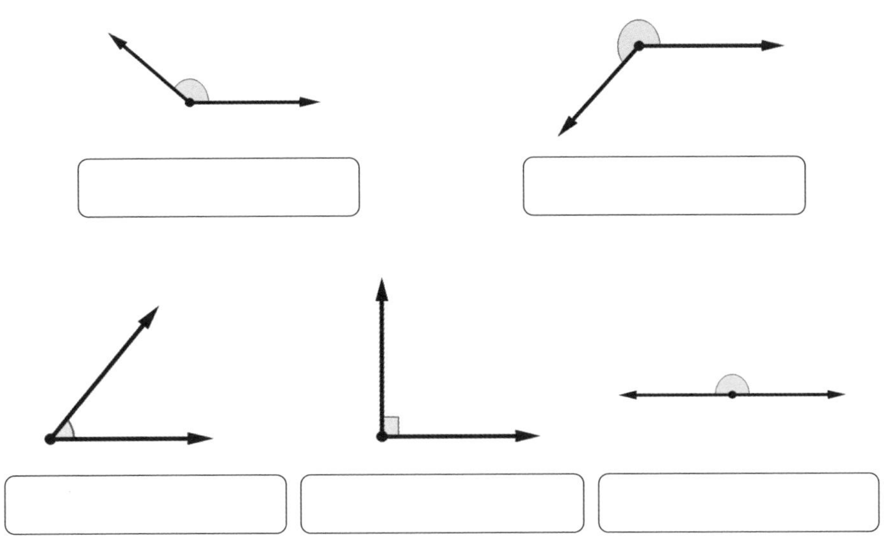

➢ An angle that measures less than $90°$ is ______________.

➢ An angle that measures greater than $90°$ but less than $180°$ is ______________.

➢ An angle that measures exactly $90°$ is ______________.

➢ An angle of exactly $180°$ is ______________.

➢ An angle greater than $180°$ is called a __________ angle.

Let's Practice!

1. Use the figure below to fill in the blanks that define angles $\angle FGK$, $\angle FGH$, and $\angle KGH$ as acute, obtuse, right, or straight.

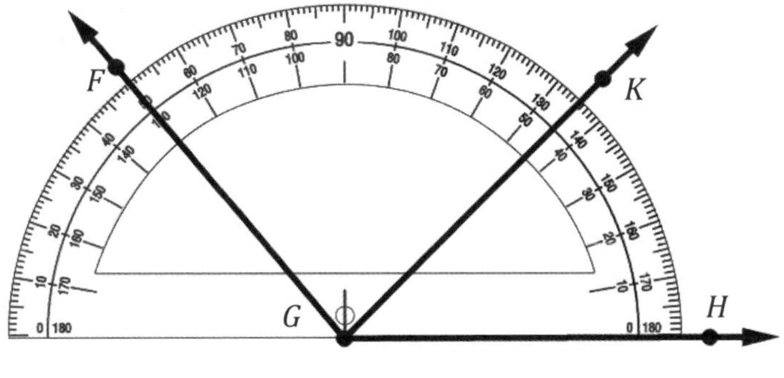

a. $\angle FGK$ is a(n) ______________ angle.

b. $\angle FGH$ is a(n) ______________ angle.

c. $\angle KGH$ is a(n) ______________ angle.

Try It!

2. A hockey stick comes into contact with the ice in such a way that the shaft makes an angle with the ice, labeled as angle B in the figure below. The angle between the shaft and the toe of the hockey stick is labeled as A.

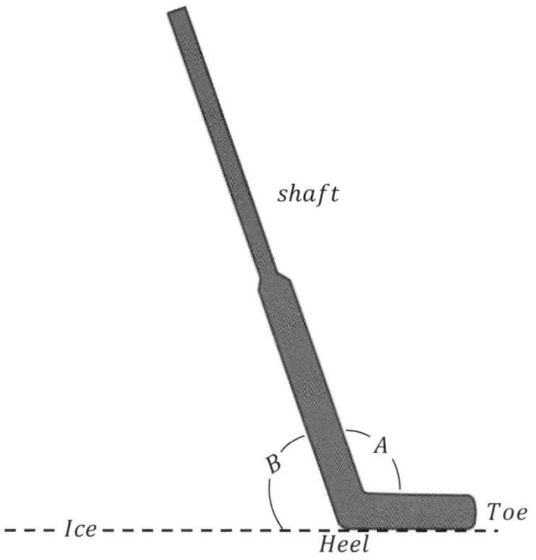

a. Determine the type of angle that is between the ice and the shaft.

b. Determine the type of angle that is between the shaft and the toe.

BEAT THE TEST!

1. Consider the figure below.

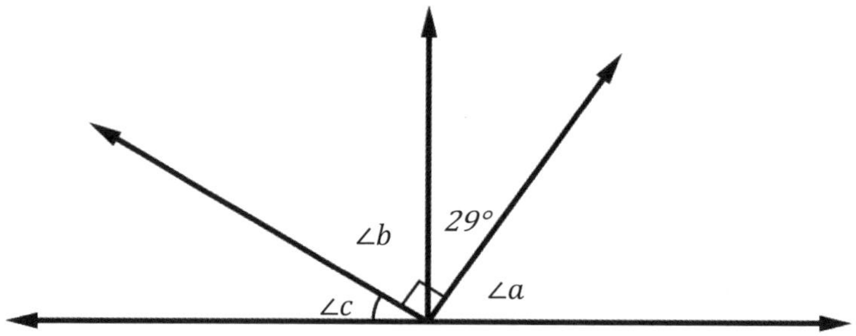

If $\angle b$ and $\angle c$ are complementary, then:

The measure of $\angle a$ is [ ] .

The sum of $m\angle a$ and $m\angle b$ is [ ] .

The sum of $m\angle a$, $m\angle b$, and $m\angle c$ is [ ] .

If $m\angle z = m\angle a + m\angle c$, then $\angle z$ is

- o acute.
- o obtuse.
- o right.
- o straight.

Section 2 – Topic 3
Angle Pairs – Part 1

Consider the following figure that presents an ***angle pair***.

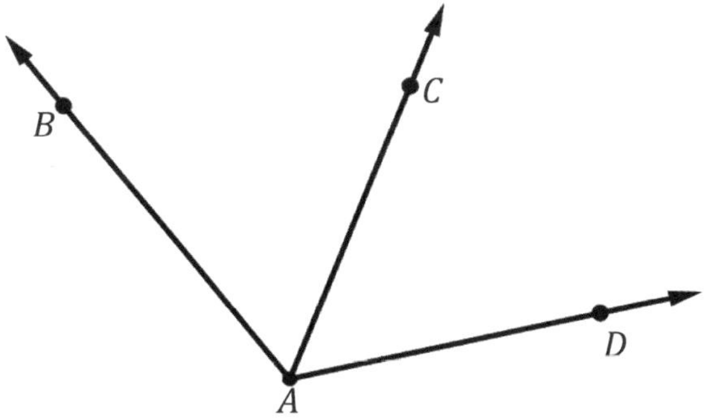

What common ray do $\angle BAC$ and $\angle CAD$ share?

Because these angle pairs share a ray, they are called __________________ angles.

Consider the following figure of ***adjacent angles***.

What observations can you make about the figure?

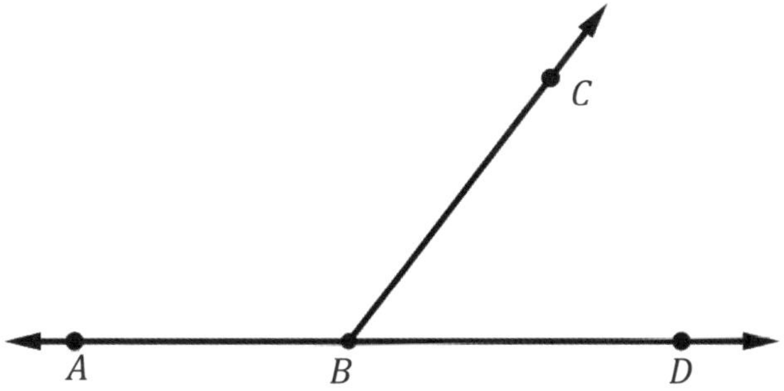

These adjacent angles are called a _____________ pair. Together, the angles form a ____________ angle.

What is the measure of a straight angle?

What is the measure of the sum of a ***linear pair***?

TAKE NOTE! *Postulates & Theorems*

Linear Pair Postulate

If two positive angles form a linear pair, then they are supplementary.

Consider the angle pairs in the figure below.

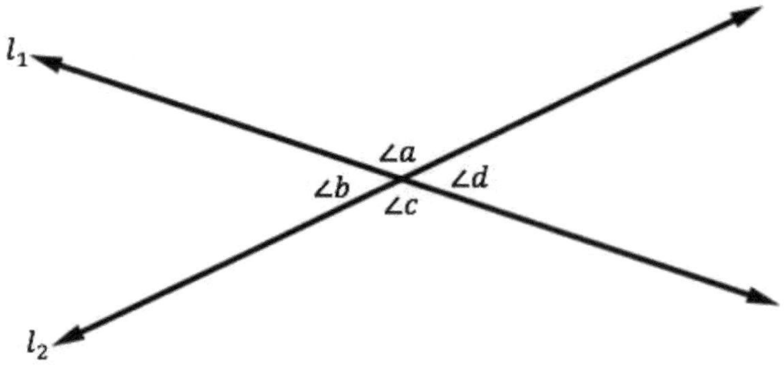

What observations can you make about $\angle a$ and $\angle c$?

What observations can you make about $\angle b$ and $\angle d$?

$\angle a$ and $\angle c$ form what we call a pair of ____________ angles.

What angle pairs form a set of ***vertical angles***?

> **TAKE NOTE!** *Postulates & Theorems*
>
> **Vertical Angles Theorem**
>
> If two angles are vertical angles, then they have equal measures.

Consider the figure below.

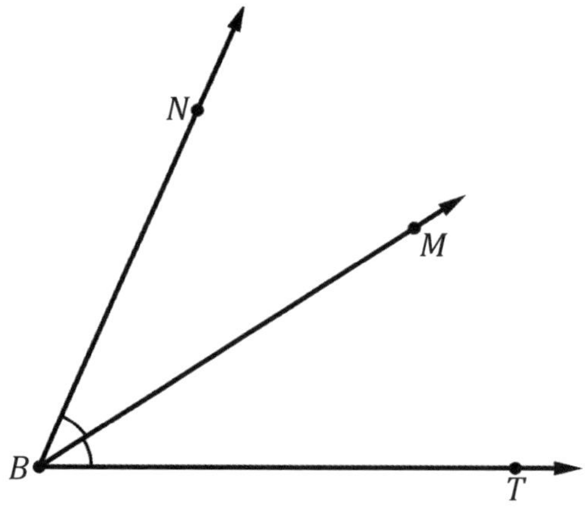

What observations can you make about the figure?

We call $\overrightarrow{BM}$ an ***angle bisector***.

Make a conjecture as to why $\overrightarrow{BM}$ is called an angle bisector.

Let's Practice!

1. Consider the figure below.

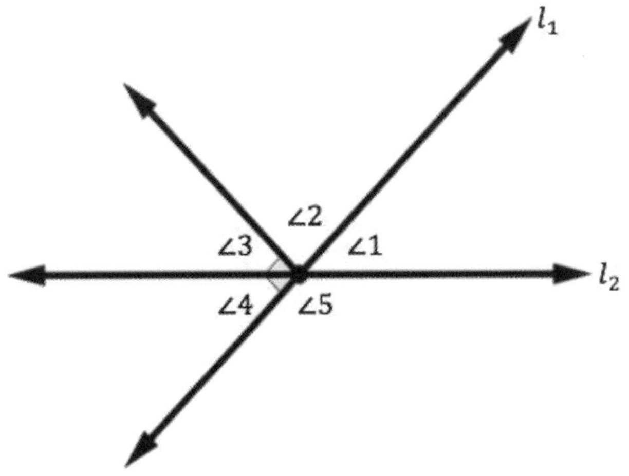

Complete the following statements:

- $\angle 1$ and $\angle 4$ are ______________ angles.
- $\angle 1$ and $\angle 2$ are ______________ angles.
- $\angle 3$ and $\angle 4$ are ______________________ angles and ______________________ angles.
- $\angle 4$ and $\angle 5$ are ______________________ angles and ______________________ angles. They also form a ______________________.

2. If $\angle ACB$ and $\angle ACE$ are linear pairs, and $m\angle ACB = 5x + 25$ and $m\angle ACE = 2x + 29$, then

   a. Determine $m\angle ACB + m\angle ACE$.

   b. Determine the measures of $m\angle ACB$ and $m\angle ACE$.

3. If $\angle MFG$ and $\angle EFN$ are vertical angles, and $m\angle MFG = 7x - 18$ and $m\angle EFN = 5x + 10$, then

   a. What can we say about $\angle MFG$ and $\angle EFN$ that will help us determine their measures?

   b. Determine the measures of $\angle MFG$ and $\angle EFN$.

Try It!

4. Consider the figure below.

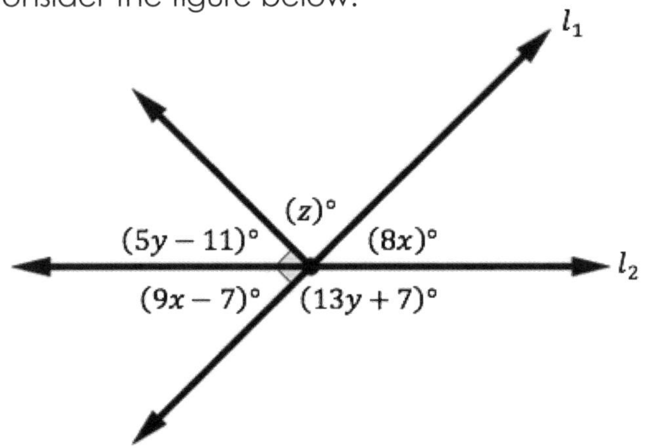

Find the value of x, y, and z.

Section 2 – Topic 4
Angle Pairs – Part 2

Consider the figure below.

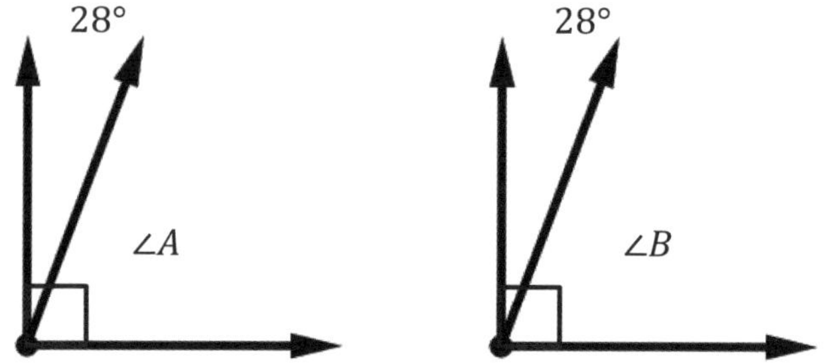

What can you observe about $\angle A$ and $\angle B$?

> ***TAKE NOTE!*** *Postulates & Theorems*
>
> **Congruent Complements Theorem**
>
> If $\angle A$ and $\angle B$ are complements of the same angle, then $\angle A$ and $\angle B$ are congruent.

Consider the figures below.

What can you observe about $\angle A$ and $\angle B$?

TAKE NOTE! *Postulates & Theorems*

Congruent Supplements Theorem

If $\angle A$ and $\angle B$ are supplements of the same angle, then $\angle A$ and $\angle B$ are congruent.

Consider the figure below.

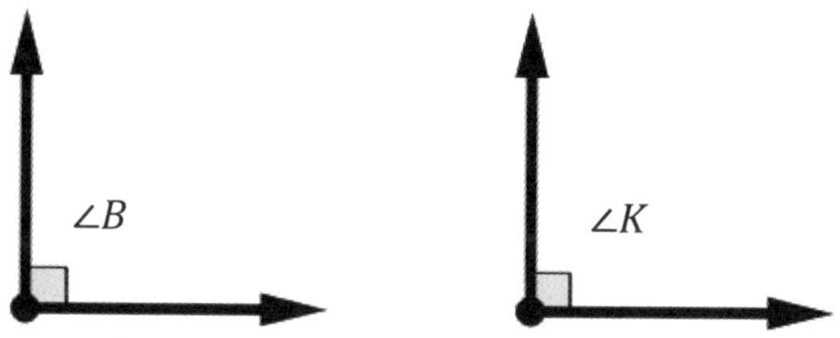

What can you observe about $\angle B$ and $\angle K$?

TAKE NOTE! *Postulates & Theorems*

Right Angles Theorem

All right angles are congruent.

Let's Practice!

1. The measure of an angle is four times greater than its complement. What is the measure of the larger angle?

Try It!

2. $\angle X$ and $\angle Y$ are supplementary. One angle measures 5 times the other angle. What is the complement of the smaller angle?

Let's Practice!

3. Consider the figure below.

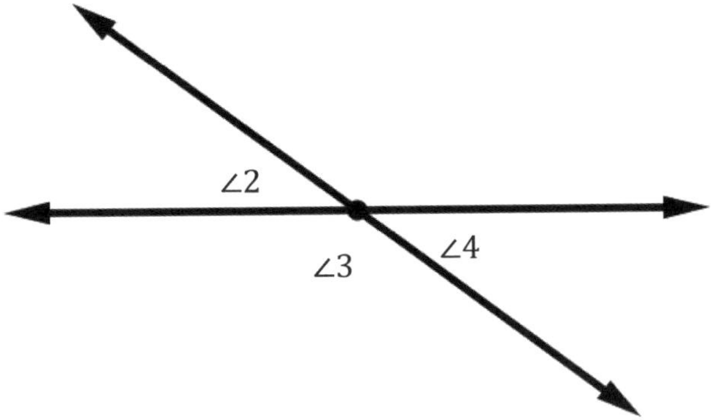

Given: ∠2 and ∠3 are a linear pair.
∠3 and ∠4 are a linear pair.

Prove: ∠2 ≅ ∠4

Complete the chart below.

Statements	Reasons
1. ∠2 and ∠3 are a linear pair. ∠3 and ∠4 are a linear pair.	**1.** Given
2. ∠2 and ∠3 are supplementary. ∠3 and ∠4 are supplementary.	**2.**
3. ∠2 ≅ ∠4	**3.**

Try It!

4. Consider the figures below.

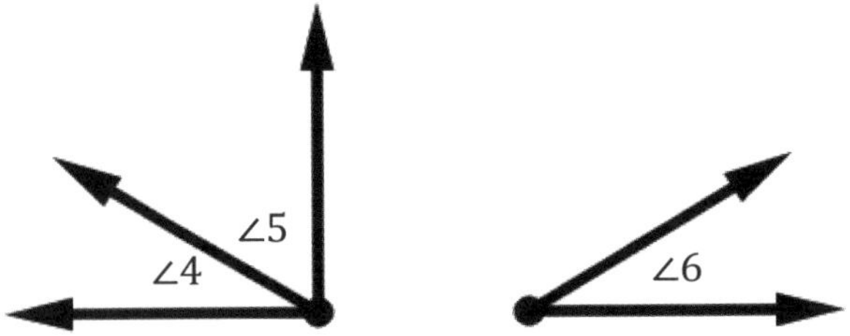

Given: ∠5 and ∠6 are complementary.
$m\angle 4 + m\angle 5 = 90°$

Prove: ∠6 ≅ ∠4

Complete the chart below.

Statements	Reasons
1.	**1.** Given
2.	**2.** Given
3. ∠4 and ∠5 are complementary	**3.**
4. ∠6 ≅ ∠4	**4.**

BEAT THE TEST!

1. $\angle LMN$ and $\angle PML$ are linear pairs, $m\angle LMN = 7x - 3$ and $m\angle PML = 13x + 3$.

   Part A: $m\angle LMN =$

   Part B: $m\angle PML =$

   Part C: If $\angle PMR$ and $\angle LMN$ form a vertical pair and $m\angle PMR = 5y + 4$, find the value of y.

2. Consider the figure below.

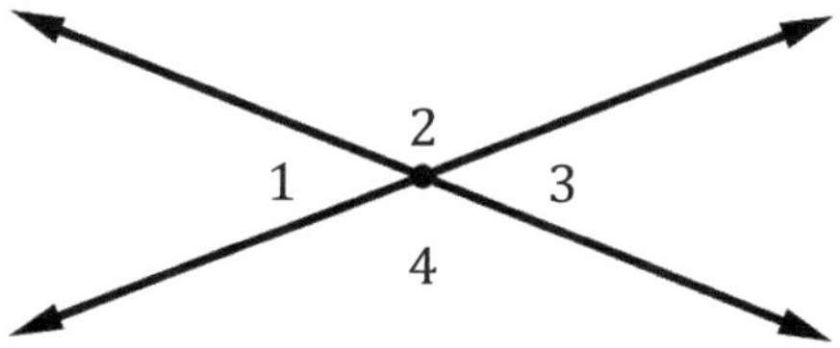

Given: $\angle 1$ and $\angle 2$ form a linear pair.
$\angle 1$ and $\angle 4$ form a linear pair.

Prove: The Vertical Angle Theorem

Use the bank of reasons below to complete the table.

Congruent Supplement Theorem	Right Angles Theorem
Congruent Complement Theorem	Linear Pair Postulate

Statements	Reasons
1. $\angle 1$ and $\angle 2$ are linear pairs. $\angle 1$ and $\angle 4$ are linear pairs.	**1.** Given
2. $\angle 1$ and $\angle 2$ are supplementary. $\angle 1$ and $\angle 4$ are supplementary.	**2.**
3. $\angle 2 \cong \angle 4$	**3.**

Section 2 – Topic 5
Special Types of Angle Pairs Formed by Transversals and Non-Parallel Lines

Many geometry problems involve the intersection of three or more lines.

Consider the figure below.

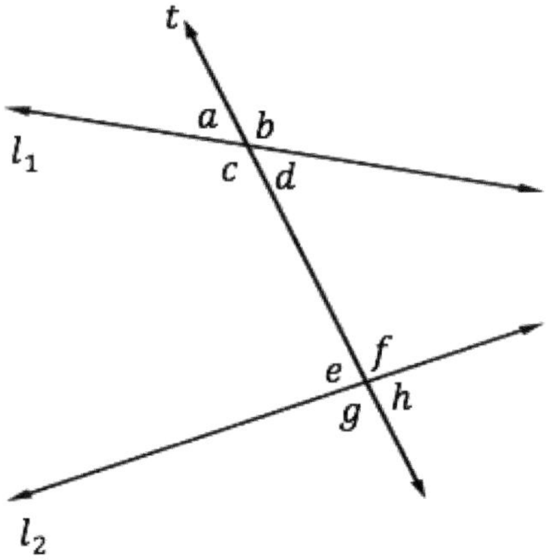

What observations can you make about the angles in the figure?

- Lines l_1 and l_2 are crossed by line t.
- Line t is called the ________________, because it intersects two other lines (l_1 and l_2).
- The intersection of line t with l_1 and l_2 forms eight angles.

Identify angles made by transversals.

Consider the figure below. $\angle a$ and $\angle b$ form a ***linear pair***.

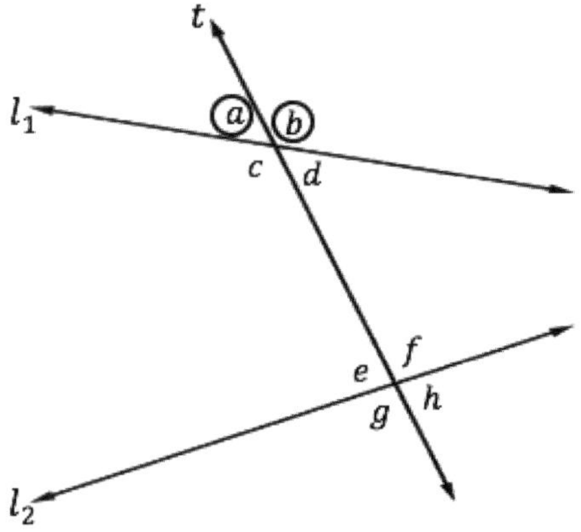

Box and name the other linear pairs in the figure.

Consider the figure below. $\angle e$ and $\angle h$ are ***vertical angles***.

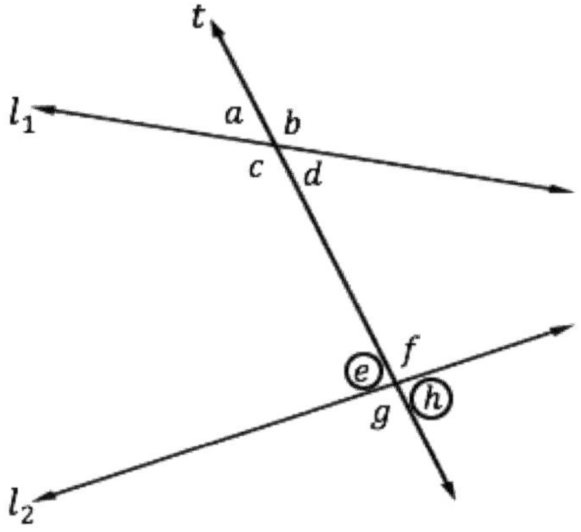

Box and name the other pairs of vertical angles in the figure.

Consider the figure below.

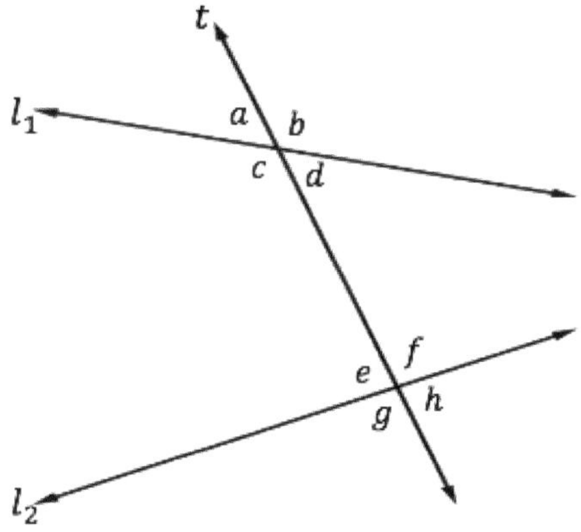

Which part of the figure do you think would be considered the interior? Draw a circle around the interior angles in the figure. Justify your answer.

Which part of the figure do you think would be considered the exterior? Draw a box around the exterior angles in the figure. Justify your answer.

Consider the figure below. $\angle d$ and $\angle e$ are ***alternate interior angles***.

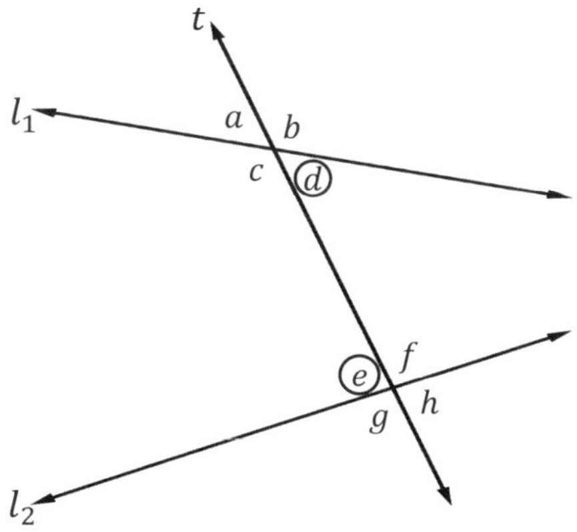

Notice how $\angle d$ and $\angle e$ are in the interior region of lines l_1 and l_2, but on opposite sides of the transversal. Draw a box around another pair of alternate interior angles in the figure.

Consider the figure below. $\angle b$ and $\angle g$ are ***alternate exterior angles***.

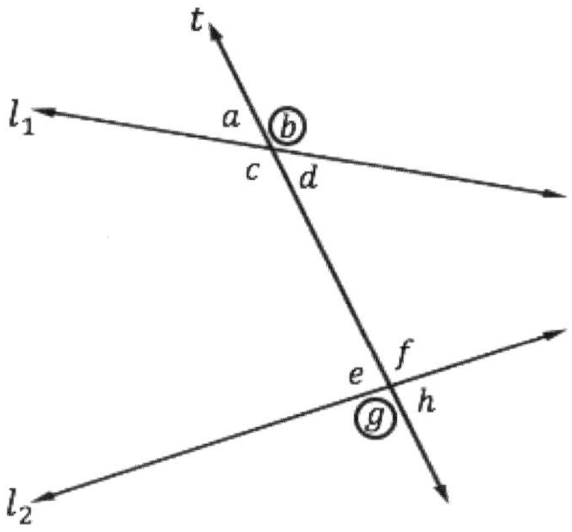

Notice how $\angle b$ and $\angle g$ are in the exterior region of lines l_1 and l_2, but on opposite sides of the transversal. Draw a box around another pair of alternate exterior angles in the figure.

Consider the figure below. $\angle b$ and $\angle f$ are ***corresponding angles***.

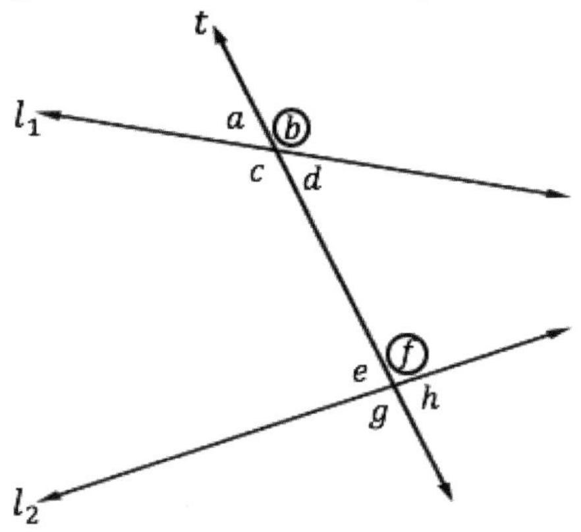

Notice how $\angle b$ and $\angle f$ have distinct vertex points and lie on the same side of the transversal. However, $\angle f$ is in the interior region of lines l_1 and l_2, and $\angle b$ is in the exterior region of lines l_1 and l_2.

Draw a box around another pair of corresponding angles in the figure and name them below.

Consider the figure below. $\angle c$ and $\angle e$ are ***consecutive*** or ***same-side interior angles***.

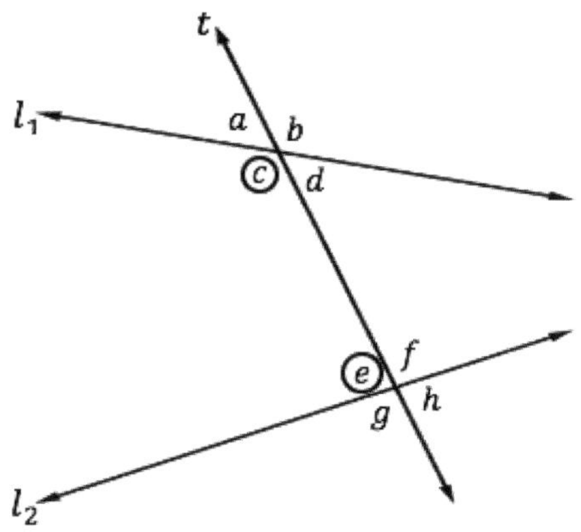

Notice how $\angle c$ and $\angle e$ have distinct vertex points and lie on the same side of the transversal. However, both angles are in the interior region of lines l_1 and l_2.

Draw a box around the other pair of consecutive interior angles.

Let's Practice!

1. On the figure below, Park Avenue and Bay City Road are non-parallel lines crossed by transversal Mt. Carmel Street.

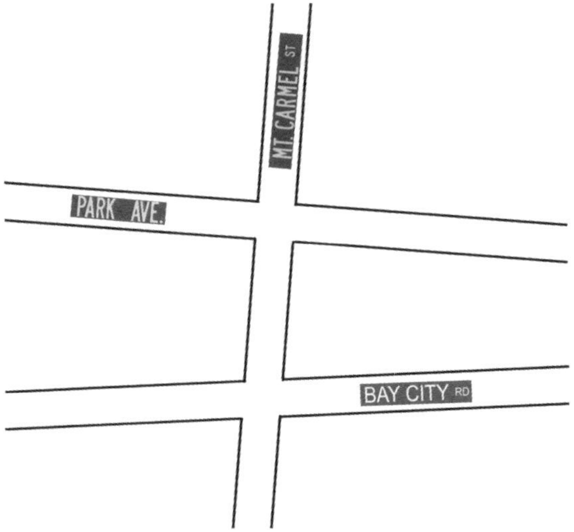

The city hired GeoNat Road Services to plan where certain buildings will be constructed and located on the map.

Position the buildings on the map by meeting the following conditions:

- The park and the city building form a linear pair.
- The city building and the police department are at vertical angles.
- The police department and the hospital are at alternate interior angles.
- The hospital and the fire department are at consecutive interior angles.
- The school is at a corresponding angle with the park and a consecutive interior angle to the police department.
- The library and the park are at alternate exterior angles.
- The church is at an exterior angle and it forms a linear pair with both the library and the school.

Try It!

2. Consider the figure below.

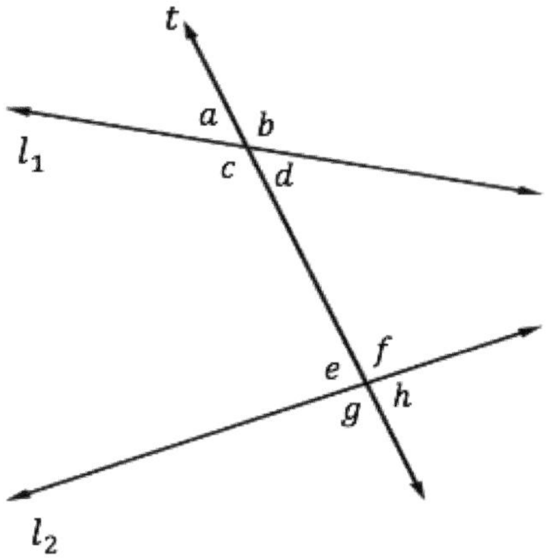

Which of the following statements is true?

Ⓐ If $\angle a$ and $\angle e$ lie on the same side of the transversal and one angle is interior and the other is exterior, then they are corresponding angles.

Ⓑ If $\angle b$ and $\angle h$ are on the exterior opposite sides of the transversal, then they are alternate exterior angles.

Ⓒ If $\angle b$ and $\angle c$ are adjacent angles lying on the same side of the transversal, then they are same-side/consecutive interior angles.

Ⓓ If $\angle b, \angle c, \angle f$ and $\angle g$ are between the non-parallel lines, then they are interior angles.

BEAT THE TEST!

1. Consider the figure below.

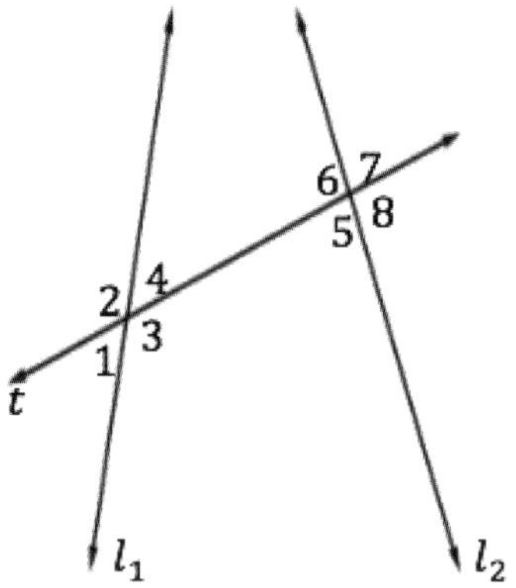

Match the angles on the left with their corresponding names on the right.

_____	∠1 and ∠7	**A.**	Alternate Interior Angles
_____	∠5 and ∠6	**B.**	Consecutive Angles
_____	∠4 and ∠6	**C.**	Corresponding Angles
_____	∠5 and ∠7	**D.**	Vertical Angles
_____	∠4 and ∠5	**E.**	Alternate Exterior Angles
_____	∠3 and ∠8	**F.**	Linear Pair

Section 2 – Topic 6
Special Types of Angle Pairs Formed by Transversals and Parallel Lines – Part 1

Consider the following figure of a transversal crossing two parallel lines.

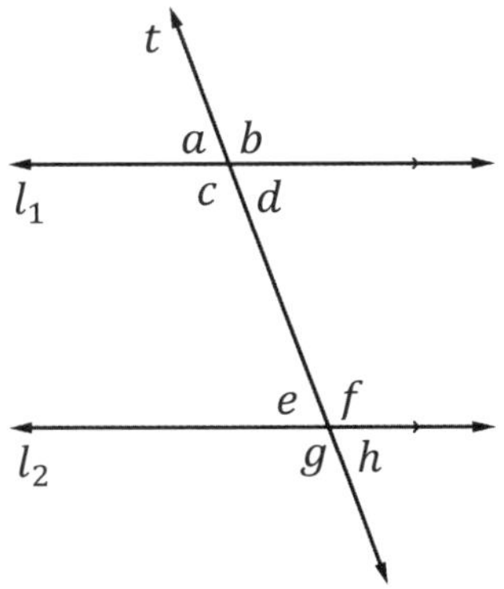

Name the acute angles in the above figure.

Name the obtuse angles in the above figure.

Which angles are congruent? Justify your answer.

Which angles are supplementary? Justify your answer.

Consider the following figures of transversal t crossing parallel lines, l_1 and l_2.

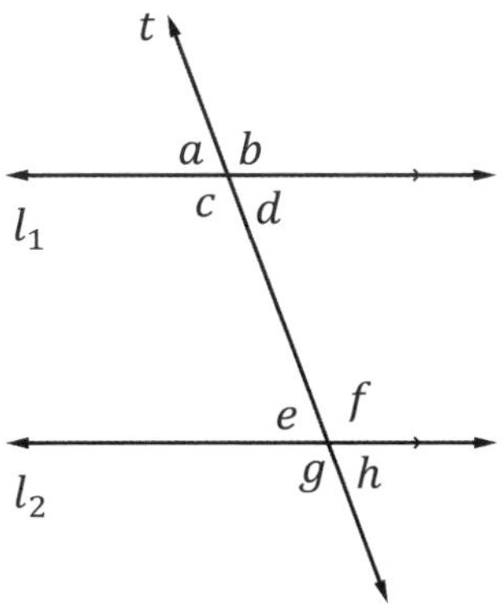

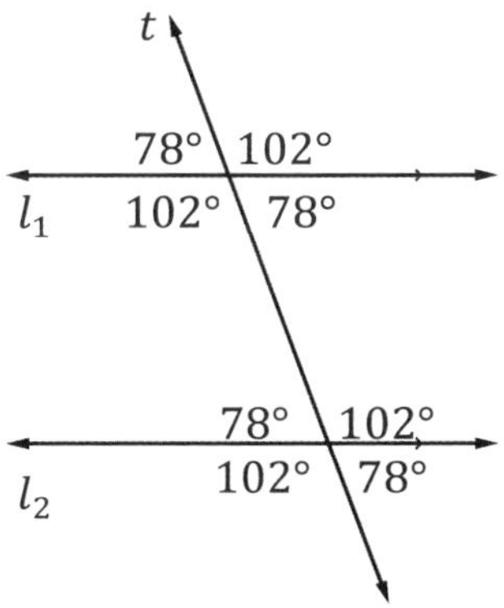

Identify an example of the Linear Pair Postulate. Use the figure above to justify your answer.

Identify an example of the Vertical Angles Theorem. Use the figure above to justify your answer.

Make a list of the interior and the exterior angles. What can you say about these angles?

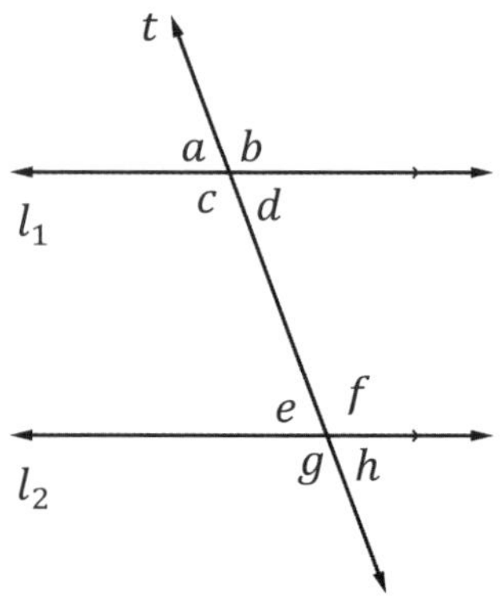

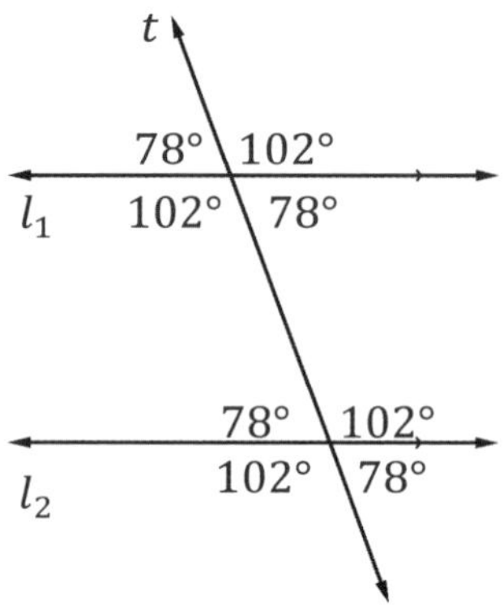

Identify each of the ***alternate interior angles*** in the above figures and determine the angles' measures.

TAKE NOTE! *Postulates & Theorems*

Alternate Interior Angles Theorem

If two parallel lines are cut by a transversal, the alternate interior angles are congruent.

Converse of the Alternate Interior Angles Theorem

If two lines are cut by a transversal and the alternate interior angles are congruent, the lines are parallel.

Identify the ***alternate exterior angles*** in the above figures and determine the angles' measures.

TAKE NOTE! *Postulates & Theorems*

Alternate Exterior Angles Theorem

If two parallel lines are cut by a transversal, the alternate exterior angles are congruent.

Converse of the Alternate Exterior Angles Theorem

If two lines are cut by a transversal and the alternate exterior angles are congruent, the lines are parallel.

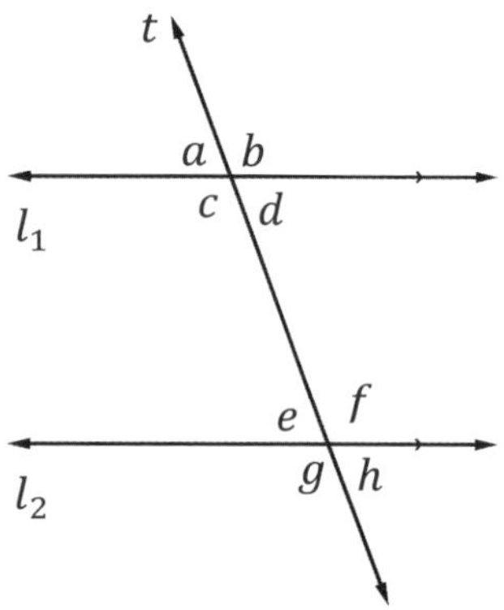

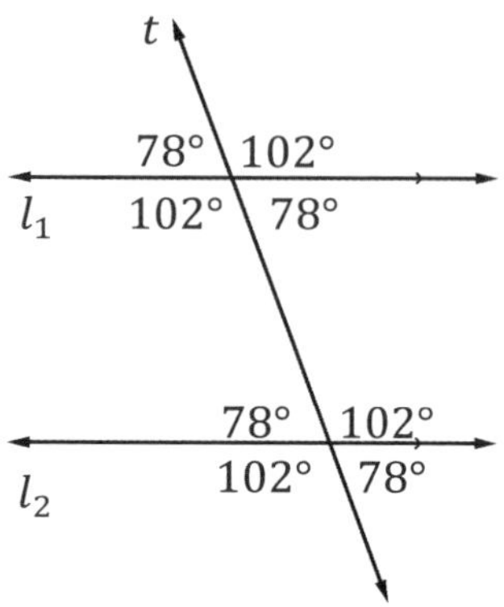

Identify the ***corresponding angles*** in the above figures. What does each angle measure?

TAKE NOTE! *Postulates & Theorems*

Corresponding Angles Theorem

If two parallel lines are cut by a transversal, the corresponding angles are congruent.

Converse of the Corresponding Angles Theorem

If two lines are cut by a transversal and the corresponding angles are congruent, the lines are parallel.

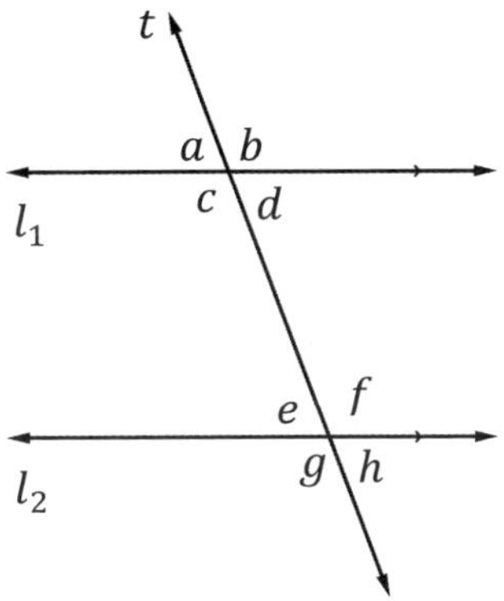

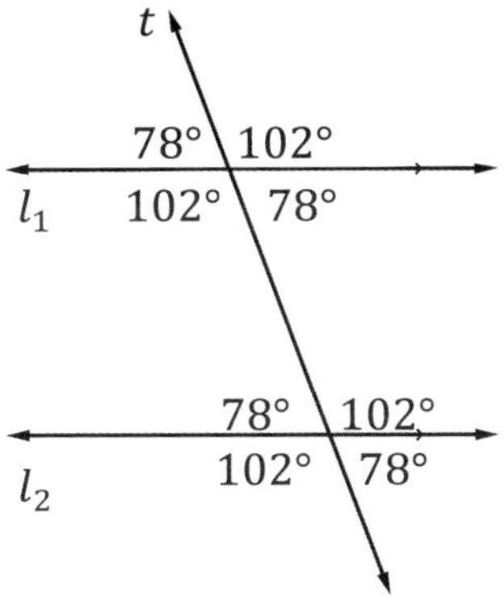

Identify the ***same-side/consecutive angles*** in the above figures. What does each angle measure?

TAKE NOTE! *Postulates & Theorems*

Same-side Consecutive Angles Theorem

If two parallel lines are cut by a transversal, the interior angles on the same side of the transversal are supplementary.

Converse of the Same-side Consecutive Angles Theorem

If two lines are cut by a transversal and the interior angles on the same side of the transversal are supplementary, the lines are parallel.

Let's Practice!

1. Which lines of the following segments are parallel?

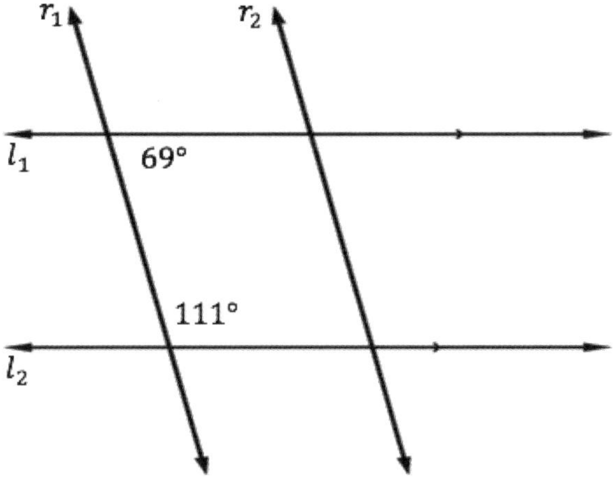

Ⓐ r_1 and r_2
Ⓑ l_1 and l_2
Ⓒ r_1 and l_2
Ⓓ l_1 and r_2

2. Which of the following is a condition for the figure below that will ***not*** prove $l_1 \parallel l_2$?

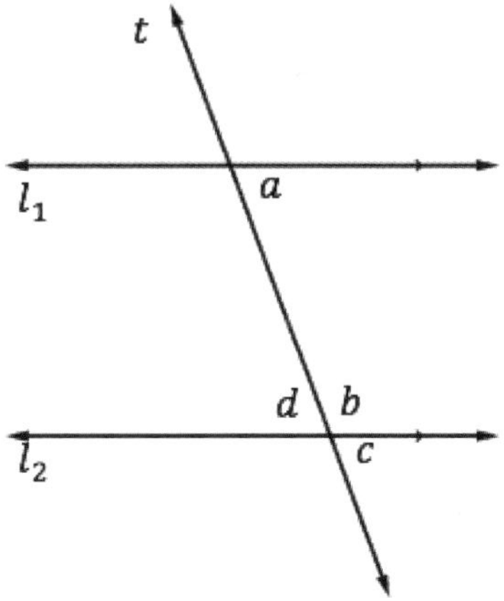

Ⓐ $\angle a \cong \angle c$
Ⓑ $m\angle b + m\angle d = 180°$
Ⓒ $\angle a \cong \angle d$
Ⓓ $m\angle a + m\angle b = 180°$

Try It!

3. Consider the figure below, where l_1 and l_2 are parallel and cut by transversals t_1 and t_2. Find the values of a, b and v.

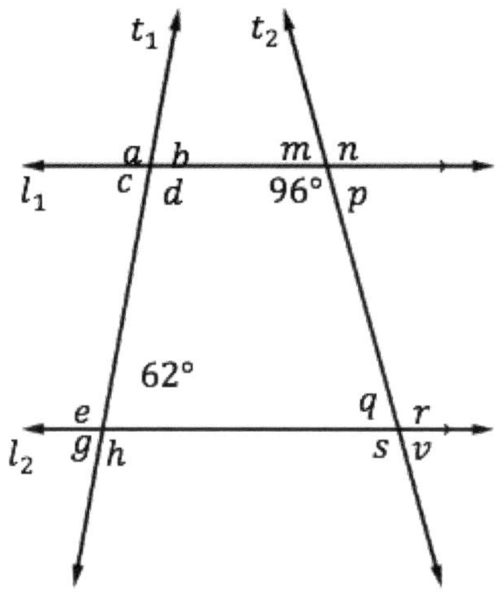

Section 2 – Topic 7
Special Types of Angle Pairs Formed by Transversals and Parallel Lines – Part 2

Let's Practice!

1. Complete the chart below using the following information.

Given:
$\angle 4$ and $\angle 7$ are supplementary.
$\angle 8$ and $\angle 16$ are congruent.

Prove: $l_1 \parallel l_2$ and $t_1 \parallel t_2$

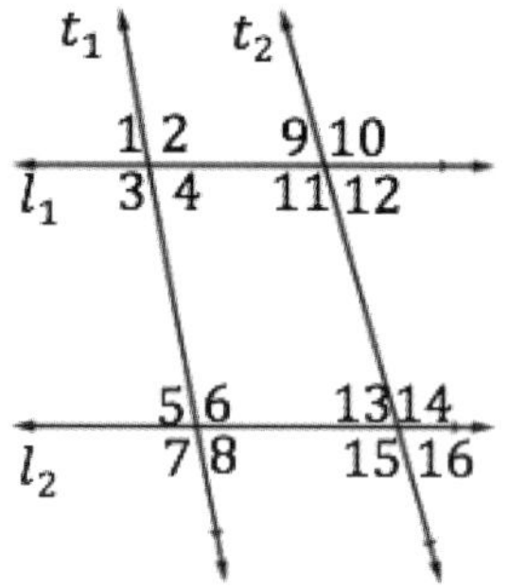

Statements	Reasons
1.	**1.** Given
2.	**2.** Given
3. $\angle 7 \cong \angle 6$; $\angle 13 \cong \angle 16$	**3.**
4.	**4.** Substitution
5. $l_1 \parallel l_2$	**5.**
6. $t_1 \parallel t_2$	**6.**

Try It!

2. Consider the figure below. Find the measures of $\angle AMS$ and $\angle CRF$, and justify your answers.

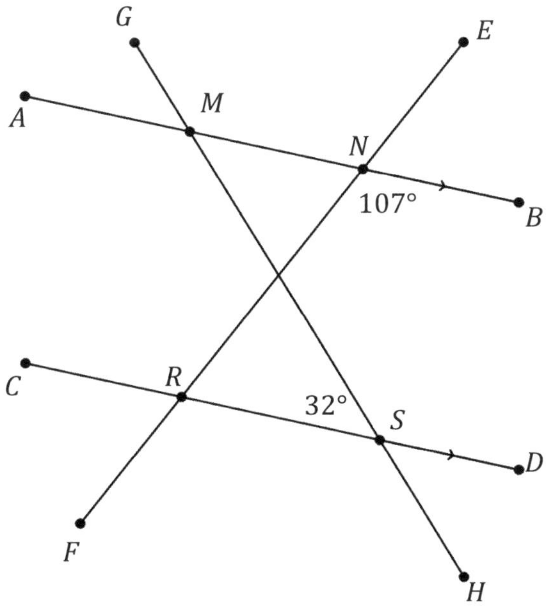

3. Complete the chart below using the following information.

Given: $l_1 \parallel l_2$

Prove: $m\angle a + m\angle g = 180°$

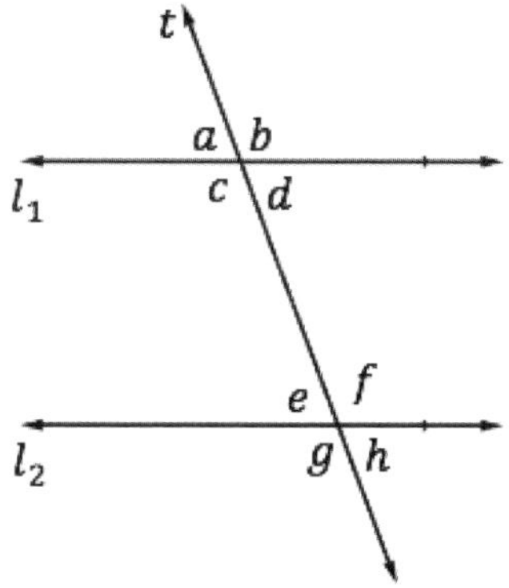

Statements	Reasons
1. $l_1 \parallel l_2$	**1.**
2.	**2.** Linear Pair Postulate
3.	**3.** Definition of Supplementary
4. $\angle c \cong \angle g$	**4.**
5.	**5.** Definition of Congruent
6. $m\angle a + m\angle g = 180°$	**6.**

BEAT THE TEST!

1. Consider the figure below in which $l_1 \parallel l_2$, $m\angle a = 13y$, $m\angle b = 31y + 4$, $m\angle r = 30x + 40$, and $m\angle s = 130x - 160$.

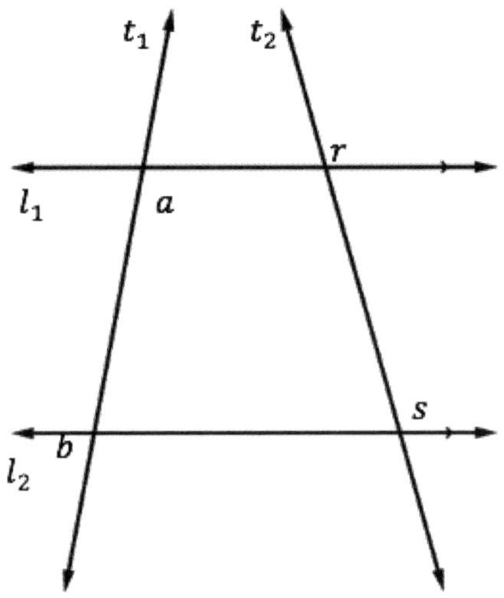

What are the values of $\angle a, \angle b, \angle r$, and $\angle s$?

$\angle a =$ $\angle b =$

$\angle r =$ $\angle s =$

2. Consider the figures below.

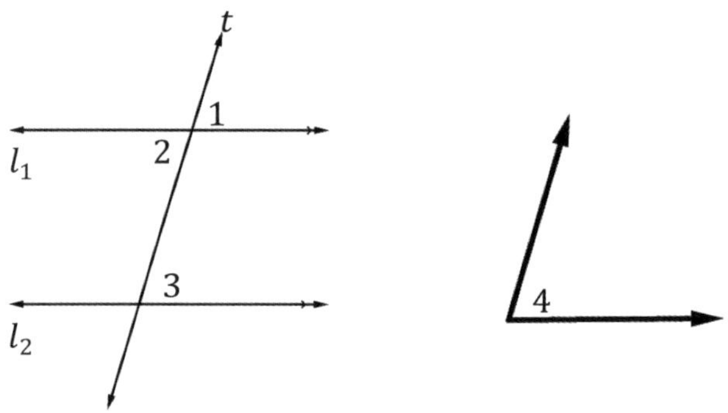

Given: $l_1 \parallel l_2$; $\angle 2 \cong \angle 4$

Prove: $\angle 1 \cong \angle 4$ and $\angle 4 \cong \angle 3$

Complete the following chart.

Statements	Reasons
1. $l_1 \parallel l_2$; $\angle 2 \cong \angle 4$	**1.** Given
2. $\angle 1 \cong \angle 2$	**2.** Vertical Angles Theorem
3. $\angle 1 \cong \angle 4$	**3.**
4. $\angle 1 \cong \angle 3$	**4.**
5. $\angle 4 \cong \angle 3$	**5.** Transitive Property of Congruence

Section 2 – Topic 8
Perpendicular Transversals

Consider the following figure of a transversal cutting parallel lines l_1 and l_2.

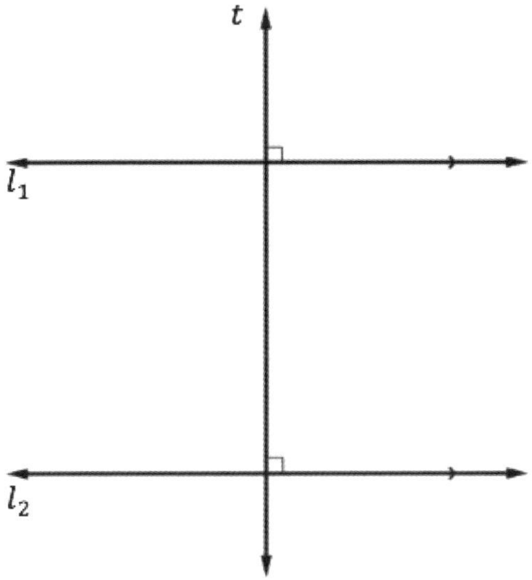

What observations can you make about the figure?

A transversal that cuts two parallel lines forming right angles is called a ________________ transversal.

TAKE NOTE! Postulates & Theorems

Perpendicular Transversal Theorem
In a plane, if a line is perpendicular to one of two parallel lines, then it is perpendicular to the other line also.

Perpendicular Transversal Theorem Corollary
If two lines are both perpendicular to a transversal, then the lines are parallel.

Consider the figure below. San Pablo Ave. and Santos Blvd. are perpendicular to one another. San Juan Ave. was constructed later and is parallel to San Pablo Ave.

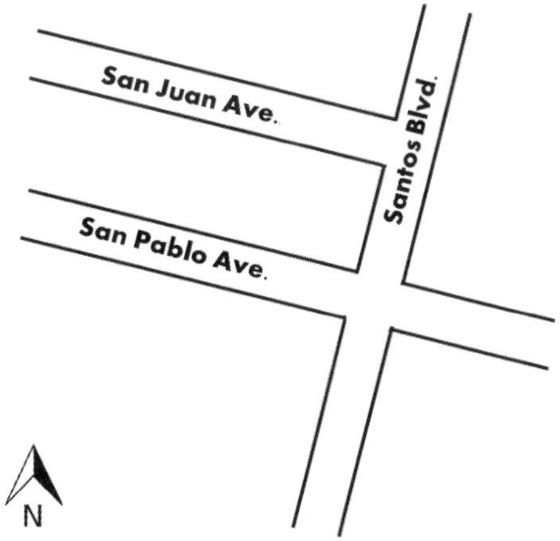

Using the ***Perpendicular Transversal Theorem***, what can you conclude about the relationship between San Juan Ave. and Santos Blvd.?

Let's Practice!

1. Consider the following information.

   Given: $p_1 \parallel p_2$, $p_2 \parallel p_3$, $l_2 \perp p_1$, and $l_1 \perp p_3$

   Prove: $l_1 \parallel l_2$

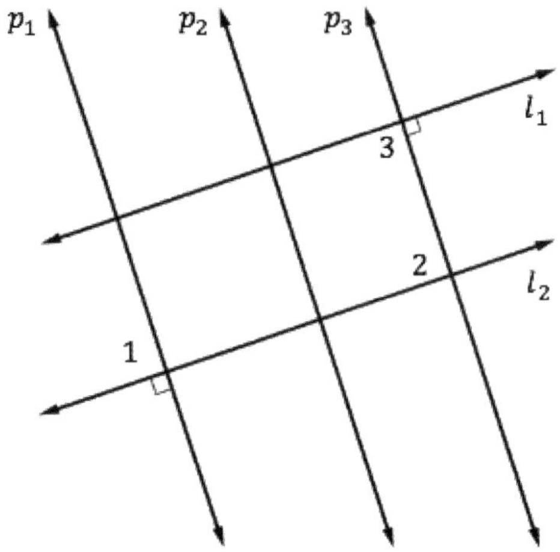

Complete the following paragraph proof.

Because it is given that $p_1 \parallel p_2$ and $p_2 \parallel p_3$, then $p_1 \parallel p_3$ by the____.

This means that $\angle 1 \cong \angle$ _____, because they are corresponding angles.

If $l_2 \perp p_1$, then $m\angle 1 = 90°$. Thus, $m\angle 2 =$ _______________.

This means $p_3 \perp l_2$, based in the definition of perpendicular lines.

It is given that $l_1 \perp p_3$, so $l_1 \parallel l_2$, based on the corollary that states ____.

Try It!

2. Consider the lines and the transversal drawn in the coordinate plane below.

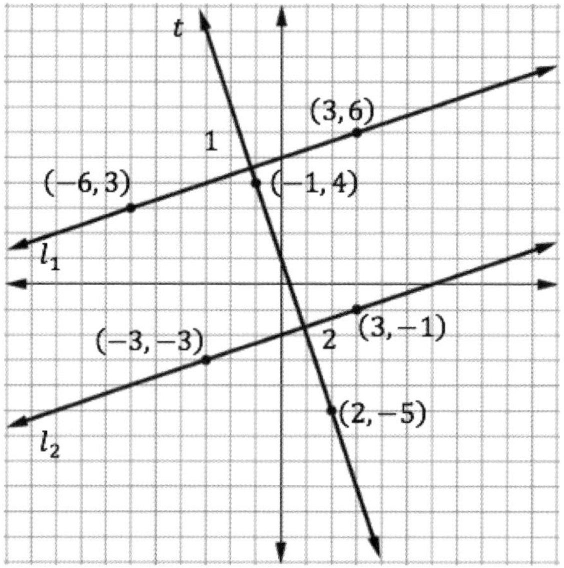

   a. Prove that $\angle 1 \cong \angle 2$. Justify your work.

   b. Prove that $m\angle 1 = m\angle 2 = 90°$. Justify your work.

BEAT THE TEST!

1. Considering the figure to the right, correct the proof of the Perpendicular Transversal Theorem.

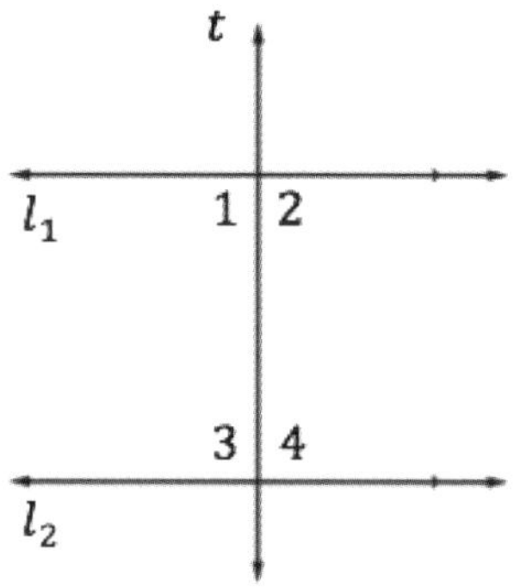

Given: $\angle 1 \cong \angle 4$ and $l_1 \perp t$ at $\angle 2$.
Prove: $l_2 \perp t$

Two of the reasons in the chart below do not correspond to the correct statements. Circle those two reasons.

Statements	Reasons
1. $\angle 1 \cong \angle 4$; $l_1 \perp t$ at $\angle 2$	**1.** Given
2. $l_1 \parallel l_2$	**2.** Consecutive Angles Theorem
3. $\angle 2$ is a right angle	**3.** Definition of perpendicular lines
4. $m\angle 2 = 90°$	**4.** Definition of right angle
5. $m\angle 2 + m\angle 4 = 180°$	**5.** Converse of Alternate Interior Angles Theorem
6. $90° + m\angle 4 = 180°$	**6.** Substitution property
7. $m\angle 4 = 90°$	**7.** Subtraction property of equality
8. $l_2 \perp t$	**8.** Definition of perpendicular lines

Section 2 – Topic 9
Proving Angle Relationships in Transversals and Parallel Lines

Consider a transversal passing through two parallel lines.

How do you know that a pair of alternate interior angles or a pair of corresponding angles are congruent under this scenario?

How do you know that same-side consecutive angles are supplementary under this scenario?

How do you prove your answers?

Let's Practice!

1. Consider the lines l_1, l_2 and l_3 in the diagram at the right.

   Given: $l_1 \parallel l_2$
   Prove: $\angle b \cong \angle h$

   Write a paragraph proof.

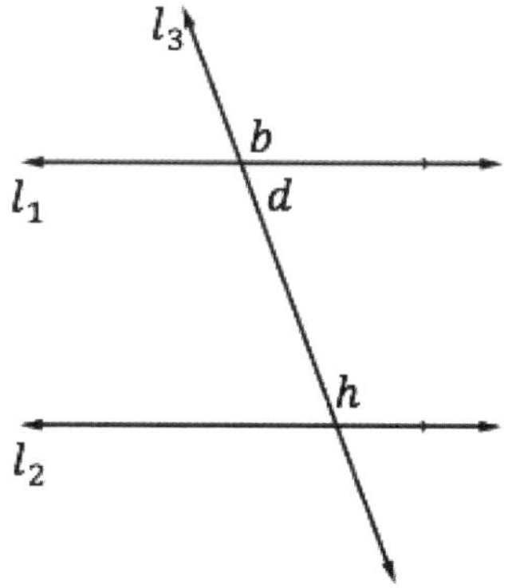

2. Reconsider the diagram and proof of exercise #1. Determine how the use of a rigid transformation is a good alternative to prove that $\angle b \cong \angle h$.

Try It!

3. Consider the lines l_1, l_2 and l_3 in the diagram to the right.

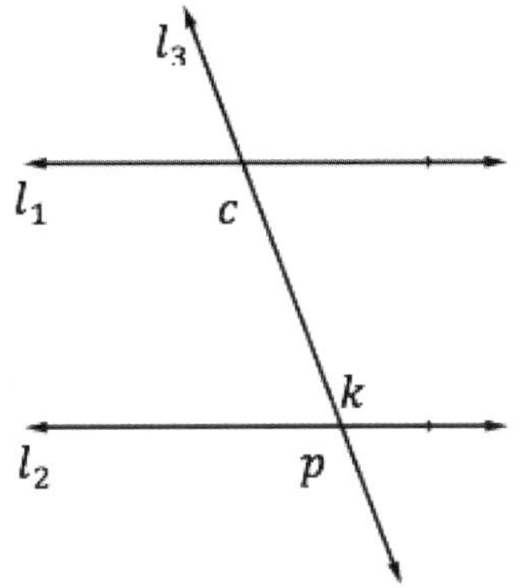

Given: $l_1 \parallel l_2$
Prove: $\angle c \cong \angle k$

Complete the following proof.

Statements	Reasons
1. $l_1 \parallel l_2$	**1.** Given
2.	**2.** Corresponding Angles Theorem
3. $\angle k \cong \angle p$	**3.**
4. $\angle c \cong \angle k$	**4.**

4. Determine how the use of a rigid transformation is good for an alternative to prove that $\angle c \cong \angle k$.

BEAT THE TEST!

1. Consider the diagram below.

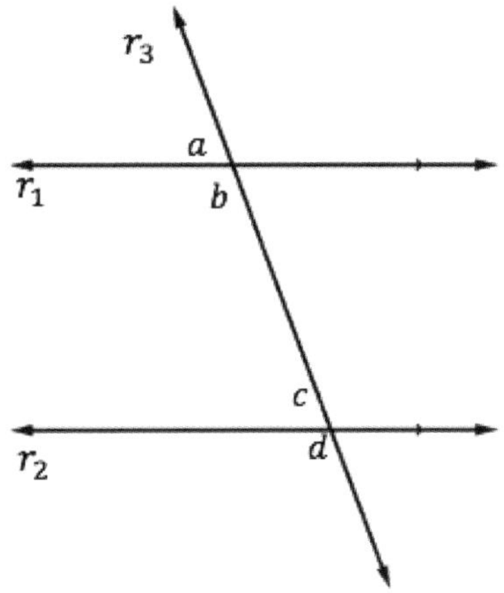

Given: $r_1 \parallel r_2$
Prove: $m\angle b + m\angle c = 180°$

Complete the following paragraph proof by circling the correct answer in each shaded part.

Since $r_1 \parallel r_2$ and r_3 is a transversal, $\angle a$ and $\angle b$ form a linear pair, same as $\angle c$ and $\angle d$ by definition. Therefore, each pair of angles ($\angle a$ and $\angle b$, and $\angle c$ and $\angle d$) are supplementary according to the Linear Pair Postulate. So, $m\angle a + m\angle b = 180°$ and $m\angle c + m\angle d = 180°$ by definition. Since $\angle a \cong \angle c$ according to the Alternate Interior | Corresponding | Vertical Angles Theorem, $m\angle a = m\angle c$ by definition of congruency. Hence, $m\angle b + m\angle c = 180°$ according to reflexive property | substitution | transitive property of congruence. This proves the Same-side Consecutive Angles Theorem.

Section 2 – Topic 10
Copying Angles and Constructing Angle Bisectors

What information or tools do we need to construct an angle?

Now, an angle already exists and we want to construct another angle that is exactly the same, then we are _______________ that angle.

Let's consider $\angle A$. Construct $\angle FDE$ to be a copy of $\angle A$.

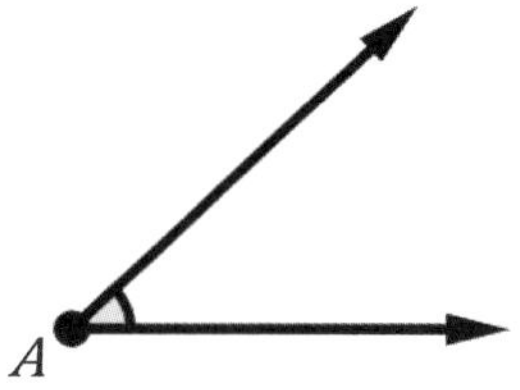

Step 1. Draw a ray that will become one of the two rays of the new angle. Label the ray $\overrightarrow{DE}$.

Step 2. Place your compass point at the vertex of $\angle A$. Create an arc that intersects both rays of $\angle A$.

Step 3. Without changing your compass setting, create an arc from point D that intersects $\overrightarrow{DE}$. Be sure to make a large arc.

Step 4. On $\angle A$, set your compass point on the intersection of the arc and ray and the pencil on the other intersection of the arc and second ray. Lock your compass.

Step 5. Place the point of the compass on the intersection of the arc and $\overrightarrow{DE}$. Mark an arc through the large arc created in step 3. Label the point of intersection of the two arc point F.

Step 6. Construct $\overrightarrow{DF}$.

Let's Practice!

1. Consider $\angle ALI$.

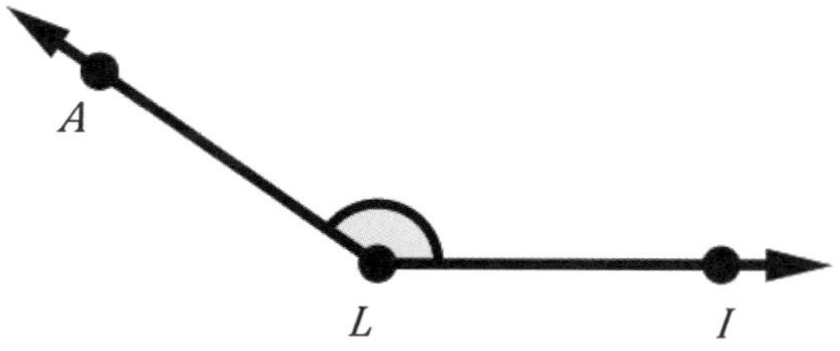

a. Construct $\angle FDE$ to be a copy of $\angle ALI$.

b. Suppose that your teacher asks you to construct an angle bisector to $\angle FDE$. How would you do it?

In order to bisect an angle, follow these steps and perform the construction of the angle bisector in $\angle FDE$ below.

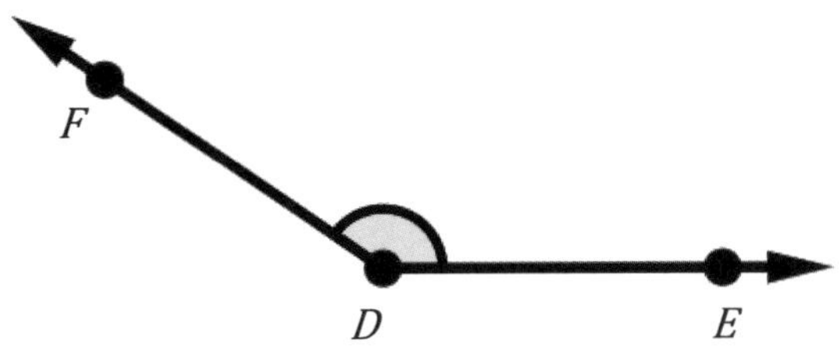

Step 1. Place the point of the compass on the angle's vertex.

Step 2. Without changing the width of the compass, draw an arc across each ray.

Step 3. Place the point of the compass on the intersection of the arc and the ray. Draw an arc in the interior of the angle.

Step 4. Without changing the compass setting, repeat step 3 for the other angle so that the two arcs intersect in the interior of the angle. Label the intersection G.

Step 5. Using a straightedge, construct a ray from the vertex D through the point where the arcs intersect, G.

Try It!

2. Consider $\angle MOW$.

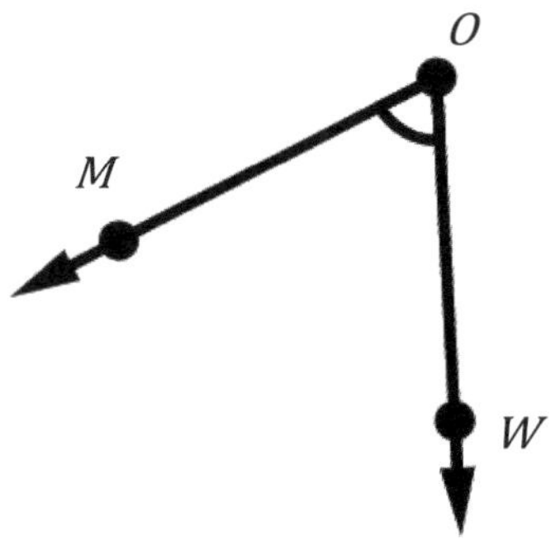

Construct $\angle CAP$ to be a copy of $\angle MOW$ and bisect $\angle CAP$ with $\overrightarrow{AK}$.

BEAT THE TEST!

1. Ernesto bisected $\angle AVI$ and his construction is shown below.

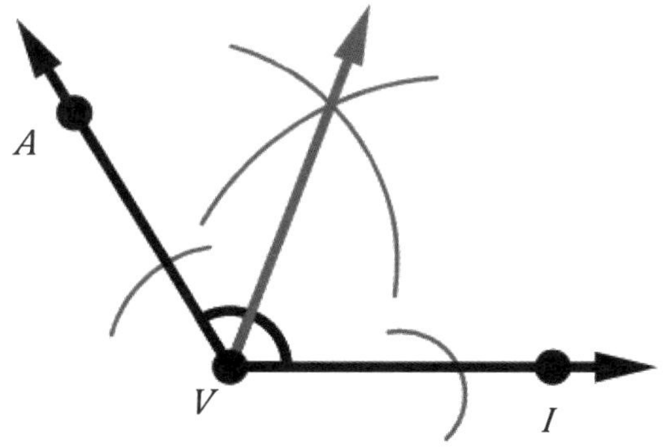

Determine if Ernesto's construction is correct. Justify your answer.

Section 2 – Topic 11
Introduction to Polygons

The word polygon can be split into two parts:

- "poly-" means ____________
- "gon" means ____________

Polygons are simple, closed, and have sides that are segments.

Draw a representation for each of the polygons below.

Name	Definition	Representation
Regular	All angles and sides of this polygon are congruent.	
Irregular	All angles and sides of this polygon are not congruent.	
Convex	This polygon has no angles pointing inwards. That is, no interior angles can be greater than 180°.	
Concave	This polygon has an interior angle greater than 180°.	
Simple	This polygon has one boundary and doesn't cross over itself.	

Try it!

1. Classify each figure as regular, concave, and/or convex by marking the appropriate box. Name each type of polygon represented by filling in each blank provided.

Figure	Regular	Concave	Convex	Name the Polygon
	☐	☐	☐	
	☐	☐	☐	
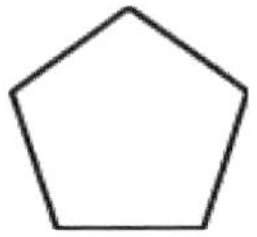	☐	☐	☐	

Consider the polygon.

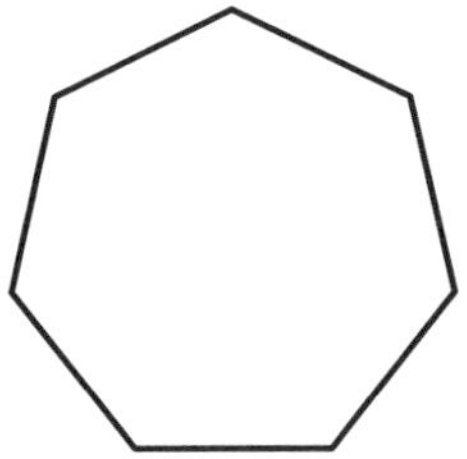

The ***interior angles of a polygon*** are the angles on the inside of the polygon formed by each pair of adjacent sides.

Use I to label the interior angles of the polygon above.

An ***exterior angle of a polygon*** is an angle that forms a linear pair with one of the interior angles of the polygon.

Use E to label the exterior angels of the polygon above.

Complete the table by using your knowledge of triangles to find the sum of the interior angles of each polygon.

Polygon	Number of sides	Sum of interior angles
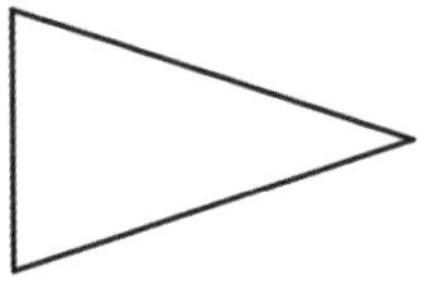	3	180°
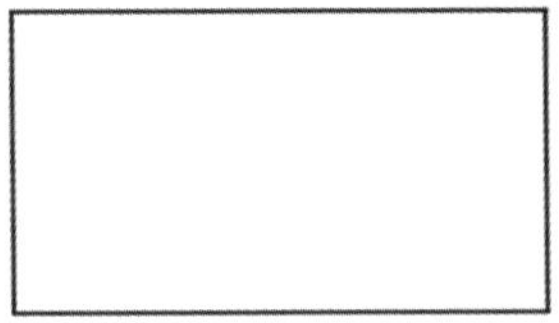	4	
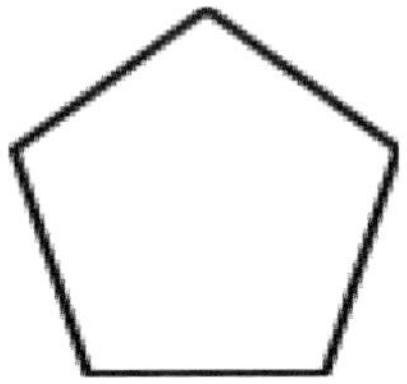	5	
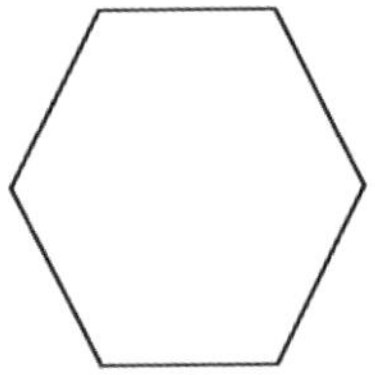	6	
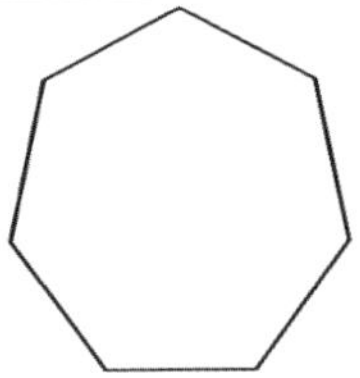	7	
	n	

Let's Practice!

2. Consider each of the following polygons. Find the sum of the exterior angles in each polygon below.

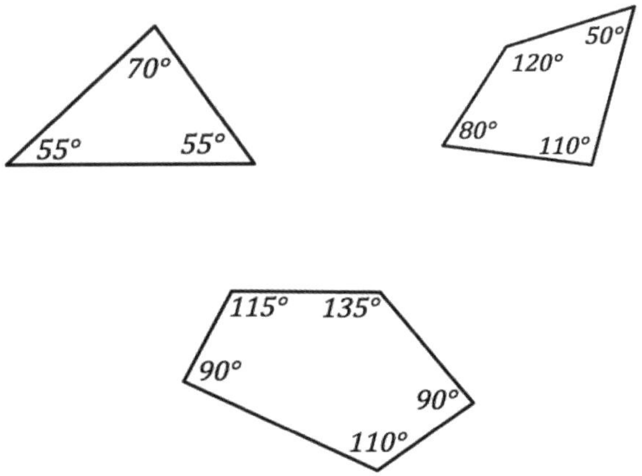

The sum of the exterior angles of any polygon equals _______.

Try it!

3. A convex pentagon has exterior angles with measures 77°, 66°, 82°, and 62°.
   a. What is the measure of the exterior angle of the pentagon at the fifth vertex?

   b. Classify the pentagon as regular or irregular. Justify your answer.

Consider the following regular heptagon.

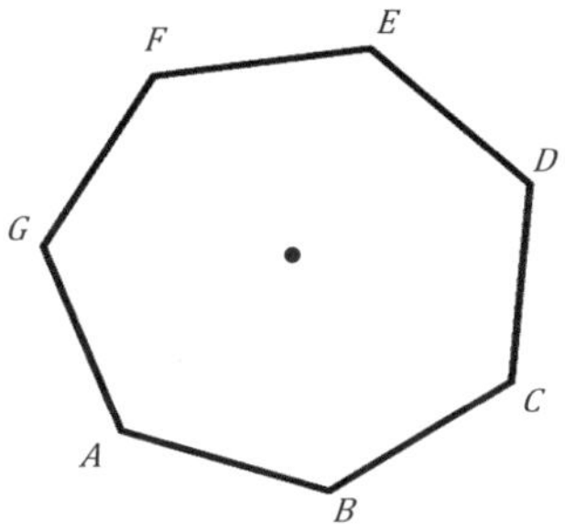

The center of the heptagon is marked.

➢ The ***circumcenter*** is the point that is ________________ from each vertex.

Draw a circle outside the heptagon that only touches the vertices of the heptagon.

➢ The "outside" circle is called a ____________________, and it connects all the vertices of the polygon.

Draw a circle inside that only touches each side of the heptagon at its midpoint.

➢ The "inside" circle is called an ____________________, and it connects all the midpoints of the sides of the polygon.

Draw a line from the center of the heptagon to one of its vertices.

➢ This is called the ______________ of the polygon, which is also the radius of the circumcircle.

Draw all the radii of the heptagon. It should result in seven isosceles triangles.

➢ The height of each isosceles triangle is also called the ____________________ of the polygon and the radius of the incircle.

BEAT THE TEST!

1. Consider the irregular hexagon below.

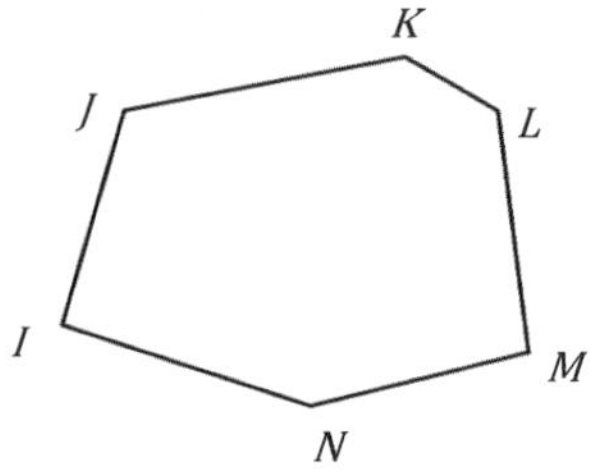

Provide one way to break up the irregular polygon above using smaller polygons. Identify each type of smaller polygon you form.

2. Rectangle $ABCD$ was cut to create pentagon $AQRPD$ in the figure below.

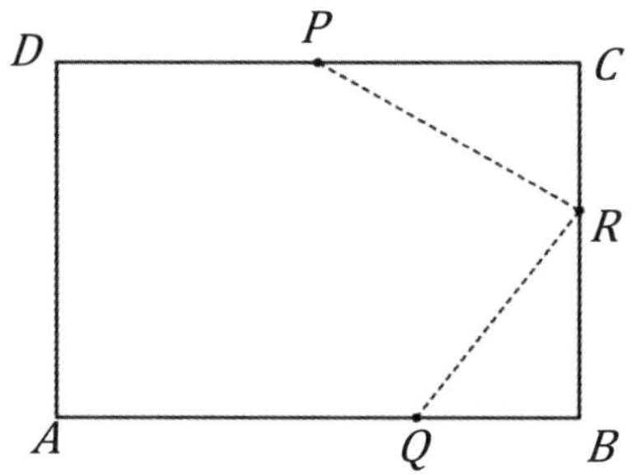

If $m\angle PRQ = 71°$ and $m\angle PRC = m\angle QRB$, verify the sum of the interior angles of pentagon $AQRPD$ using two different methods. Justify your answers.

Section 2 – Topic 12
Angles of Polygons

In the previous video, you learned the formula to find the sum of the angles of a polygon.

How can you use the sum of interior angles formula to find the number of sides of a polygon?

How can you use the sum of interior angles formula to find the measure of one angle of a regular polygon?

Can the same process be used to find the measure of one angle of an irregular polygon? Explain your reasoning.

Let's Practice!

1. What are the measures of each interior angle and each exterior angle of regular hexagon $MARLON$?

2. The sum of the interior angles of a regular polygon is $1080°$.

    a. Classify the polygon by the number of sides.

    b. What is the measure of one interior angle of the polygon?

    c. What is the measure of one exterior angle of the polygon?

3. Consider pentagon $ABCDE$.

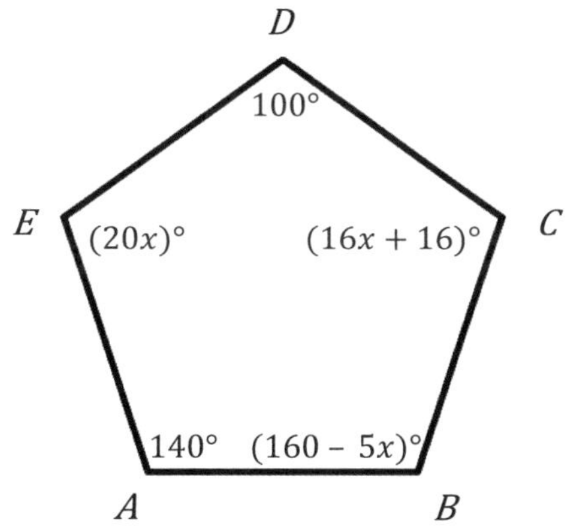

    a. Find the value of x.

    b. Find the value of the following angles: $\angle A$, $\angle B$, $\angle C$, $\angle D$, and $\angle E$.

    c. Find the value of each exterior angle.

Try It!

4. Consider the regular hexagon below.

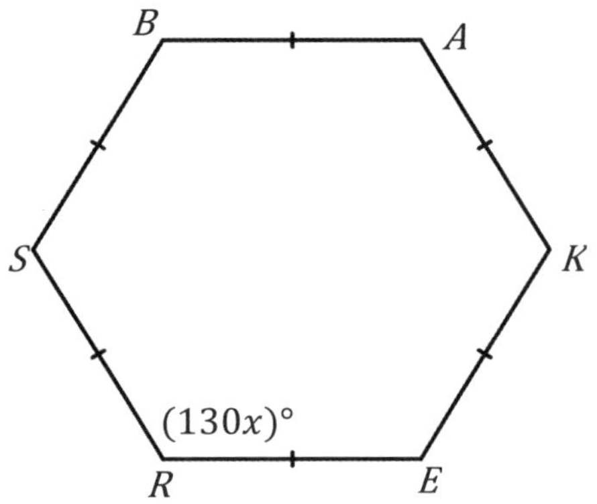

Find the value of x and determine the value of each interior and exterior angle.

5. If the measure of an exterior angle of a regular polygon is $24°$, how many sides does the polygon have?

6. Given a regular decagon and a regular dodecagon, which one has a greater exterior angle? By how much is the angle greater?

BEAT THE TEST!

1. A teacher showed the following exit ticket on the projector.

> 1. What is the sum of the interior angle measures of a regular 24-gon?
> 2. Pentagon ABCDE has interior angles that measure $60°$ and $160°$ and another pair of interior angles that measure $130°$ each. What is the measure of an interior angle at the fifth vertex?

A student completed the following exit ticket.

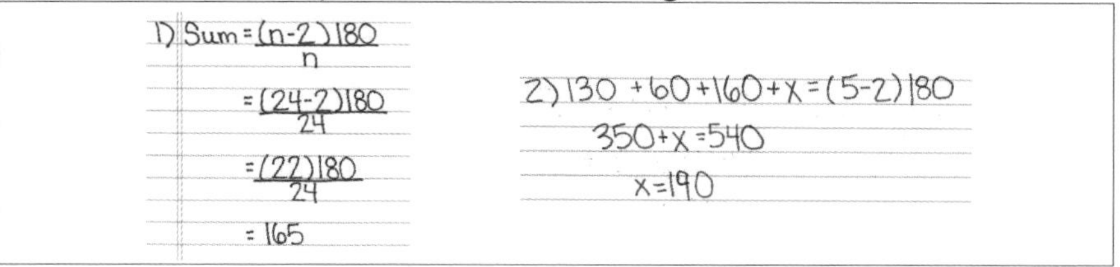

Which of the following statements is true?

Ⓐ Both answers are correct.

Ⓑ Answer #1 is incorrect. The student found the individual angle, not the sum of the angles. The answer should be $3960°$. Answer #2 is correct.

Ⓒ Answer #1 is correct. Answer #2 is incorrect. There are two angles measuring $130°$, but only one was counted in the sum. The answer should be $60°$.

Ⓓ Both answers are incorrect. In #1 the student found the individual angle, not the sum of the angles. The answer is $3960°$. In #2 there are two angles measuring $130°$, but only one was counted in the sum. The answer should be $60°$.

2. Consider the figure below.

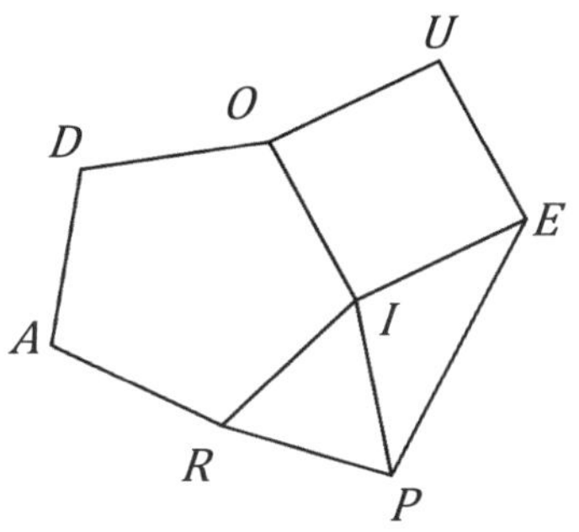

$DARIO$ is a regular pentagon, RIP is an equilateral triangle, and $EIOU$ is a square.

Part A: What is the measure of $\angle IPE$?

Part B: Find $m\angle DOU$.

Section 2 – Topic 13
Angles of Other Polygons

Use the following diagram, where point A and square $BCDE$ with center at F are shown, to answer the questions below.

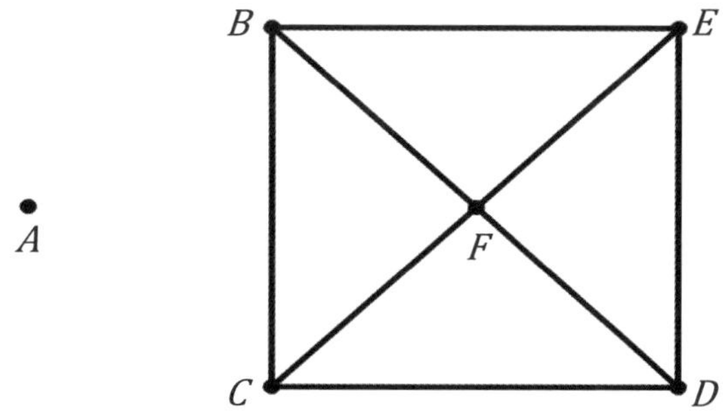

What is the angle measure surrounding point A?

What are the angle measures surrounding point F?

What is the difference between points A and F?

Some important facts about the angles of a polygon:

- The ***center*** of a polygon is the point ______________ from every vertex.
- The ***central angle*** of a polygon is the angle made at the center of the polygon by any two ____________ vertices of the polygon.
- The sum of the central angles of a polygon is __________ (a full circle).
- The measure of the central angle of a regular polygon is $360°$ divided by the number of _______________.

Let's Practice!

1. Consider the following diagram of the regular polygons.

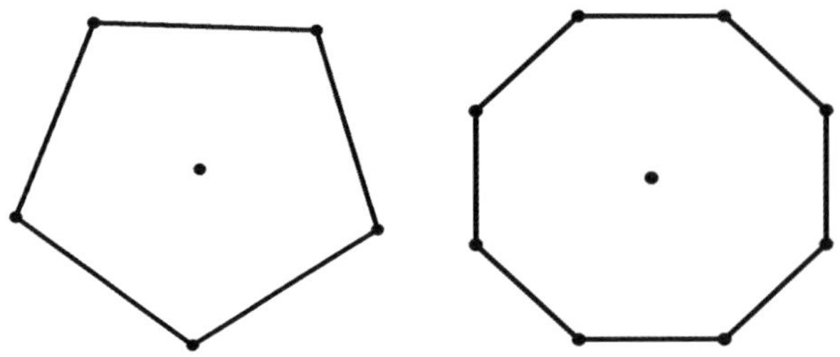

   a. Draw a central angle in each of the above polygons and calculate the measure of a central angle in each polygon.

   b. What are the measures of the base angles of each isosceles triangle in the pentagon?

   c. What are the measures of the base angles of each isosceles triangle in the octagon?

The base angles of each isosceles triangle in a regular polygon can be calculated in two ways.

- Base angles of an isosceles triangle are equal. Therefore, each base angle can be calculated by $\frac{180-c}{2}$, where c is a central angle.

- The radius of a polygon bisects the angle at the vertex and each interior angle of a regular polygon is $\frac{180(n-2)}{n}$, where n is the number of sides of the regular polygon.

2. Consider the following regular octagon, and use it to complete the questions below.

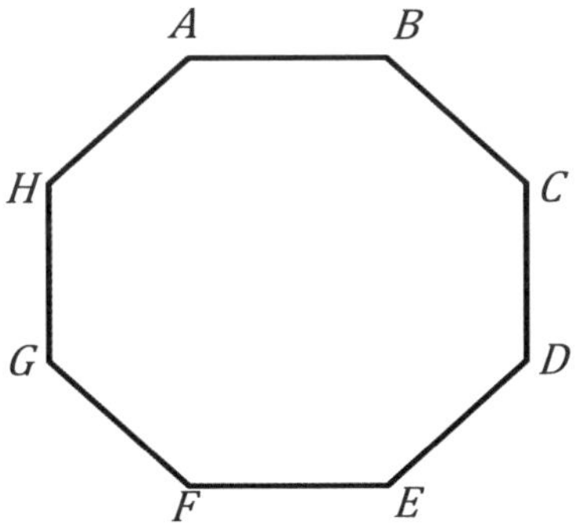

a. Prove that the sum of all exterior angles is $360°$ in a regular octagon.

b. Prove that the sum of all interior angles at each vertex is $180(n-2)$ in a regular octagon.

3. A student claims that the sum of the measures of the exterior angles of a hendecagon is greater than the sum of the measures of the exterior angles of a nonagon. The student justifies this claim by saying that a hendecagon has two more sides than the nonagon.

Describe and correct the student's error.

4. Determine if an irregular polygon has a central angle. Justify your answer.

5. Does an irregular polygon have exterior angles? If so, how do we calculate the exterior angles? Justify your answer.

STUDY EDGE TIP

Irregular polygons do not have a center, and they do not have a central angle; however, they do have interior and exterior angles.

Try It!

6. Consider the following irregular hexagon and answer the questions below it.

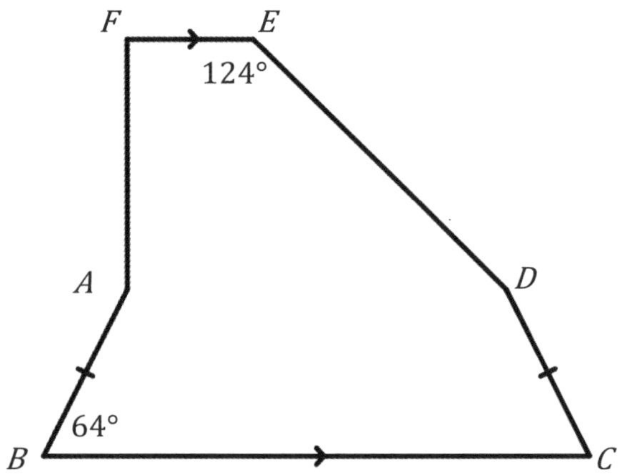

a. If $\overline{AF} \perp \overline{EF}$ and $\overline{AF} \perp \overline{AD}$, find the measure of each interior angle of the irregular polygon above.

b. Does the same exterior angles rule for regular polygons apply to irregular polygons? Justify your answer.

BEAT THE TEST!

1. Consider the following diagram where the regular polygon $ABCDE$ has center at M, polygon $DEHGF$ is irregular, and point D is on $\overline{CF}$.

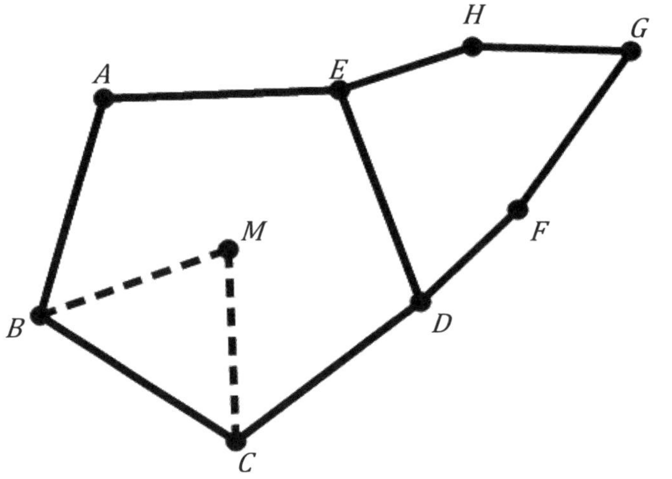

Which of the following statements are correct? Select all that apply.

- ☐ $m\angle BMC = m\angle EDF$
- ☐ $m\angle EDC = 72°$
- ☐ The sum of the exterior angles of $ABCDE$ is less than the sum of the exterior angles of $DEHGF$.
- ☐ The sum of the interior angles of polygon $ABCDE$ with the sum of the exterior angles of polygon $DEHGF$ equals 900°.
- ☐ $m\angle ABM = m\angle BMC = m\angle DCM$

Test Yourself! Practice Tool

Great job! You have reached the end of this section. Now it's time to try the "Test Yourself! Practice Tool," where you can practice all the skills and concepts you learned in this section. Log in to Math Nation and try out the "Test Yourself! Practice Tool" so you can see how well you know these topics!

Section 3: Rigid Transformations and Symmetry

Topic 1: Introduction to Transformations 79
Standards Covered: G-CO.2, G-CO.4, G-CO.5
- ☐ I can determine if a transformation is rigid or non-rigid.

Topic 2: Examining and Using Translations 82
Standards Covered: G-CO.2
- ☐ I can determine the relationship between the coordinates of vertices of a figure and the coordinates of vertices of the figure's image generated by translations.

Topic 3: Translations of Polygons 84
Standards Covered: G-CO.2
- ☐ I can perform a translation of a polygon on a coordinate plane and find the coordinates or location of the image and the pre-image.

Topic 4: Examining and Using Reflections 87
Standards Covered: G-CO.2
- ☐ I can perform a reflection of points and line segments on a coordinate plane.

Topic 5: Reflections of Polygons 89
Standards Covered: G-CO.5
- ☐ I can perform reflections of polygons on a coordinate plane and find the coordinates or location of the image and the pre-image.

Topic 6: Examining and Using Rotations 92
Standards Covered: G-CO.2
- ☐ I can perform rotations of points and line segments on a coordinate plane..

Topic 7: Rotations of Polygons – Part 1 95
Standards Covered: G-CO.2
- ☐ I can perform rotations of polygons on a coordinate plane and find the coordinates or location of the image and pre-image.

Topic 8: Rotations of Polygons – Part 2 97
Standards Covered: G-CO.2
- ☐ I can perform rotations of polygons on a coordinate plane and find the coordinates or location of the image and pre-image.

Topic 9: Angle-Preserving Transformations 100
Standards Covered: G-CO.2
- ☐ I can apply transformations to figures formed by parallel lines crossed by a transversal..

Topic 10: Symmetries of Regular Polygons 104
Standards Covered: G-CO.3
- ☐ I can map a regular polygon onto itself.

Visit MathNation.com or search "Math Nation" in your phone or tablet's app store to watch the videos that go along with this workbook!

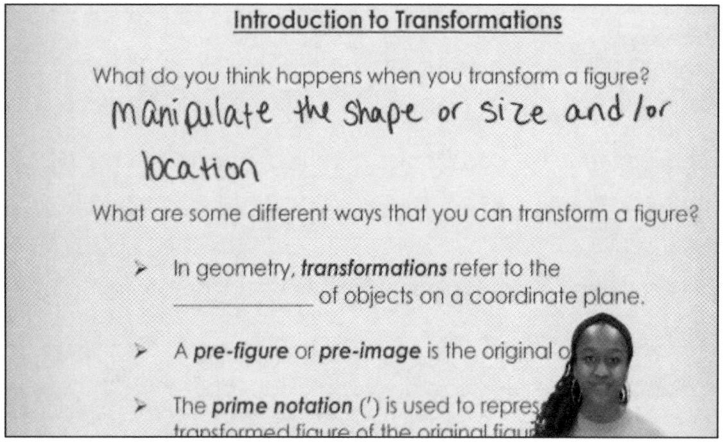
Introduction to Transformations
What do you think happens when you transform a figure?
manipulate the shape or size and/or
location
What are some different ways that you can transform a figure?
In geometry, transformations refer to the
of objects on a coordinate plane.
A pre-figure or pre-image is the original
The prime notation (') is used to repres

The following Michigan Mathematics Standards will be covered in this section:
G-CO.2 - Represent transformations in the plane using, e.g., transparencies and geometry software; describe transformations as functions that take points in the plane as inputs and give other points as outputs. Compare transformations that preserve distance and angle to those that do not.
G-CO.3 - Given a rectangle, parallelogram, trapezoid, or regular polygon, describe the rotations and reflections that carry it onto itself.
G-CO.4 - Develop definitions of rotations, reflections, and translations in terms of angles, circles, perpendicular lines, parallel lines, and line segments.
G-CO.5 - Given a geometric figure and a rotation, reflection, or translation, draw the transformed figure. Specify a sequence of transformations that will carry a given figure onto itself.

Section 3: Rigid Transformations and Symmetry
Section 3 – Topic 1
Introduction to Transformations

What do you think happens when you transform a figure?

What are some different ways that you can transform a figure?

- In geometry, ***transformations*** refer to the ______________ of objects on a coordinate plane.
- A ***pre-figure*** or ***pre-image*** is the original object.
- The ***prime notation*** (′) is used to represent a transformed figure of the original figure.

Consider the graph below, circle the pre-image and box the transformed image. Describe the transformation.

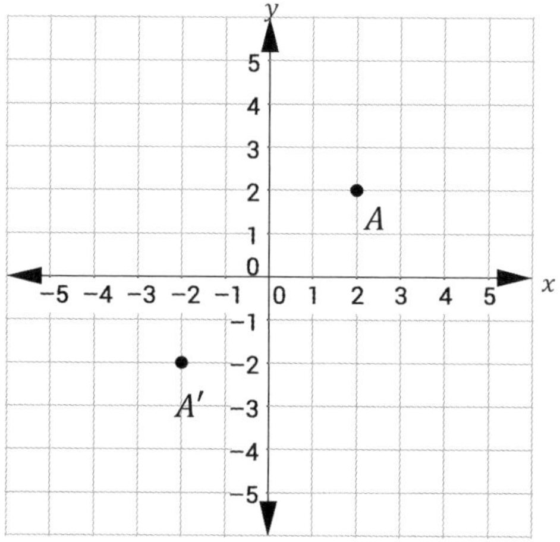

There are two main categories of transformations: ***rigid*** and ***non-rigid***.

- A __________________ transformation changes the size of the pre-image.
- A __________________ transformation does not change the size of the pre-image.

Write a real-world example of a rigid transformation.

Write a real-world example of a non-rigid transformation.

There are four common types of transformations:

- A ***rotation*** turns the shape around a center point.
- A ***translation*** slides the shape in any direction.
- A ***dilation*** changes the size of an object through an enlargement or a reduction.
- A ***reflection*** flips the object over a line (as in a mirror image).

In the table below, indicate whether the transformation is rigid or non-rigid and justify your answer.

Transformation	Rigid/Non-Rigid	Justification
Translation	○ Rigid ○ Non-Rigid	
Reflection	○ Rigid ○ Non-Rigid	
Rotation	○ Rigid ○ Non-Rigid	
Dilation	○ Rigid ○ Non-Rigid	

Now, identify the transformations shown in the following graphs and write the names of the transformations in the corresponding boxes under each graph.

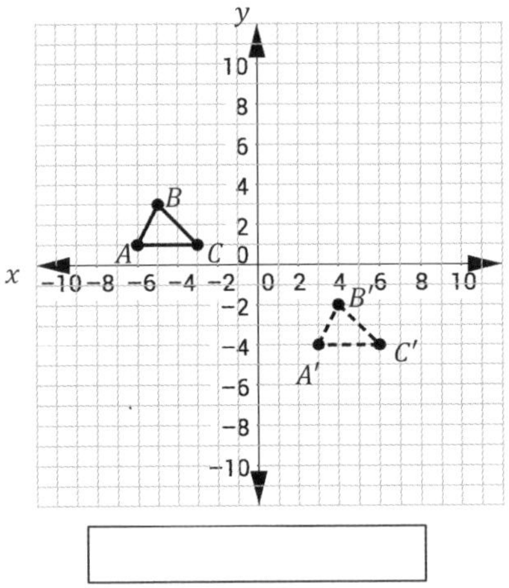

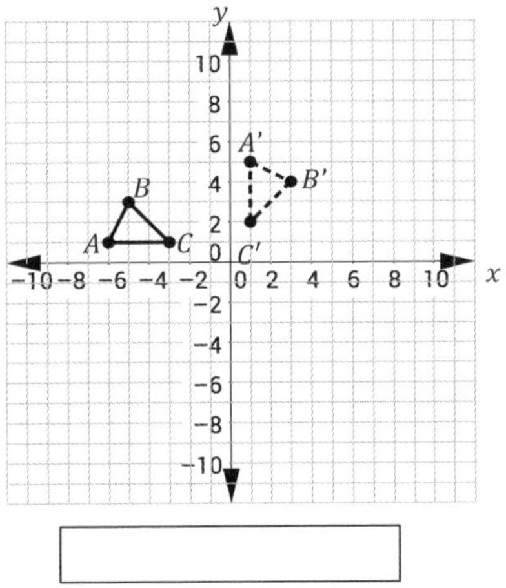

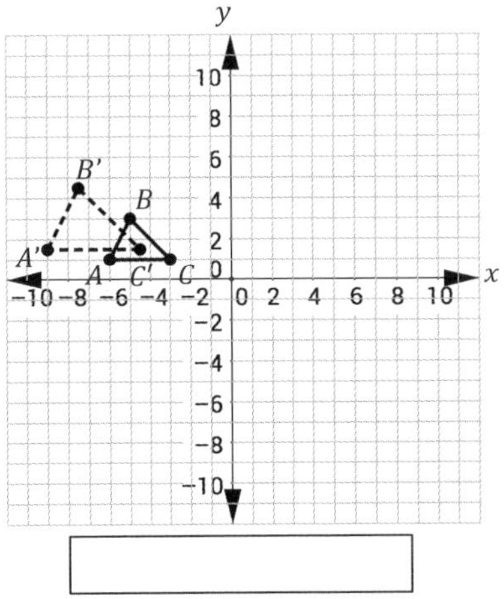

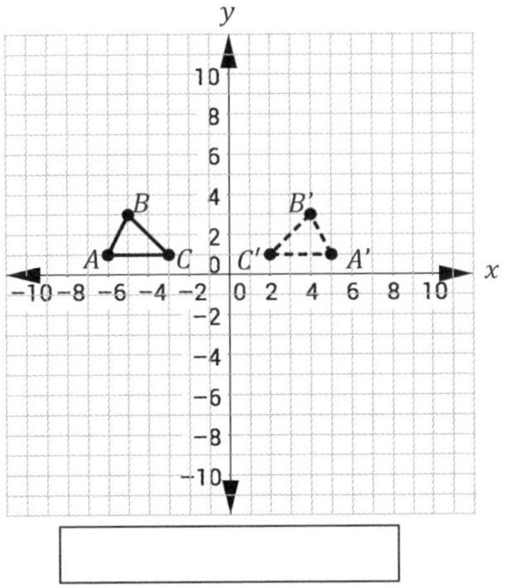

Let's Practice!

1. Consider $\overline{AB}$ in the coordinate plane below.

   a. Write the coordinates of each endpoint, the length of the segment, and the midpoint of the segment.

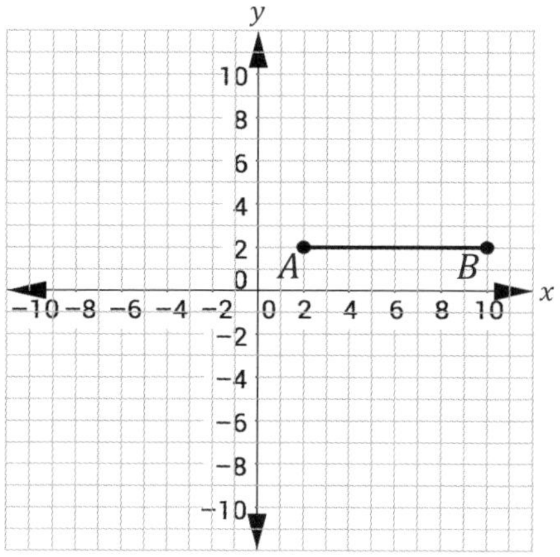

$A($_____, _____$)$

$B($_____, _____$)$

Length: ______ units

Midpoint: (_____, _____)

   b. Write the coordinates of A′ and B′ after the following transformations.

Transformations	A'	B'
$\overline{AB}$ is translated 5 units up and 3 units to the left.		
$\overline{AB}$ is rotated 180° clockwise about the origin.		

Try It!

2. Consider the transformations of $\overline{AB}$ in the previous problem.

   a. Trace the lines and identify the transformations on the graph.

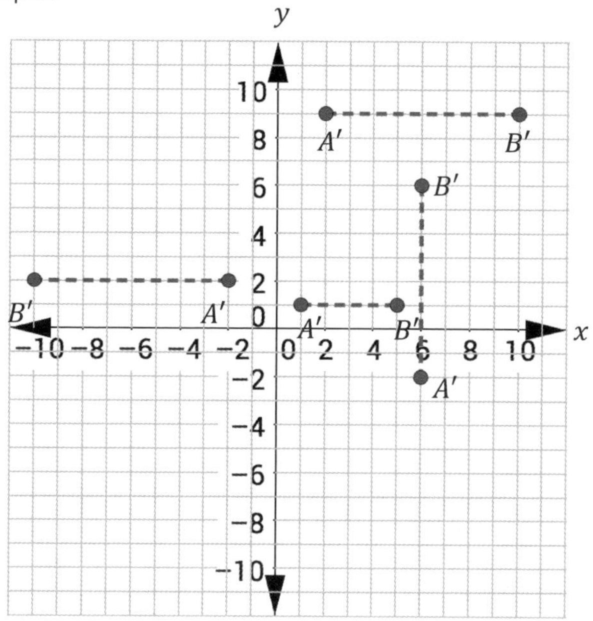

   b. What are the A' and B' coordinates for each transformation below? Fill in the length and midpoint of each segment indicated in the chart.

Transformation	Coordinates	Length	Midpoint
Translation	$A'($___, ___$); B'($___, ___$)$		
Dilation	$A'($___, ___$); B'($___, ___$)$		
Rotation	$A'($___, ___$); B'($___, ___$)$		
Reflection	$A'($___, ___$); B'($___, ___$)$		

BEAT THE TEST!

1. Three rays share the same vertex $(5,4)$ as shown in the coordinate plane below.

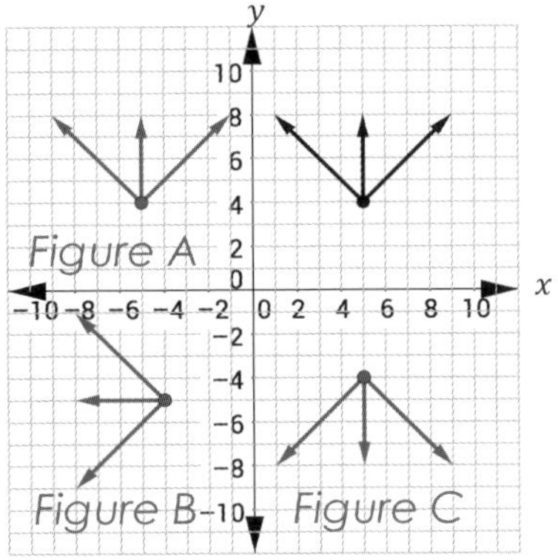

Part A: Which figure represents a reflection across the y-axis?

Part B: Which of the following statements are true about the figure? Select all that apply.

- ☐ A rotation of $360°$ will carry the object onto itself.
- ☐ A reflection of the figure along the x-axis carries the figure to Quadrant II.
- ☐ In Figure A, $(x',y') = (x+10,y)$.
- ☐ If the vertex of Figure A is translated $(x+1,y-9)$, it will carry onto the vertex of Figure B.
- ☐ Figure C is a reflection on the x-axis of Figure A.

Section 3 – Topic 2
Examining and Using Translations

A ***translation*** is a rigid transformation that "slides" an object a fixed distance in a given direction while preserving the __________ and __________ of the object.

Suppose a geometric figure is translated h units along the x-axis and k units along the y-axis. We use the following notation to represent the transformation:

$$T_{h,k}(x,y) = (x+h, y+k) \text{ or } (x,y) \to (x+h, y+k)$$

- $(x,y) \to (x+2, y-5)$ translates the point (x,y) 2 units ______ and 5 units _______.

- What is the algebraic description for a transformation that translates the point (x,y) 2 units to the left and 3 units upward?

- What is the algebraic description for a transformation that translates the point (x,y) 3 units to the right and 2 units downward?

Let's Practice!

1. Transform triangle ABC according to $(x, y) \rightarrow (x + 3, y - 2)$. Write the coordinates for triangle $A'B'C'$.

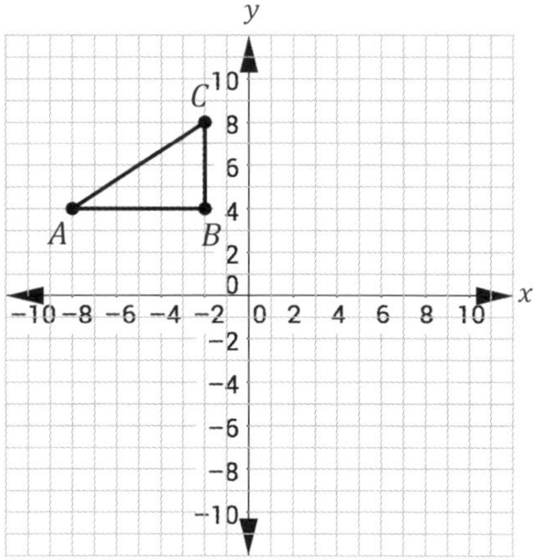

A'(_____,_____)

B'(_____,_____)

C'(_____,_____)

2. When the transformation $(x, y) \rightarrow (x + 10, y + 5)$ is performed on point A, its image, point A', is on the origin. What are the coordinates of A? Justify your answer.

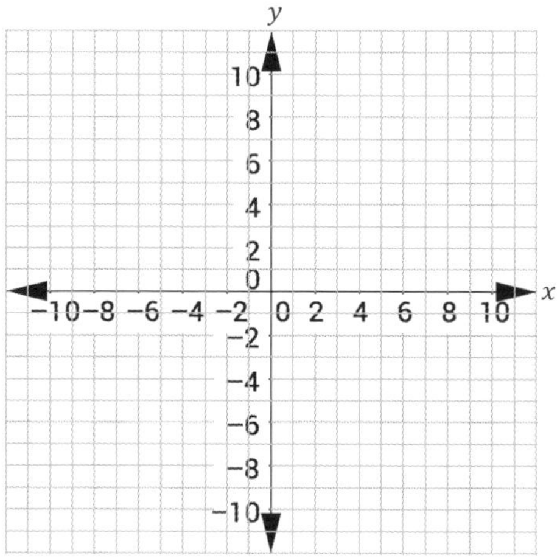

Try It!

3. $\overline{AP}$ undergoes the translation $T_{h,k}(x, y)$, such that $A'(1, 1)$ and $P'(4, 3)$.

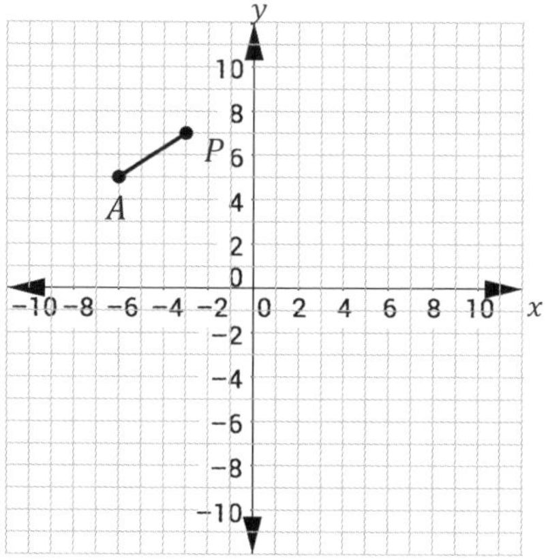

a. What are the values of h and k?

$h =$ ________ units

$k =$ ________ units

b. Which of the following statements is true?

Ⓐ $\overline{AP}$ and $\overline{A'P'}$ have different locations.
Ⓑ $\overline{AP}$ and $\overline{A'P'}$ have different shapes.
Ⓒ $\overline{AP}$ and $\overline{A'P'}$ have different sizes.
Ⓓ $\overline{AP}$ and $\overline{A'P'}$ have different directions.

BEAT THE TEST!

1. When the transformation $(x, y) \rightarrow (x - 4, y + 7)$ is performed on point P, its image is point $P'(-3, 4)$. What are the coordinates of P?

   Ⓐ $(-7, 11)$
   Ⓑ $(-1, 3)$
   Ⓒ $(1, -3)$
   Ⓓ $(7, -11)$

2. Consider the following points.

   $R(-6, 5)$ and $U(5, -6)$

   $\overline{RU}$ undergoes the translation $(x, y) \rightarrow (x + h, y + k)$, such that $R'(5, 1)$ and $U'(16, -10)$.

   Part A: Complete the following algebraic description.

   $(x, y) \rightarrow (x + \square, y + \square)$

   Part B: What is the difference between $\overline{RU}$ and $\overline{R'U'}$?

Section 3 – Topic 3
Translations of Polygons

Describe the translation of rectangle $PINE$.

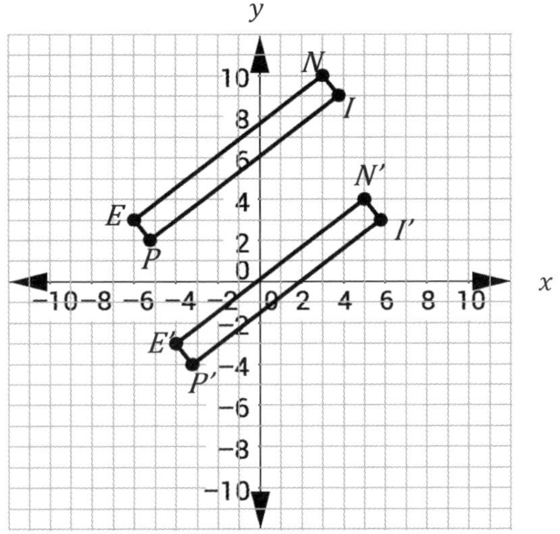

- ➢ The original object and its image are ______________.
- ➢ In other words, the two objects are identical in every respect except for their ____________.

Draw line segments linking a vertex in the original image to the corresponding vertex in the translated image. Make observations about the line segments.

Let's Practice!

1. Consider the two right triangles below.

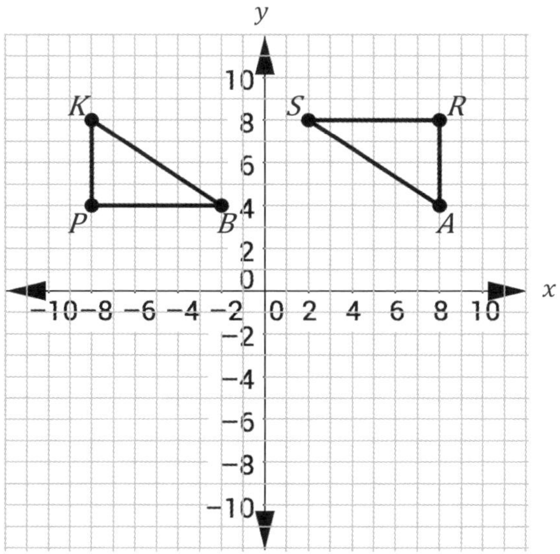

Rectangle $PARK$ is formed when right triangles PBK and RSA are translated. $PARK$ has vertices at $P(-3,4)$, $A(3,4)$, $R(3,8)$, and $K(-3,8)$.

Describe how rectangle $PARK$'s location on the coordinate plane is possible with only one translation for PBK and one translation for RSA.

Try It!

2. $C(0,-1)$, $A(-2,2)$, $M(2,4)$, $P(3,0)$ is transformed by $(x,y) \rightarrow (x-2, y-1)$.

   a. What is the x – coordinate of A'?

   b. What is the y – coordinate of P'?

   c. Show the translation on the coordinate plane below.

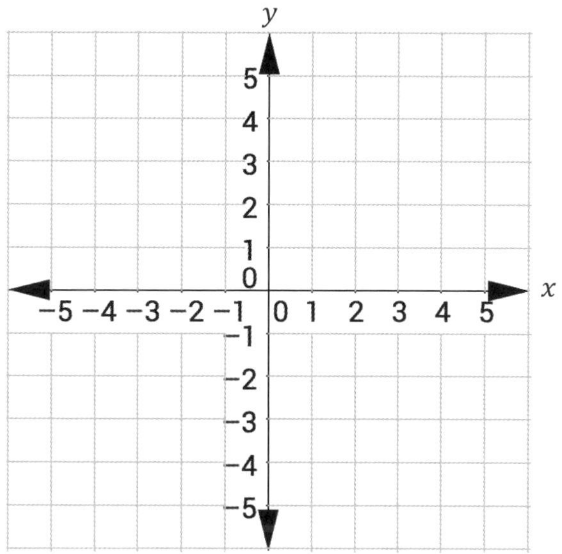

3. Polygon $A'M'O'R'E'S'$ is the image of polygon $AMORES$ after a translation $(x+8, y-7)$.

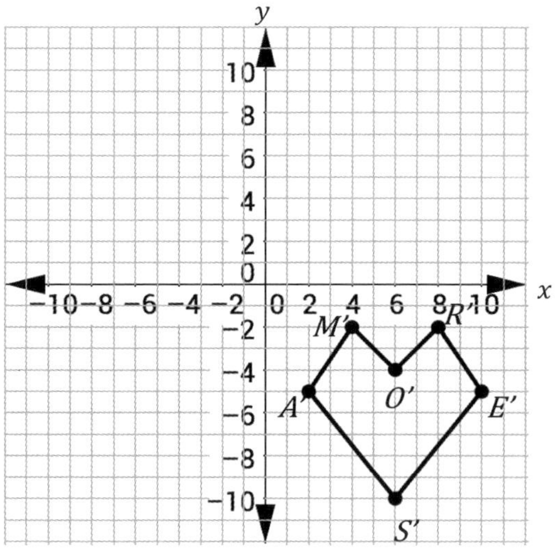

What are the original coordinates of each point of polygon $AMORES$?

BEAT THE TEST!

1. Consider the figure below.

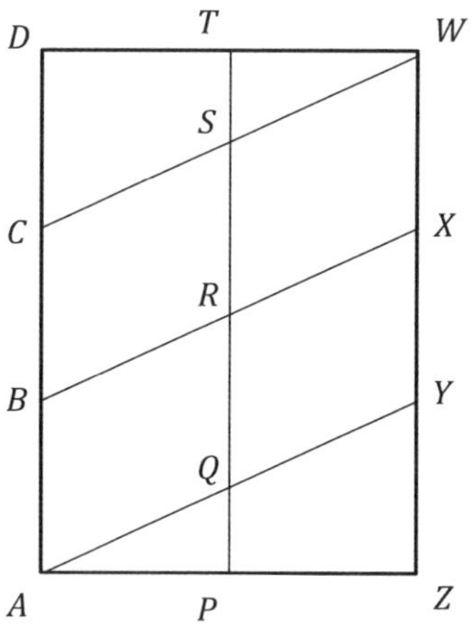

If R is the image of A after a translation, then which point is the image of Q after the same translation?

Section 3 – Topic 4
Examining and Using Reflections

A ***reflection*** is a mirrored version of an object. The image does not change __________, but the figure itself reverses.

The function $r_{line}(x, y)$ reflects the point (x, y) over the given line. For instance, $r_{x-axis}(3, 2)$ reflects the point $(3, 2)$ over the x-axis.

Let's examine the line reflections of the point $(3, 2)$ over the x-axis, y-axis, $y = x$, and $y = -x$.

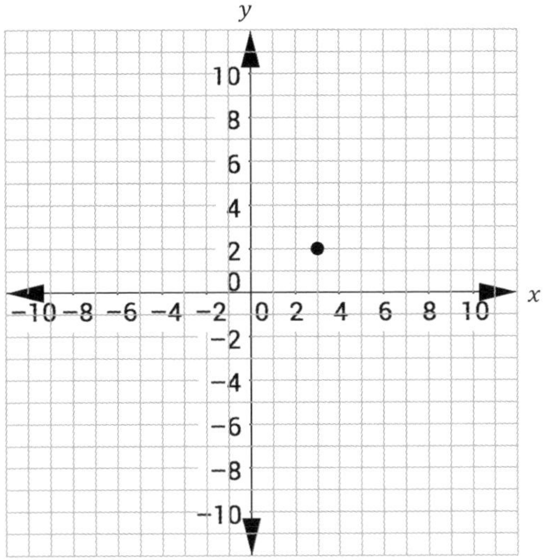

Reflection over	Notation	New coordinates
x-axis	$r_{x-axis}(3, 2)$	
y-axis	$r_{y-axis}(3, 2)$	
$y = x$	$r_{y=x}(3, 2)$	
$y = -x$	$r_{y=-x}(3, 2)$	

Make generalizations about reflections to complete the following table.

Reflection over	Notation	New coordinates
x-axis	$r_{x-axis}(x, y)$	
y-axis	$r_{y-axis}(x, y)$	
$y = x$	$r_{y=x}(x, y)$	
$y = -x$	$r_{y=-x}(x, y)$	

Let's Practice!

1. Suppose the line segment with endpoints $C(1, 3)$ and $D(5, 2)$ is reflected over the y-axis, and then reflected again over $y = x$. What are the coordinates $C"$ and $D"$?

Try It!

2. Suppose a line segment with endpoints $A(-10,-5)$ and $B(-4,2)$ is reflected over $y=-x$.

   a. What are the coordinates of $A'(\_\_,\_\_)$ and $B'(\_\_,\_\_)$?

   b. Graph $\overline{A'B'}$ on the coordinate plane below.

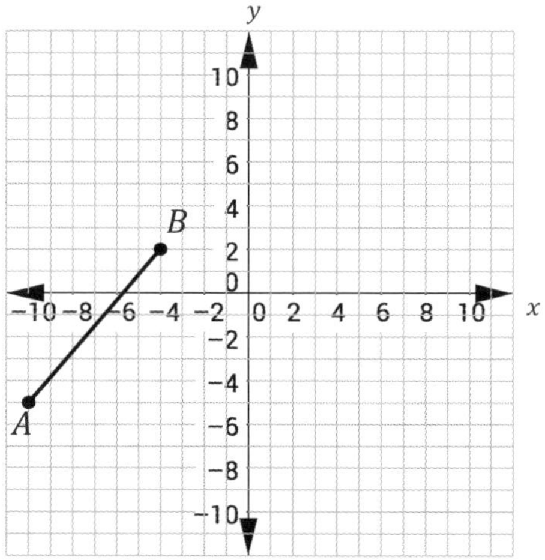

BEAT THE TEST!

1. Consider the following points.

   $F(-3,-10)$ and $E(10,-3)$

   Let $\overline{F'E'}$ be the image of $\overline{FE}$ after a reflection across line l. Suppose that F' is located at $(-3,10)$ and E' is located at $(10,3)$. Which of the following is true about line l?

   Ⓐ Line l is represented by $y=-x$.
   Ⓑ Line l is represented by $y=x$.
   Ⓒ Line l is represented by the x-axis.
   Ⓓ Line l is represented by the y-axis.

2. Suppose a line segment whose endpoints are $G(8,2)$ and $H(14,-8)$ is reflected over $y=x$.

   What are the coordinates of $G'(\_\_,\_\_)$ and $H'(\_\_,\_\_)$?

Section 3 – Topic 5
Reflections of Polygons

Think back to what you know about reflections to answer the questions below.

What are the mirror lines? Draw a representation of a mirror line.

What is a mirror point? Draw a representation of a mirror point.

What are the most common mirror point(s) and line(s)?

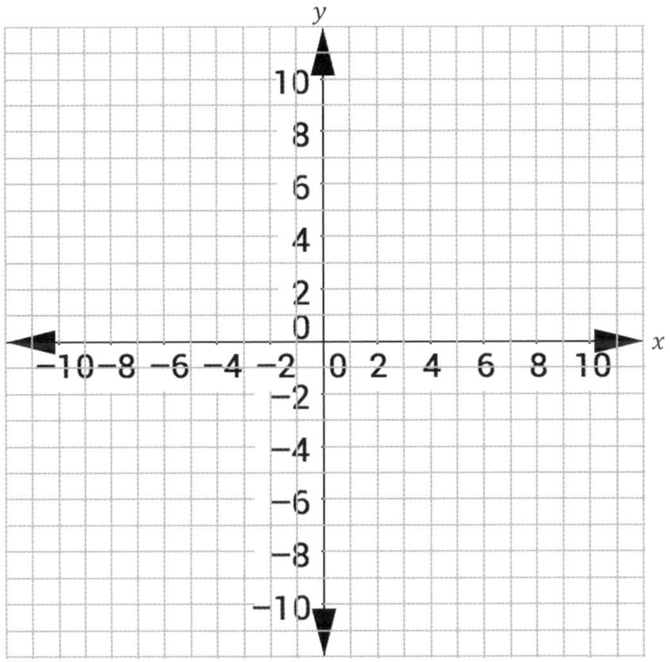

Let's Practice!

1. Consider rectangle $ROPE$ on the coordinate plane.

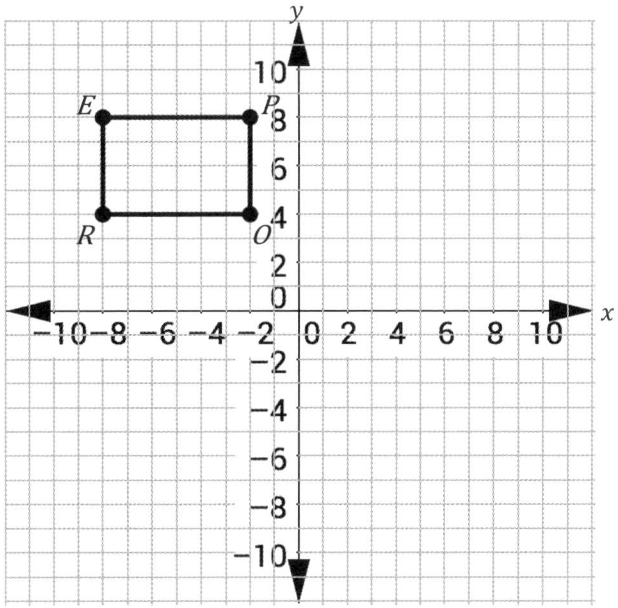

   a. Draw a reflection over the x-axis. Write down the coordinates of the reflected figure.

   b. Draw a reflection over the y-axis. Write down the coordinates of the reflected figure.

Try It!

2. The pentagon below was reflected three different times and resulted in the dashed pentagons labeled as $1, 2,$ and 3.

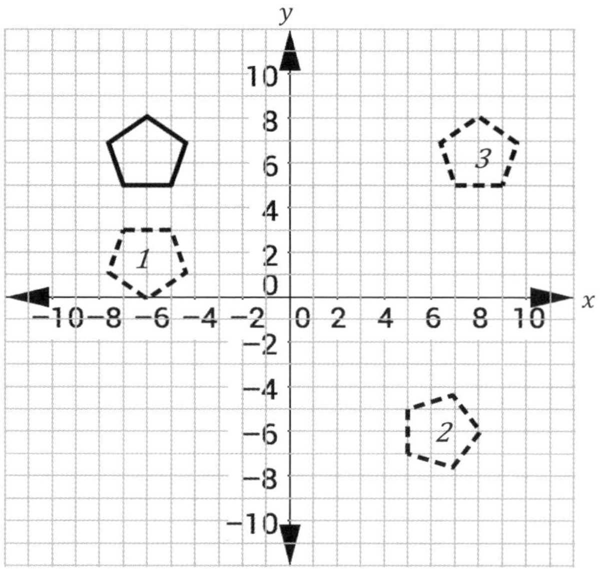

Describe each reflection in the table below.

Reflection 1	Reflection 2	Reflection 3

Let's Practice!

3. Reflect the following image over $y = x$.

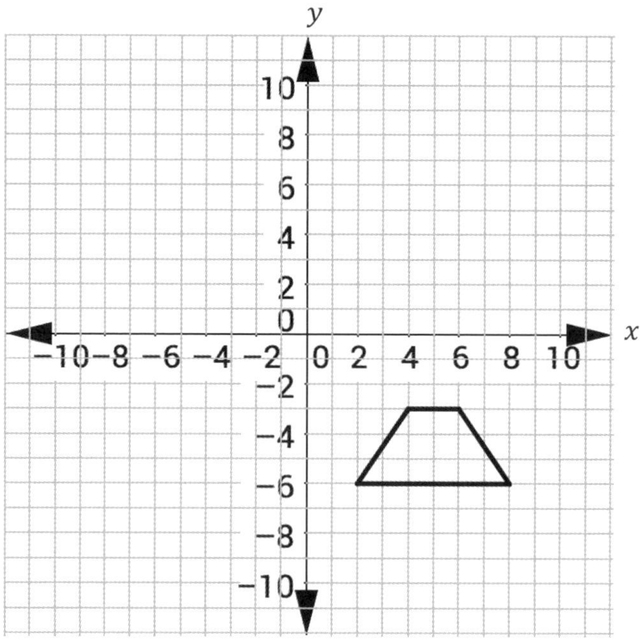

Try It!

4. Reflect the following image over $y = -x$.

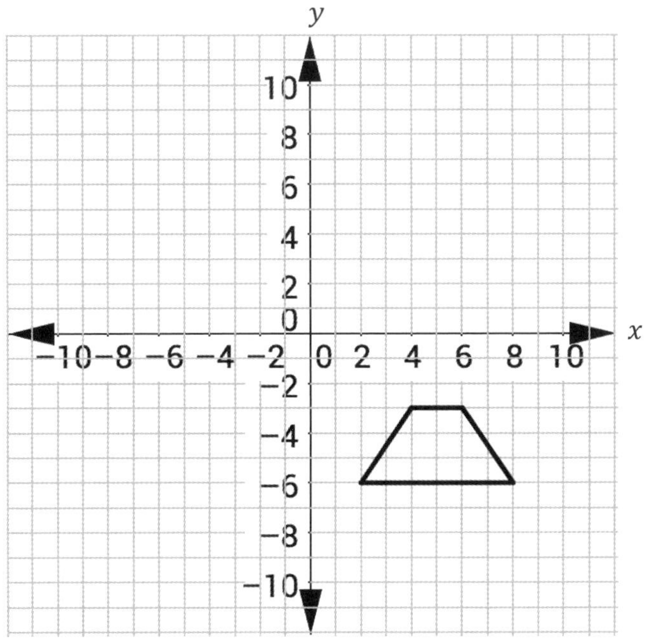

How is reflecting over the axis different from reflecting over other linear functions?

How is reflecting over the axis similar from reflecting over other linear functions?

5. Pentagon $CALOR$ is the result of a reflection of pentagon $FRISA$ over $y = x$. $CALOR$ has vertices at $C(2, -2), A(0, -4)$, $L(1, -6)$, $O(3, -6)$, and $R(4, -4)$. In which quadrant was pentagon $FRISA$ located before being reflected to create $CALOR$?

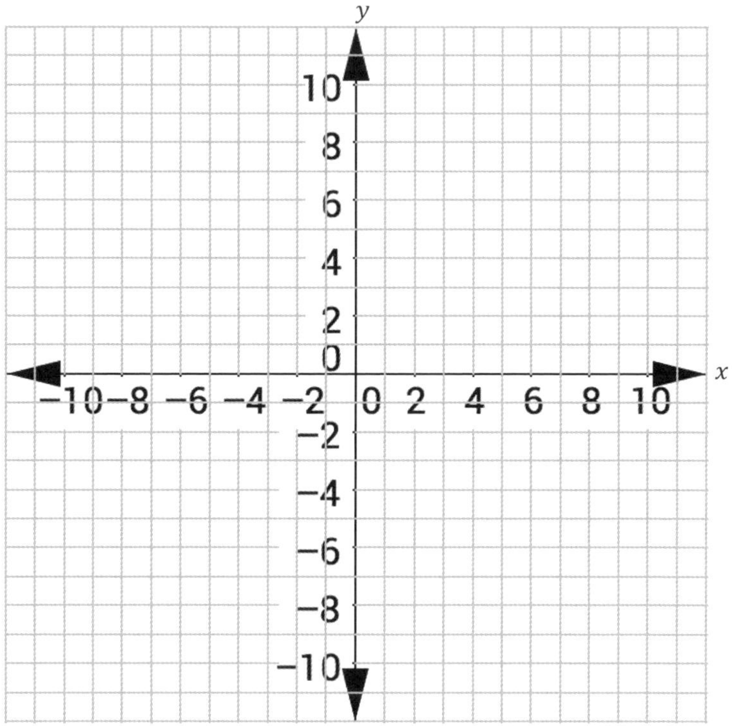

BEAT THE TEST!

1. Draw the line(s) of reflection of the following figures.

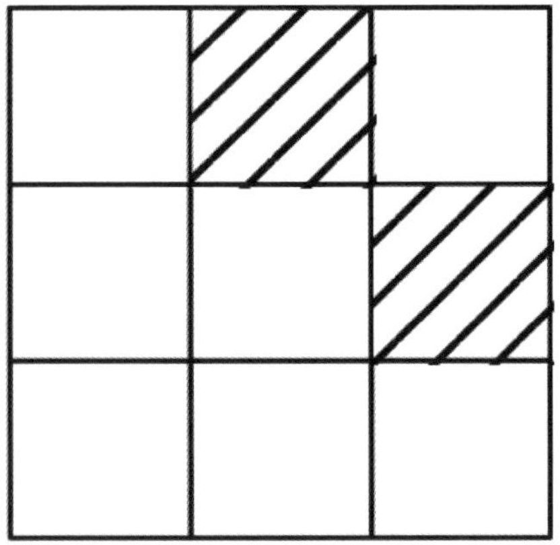

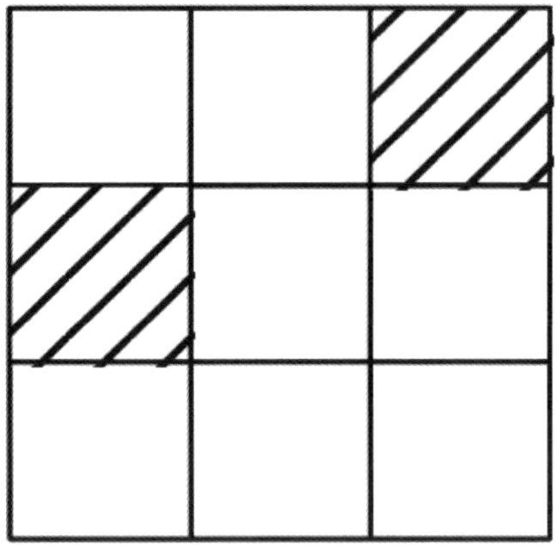

Section 3 – Topic 6
Examining and Using Rotations

A ***rotation*** changes the ____________ of a figure by moving it around a fixed point to the right (clockwise) or to the left (counterclockwise).

Let's consider the following graph.

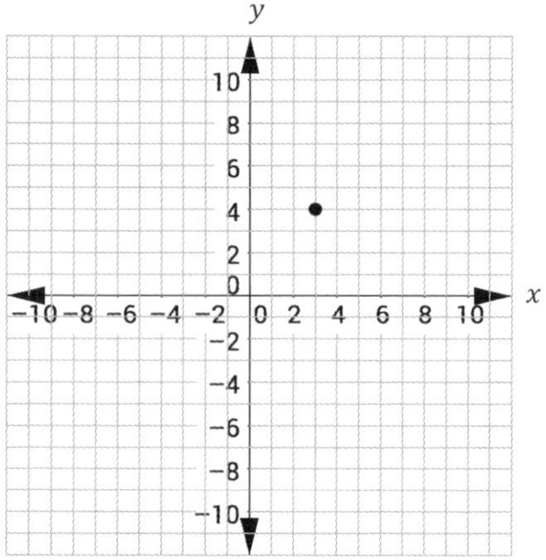

Use the graph to help you determine the coordinates for (x', y') after the following rotations about the origin.

Degree	Counterclockwise	Clockwise
90° Rotation:	$R_{90°}(3,4) =$ ______	$R_{-90°}(3,4) =$ ______
180° Rotation:	$R_{180°}(3,4) =$ ______	$R_{-180°}(3,4) =$ ______
270° Rotation:	$R_{270°}(3,4) =$ ______	$R_{-270°}(3,4) =$ ______
360° Rotation:	$R_{360°}(3,4) =$ ______	$R_{-360°}(3,4) =$ ______

The function $R_t(x, y)$ rotates the point (x, y) $t°$ ________________ about the origin.

The function $R_{-t}(x, y)$ rotates the point (x, y) $t°$ ________________ about the origin.

STUDY EDGE TIP

Rotations are always performed in the counterclockwise (positive) direction unless otherwise stated.

Make generalizations regarding rotations about the origin to complete the following table.

Degree	Counterclockwise	Clockwise
$90°$ Rotation:	$(x, y) \rightarrow$ ________	$(x, y) \rightarrow$ ________
$180°$ Rotation:	$(x, y) \rightarrow$ ________	$(x, y) \rightarrow$ ________
$270°$ Rotation:	$(x, y) \rightarrow$ ________	$(x, y) \rightarrow$ ________
$360°$ Rotation:	$(x, y) \rightarrow$ ________	$(x, y) \rightarrow$ ________

Describe a rotation that will carry a line segment onto itself.

What happens if the center of rotation is not at the origin?

What happens if the degree of rotation is a degree other than $90°, 180°, 270°$, or $360°$?

Let's Practice!

1. $\overline{RT}$ has endpoints $R(0,3)$ and $T(4,1)$. Rotate $\overline{RT}$ about the origin $-90°$.

   a. Which direction is $\overline{RT}$ being rotated?

   b. Write an algebraic description of the transformation of $\overline{RT}$.

   c. What are the endpoints of the new line segment?

2. Let's consider the following graph.

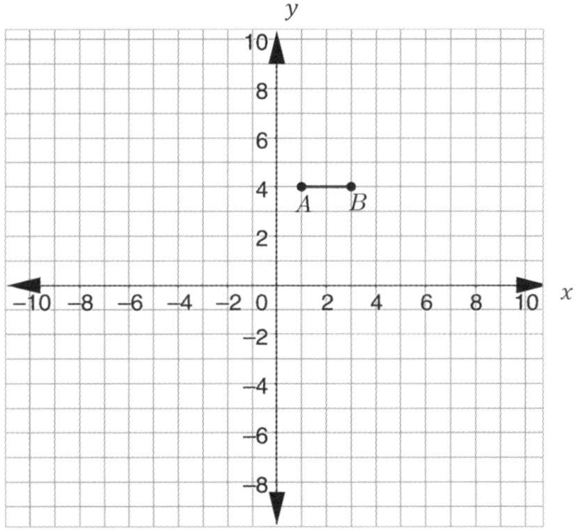

Rotate $\overline{AB}$ $90°$ about $(5,7)$.

Try It!

3. Consider the following graph.

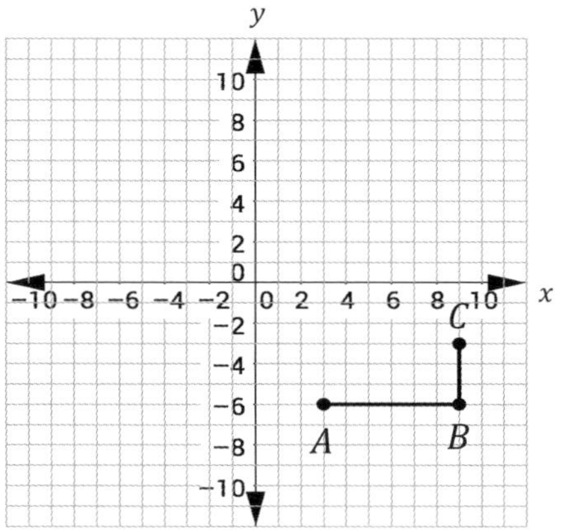

a. Rotate figure ABC $990°$ about the origin. Graph the new figure on the coordinate plane, and complete each blank below with the appropriate coordinates.

A (___,___) → A'(___,___)
B (___,___) → B'(___,___)
C (___,___) → C'(___,___)

b. Rotate figure ABC $-1170°$ about the origin. Graph the new figure on the coordinate plane and complete each blank below with the appropriate coordinates.

A (___,___) → A'(___,___)
B (___,___) → B'(___,___)
C (___,___) → C'(___,___)

BEAT THE TEST!

1. $\overline{PQ}$ has endpoints $P(-2,-1)$ and $Q(6,-5)$. Consider the transformation $(x,y) \rightarrow (y,-x)$ for $\overline{PQ}$.
   a. Is this a rigid transformation? Explain how you know.

   b. What are the coordinates of $\overline{P'Q'}$?

2. The school step team is choreographing their spring dance routine. They begin in a line, as indicated in the graph, and then rotate $-90°$ about person A. Next, they rotate $180°$ about person B. Label the final position of person D on the graph. Explain your reasoning.

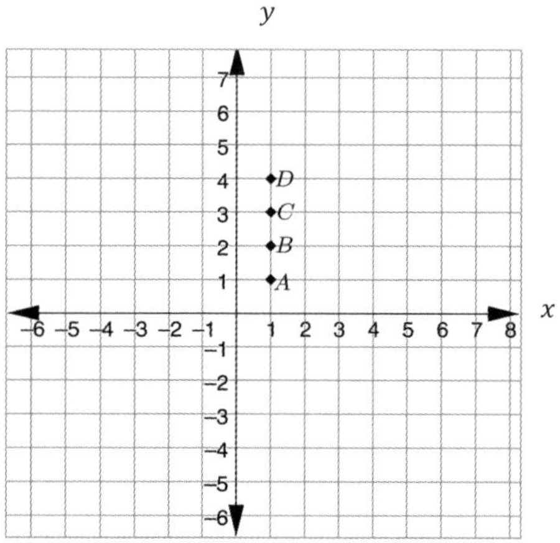

Section 3 – Topic 7
Rotations of Polygons – Part 1

Consider polygon $ABCD$ and the transformed polygon that is rotated 90°, 180°, 270°, and 360° clockwise about the origin.

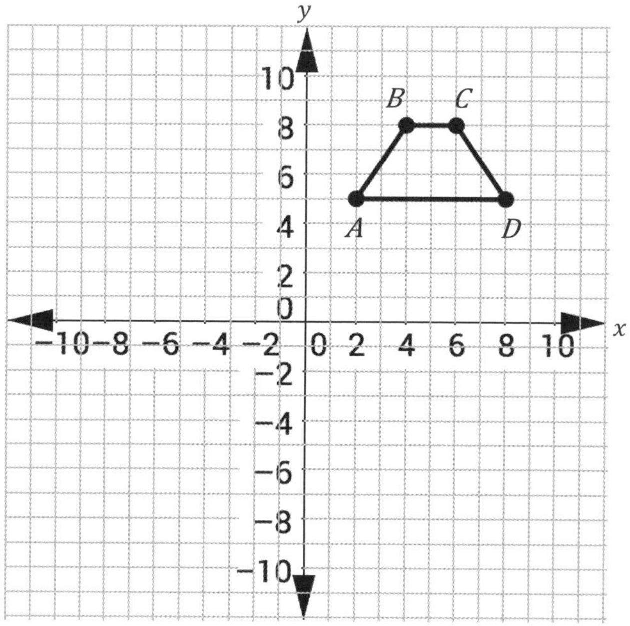

Vertices of $ABCD$	Vertices of 90° rotation	Vertices of 180° rotation	Vertices of 270° rotation	Vertices of 360° rotation
$(2, 5)$				
$(4, 8)$				
$(6, 8)$				
$(8, 5)$				

Consider polygon $ABCD$ and the transformed polygon that is rotated 90°, 180°, 270°, and 360° counterclockwise about the origin.

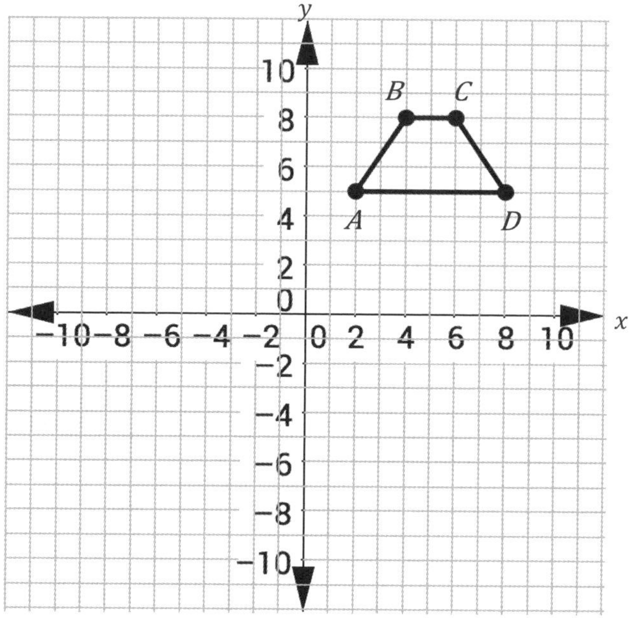

Vertices of $ABCD$	Vertices of 90° rotation	Vertices of 180° rotation	Vertices of 270° rotation	Vertices of 360° rotation
$(2, 5)$				
$(4, 8)$				
$(6, 8)$				
$(8, 5)$				

Let's Practice!

1. Rotate and draw $COMA$ $90°$ counterclockwise about the origin if the vertices are $C(1,-2), O(0,2), M(3,2), A(3,-3)$.

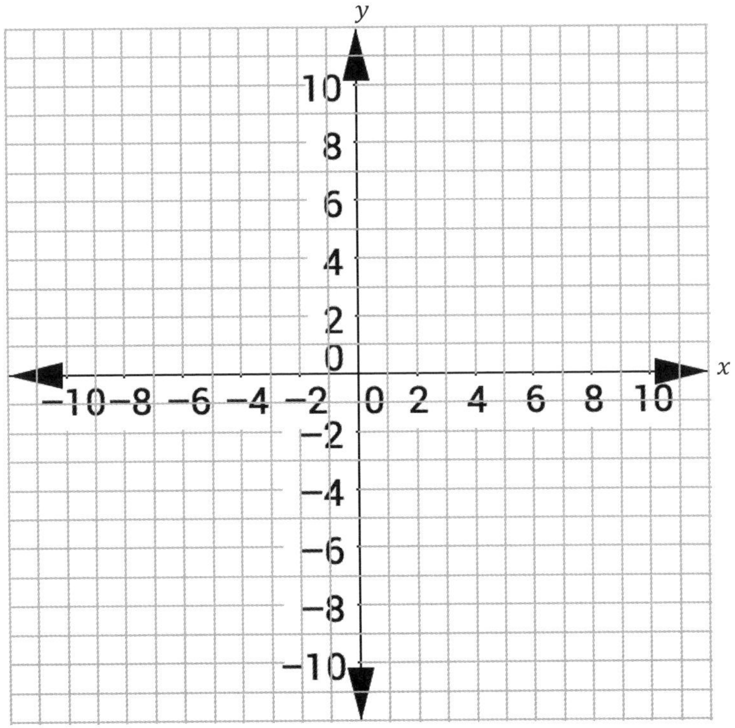

What are the coordinates of $C'O'M'A'$?

Try It!

2. Samuel rotated $AMEN$ $270°$ clockwise about the origin to generate $A'M'E'N'$ with vertices at $A'(1,5), M'(1,0)$, $E'(-1,-1)$, and $N'(-3,2)$.

   What is the sum of all y-coordinates of $AMEN$?

3. What happens if we rotate a figure around a different center point instead of rotating it around the origin?

Section 3 – Topic 8
Rotations of Polygons – Part 2

Use the following steps to rotate polygon $ABCD$ $155°$ clockwise about C. Use the figure on the following page.

Step 1. Extend the line segment between the point of rotation, C, and another vertex on the polygon, towards the opposite direction of the rotation.

Step 2. Place the center of the protractor on the point of rotation and line it up with the segment drawn in step 1. Measure the angle of rotation at C. Mark a point at the angle of rotation and draw a segment with your straightedge by connecting the point with the center of rotation, C.

Step 3. Use a compass to measure the segment used in step 1. Keeping the same setting, place the compass on the segment drawn in step 2 and draw an arc where the new point will be located. Label the new point with a prime notation.

Step 4. Copy the angle adjacent to the angle of rotation. Mark a point at the copied angle in the new figure. Draw a segment by connecting the point at the new angle with the point created in step 3.

Step 5. Use a compass to measure the segment adjacent to the one used in step 1. Keeping the same setting, place the compass on the segment drawn in step 4 and draw an arc where the new point will be located. Label the new point with a prime notation.

Step 6. Repeat steps 4-5 with the two other angles to complete the construction of the rotated polygon.

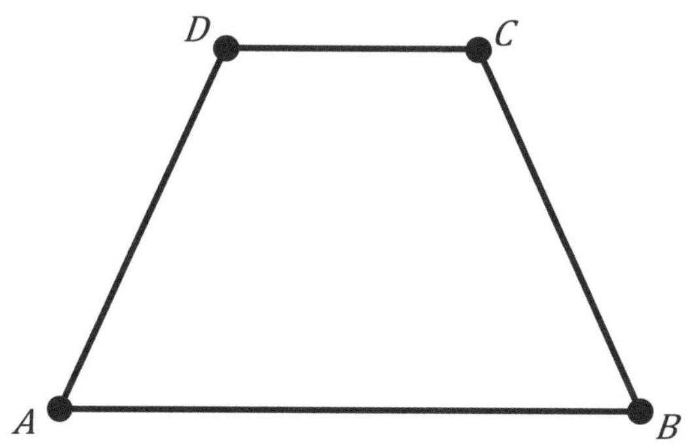

Consider the figure below.

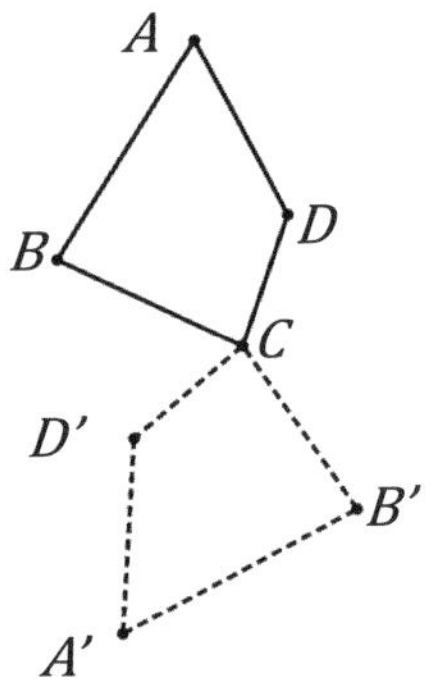

What is the point of rotation? How do you know?

Do you have enough information to determine if the rotation is clockwise or counterclockwise?

If the rotation is clockwise, which of the following degree ranges would it fall in?

Ⓐ $0° - 90°$
Ⓑ $90° - 180°$
Ⓒ $180° - 270°$
Ⓓ $270° - 360°$

If the rotation is counterclockwise, which of the following degree ranges would it fall in?

Ⓐ $0° - 90°$
Ⓑ $90° - 180°$
Ⓒ $180° - 270°$
Ⓓ $270° - 360°$

Let's Practice!

1. Consider the figure below.

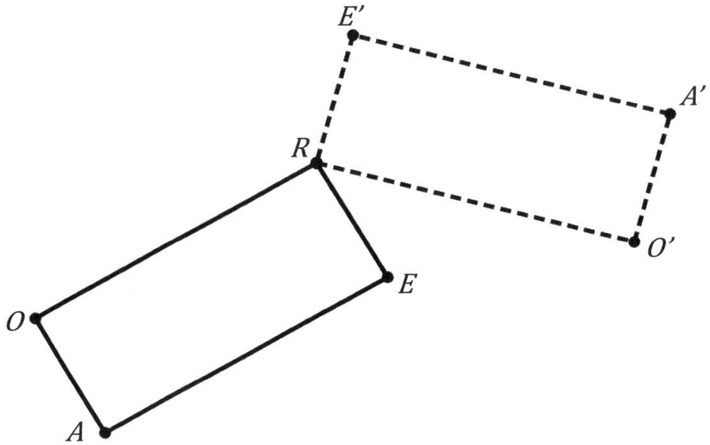

Which of the following statements is true?

Ⓐ The figure shows quadrilateral $AERO$ rotated $45°$ counterclockwise about R and $90°$ clockwise about R.
Ⓑ The figure shows quadrilateral $AERO$ rotated $45°$ clockwise about R and $90°$ counterclockwise about R.
Ⓒ The figure shows quadrilateral $AERO$ rotated $135°$ clockwise about R and $225°$ counterclockwise about R.
Ⓓ The figure shows quadrilateral $AERO$ rotated $135°$ counterclockwise about R and $225°$ clockwise about R.

Try It!

2. Consider quadrilateral $PQRS$ on the coordinate plane below.

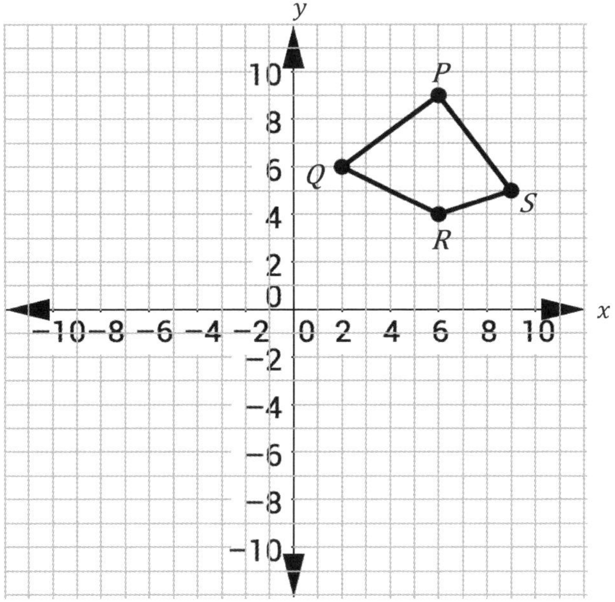

After a rotation of $PQRS$ $90°$ clockwise about the origin, answer each of the following questions.

a. Which vertex will be at point $(-9, 6)$?

b. What will be the coordinates of point R'?

BEAT THE TEST!

1. Consider the quadrilateral below and choose the figure that shows the same quadrilateral after an $80°$ counterclockwise rotation about point A.

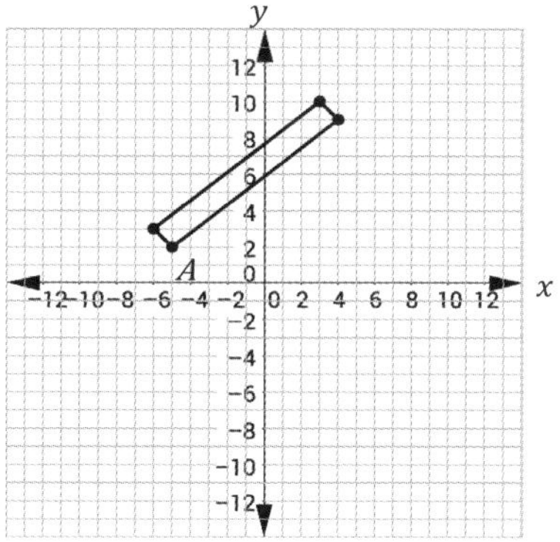

Ⓐ

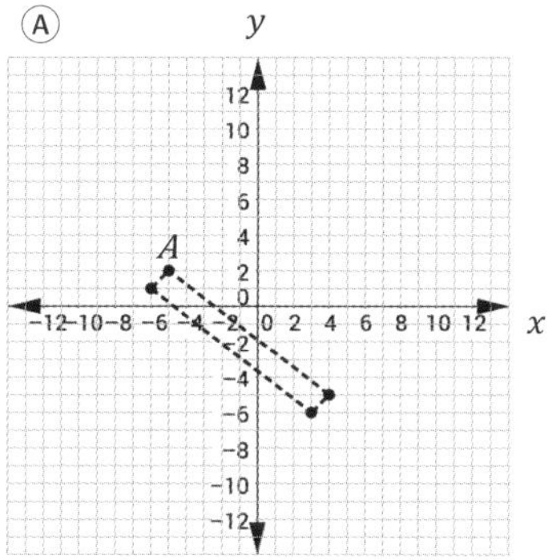

Ⓑ

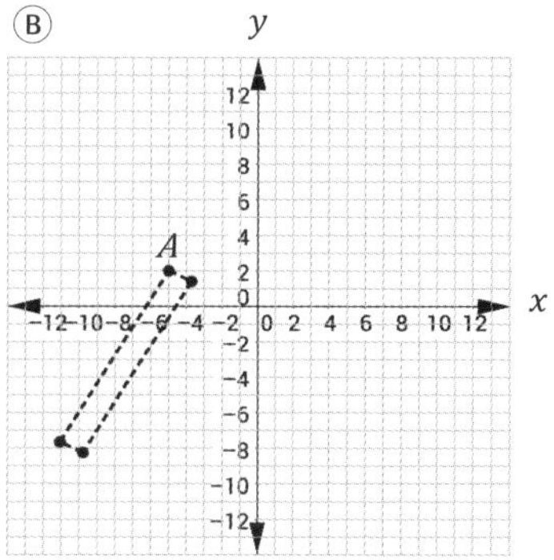

Ⓒ

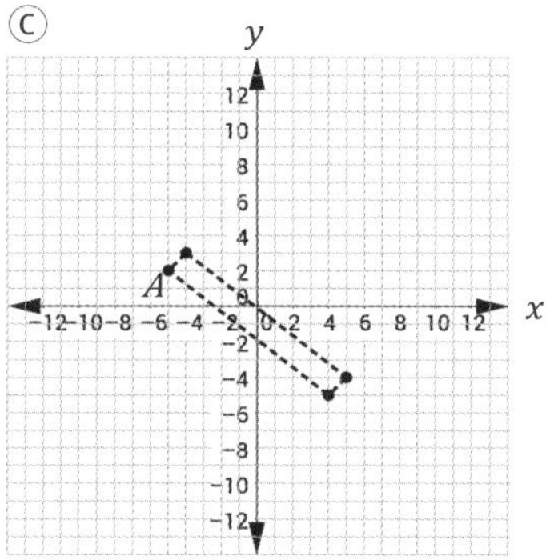

Ⓓ

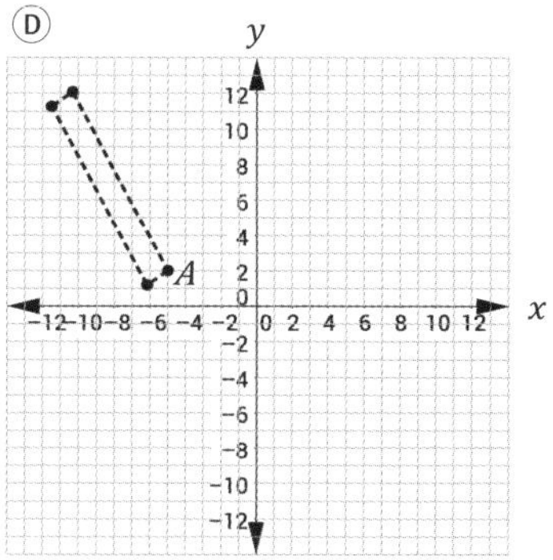

Section 3 – Topic 9
Angle-Preserving Transformations

Consider the figures below. The lines l_1 and l_2 are parallel, and Figure B is a rotation of Figure A.

Figure A

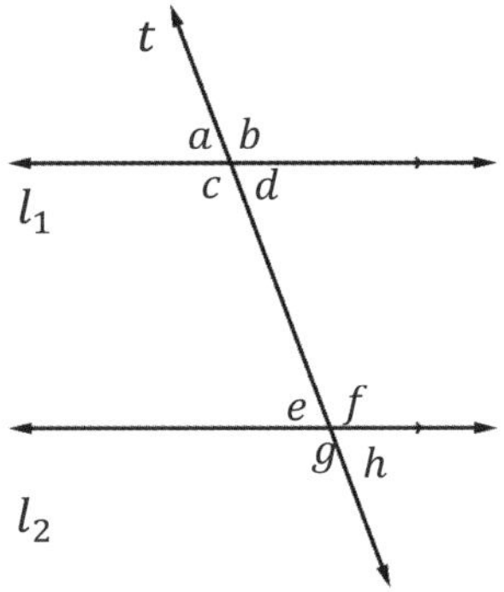

Figure B

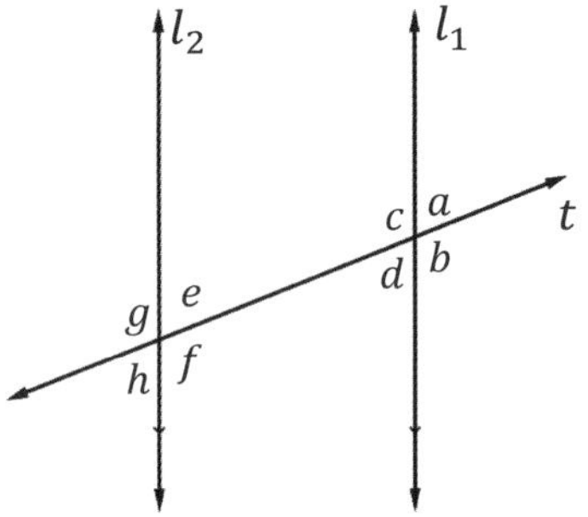

The figures above represent an ***angle-preserving transformation***.

What do you think it means for something to be an angle-preserving transformation?

Does the transformation preserve parallelism? Justify your answer.

Angle-preserving transformations refer to reflection, translation, rotation, and dilation that preserve ________________ ____________ and ____________after the transformation.

The conditions for parallelism of two lines cut by a transversal are:

- Corresponding angles
- Alternate interior angles
- Alternate exterior angles

} are ______________.

- Same-side/consecutive angles are ______________.

Since the transformations preserve angle measures, these conditions are also preserved. Therefore, parallel lines will remain parallel after any of these four transformations.

Let's Practice!

1. Consider the figure below in which $l_1 \parallel l_2$.

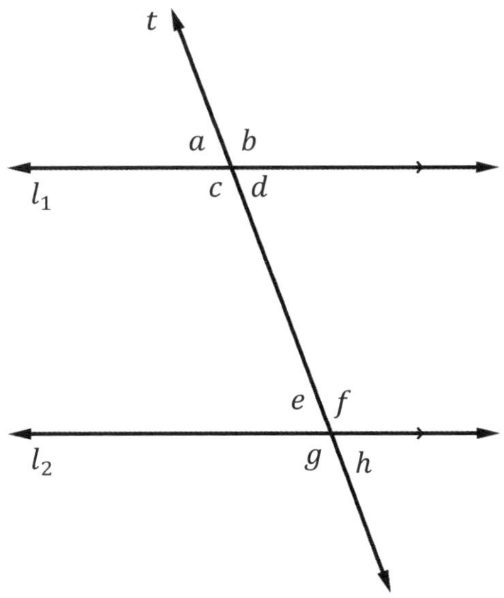

   a. Determine the angles that are congruent with $\angle a$ after a translation of $\angle a$.

   b. Determine the angles that are supplementary with $\angle a$ and $\angle e$ after a 180° rotation of $\angle a$.

Try It!

2. Consider the following figure.

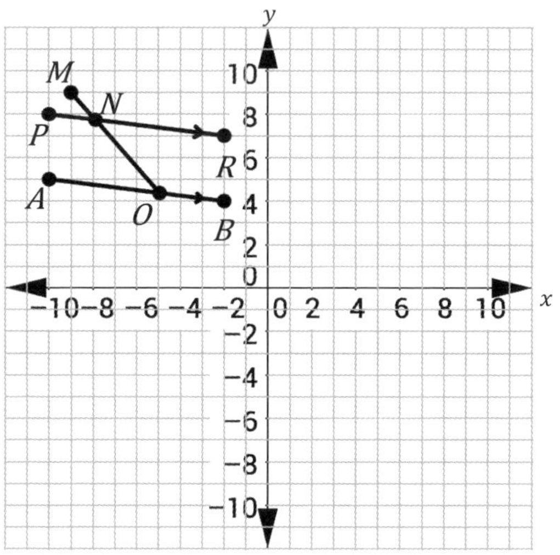

   a. Reflect the above image across $y = x$.

   b. If $m\angle MOB = 117°$ and $m\angle M'N'P' = 63°$, prove that after the reflection, $m\angle M'O'B' = 117°$.

Let's Practice!

3. The figure in Quadrant III of the coordinate plane below is a transformation of the figure in Quadrant II.

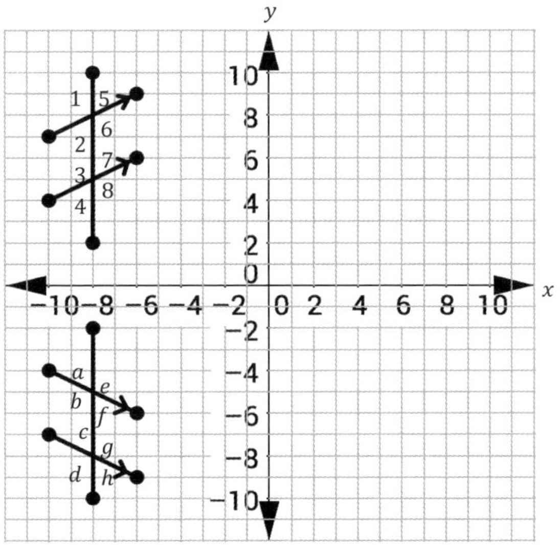

   a. What type of transformation is shown above? Justify your answer.

   b. Write a paragraph proof to prove that $\angle 6$ and $\angle f$ are supplementary.

Try It!

4. The figure in Quadrant IV of the coordinate plane below is a transformation of the figure in Quadrant II.

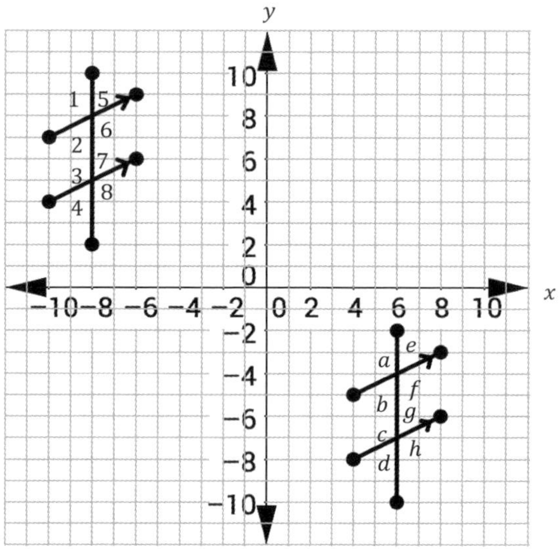

   a. What type of transformation is shown above? Justify your answer.

   b. Write a paragraph proof to prove that $\angle 4$ and $\angle e$ are congruent.

5. Consider the figure and the statements below.

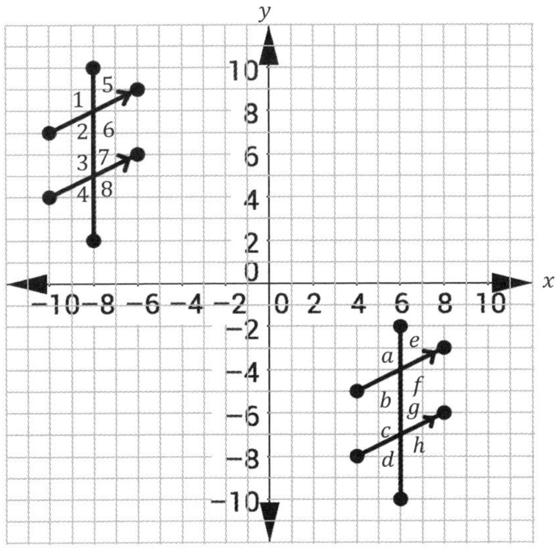

$m\angle 2 = 4x - 11$

$m\angle 4 = 4y + 1$

$m\angle g = 3x + 3$

$m\angle h = 13y - 8$

Find the following values. Explain how you found the answers.

$x =$

$y =$

$m\angle 1 =$

$m\angle d =$

BEAT THE TEST!

1. The figure in the second quadrant of the coordinate plane below was transformed into the figure in the first quadrant. Mark the most appropriate answer in each shape below.

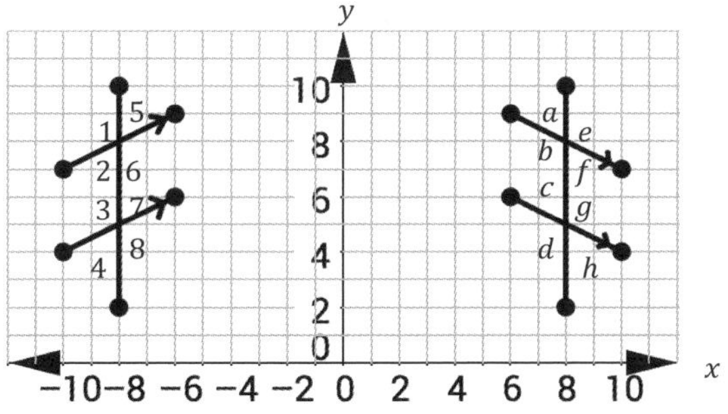

Part A: The figure was

- o dilated
- o rotated
- o reflected
- o translated

- o across the x-axis.
- o across the y-axis.
- o around the origin.
- o by a scale factor of -1.
- o sixteen units to the right.

Part B: $\angle 1$ is

- o complementary
- o congruent
- o corresponding
- o supplementary

to $\angle c$.

Part C: $\angle 6$ is

- o complementary
- o congruent
- o corresponding
- o supplementary

to $\angle g$.

2. Consider the same figure as in the previous question.

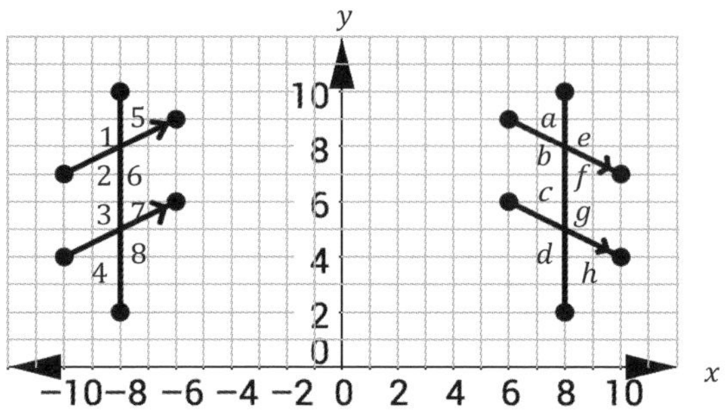

If $m\angle 7 = 2x - 4$ and $m\angle b = 6x$, then $m\angle 8 =$ _____ and $m\angle h =$ _____.

Section 3 – Topic 10
Symmetries of Regular Polygons

Which of the following are symmetrical? Circle the figure(s) that are symmetrical.

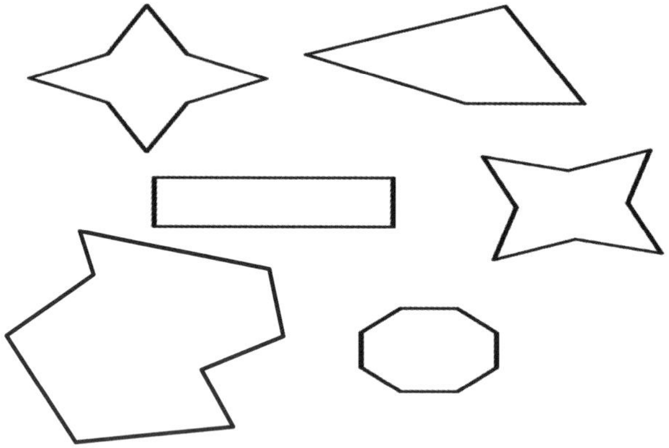

What do you think it means to map a figure onto itself?

Draw a figure and give an example of a single transformation that carries the image onto itself.

Consider the rectangle shown below in the coordinate plane. We need to identify the equation of the line that maps the figure onto itself after a reflection across that line.

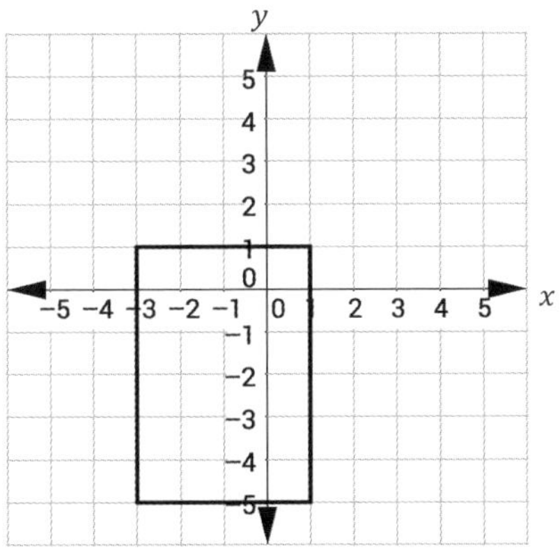

Reflect the image across the line $x = -1$. Does the transformation result in the original pre-image?

Reflect the image across the line $y = -1$. Does the transformation result in the original pre-image?

Reflect the image across the line $y = x - 1$. Does the transformation result in the original pre-image?

Reflect the image across the line $y = -2$. Does the transformation result in the original pre-image?

The equations of the lines that map the rectangle above onto itself are ______________ and ______________.

Reflecting a regular n-gon across a line of symmetry carries the n-gon onto itself.

Let's explore lines of symmetry.

In regular polygons, if n is odd, the lines of symmetry will pass through a vertex and the midpoint of the opposite side. Draw the lines of symmetry on the polygon below.

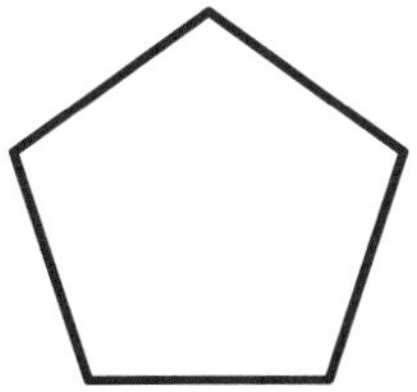

In regular polygons, if n is even, there are two scenarios.

- The lines of symmetry will pass through two opposite vertices.
- The lines of symmetry will pass through the midpoints of two opposite sides.

Draw the lines of symmetry on the polygon below.

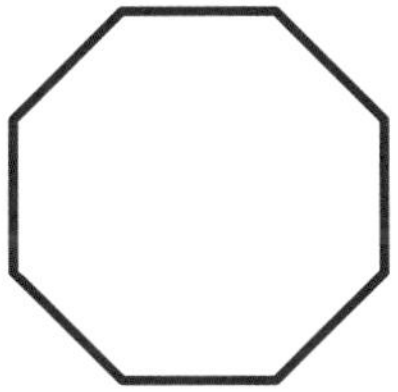

Let's Practice!

1. Consider the trapezoid below.

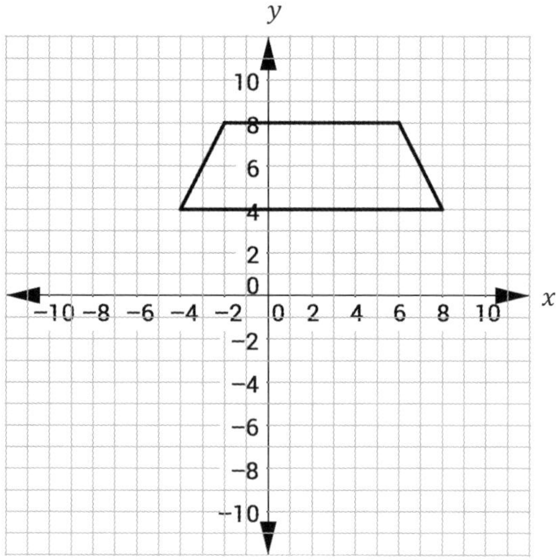

Which line will carry the figure onto itself?

Ⓐ $x = 1$
Ⓑ $x = 2$
Ⓒ $y = 4$
Ⓓ $y = 6$

Try It!

2. Which of the following transformations carries this regular polygon onto itself?

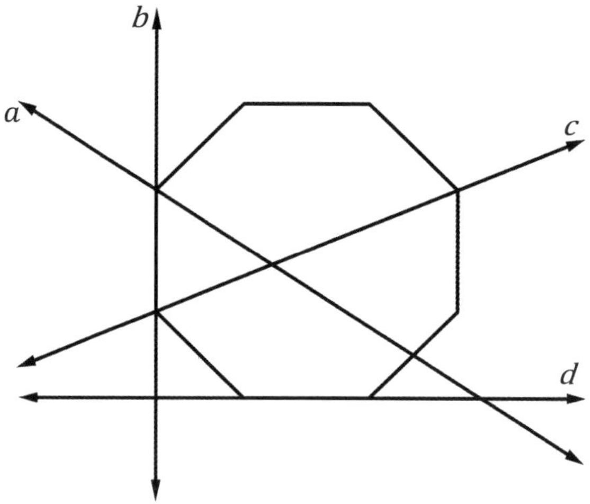

Ⓐ Reflection across line a
Ⓑ Reflection across line b
Ⓒ Reflection across line c
Ⓓ Reflection across line d

3. How many ways can you reflect each of the following figures onto itself?

a. Regular heptagon: ________

b. Regular octagon: ________

Rotations also carry a geometric figure onto itself.

What rotations will carry a regular polygon onto itself?

About which location do you rotate a figure in order to carry it onto itself?

What rotation would carry this regular hexagon onto itself?

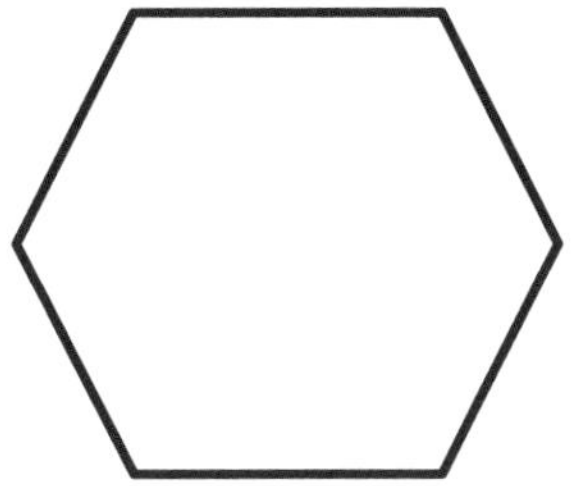

STUDY EDGE TIP

Rotating a regular n-gon by a multiple of $\frac{360°}{n}$ carries the n-gon onto itself.

Let's Practice!

4. Consider the regular octagon below with center at the origin and a vertex at $(4, 0)$.

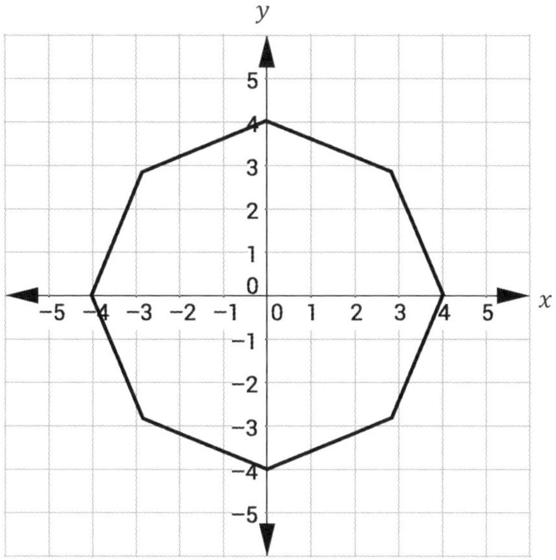

Describe a rotation that will map this regular octagon onto itself.

Try It!

5. Which rotations will carry this regular polygon onto itself?

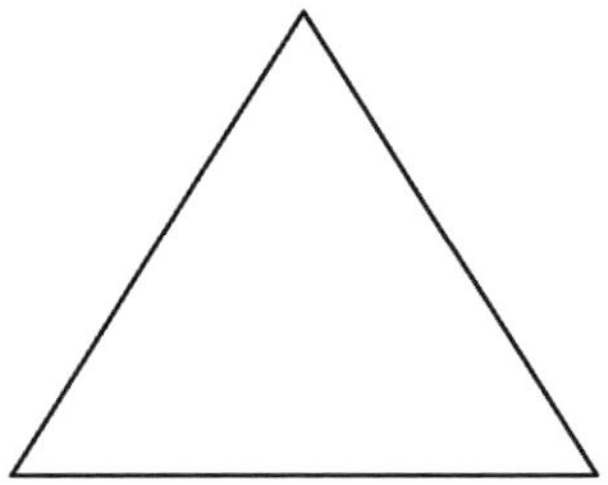

6. Consider the two rectangles below.

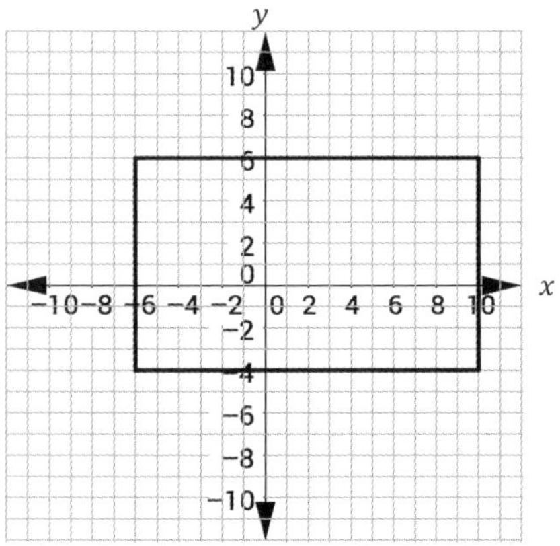

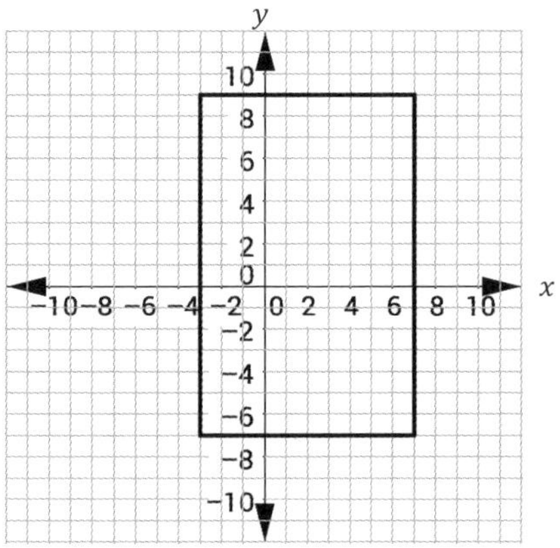

The degree of rotation that maps each figure onto itself is a rotation _______ degrees about the point

(,).

BEAT THE TEST!

1. Which of the following transformations carry this regular polygon onto itself? Select all that apply.

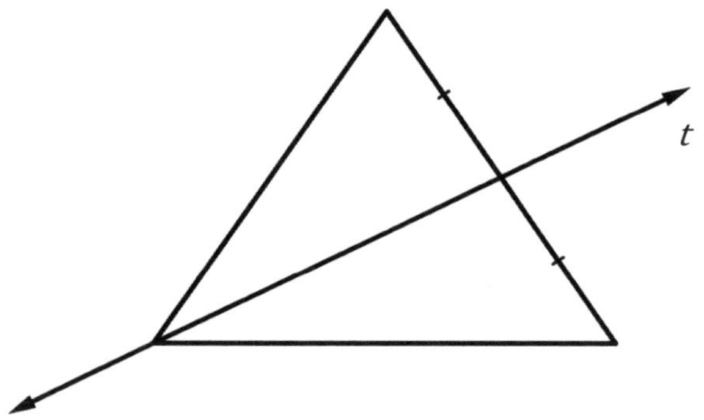

- ☐ Reflection across line t
- ☐ Reflection across its base
- ☐ Rotation of 40° counterclockwise
- ☐ Rotation of 90° counterclockwise
- ☐ Rotation of 120° clockwise
- ☐ Rotation of 240° counterclockwise

Test Yourself! Practice Tool

Great job! You have reached the end of this section. Now it's time to try the "Test Yourself! Practice Tool," where you can practice all the skills and concepts you learned in this section. Log in to Math Nation and try out the "Test Yourself! Practice Tool" so you can see how well you know these topics!

Section 4: Non-Rigid Transformations, Congruence, and Similarity

Topic 1: Examining and Using Dilations – Part 1 111
Standards Covered: G-SRT.1
- ☐ I can change a figure's size without changing its shape.

Topic 2: Examining and Using Dilations – Part 2 113
Standards Covered: G-SRT.1
- ☐ I can perform dilations of points and line segments on a coordinate plane.

Topic 3: Dilations of Polygons 115
Standards Covered: G-SRT.1
- ☐ I can perform dilations of polygons on a coordinate plane and find the coordinates of the image and the pre-image.

Topic 4: Compositions of Transformations of Polygons – Part 1 118
Standards Covered: G-CO.5
- ☐ I can describe a single transformation as a composition of two transformations.

Topic 5: Compositions of Transformations of Polygons – Part 2 121
Standards Covered: G-CO.5
- ☐ I can determine the coordinates of a dilated image centered at the origin using the coordinates of a preimage.

Topic 6: Congruence of Polygons 123
Standards Covered: G-CO.6, G-CO.7
- ☐ I can recognize and use transformations to produce a congruent image.

Topic 7: Similarity of Polygons 125
Standards Covered: G-SRT.2
- ☐ I can recognize and use transformations to produce a similar image.

Visit MathNation.com or search "Math Nation" in your phone or tablet's app store to watch the videos that go along with this workbook!

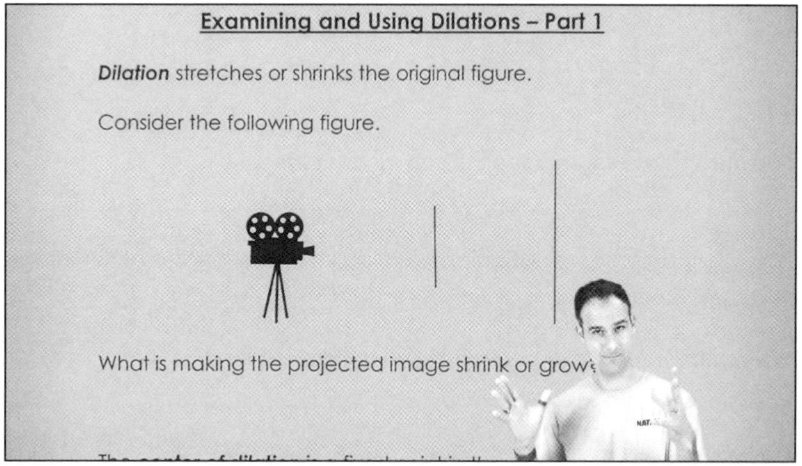
Examining and Using Dilations – Part 1
Dilation stretches or shrinks the original figure.
Consider the following figure.
What is making the projected image shrink or grow

The following Michigan Mathematics Standards will be covered in this section:
G-CO.5 - Given a geometric figure and a rotation, reflection, or translation, draw the transformed figure. Specify a sequence of transformations that will carry a given figure onto itself.
G-CO.6 - Use geometric descriptions of rigid motions to transform figures and to predict the effect of a given rigid motion on a given figure; given two figures, use the definition of congruence in terms of rigid motions to decide if they are congruent.
G-CO.7 - Use the definition of congruence in terms of rigid motions to show that two triangles are congruent if and only if corresponding pairs of sides and corresponding pairs of angles are congruent.
G-SRT.1 - Verify experimentally the properties of dilations given by a center and a scale factor: a. A dilation takes a line not passing through the center of the dilation to a parallel line and leaves a line passing through the center unchanged. b. The dilation of a line segment is longer or shorter in the ratio given by the scale factor.
G-SRT.2 - Given two figures, use the definition of similarity transformations to decide if they are similar; explain using similarity transformations the meaning of similarity for triangles as the equality of all corresponding pairs of angles and the proportionality of all corresponding pairs of sides.

Section 4: Non-Rigid Transformations, Congruence, and Similarity

Section 4 – Topic 1
Examining and Using Dilations – Part 1

Dilation stretches or shrinks the original figure.

Consider the following figure.

What is making the projected image shrink or grow?

The ***center of dilation*** is a fixed point in the plane about which all points are expanded or contracted.

How different is one line from the other in the above figure?

The ***scale factor*** refers to how much the figure grows or shrinks, and it is denoted by k.

- If $0 < k < 1$, the image gets smaller and closer to the center of dilation.
- If $k > 1$, the image gets larger and farther from the center of dilation.

Consider the following graph.

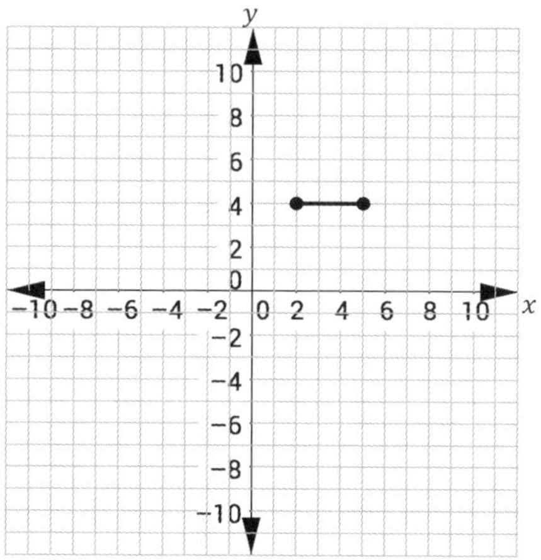

How do you dilate the line segment on the above graph centered at a point on the same line?

Use $(2, 4)$ as the center of dilation and complete the following:

- If $k = 2$, then the dilated line segment will have coordinates: ____________ and ____________.
- If $k = \frac{1}{2}$, then the dilated line segment will have coordinates: ____________ and ____________.
- When dilating a line that passes through the center of dilation, the line is ____________.

Consider the following graph.

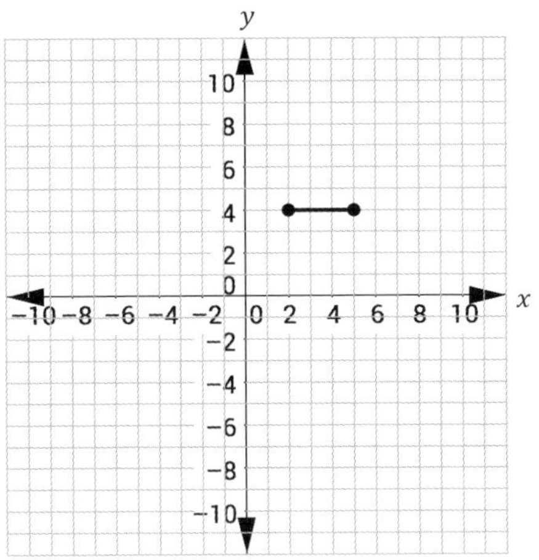

How do you dilate the line segment on the above graph centered at the origin?

➢ If $k = 2$, then the dilated line segment will have coordinates: ____________ and ____________.

➢ If $k = \frac{1}{2}$, then the dilated line segment will have coordinates: ____________ and ____________.

➢ When dilating a line that does not pass through the center of dilation, the dilated line is ______________ to the original.

➢ $(x, y) \rightarrow (kx, ky)$ changes the size of the figure by a factor of k when the center of dilation is the origin.

Consider the following graph.

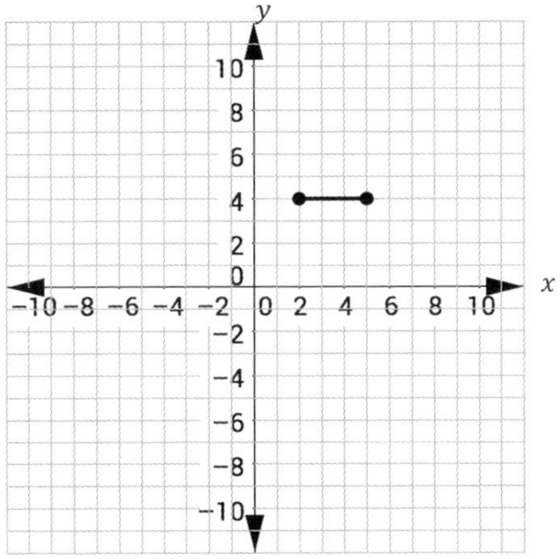

Use $(3, 6)$ as the center of dilation and complete the following statements:

➢ If $k = 4$, then the dilated line segment will have the coordinates ____________ and ____________.

➢ If $k = \frac{1}{4}$, then the dilated line segment will have the coordinates ____________ and ____________.

In conclusion,

➢ A dilation produces an image that is the same ________ as the original, but is a different ________.

➢ When dilating a line segment, the dilated line segment is longer or shorter with respect to the ___________ _______________.

Section 4 – Topic 2
Examining and Using Dilations – Part 2

Let's Practice!

1. $\overline{AB}$ has coordinates $A(-3,9)$ and $B(6,-12)$. $\overline{PQ}$ has coordinates $P(3,-6)$ and $Q(3,9)$.

   a. Find the coordinates of $\overline{A'B'}$ after a dilation with a scale factor of $\frac{2}{3}$ centered at the origin.

   b. Find the coordinates of $\overline{P'Q'}$ after a dilation with a scale factor of $\frac{1}{5}$ centered at $(3,-1)$.

2. Line l is mapped onto the line t by a dilation centered at the origin with a scale factor of 3. The equation of line l is $2x - y = 7$. What is the equation for line t?

   Ⓐ $6x - 3y = 21$
   Ⓑ $\frac{1}{6}x - y = \frac{1}{21}$
   Ⓒ $y = 2x - 21$
   Ⓓ $y = 6x - 21$

3. Suppose the line l represented by $f(x) = 2x - 1$ is transformed into $g(x) = 2(f(x+1)) - 7$.

   a. Describe the transformation from $f(x)$ to $g(x)$.

   b. What is the y-coordinate of $g(0)$?

Try It!

4. What is the scale factor for the dilation of ABC into $A'B'C'$?

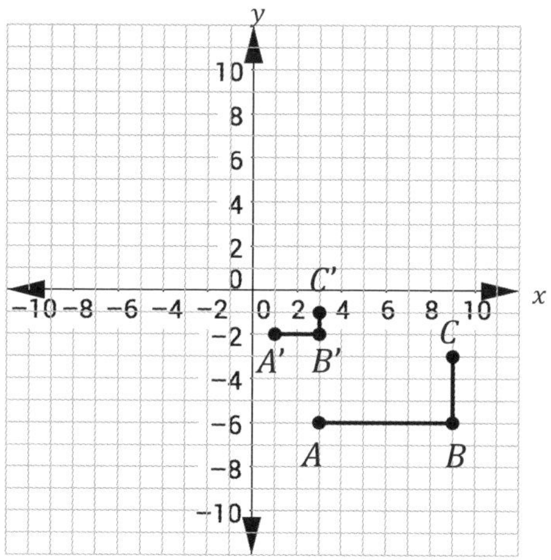

$k =$

5. $\overline{CD}$ has coordinates $C(-8,-2)$ and $D(-4,-12)$.

   a. Determine the coordinates of $\overline{C'D'}$ if $(x,y) \rightarrow (3x,3y)$.

   b. Find the coordinates of $\overline{C'D'}$ after a dilation with a scale factor of 2 centered at $(2,2)$.

BEAT THE TEST!

1. $\overline{M'T'}$ has coordinates $M'(-8, 10)$ and $T'(2, -4)$, and it is the result of the dilation of $\overline{MT}$ centered at the origin. The coordinates of $\overline{MT}$ are $M(-4, 5)$ and $T(1, -2)$. Complete the following algebraic description so that it represents the transformation of $\overline{MT}$.

$(x, y) \rightarrow (\square\, x, \square\, y)$

2. Line l is mapped onto line m by a dilation centered at the origin with a scale factor of $\frac{4}{5}$. Line m is represented by $y = 3x + 8$ and it passes through the point whose coordinates are $(-4, -4)$. Which of the following is true about line l?

Ⓐ Line l is parallel to line m.
Ⓑ Line l is perpendicular to line m.
Ⓒ Line l passes through the origin.
Ⓓ Line l is the same as line m.

3. $P(-6, -10)$, $Q(-10, -4)$, and $R(-4, 2)$ form figure PQR.

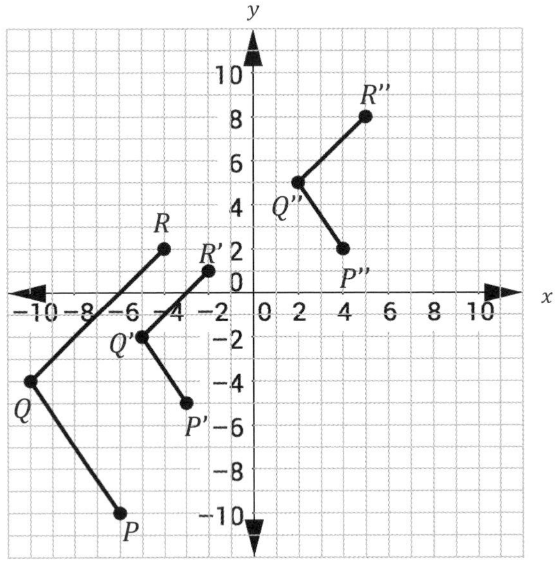

Part A: Gladys transformed figure PQR into $P'Q'R'$. Which of the following represents her transformation?

Ⓐ $(x, y) \rightarrow (\frac{1}{2}x, \frac{1}{2}y)$
Ⓑ $(x, y) \rightarrow (2x, 2y)$
Ⓒ $(x, y) \rightarrow (x + 3, y + 5)$
Ⓓ $(x, y) \rightarrow (x - 3, y - 5)$

Part B: She then transformed $P'Q'R'$ into $P''Q''R''$. What is the transformation?

$(x, y) \rightarrow (\_\_\_\_\_\_\_\_\_\_, \_\_\_\_\_\_\_\_\_\_)$

Section 4 – Topic 3
Dilations of Polygons

How is a ***dilation*** different from a translation, reflection, or rotation?

Consider the figures below.

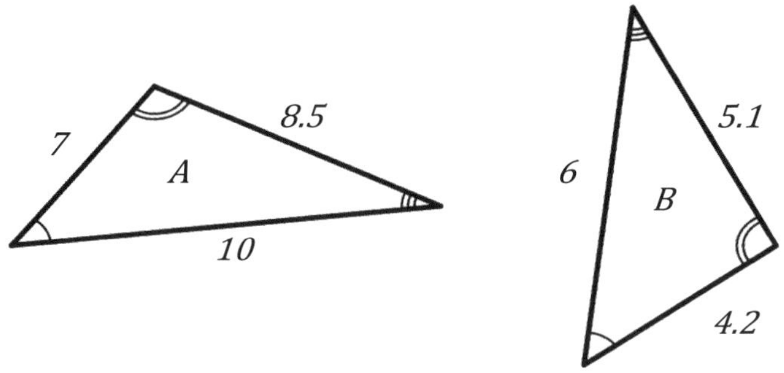

Is Figure B a dilation of Figure A? Justify your answer.

What is the scale factor?

Is Figure A a dilation of Figure B? Justify your answer.

What is the scale factor?

We often represent a dilation with the following notation:

$$D_k = k(x, y)$$

Consider the dilation of quadrilateral $ABCD$ below.

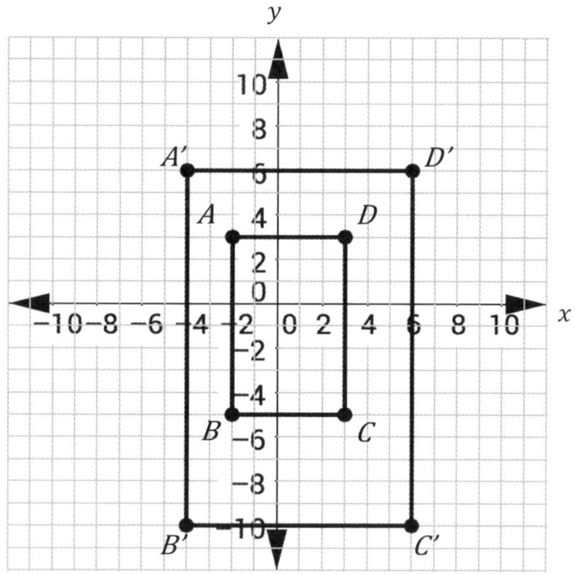

What do you notice about the dilation represented in the figure above?

Let's Practice!

1. Pentagon $PENTA$ has coordinates $P(0,0), E(4,4), N(8,4),$ $T(8,-4)$, and $A(4,-4)$ and is dilated at the origin with a scale factor of $\frac{3}{4}$.

   What are the coordinates of $P'E'N'T'A'$?

Try It!

2. Quadrilateral $PINT$ is dilated at the origin with a scale factor of $\frac{5}{3}$.

   Describe quadrilateral $PINT$ and quadrilateral $P'I'N'T'$ by filling in the table below with the most appropriate answer.

Quadrilateral $PINT$	Quadrilateral $P'I'N'T'$
(x, y)	$(\qquad , \qquad)$
$P(3,3)$	$P'(\qquad , \qquad)$
$I(\qquad , \qquad)$	$I'(10,15)$
$N(\qquad , \qquad)$	$N'(15,-5)$
$T(-3,-6)$	$T'(\qquad , \qquad)$

3. Consider rectangle $ABCD$.

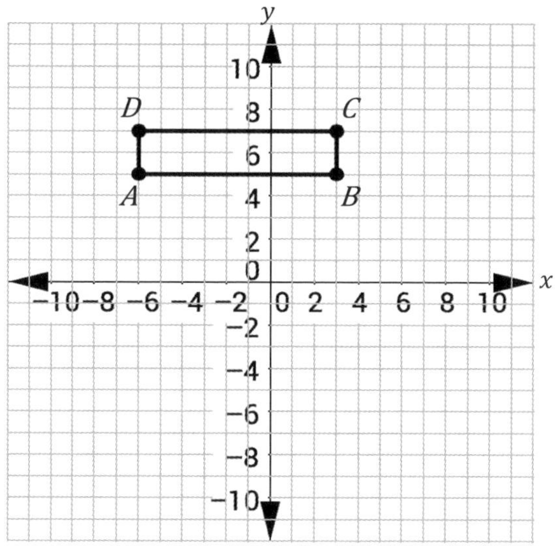

Dilate $ABCD$ by a scale factor of $\frac{1}{2}$ using a center of dilation of $(1,1)$. Draw $A'B'C'D'$ on the same coordinate plane.

BEAT THE TEST!

1. Consider quadrilateral $MATH$ on the figure below.

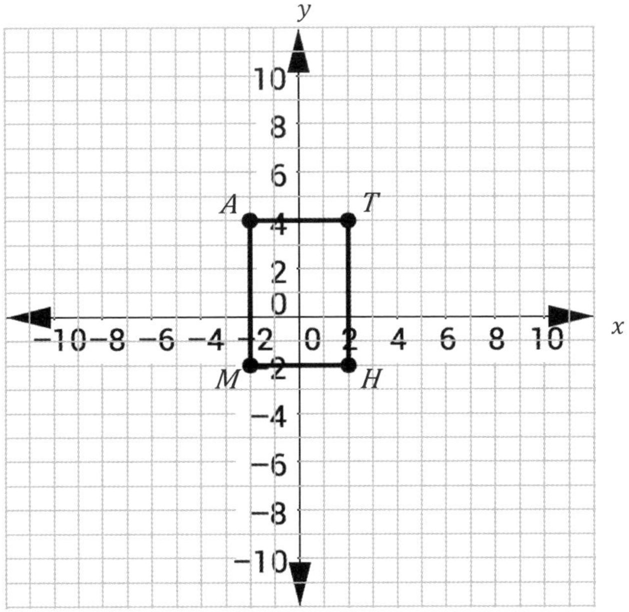

Quadrilateral $MATH$ is dilated by a scale factor of 0.5 centered at $(-2,-2)$ to create quadrilateral $M'A'T'H'$.

What is the difference between the y-coordinate of A' and the y-coordinate of T'?

The difference is ☐ units.

2. Triangle PRA was dilated by a scale factor of 3 centered at the origin to create triangle $P'R'A'$, which has coordinates $P'(-6,-12), R'(-18,-6), A'(-6,-6)$. Write the coordinates of the vertices of triangle PRA in the spaces provided below.

$P($_____, _____$)$

$R($_____, _____$)$

$A($_____, _____$)$

Section 4 – Topic 4
Compositions of Transformations of Polygons – Part 1

Is there a single transformation that will carry ΔABC onto $\Delta A'B'C'$? Justify your answer.

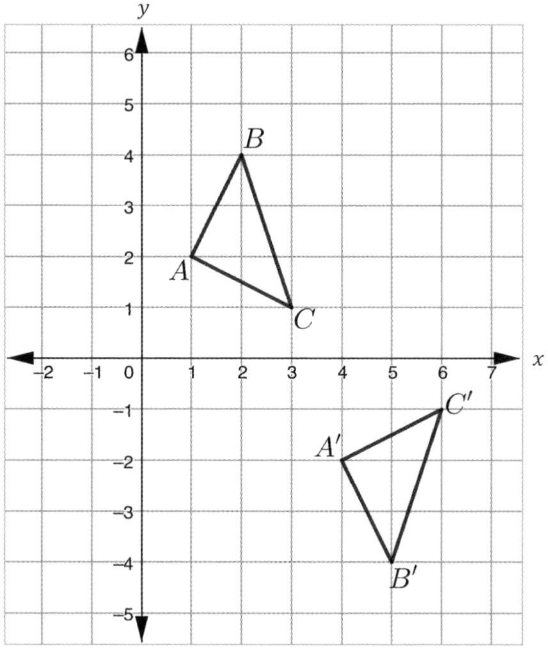

If there is not a single transformation that carries one figure onto the next, then we use a composition of transformations. What do you think "***composition of transformations***" means?

Quadrilateral $WXYZ$ is shown with vertices $W\ (-3,5)$, $X\ (-2,6)$, $Y\ (-2,2)$, and $Z\ (-3,3)$. Reflect the quadrilateral $WXYZ$ over the line $y = x$, then apply the transformation $(x,y) \to (x, y+1)$ to quadrilateral $W'X'Y'Z'$. Draw quadrilateral $W''X''Y''Z''$ on the coordinate grid.

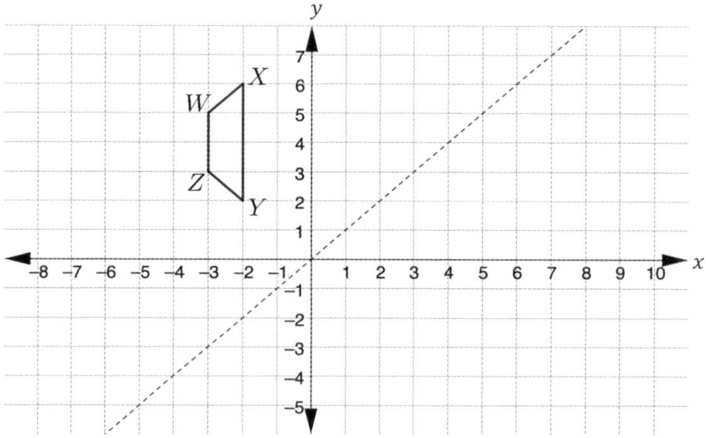

Quadrilateral $WXYZ$ is shown with vertices $W\ (-3,5)$, $X\ (-2,6)$, $Y\ (-2,2)$, and $Z\ (-3,3)$. Apply the transformation $(x,y) \to (x, y+1)$ to quadrilateral $WXYZ$, then reflect the quadrilateral $W'X'Y'Z'$ over the line $y = x$. Draw quadrilateral $W''X''Y''Z''$ on the coordinate grid.

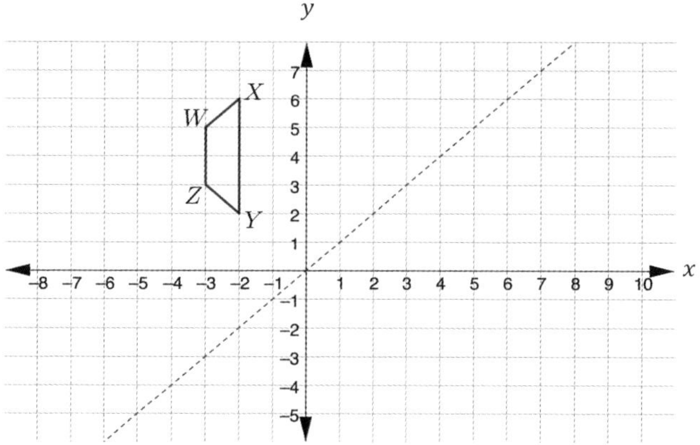

What do you notice about $W''X''Y''Z''$ in each graph on the previous page?

Reflect ΔABC across line w, then reflect $\Delta A'B'C'$ across line z.

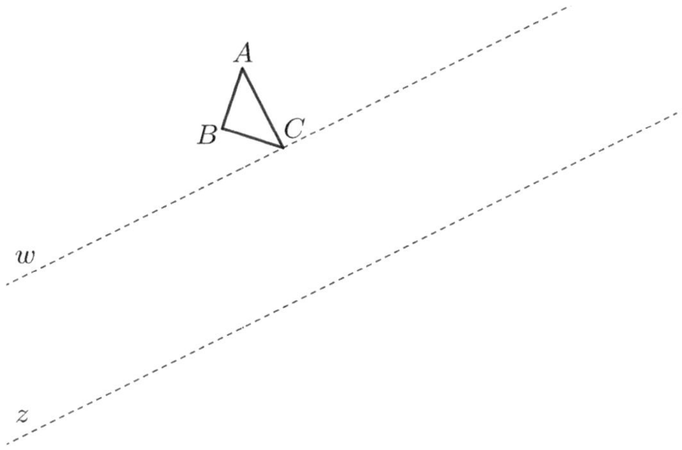

It is possible to use one transformation so that the result is in the same position as reflecting ΔABC across line w and then across line z. Find that one transformation.

Reflect ΔABC across line h, then reflect $\Delta A'B'C'$ across line k.

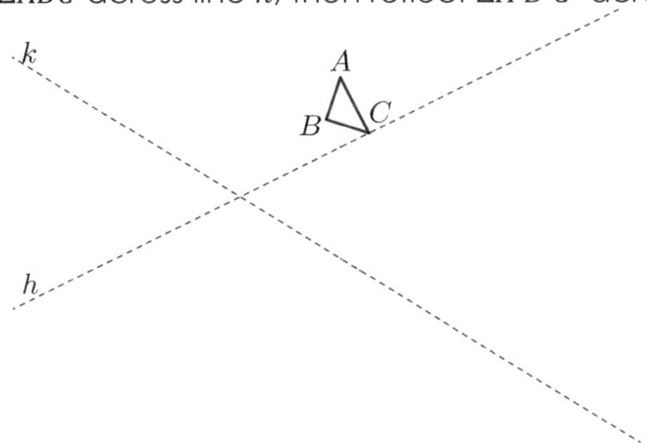

It is possible to use one transformation so that the result is in the same position as reflecting ΔABC across line h and then across line k. Find that one transformation.

In summary, in most cases changing the order of a series of transformations will not have the same result. In some cases a series of transformations could have an equivalent single transformation.

Let's Practice!

1. Trapezoid $VFPZ$ is shown with vertices $V\,(-1,1), F(-2,-5), P(-3,-5)$, and $Z\,(-4,1)$. Reflect trapezoid $VFPZ$ across the line $x = 1$. Then rotate the quadrilateral $V'F'P'Z'$ $270°$ clockwise around the origin.

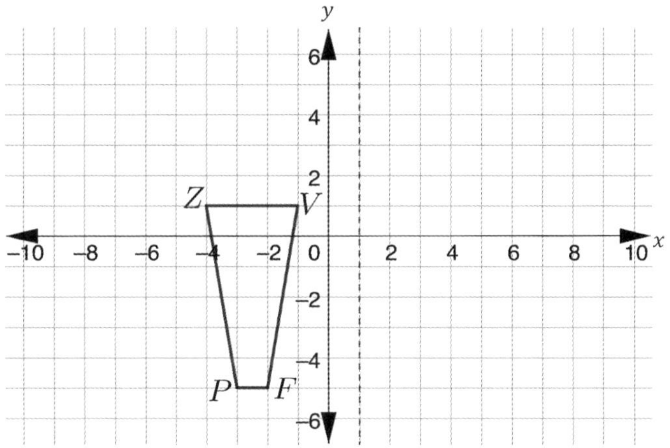

2. Consider the quadrilateral below. Quadrilateral $WXYZ$ is shown with vertices $W\ (-4,-2), X\ (-1,-2), Y\ (-2,-5)$, and $Z\ (-5,-5)$. Dilate the quadrilateral about the origin with a scale factor of $\frac{1}{2}$ and then reflect the figure over the line $y=-x$.

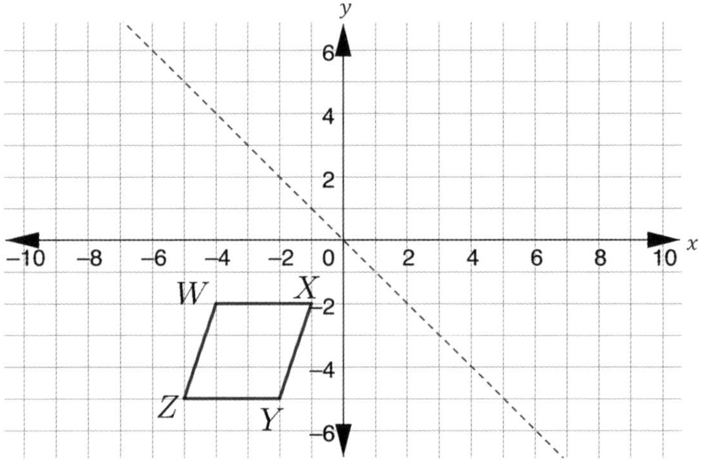

3. Do the transformations in the previous two questions represent a composition of transformations that preserve both segment length and angle measure? Justify your answer.

Try It!

4. Trapezoid $ABCD$ is shown with vertices $A\ (2,5), B\ (4,8), C(6,8)$, and $D\ (8,5)$. Describe the composition of transformations that carry the trapezoid onto itself. Use no more than three transformations.

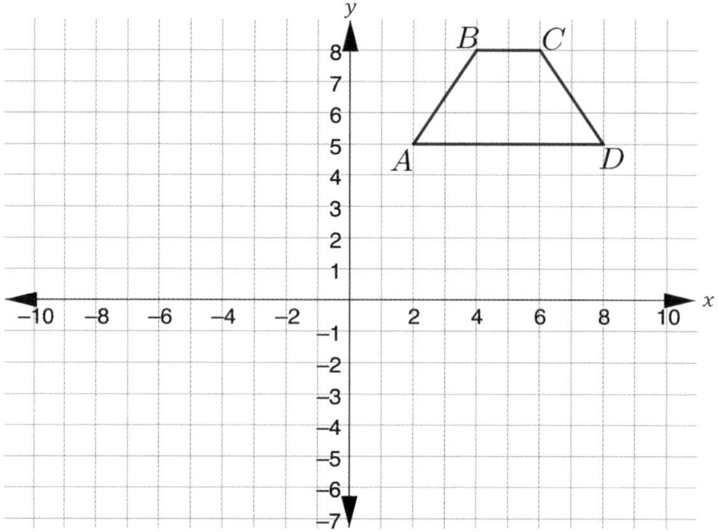

Section 4 – Topic 5
Compositions of Transformations of Polygons – Part 2

Let's Practice!

1. Consider the following information.

A pre-image of $SPOT$ with coordinates
$S(7,2)$, $P(0,9)$, $O(-6,-5)$, and $T(1,-12)$

a. If we reflect $SPOT$ over the x-axis then rotate it $90°$ counterclockwise about the origin, what are the coordinates of $S''P''O''T''$? Write each answer in the space provided below.

$S(7,2) \rightarrow S'(\_\_\_\_,\_\_\_\_) \rightarrow S''(\_\_\_\_,\_\_\_\_)$

$P(0,9) \rightarrow P'(\_\_\_\_,\_\_\_\_) \rightarrow P''(\_\_\_\_,\_\_\_\_)$

$O(-6,-5) \rightarrow O'(\_\_\_\_,\_\_\_\_) \rightarrow O''(\_\_\_\_,\_\_\_\_)$

$T(1,-12) \rightarrow T'(\_\_\_\_,\_\_\_\_) \rightarrow T''(\_\_\_\_,\_\_\_\_)$

b. If you take $S''P''O''T''$ and dilate it by a scale factor of 3 centered at the origin, what are the coordinates of $S'''P'''O'''T'''$? Justify your answer.

Try It!

2. Consider the figure below and the following rotation. Rectangle $PATH$ is rotated $270°$ counterclockwise around the origin and then reflected across the y-axis.

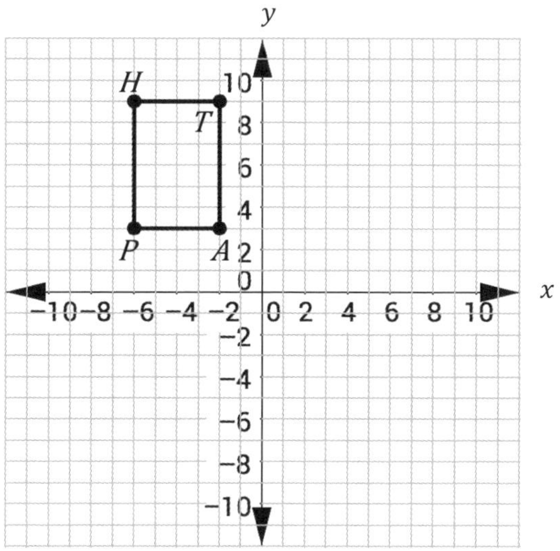

Tatum argues that the image created above will be the same as the pre-image. Marla refutes the answer by arguing that the images will not be the same. Who is correct? Justify your answer.

BEAT THE TEST!

1. Point $P"(-9,0)$ is a vertex of triangle $P"I"E"$. The original image was rotated $90°$ clockwise and then translated $(x, y) \rightarrow (x-8, y+5)$. What are the coordinates of the original image's point P before the composition of transformations?

   Ⓐ $(-1,-5)$
   Ⓑ $(0,-4)$
   Ⓒ $(1,-5)$
   Ⓓ $(5,-1)$

2. Consider the following polygon after a composition of transformations represented by the dashed lines below.

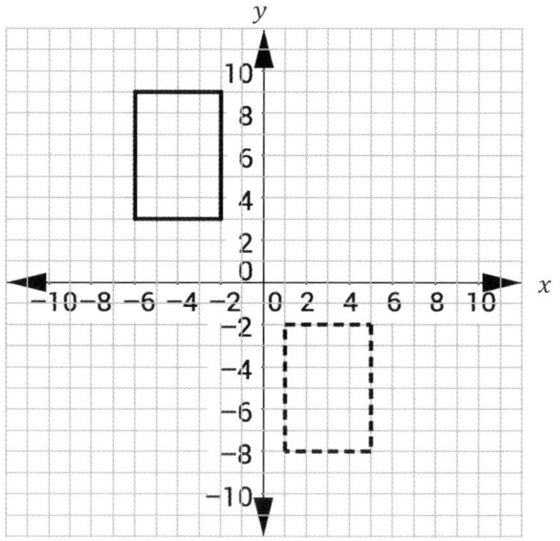

   Which composition of isometries did the polygon have?

   Ⓐ A reflection over the x-axis and a translation $(x+7, y+1)$.
   Ⓑ A reflection over $y=1$ and a translation $(x+7, y)$.
   Ⓒ A translation $(x+8, y-3)$ and a rotation of $90°$ clockwise about $(1,1)$.
   Ⓓ A translation $(x+10, y)$ and a reflection over $y=-x$.

Section 4 – Topic 6
Congruence of Polygons

Consider the figures below.

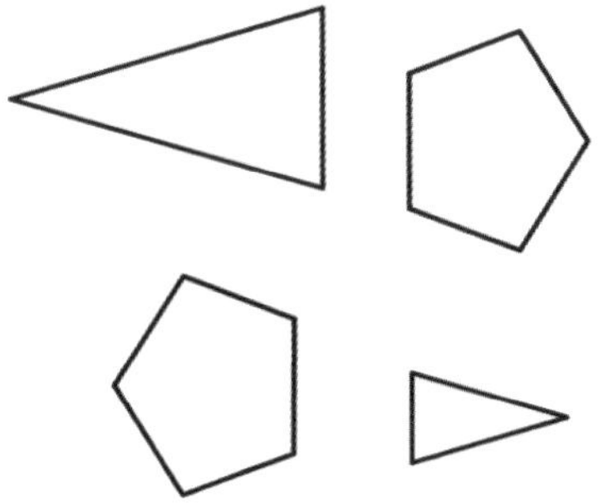

Explain which figures are congruent, if any.

Let's state some properties of congruent polygons.

- The symbol __________ represents congruency.
- Congruent polygons have the same number of _______________ and _______________.
- Corresponding _______________ of congruent polygons are congruent.
- Corresponding interior _______________ of congruent polygons are congruent.

Will rigid or non-rigid transformations produce congruent figures? Explain your reasoning.

STUDY EDGE TIP Two figures are ***congruent*** if there is a sequence of rigid transformations that maps one figure to the other.

Let's Practice!

1. Quadrilateral $LION$ is reflected across line f to create quadrilateral $BEAR$.

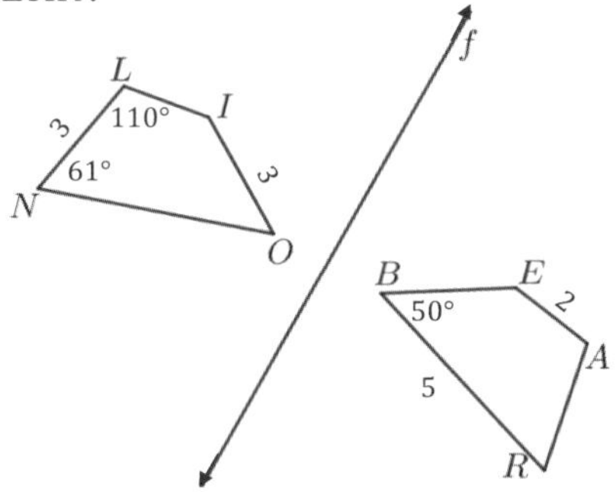

   a. What do we know about quadrilateral $LION$ and quadrilateral $BEAR$?

   b. What is $m\angle E$?

   c. What is the perimeter of quadrilateral $BEAR$?

2. Use the definition of congruence in terms of rigid motions to prove rectangle $ABCD$ is congruent to rectangle $A'B'C'D'$.

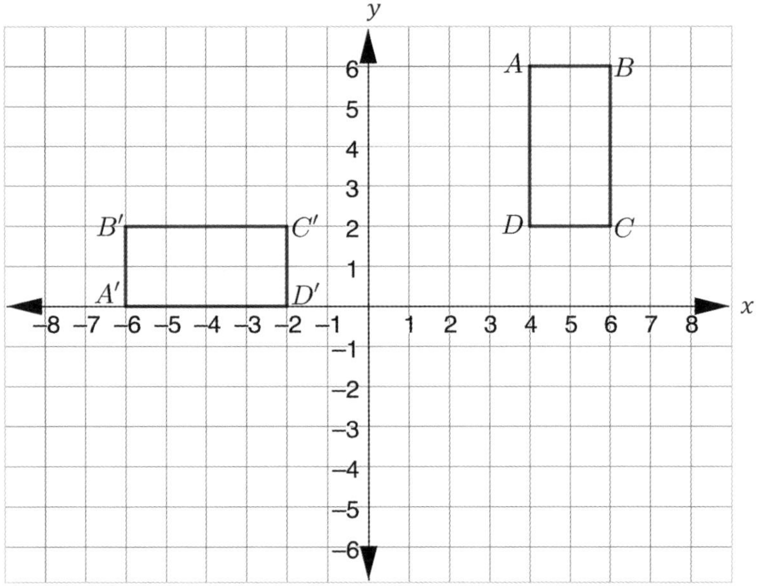

Try It!

3. How can Romeo use rigid transformations to show that all the petals on the flower are congruent to each other?

4. In the graph below, ΔMON is the image of ΔBAC after a rotation of $270°$ counterclockwise about the origin.

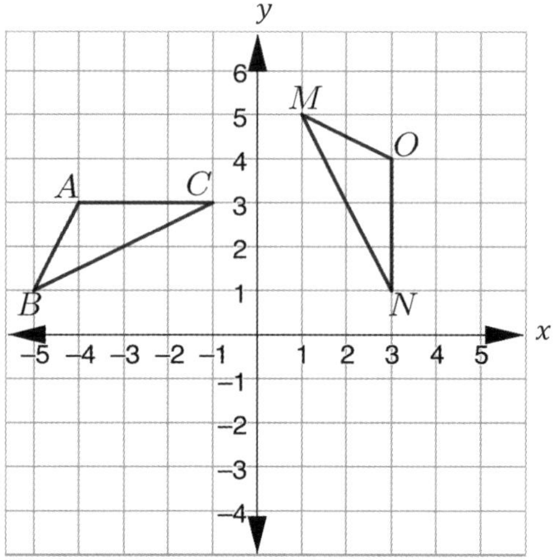

Which statements below are true? Select all that apply.

- ☐ $\overline{AB} \cong \overline{ON}$
- ☐ $\overline{BC} \cong \overline{MN}$
- ☐ $\angle B \cong \angle M$
- ☐ $\angle N \cong \angle C$
- ☐ $\overline{MO} \cong \overline{AB}$
- ☐ $\Delta ACB \cong \Delta MON$

BEAT THE TEST!

1. Consider the graph of $FRIES$ below.

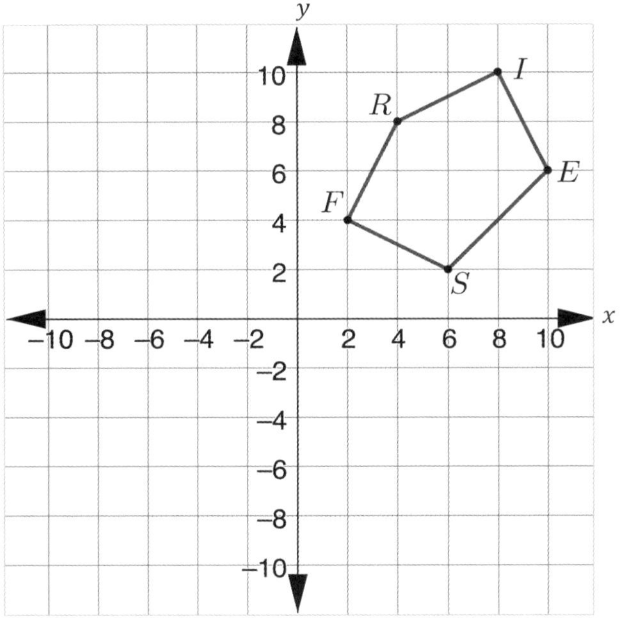

Camilla transformed $FRIES$ so that the image of point E is at $(-6, 10)$ and the image of point F is at $(-4, 2)$. Which transformation could Camilla have used to show that $FRIES$ and its image are congruent?

Ⓐ $FRIES$ was rotated $270°$ counterclockwise.
Ⓑ $FRIES$ was translated left 6 units and down 2 units.
Ⓒ $FRIES$ was reflected across the y-axis.
Ⓓ $FRIES$ was rotated $90°$ counterclockwise.

Section 4 – Topic 7
Similarity of Polygons

Consider the following similar shapes.

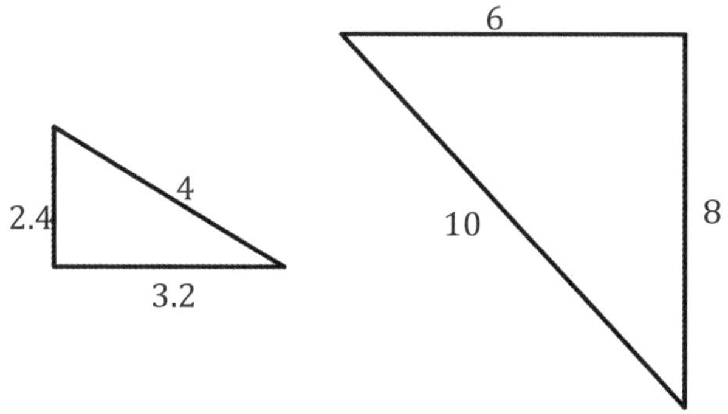

Why do we classify these shapes as "similar" instead of congruent?

Let's state properties of similar polygons.

- The symbol __________ represents similarity.
- Similar polygons have the same number of ________________ and ________________.
- Corresponding interior ________________ of similar polygons are congruent.
- Corresponding ________________ of similar polygons are proportional.

Will rigid or non-rigid transformations produce similar figures? Explain your reasoning.

Let's Practice!

1. Rectangle $ABCD$ is similar to rectangle $A'B'C'D'$. Find a composition of transformations that will map rectangle $ABCD$ to rectangle $A'B'C'D'$.

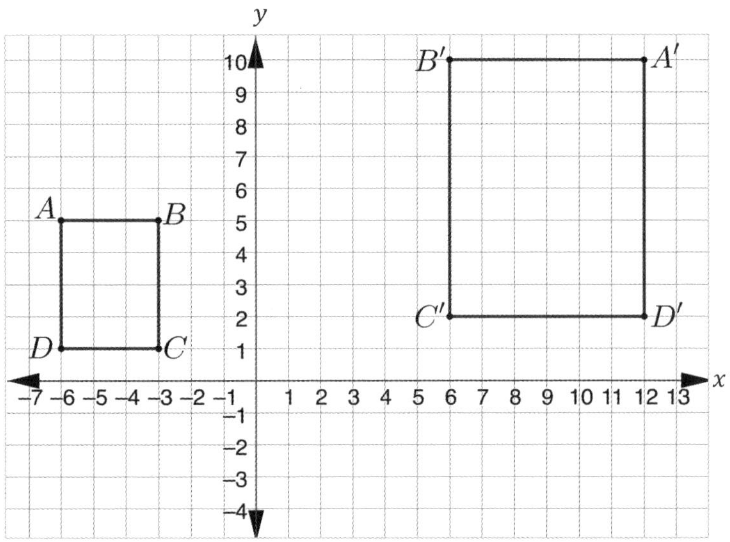

> **STUDY EDGE TIP**
> A *sequence of similarity transformations* is a composition of one or more rigid transformations followed by a dilation.

2. Mrs. Kemp's rectangular garden has a length of 20 meters and a width of 15 meters. Her neighbor, Mr. Pippen, has a garden similar in shape with a scale factor of 3.

   a. What is the width of Mr. Pippen's garden?

   b. How do the areas of the gardens relate to one another?

> **STUDY EDGE TIP**
> Each corresponding side of a polygon can be multiplied by the ***scale factor*** to get the length of its corresponding side on a similar polygon. Then, the ratio of the areas is the square of the scale factor while the ratio of perimeters is the scale factor.

Try It!

3. A right triangle has a base of 11 yards and a height of 7 yards. If you were to construct a similar but not congruent right triangle with an area of 616 square yards, what would the dimensions of the new triangle be?

4. What conjectures can you make if two similar polygons have a similarity ratio of 1? Draw an example to justify your conjectures.

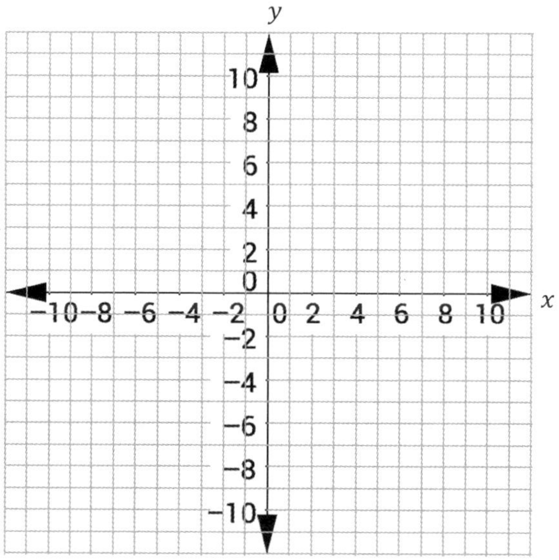

5. Consider the graph below of square $ABCD$ and square $GHIJ$.

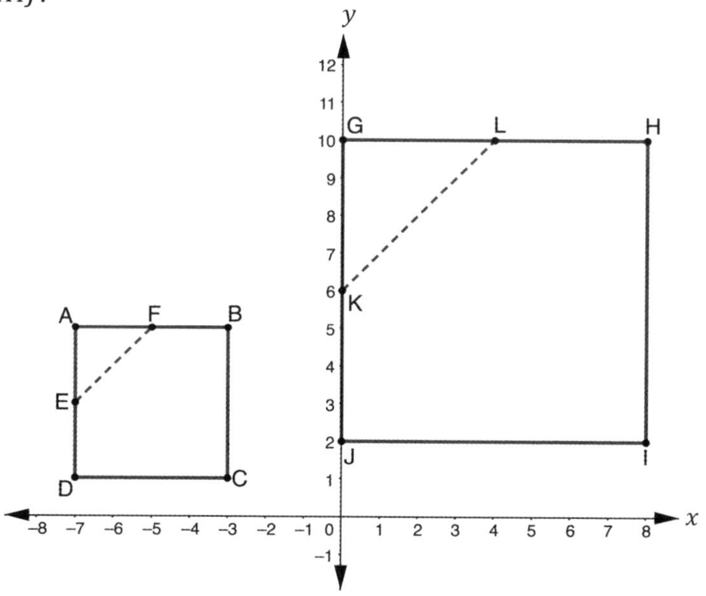

a. Prove square $ABCD$ and square $GHIJ$ are similar using a sequence of similarity transformations.

b. Square $ABCD$ is cut along the line $\overline{EF}$ to create pentagon $FBCDE$ such that $m\angle AEF = 45°$. If $FBCDE \sim LHIJK$, find $m\angle KLH$.

BEAT THE TEST!

1. Which transformation would result in the perimeter of a polygon being different from the perimeter of its pre-image?

   Ⓐ $(x, y) \to (-x, -y)$
   Ⓑ $(x, y) \to (y, x)$
   Ⓒ $(x, y) \to (3x, 3y)$
   Ⓓ $(x, y) \to (x - 3, y + 1)$

2. In triangle ABC, $m\angle A = 90°$ and $m\angle B = 35°$. In triangle DEF, $m\angle E = 35°$ and $m\angle F = 55°$. Are the triangles similar? Prove your answer.

3. ΔTOY is reflected across the x-axis and then dilated by a scale factor of $\frac{1}{2}$ centered at the origin to obtain $\Delta T''O''Y''$.

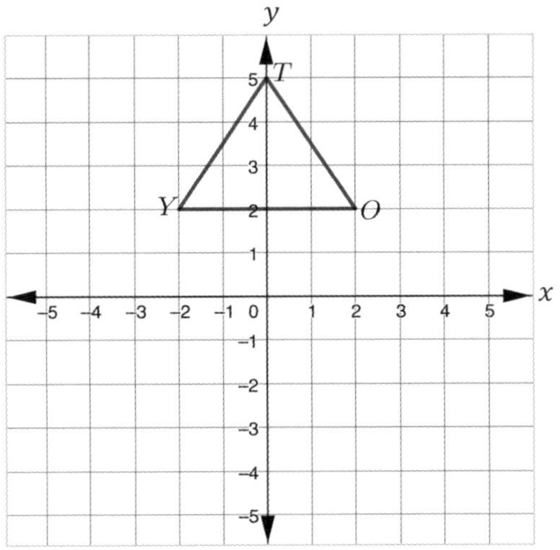

   a. What are the coordinates of point Y''?

   b. What is the length of line $\overline{T''Y''}$?

Test Yourself! Practice Tool

Great job! You have reached the end of this section. Now it's time to try the "Test Yourself! Practice Tool," where you can practice all the skills and concepts you learned in this section. Log in to Math Nation and try out the "Test Yourself! Practice Tool" so you can see how well you know these topics!

Section 5: Triangles – Part 1

Topic 1: Introduction to Triangles – Part 1 131
*Standards Covered:*G-CO.10
- ☐ I can classify triangles by sides and angles.
- ☐ I can use a triangle's characteristics to find missing sides and angles.

Topic 2: Introduction to Triangles – Part 2 133
Standards Covered: G-CO.10
- ☐ I can classify triangles by sides and angles.
- ☐ I can use a triangle's characteristics to find missing sides and angles.

Topic 3: Triangles in the Coordinate Plane 136
*Standards Covered:*G-PE.7
- ☐ I can calculate the area and perimeter of a triangle.

Topic 4: Triangle Congruence – SSS and SAS – Part 1 138
*Standards Covered:*G-SRT.5
- ☐ I can use the Side-Side-Side or Side-Angle-Side theorems to find missing sides or angles and prove triangles are congruent.

Topic 5: Triangle Congruence – SSS and SAS – Part 2 140
Standards Covered: G-CO.8, G-SRT.5
- ☐ I can use the Side-Side-Side or Side-Angle-Side theorems to find missing sides or angles and prove triangles are congruent.

Topic 6: Triangle Congruence – ASA and AAS – Part 1 143
Standards Covered: G-CO.8, G-SRT.5
- ☐ I can use Angle-Side-Angle and Angle-Angle-Side theorems to find missing sides or angles and provide certain characteristics of triangles.

Topic 7: Triangle Congruence – ASA and AAS – Part 2 146
Standards Covered: G-CO.7, G-CO.8, G-SRT.5
- ☐ I can use Angle-Side-Angle and Angle-Angle-Side theorems to find missing sides or angles and provide certain characteristics of triangles.

Topic 8: Base Angle of Isosceles Triangles 148
*Standards Covered:*G-SRT.4
- ☐ I can use properties of isosceles triangles to find missing angle and/or side measures.

Topic 9: Using the Definition of Triangle Congruence in Terms of Rigid Motions 151
Standards Covered: G-CO.6
- ☐ I can write two-column proofs to show that two triangles are congruent.

Topic 10: Using Triangle Congruency to Find Missing Variables 153
Standards Covered: G-SRT.5
- ☐ I can use Triangle Congruence Theorems to find missing sides.

Visit MathNation.com or search "Math Nation" in your phone or tablet's app store to watch the videos that go along with this workbook!

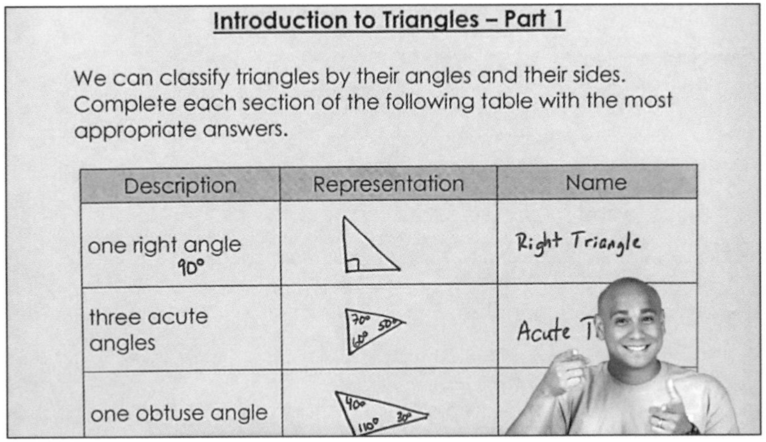
Introduction to Triangles – Part 1
We can classify triangles by their angles and their sides. Complete each section of the following table with the most appropriate answers.
Description
Representation
Name
one right angle
90°
Right Triangle
three acute angles
Acute T
one obtuse angle

The following Michigan Mathematics Standards will be covered in this section:
G-CO.6 - Use geometric descriptions of rigid motions to transform figures and to predict the effect of a given rigid motion on a given figure; given two figures, use the definition of congruence in terms of rigid motions to decide if they are congruent.
G-CO.7 - Use the definition of congruence in terms of rigid motions to show that two triangles are congruent if and only if corresponding pairs of sides and corresponding pairs of angles are congruent.
G-CO.8 - Explain how the criteria for triangle congruence (ASA, SAS, SSS, and Hypotenuse-Leg) follow from the definition of congruence in terms of rigid motions.
G-CO.10 - Prove theorems about triangles; use theorems about triangles to solve problems.
G-GPE.7 - Use coordinates to compute perimeters of polygons and areas of triangles and rectangles.
G-SRT.4 - Prove theorems about triangles.
G-SRT.5 - Use congruence and similarity criteria for triangles to solve problems and to prove relationships in geometric figures.

Section 5: Triangles – Part 1
Section 5 – Topic 1
Introduction to Triangles – Part 1

We can classify triangles by their angles and their sides. Complete each section of the following table with the most appropriate answers.

Description	Representation	Name
One right angle		
Three acute angles		
One obtuse angle		
All 60° angles		
Two congruent sides		
No congruent sides		
Three congruent sides		

Can a triangle be both acute and isosceles? Justify your reasoning.

Can a triangle be both equiangular and obtuse? Justify your reasoning.

Let's Practice!

1. Consider the diagram below of an equilateral triangle.

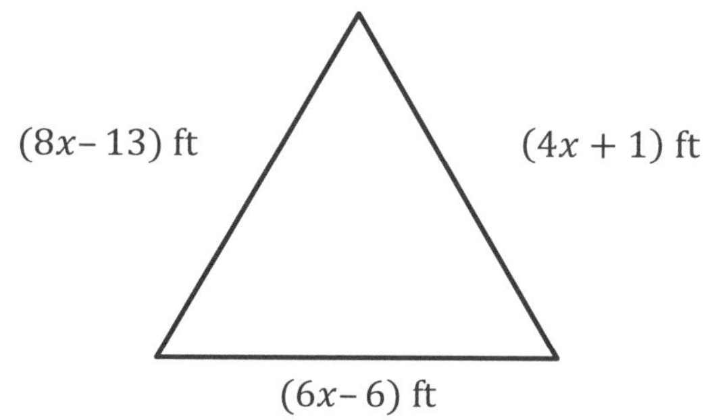

How long is each side of the triangle? Justify your answer.

Try It!

2. Consider the triangle below.

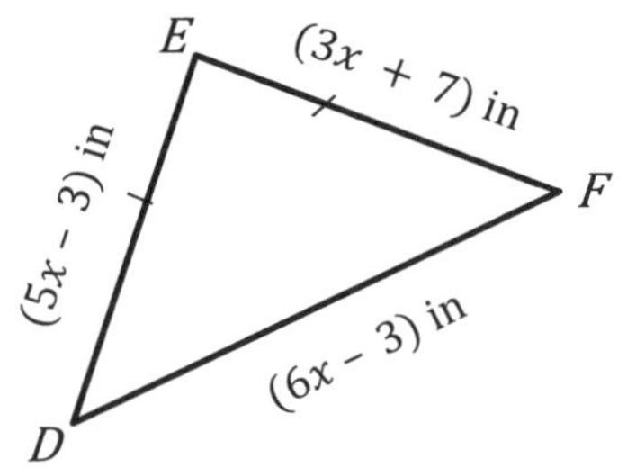

a. If ΔDEF is an isosceles triangle with base $\overline{DF}$, what is the value of x? Justify your answer.

b. What is the length of each leg?

c. What is the length of the base?

3. How can you determine if a triangle on the coordinate plane is a right triangle?

Let's Practice!

4. Consider the figure below.

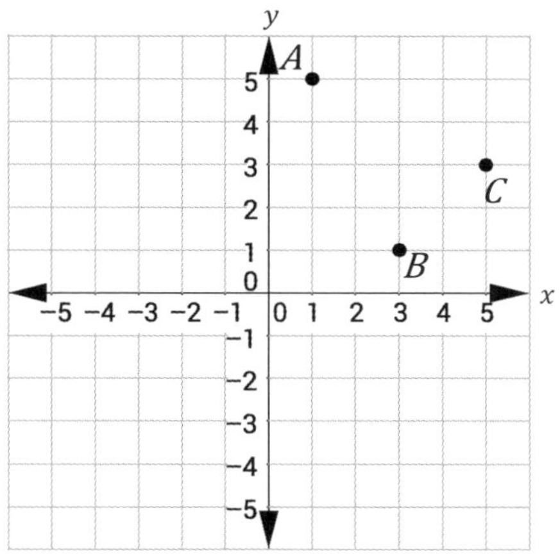

a. After connecting the points on the plane, Marcos claims that angle B is a right angle. Is Marcos correct? Explain your reasoning.

b. How can you classify a triangle on the coordinate plane by its sides?

Try It!

5. Consider the figure below.

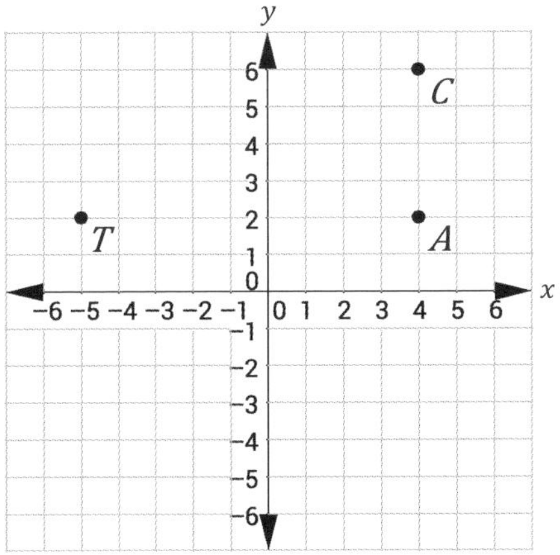

Connect the points on the plane and classify the resulting triangle. Use two different approaches to justify your answer.

Section 5 – Topic 2
Introduction to Triangles – Part 2

What is the sum of the measures of the interior angles of a triangle?

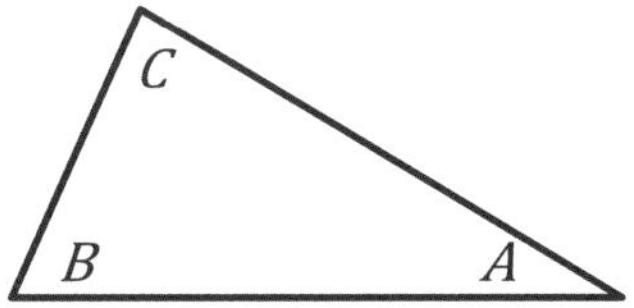

Formulate how you can prove the sum of measures, if possible.

TAKE NOTE! *Postulates & Theorems*

Triangle Sum Theorem

The sum of the interior angles in a triangle is 180°.

Consider the following figure and complete the following proof.

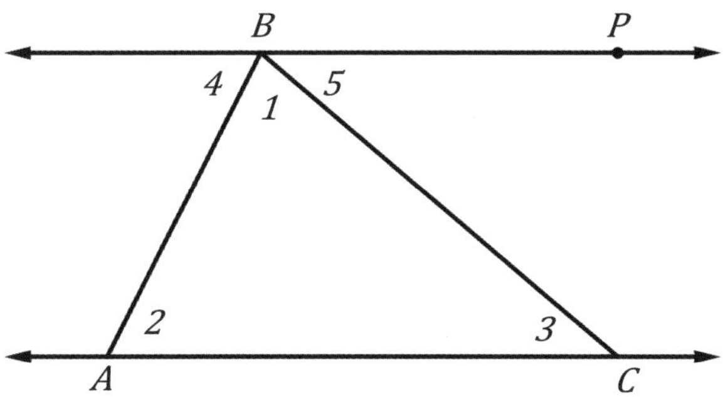

Given: ΔABC and $\overline{BP}$ is parallel to $\overline{AC}$.
Prove: $m\angle 1 + m\angle 2 + m\angle 3 = 180°$

Statements	Reasons
1. ABC is a triangle.	**1.**
2. $\overline{BP} \parallel \overline{AC}$	**2.**
3. $m\angle 1 + m\angle 5 = m\angle PBA$	**3.**
4. $m\angle PBA + m\angle 4 = 180°$	**4.**
5. $m\angle 1 + m\angle 5 + m\angle 4 = 180°$	**5.**
6. $\angle 2 \cong \angle 4$; $\angle 3 \cong \angle 5$	**6.**
7. $m\angle 2 = m\angle 4$; $m\angle 3 = m\angle 5$	**7.**
8. $m\angle 1 + m\angle 2 + m\angle 3 = 180°$	**8.**

Let's Practice!

1. Joan knows the measures of two of the interior angles in a triangle. How could she find the third measure? Explain your reasoning.

Try It!

2. Consider the figure below.

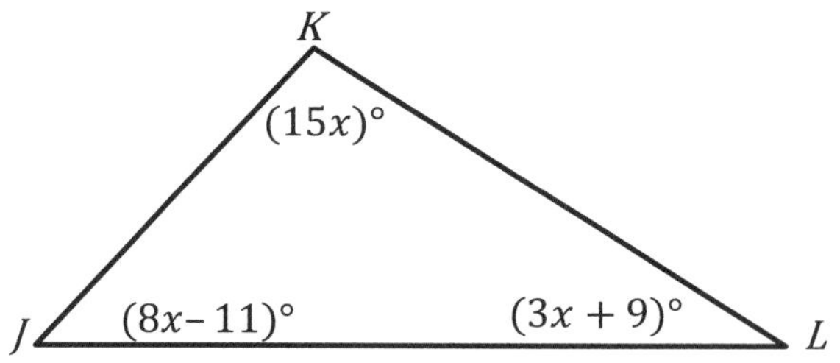

Timothy was trying to find the measure of $\angle K$ in the triangle above. His answer was 7°. He is confused as he cannot understand why $m\angle K = 7°$. Is Timothy's answer correct? Justify your answer.

BEAT THE TEST!

1. Triangle DOG has vertices at $D(5,8)$, $O(-3,10)$, and $G(-3,6)$.

   Part A: Determine what type of triangle DOG is and mark the most appropriate answer.

   Ⓐ Scalene
   Ⓑ Isosceles
   Ⓒ Equilateral
   Ⓓ Right

   Part B: If you move vertex D four units to the left, will the classification of triangle DOG change? If so, what type of triangle will it be? Justify your answer.

2. Stephen is fencing in his triangular garden as shown by the diagram below.

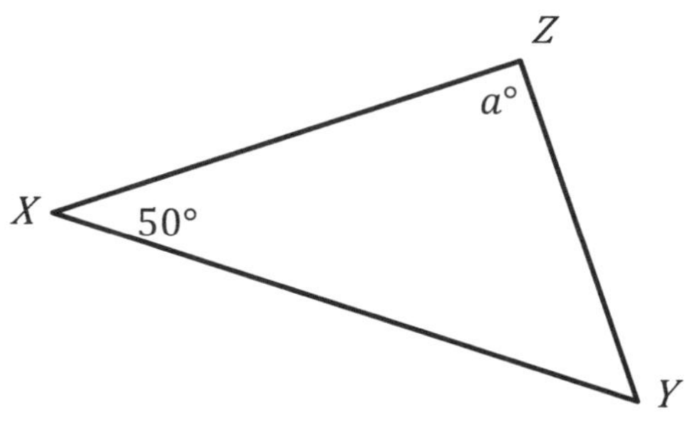

   Part A: Write an expression for the measure of angle Y.

   Part B: Stephen measured angle Z as $90°$. He measures angle Y as $38°$. Did he measure correctly? Justify your answer.

Section 5 – Topic 3
Triangles in the Coordinate Plane

How can we find area and perimeter when a figure is on the coordinate plane?

Let's Practice!

1. Consider the triangle BAT below.

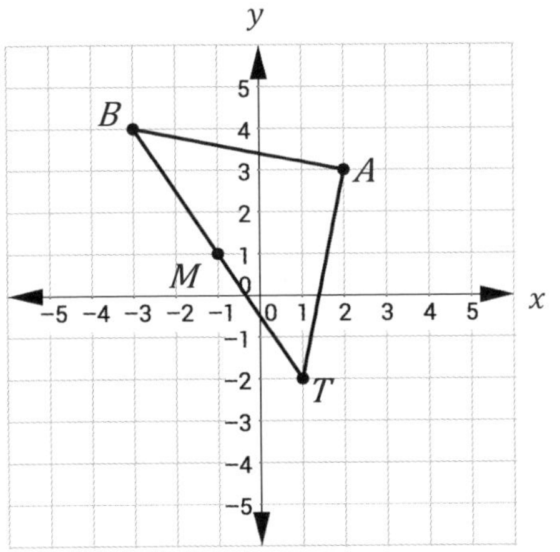

a. Which side should be considered the base? Justify your answer.

b. Find the area and perimeter of the triangle.

Try It!

2. Consider the figure below.

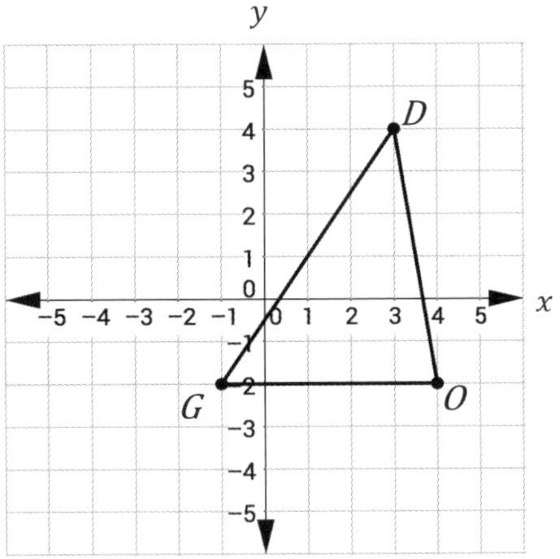

Deena's mother is helping her sew a large flag for color guard. Each square on Deena's plan above represents a square foot.

a. Determine the amount of fabric Deena needs in square feet.

b. The flag will be sewn along the edges.
How much ribbon will be needed to the nearest tenth of a foot?

BEAT THE TEST!

1. Consider the right triangle below.

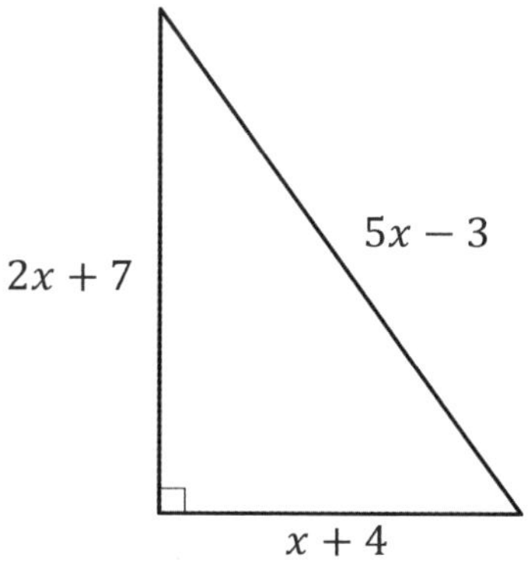

If the perimeter is 40 units, find the value of x and the area of the triangle.

The value of x is ☐ .

The area is ☐ square units.

2. Dallas is putting down hardwood floors in his home. His living room is pentagonal. Each unit on the coordinate plane represents 5 feet. Find the area of flooring needed in square feet.

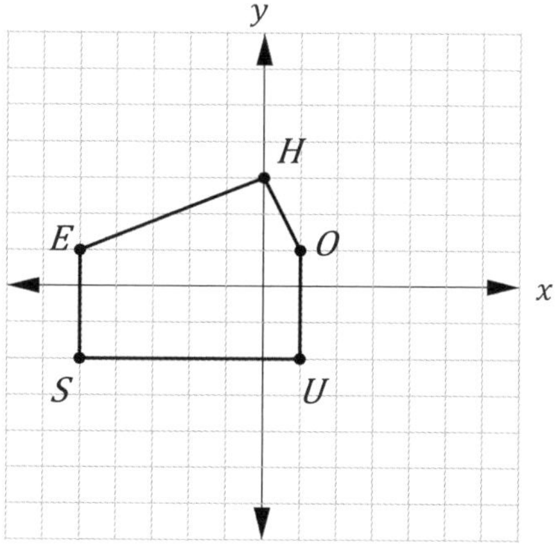

Which of the following is the total area of the living room?

Ⓐ 18 ft^2
Ⓑ 24 ft^2
Ⓒ 450 ft^2
Ⓓ 600 ft^2

Section 5 – Topic 4
Triangle Congruence – SSS and SAS – Part 1

What information do we need in order to determine whether two different triangles are congruent?

When we state triangle congruency, the order of the letters in the names of the triangles is *extremely* important.

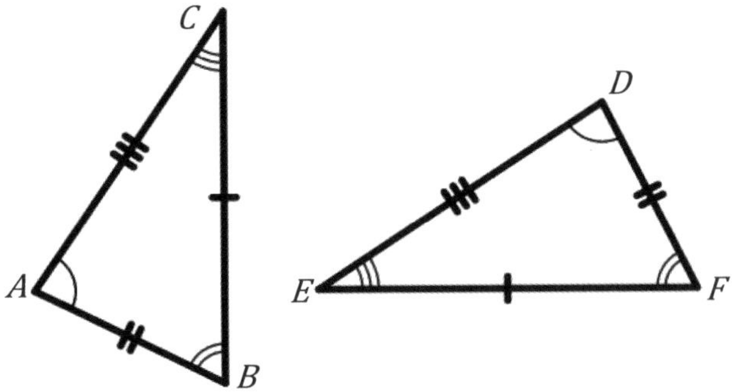

How can this congruency be stated?

Let's Practice!

1. If $\Delta JKL \cong \Delta COT$, finish the following congruence statements and mark the corresponding congruent sides and the corresponding congruent angles.

$\overline{JK} \cong$ ______	$\angle J \cong$ ______
______ $\cong \overline{CT}$	______ $\cong \angle T$
$\overline{KL} \cong$ ______	$\angle K \cong$ ______

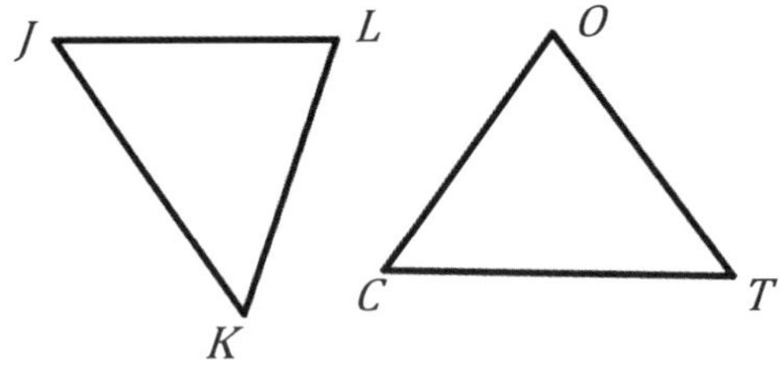

2. Complete the congruence statements for the triangles below.

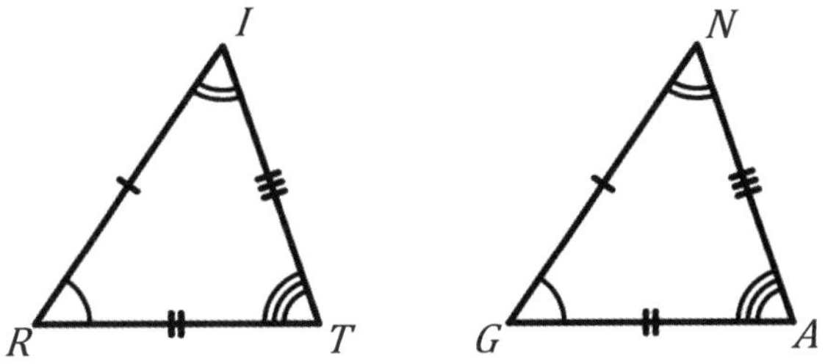

$\Delta TRI \cong \Delta$______ $\quad\quad \angle I \cong \angle$______

Try It!

3. Let's consider the same triangles where $\Delta TRI \cong \Delta GNA$.

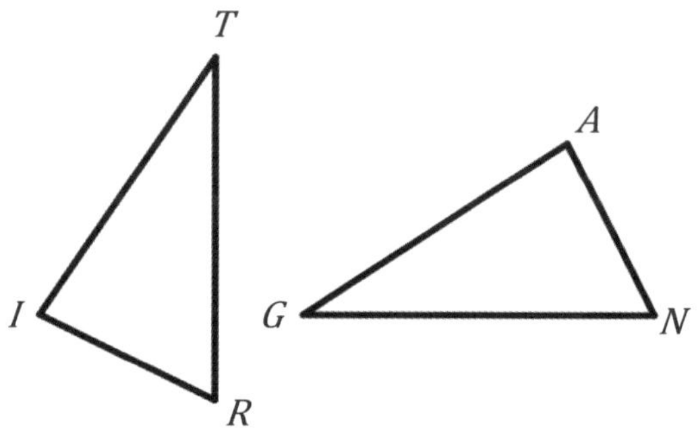

a. Mark the corresponding congruent sides with hash marks and the corresponding congruent angles with arcs.

b. To state that two triangles are congruent, we don't need to know that all three sides and all three angles are congruent. Four postulates help us determine triangle congruency.

1.

2.

3.

4.

TAKE NOTE! *Postulates & Theorems*

Side-Side-Side (SSS) Congruence Postulate

If three sides of one triangle are congruent to three sides of a second triangle, then the two triangles are congruent.

We can prove the following triangles are congruent by the SSS Congruence Postulate.

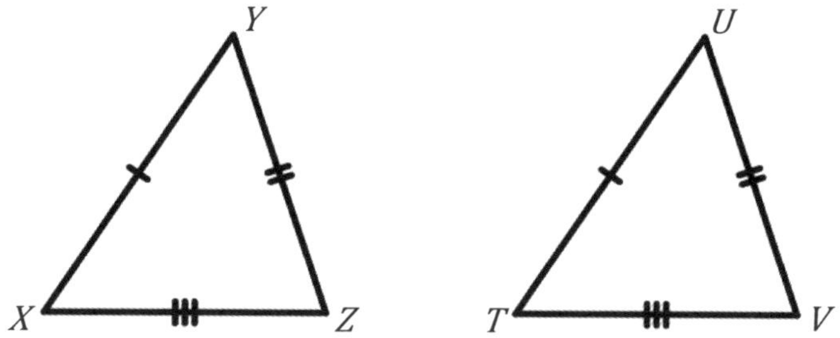

Write the congruency statement for the triangles above.

Determine if Angle-Angle-Angle congruence exists and explain why it does or does not.

TAKE NOTE! *Postulates & Theorems*

Side-Angle-Side (SAS) Congruence Postulate

If two sides and the included angle of one triangle are congruent to two sides and the included angle of a second triangle, then the two triangles are congruent.

We can prove the following triangles are congruent by the SAS Congruence Postulate.

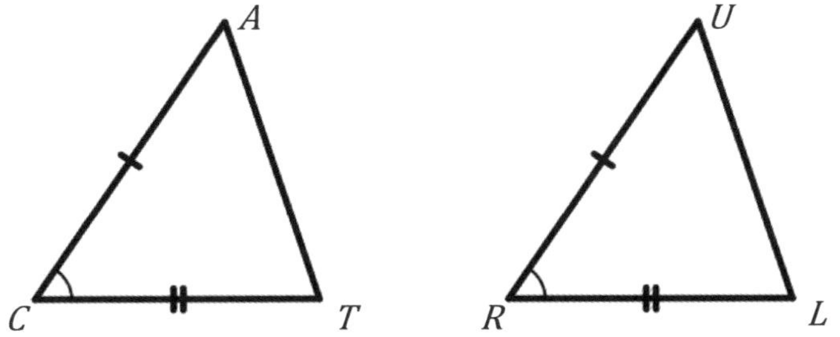

Write the congruency statement for the triangles above.

Determine if Side-Side-Angle congruence exists and explain why it does or does not.

Section 5 – Topic 5
Triangle Congruence – SSS and SAS – Part 2

Let's Practice!

1. What information is needed to prove the triangles below are congruent using the SSS Congruence Postulate?

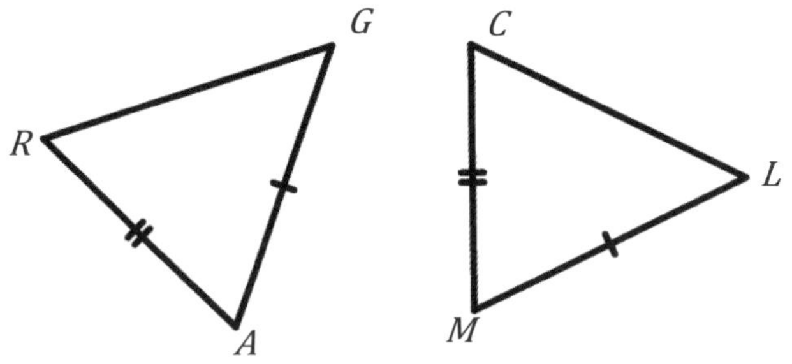

2. What information is needed to prove the triangles below are congruent using the SAS Congruence Postulate?

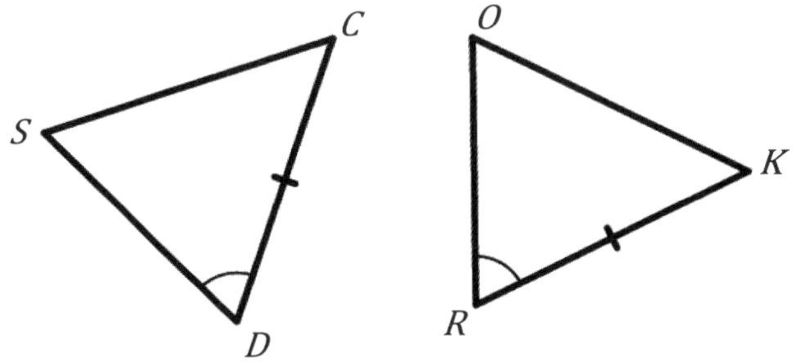

3. What information is needed to prove the triangles below are congruent using the SSS Congruence Postulate?

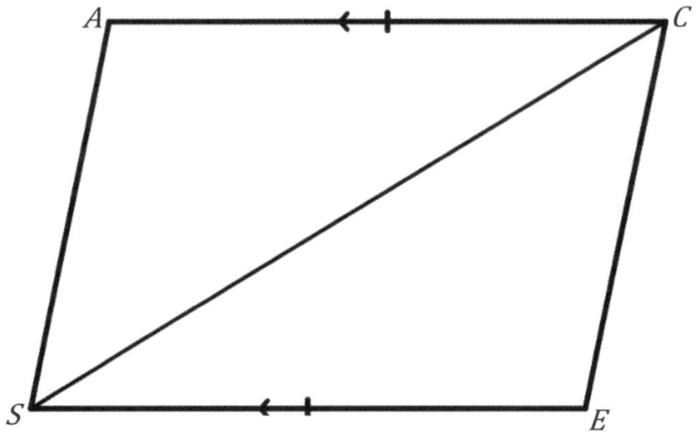

Try It!

4. Consider ΔCAR and ΔCER in the figure below.

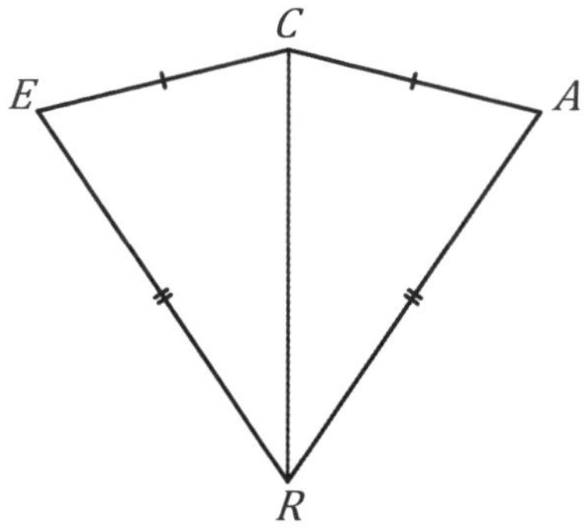

Given: $\overline{CE} \cong \overline{AC}$ and $\overline{ER} \cong \overline{AR}$
Prove: $\Delta CAR \cong \Delta CER$

Based on the above figure and the information below, complete the following two-column proof.

Statements	Reasons
1. $\overline{CE} \cong \overline{AC}$	**1.** Given
2. $\overline{ER} \cong \overline{AR}$	**2.** Given
3.	**3.** Reflexive Property of Congruence
4. $\Delta CAR \cong \Delta CER$	**4.**

5. Consider ΔGRT and ΔARE in the diagram below.

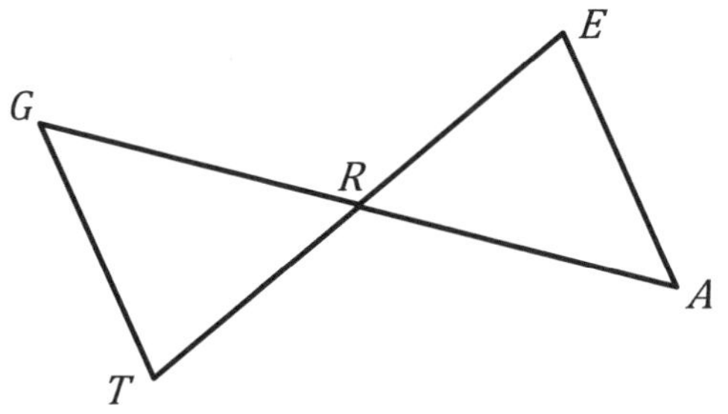

Given: R is the midpoint of $\overline{AG}$ and $\overline{ET}$.
Prove: $\Delta GRT \cong \Delta ARE$

Complete the following two-column proof.

Statements	Reasons
1. R is the midpoint of $\overline{AG}$ and $\overline{ET}$	**1.** Given
2.	**2.** Definition of Midpoint
3.	**3.** Definition of Midpoint
4. $\angle GRT \cong \angle ARE$	**4.**
5. $\Delta GRT \cong \Delta ARE$	**5.**

BEAT THE TEST!

1. Moshi is making a quilt using the pattern below and wants to be sure her triangles are congruent before cutting the fabric. She measures and finds that $\overline{NV} \cong \overline{VO}$ and $\angle N \cong \angle O$.

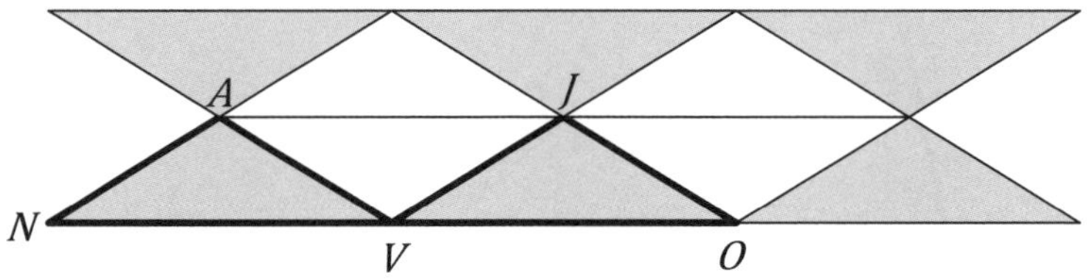

Can Moshi determine if the triangles are congruent with the given information? If not, what other information would allow her to do so? Justify your answer.

2. Iskra is a structural engineer, designing a tri-bearing truss for the roof of a new building. She must determine if the triangles below are congruent for the stability of the roof.

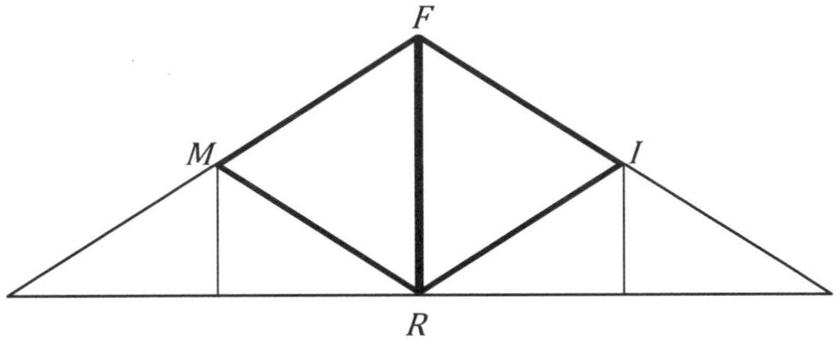

Given: $\overline{FM} \cong \overline{FI}$; $\overline{FR}$ bisects $\angle MFI$
Prove: $\Delta FMR \cong \Delta FIR$

Which of the reasons for statement 5 is correct?

Statements	Reasons
1. $\overline{FM} \cong \overline{FI}$	**1.** Given
2. $\overline{FR}$ bisects $\angle MFI$	**2.** Given
3. $\angle MFR \cong \angle IFR$	**3.** Definition of angle bisector
4. $\overline{FR} \cong \overline{FR}$	**4.** Reflective Property of Congruence
5. $\Delta FMR \cong \Delta FIR$	**5.** Ⓐ AAA Ⓑ SAS Ⓒ SSS Ⓓ Can't prove congruency

Section 5 – Topic 6
Triangle Congruence – ASA and AAS – Part 1

Consider the figures below.

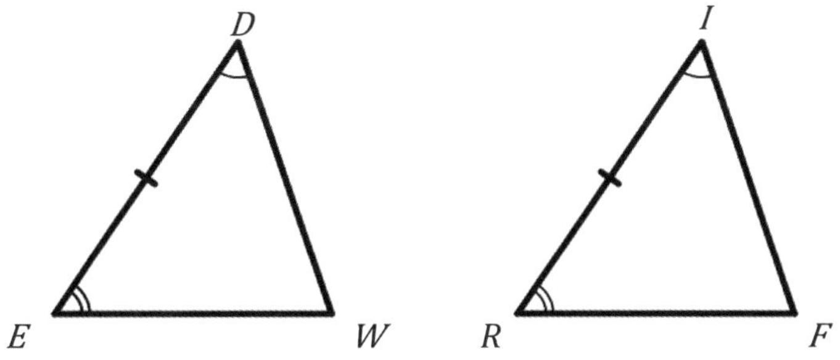

In the above diagram, $\Delta WED \cong \Delta FRI$ based on the ASA Congruence Postulate.

Name the congruent sides and angles in these two triangles.

TAKE NOTE! Postulates & Theorems

Angle-Side-Angle (ASA) Congruence Postulate
If two angles and the included side of one triangle are congruent to two angles and the included side of a second triangle, then the two triangles are congruent.

Consider the figures below.

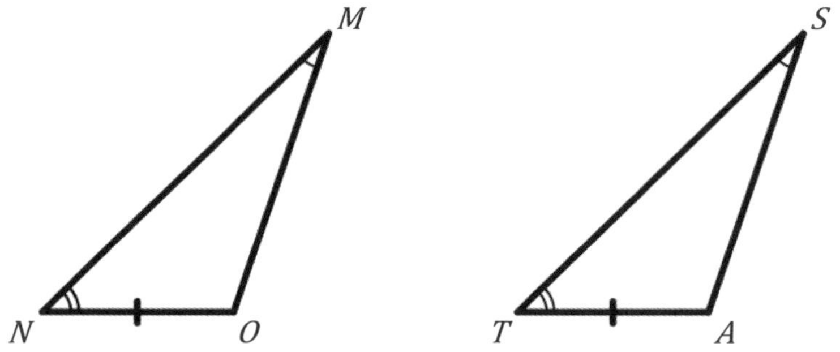

In the above diagram, $\Delta MON \cong \Delta SAT$ based on the AAS Congruence Postulate.

Name the congruent sides and angles in these two triangles.

TAKE NOTE! *Postulates & Theorems*

Angle-Angle-Side (AAS) Congruence Postulate

If two angles and a non-included side of one triangle are congruent to two angles and a non-included side of a second triangle, then the two triangles are congruent.

Consider the triangles below.

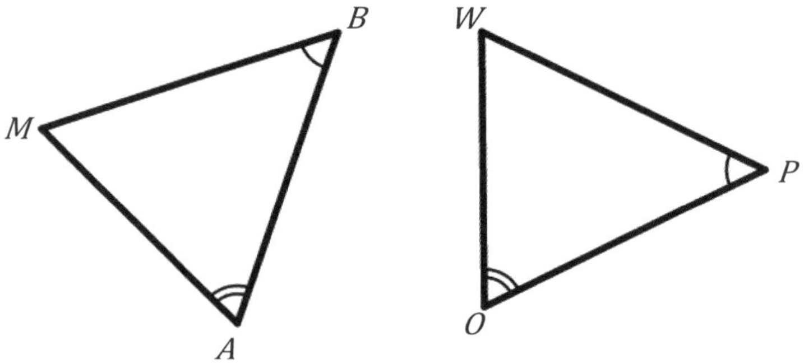

Identify the postulate you could use to prove that the two triangles are congruent, given each additional congruence statement below.

Congruency Statement	Postulate
$\overline{BM} \cong \overline{PW}$	
$\overline{AB} \cong \overline{OP}$	
$\overline{AM} \cong \overline{OW}$	

Consider the figure below.

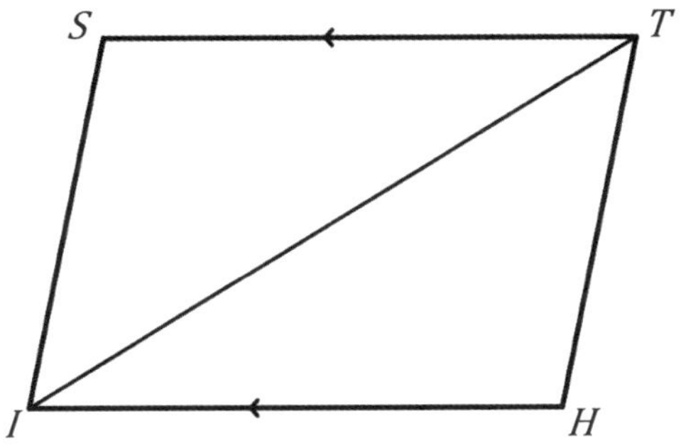

Nadia would like to use the AAS Congruence Postulate to prove that $\Delta TIS \cong \Delta ITH$. Would knowing that $\angle S \cong \angle H$ be enough information for Nadia to use this postulate? If not, find the missing congruence statement.

Let's Practice!

1. Consider ΔPAI and ΔTNI in the diagram below.

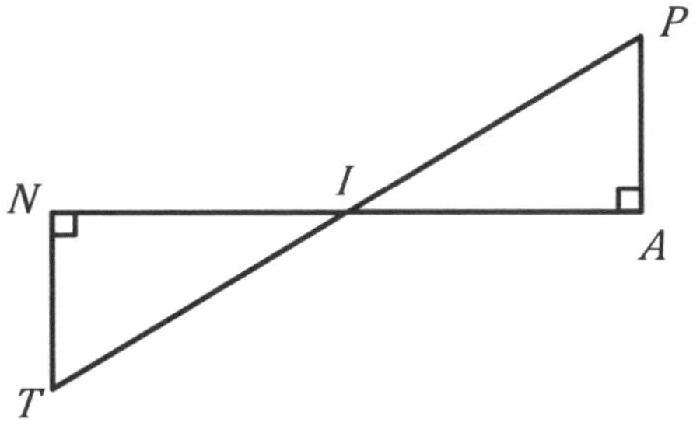

Given: $\angle N$ and $\angle A$ are right angles; I is the midpoint of $\overline{PT}$

Prove: $\Delta PAI \cong \Delta TNI$

Complete the following two-column proof.

Statements	Reasons
1. $\angle N$ and $\angle A$ are right angles	**1.** Given
2. $\angle N \cong \angle A$	**2.**
3. I is the midpoint of $\overline{PT}$	**3.** Given
4.	**4.** Definition of midpoint
5. $\angle TIN \cong \angle AIP$	**5.**
6. $\Delta PAI \cong \Delta TNI$	**6.**

Try It!

2. Consider ΔOHP and ΔEPH in the diagram below.

Given: $\overline{OH} \parallel \overline{EP}$; $\overline{EH} \parallel \overline{OP}$
Prove: $\Delta OHP \cong \Delta EPH$

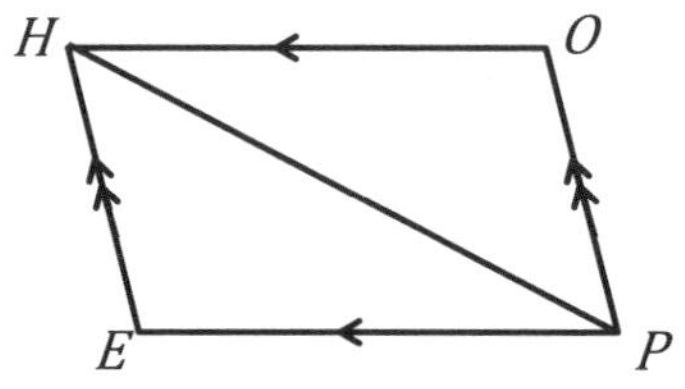

Complete the following two-column proof.

Statements	Reasons
1. $\overline{OH} \parallel \overline{EP}$	**1.** Given
2.	**2.** Alternate interior angles theorem
3. $\overline{EH} \parallel \overline{OP}$	**3.** Given
4. $\angle PHE \cong \angle HPO$	**4.**
5.	**5.** Reflexive property
6. $\Delta OHP \cong \Delta EPH$	**6.**

Section 5 – Topic 7
Triangle Congruence – ASA and AAS – Part 2

Let's Practice!

1. Consider the figure to the right.

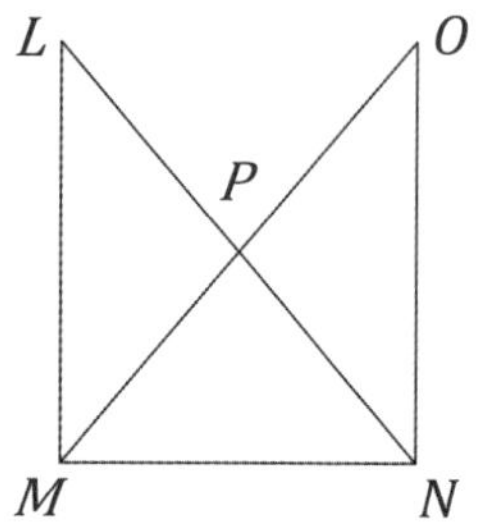

Given: $\overline{PM} \cong \overline{PN}, \overline{LM} \perp \overline{MN}, \overline{MN} \perp \overline{ON}$
$\overline{LN}$ bisects $\angle MNO$, $\overline{OM}$ bisects $\angle LMN$.
Prove: $\Delta MPL \cong \Delta NPO$

Complete the following two-column proof.

Statements	Reasons
1. $\overline{PM} \cong \overline{PN}$	**1.** Given
2. $\overline{LM} \perp \overline{MN}, \overline{MN} \perp \overline{ON}$	**2.** Given
3. $\overline{LN}$ bisects $\angle MNO$ and $\overline{OM}$ bisects $\angle LMN$.	**3.** Given
4.	**4.** Definition of $\perp$ lines.
5. $m\angle LMP = m\angle ONP = 45°$	**5.**
6.	**6.** Vertical Angles
7. $\Delta MPL \cong \Delta NPO$	**7.**

Try It!

2. Consider the figures below.

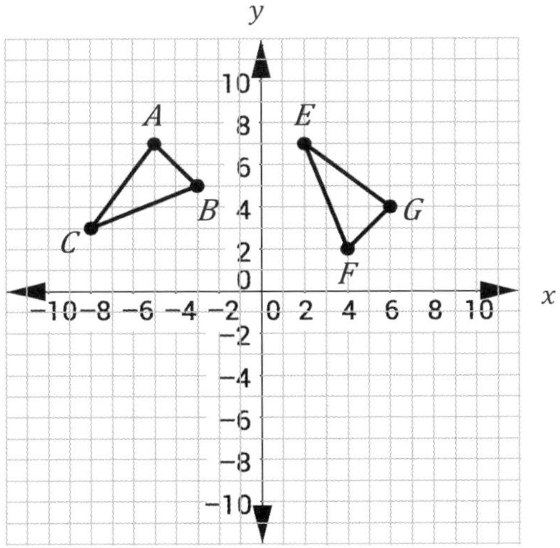

How would you prove $\Delta ABC \cong \Delta GFE$ by applying ideas of transformations?

BEAT THE TEST!

1. Consider the diagram below.

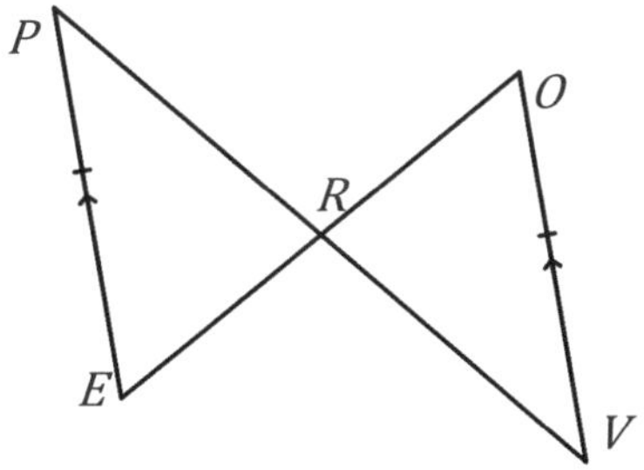

Given: $\overline{PE} \cong \overline{OV}$; $\overline{PE} \parallel \overline{OV}$

Prove: $\Delta PRE \cong \Delta VRO$

Select the most appropriate reason for #5.

Statements	Reasons
1. $\overline{PE} \cong \overline{OV}$	**1.** Given
2. $\overline{PE} \parallel \overline{OV}$	**2.** Given
3. $\angle PER \cong \angle VOR$	**3.** Alternate Interior Angles Theorem
4. $\angle ERP \cong \angle ORV$	**4.** Vertical angle theorem
5. $\Delta PRE \cong \Delta VRO$	**5.** Ⓐ AAS Ⓑ ASA Ⓒ SAS Ⓓ SSS

2. Consider the figure below.

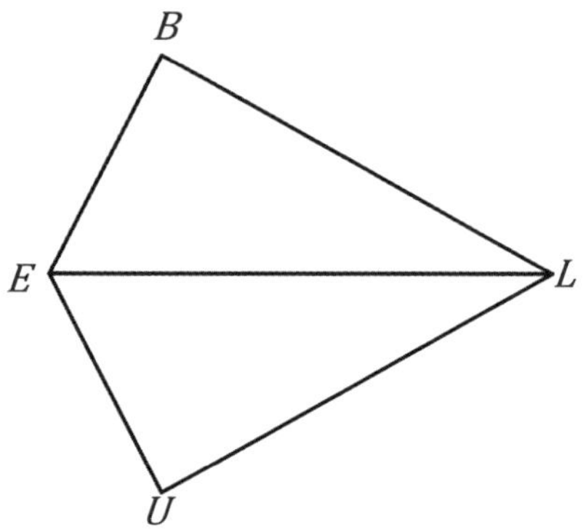

Part A: What transformation(s) will prove $\Delta BLE \cong \Delta ULE$? Justify your answer.

Part B: If $\overline{EL}$ is the angle bisector of $\angle BEU$, what additional information is needed to prove that $\Delta BLE \cong \Delta ULE$ using ASA?

Ⓐ $\overline{BE} \cong \overline{EU}$
Ⓑ $\angle BLE \cong \angle EUL$
Ⓒ $\angle EBL \cong \angle EUL$
Ⓓ $\angle ELB \cong \angle ULE$

Section 5 – Topic 8
Base Angle of Isosceles Triangles

By definition, an ________________ ________________ is a triangle with two equal sides.

Consider $\triangle UVA$ below.

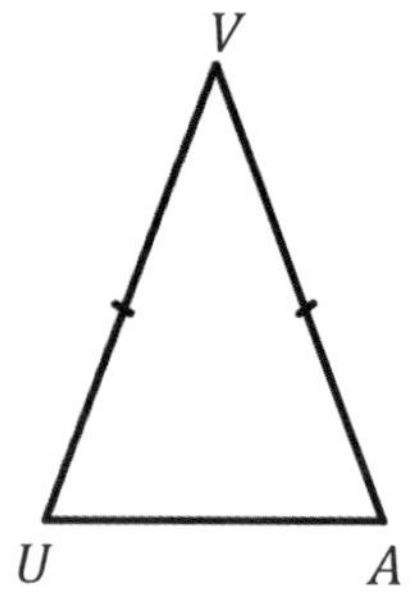

Draw the angle bisector $\overline{VP}$ of $\angle V$, where P is the intersection of the bisector and $\overline{UA}$.

Use paragraph proofs to show that $m\angle U = m\angle A$ in two ways: by using transformations and triangle congruence postulates.

Transformations	Triangle Congruence Postulates

Let's Practice!

1. Consider the diagram below.

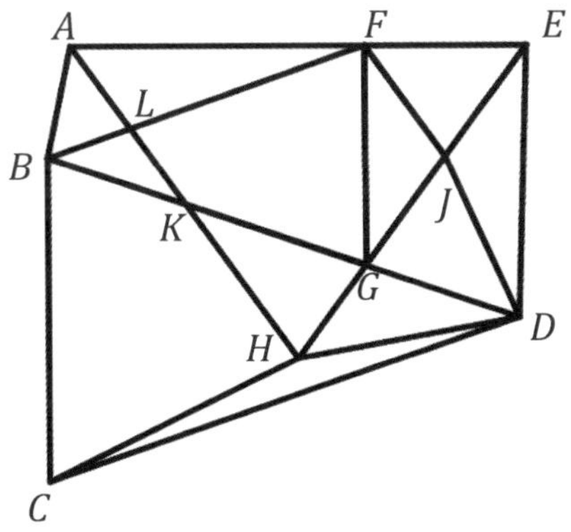

For each of the following congruence statements, name the isosceles triangle and the pair of congruent angles for the triangle based on the diagram above.

a. $\overline{CD} \cong \overline{BD}$

b. $\overline{FJ} \cong \overline{GJ}$

c. $\overline{AH} \cong \overline{EH}$

d. $\overline{EJ} \cong \overline{FJ}$

e. $\overline{FB} \cong \overline{GB}$

TAKE NOTE! *Postulates & Theorems*

Base Angle Theorem and its Converse

The Base Angle Theorem states that if two sides in a triangle are congruent, then the angles opposite to these sides are also congruent. The converse of this theorem is also true. If two angles of a triangle are congruent, then the sides opposite to these angles are congruent.

2. Consider the figure below.

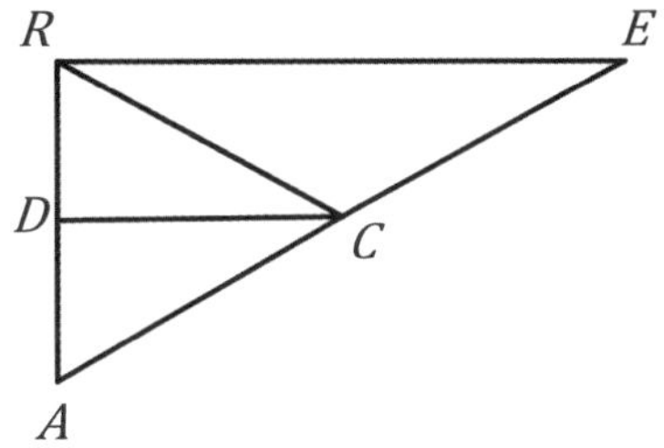

Given: $\triangle REA$, $\overline{DC}$ is the angle bisector of $\angle RCA$, and $\overline{RE} \parallel \overline{DC}$

Prove: $CR = CE$

Complete the following two-column proof.

Statements	Reasons
1. $\overline{RE} \parallel \overline{DC}$	**1.** Given
2. $\angle DCR \cong \angle ERC$	**2.**
3.	**3.** Corresponding Angles Theorem
4. $\angle DCA \cong \angle DCR$	**4.**
5.	**5.** Transitive Property
6.	**6.** Definition of Congruence
7. $CR = CE$	**7.**

Try It!

3. Consider the figure below.

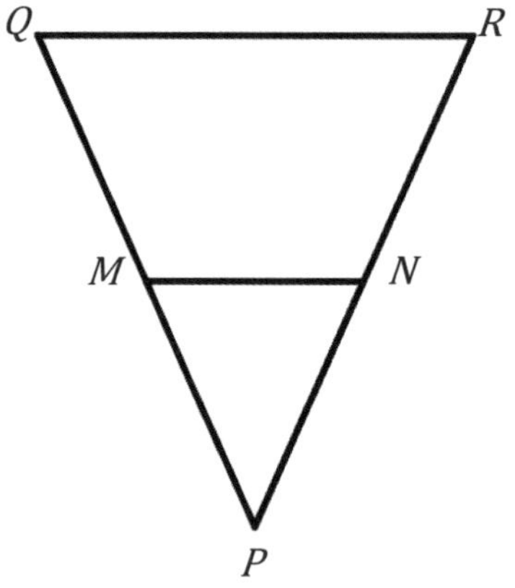

Given: $PQ = PR$ and $\overline{MN} \parallel \overline{QR}$ **Prove:** $PM = PN$

Complete the following two-column proof.

Statements	Reasons
1. $PQ = PR$	**1.** Given
2. $\triangle PQR$ is isosceles.	**2.**
3.	**3.** Base Angle Theorem
4. $\overline{MN} \parallel \overline{QR}$	**4.** Given
5. $\angle NMP \cong \angle RQP$ and $\angle MNP \cong \angle QRP$	**5.**
6.	**6.** Transitive Property
7.	**7.** Definition of Congruence
8. $PM = PN$	**8.**

BEAT THE TEST!

1. Consider the following $\triangle TOW$, with $m\angle OWT = m\angle WTO$.

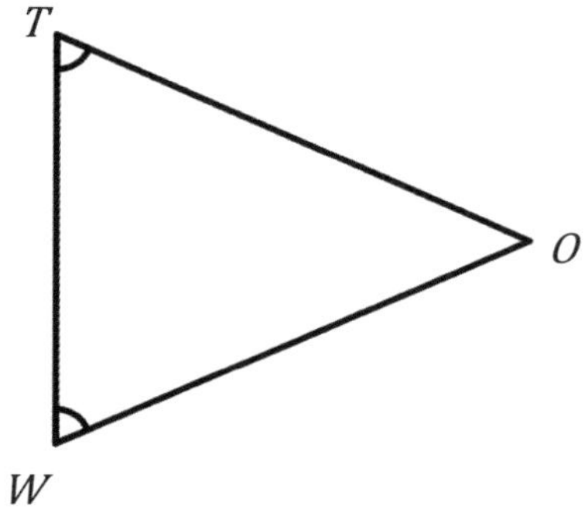

Waseem was asked to prove that $TO = WO$. His work is shown below. There is at least one error in Waseem's work. Describe and explain his error(s).

We can prove that TO=WO by using two approaches. Construct the perpendicular bisector $\overline{OP}$ to $\overline{TW}$. Then, rotate the triangle 210 degrees counter clockwise about point P. Since all points on the perpendicular bisector are equidistant from T and W, then TO=WO. The second approach will be just using the Base Angle Theorem to conclude that TOW is an isosceles triangle.

Section 5 – Topic 9
Using the Definition of Triangle Congruence in Terms of Rigid Motions

How can rigid motion(s) be used to determine congruence?

- Rigid motions move figures to a new location without altering their ____________ or ____________, thus maintaining the conditions for the figures to be congruent.

By definition, two figures are ____________ if and only if there exists one, or more, rigid motions which will map one figure onto the other.

Consider the diagram below.

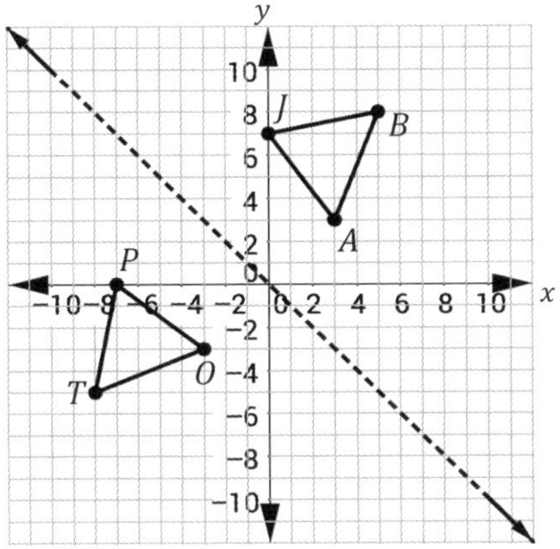

Find a rigid motion that will map $\triangle POT$ onto $\triangle JAB$.

Justify the use of the SSS Congruence Postulate to prove that $\triangle POT \cong \triangle JAB$.

Let's Practice!

1. Consider the diagram below.

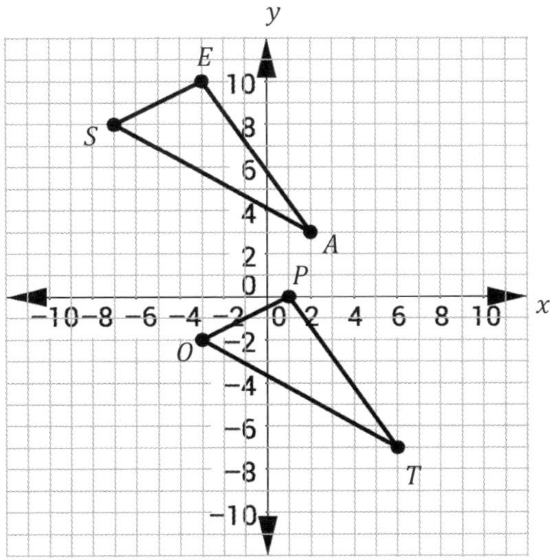

Find a rigid motion that will map $\triangle SEA$ onto $\triangle OPT$.

Try It!

2. Consider the diagram below.

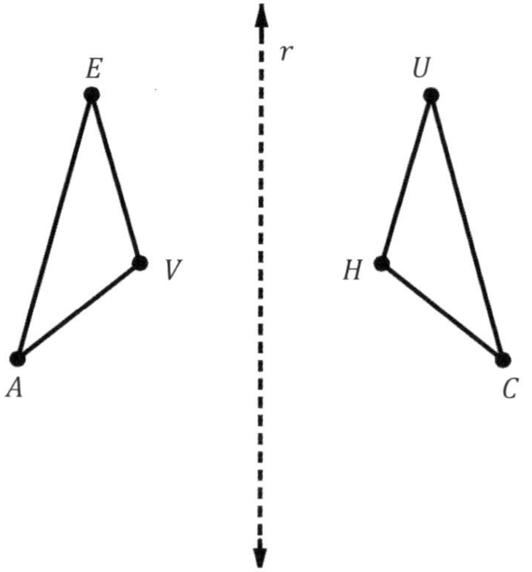

a. Find a rigid motion that will map $\triangle AVE$ onto $\triangle CHU$.

b. Suppose that $m\angle AVE = 112.71°$, $AV = 6.4''$, and $VE = 7.28''$. Justify the use of the SAS Congruence Postulate to prove that $\triangle AVE \cong \triangle CHU$.

c. Suppose that your friend suggests a translation as the rigid motion that maps $\triangle AVE$ onto $\triangle CHU$. Is your friend correct? Justify your answer.

3. Consider the diagram below.

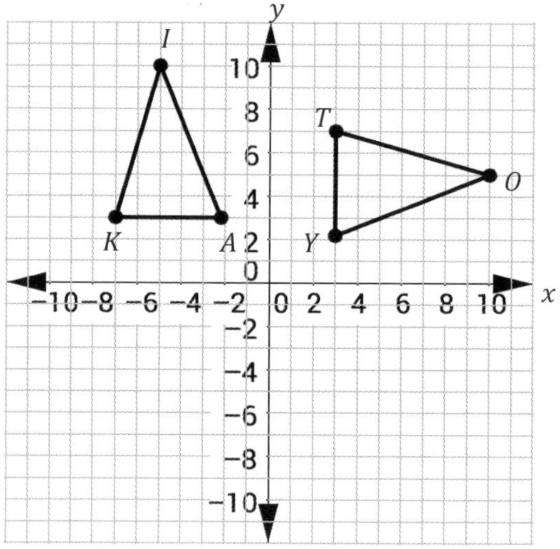

Which of the following rigid motions will map $\triangle TOY$ onto $\triangle KIA$? Select all that apply.

- ☐ A reflection over the y-axis
- ☐ A rotation of $270°$ clockwise about the origin
- ☐ The translation $(x, y) \to (x + 5, y - 1)$
- ☐ A reflection over the line $y = -x$ followed by a rotation of $180°$ clockwise about the origin
- ☐ The translation $(x, y) \to (x - 5, y + 1)$ followed by a rotation of $90°$ counterclockwise about vertex Y

BEAT THE TEST!

1. Consider the diagram below.

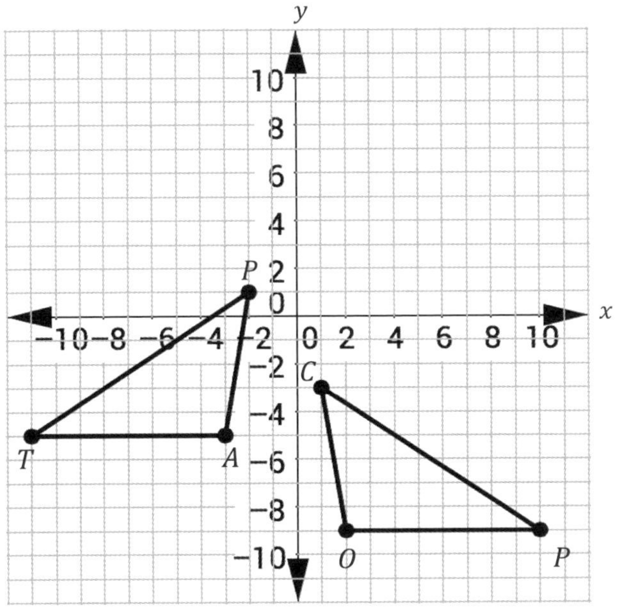

Find a combination of rigid motions that will map $\triangle COP$ onto $\triangle PAT$ and determine if $\triangle COP \cong \triangle PAT$.

Section 5 – Topic 10
Using Triangle Congruency to Find Missing Variables

Consider the figures below.

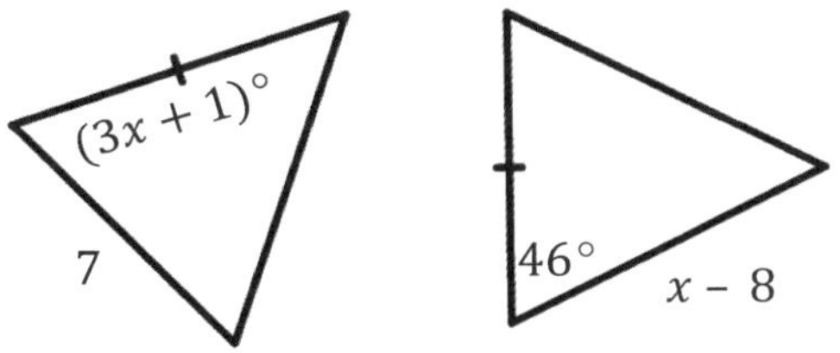

Find the value of x in order to prove that the two triangles are congruent by the SAS Congruence Postulate. Justify your work.

Let's Practice!

1. Consider the figures below.

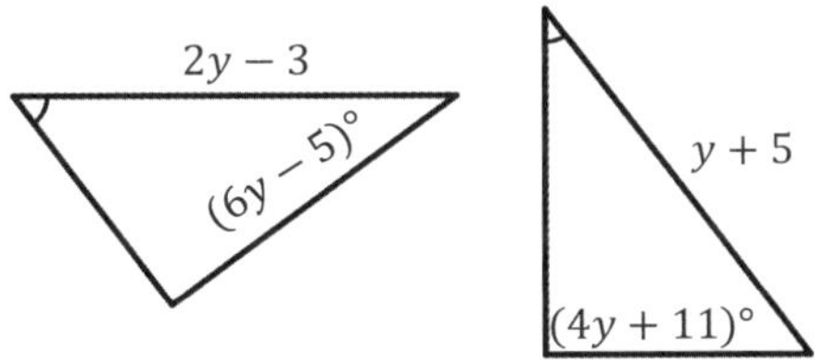

Find the value of y in order to prove that the two triangles are congruent using the ASA Congruence Postulate. Justify your work.

Try It!

2. Consider the figure below.

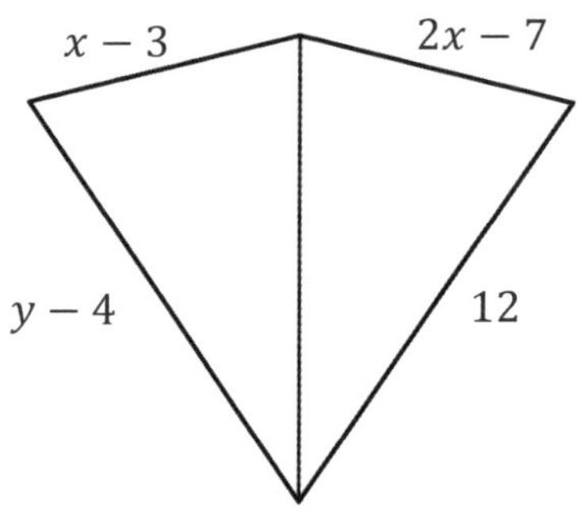

Find the values of x and y that prove the two triangles are congruent using the SSS Congruence Postulate.

3. Consider the figure below.

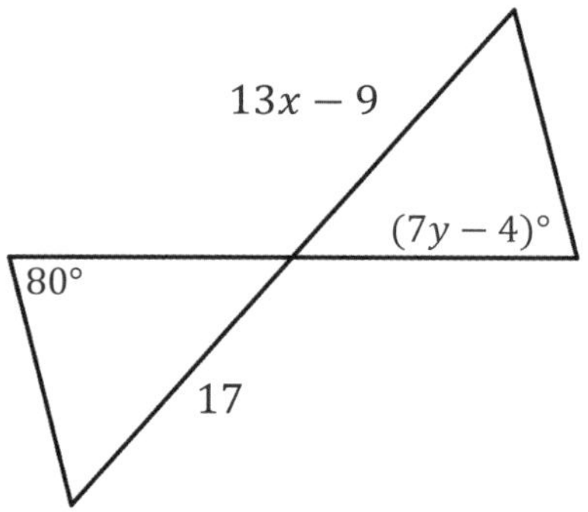

Find the values of x and y that prove the two triangles are congruent using the AAS Congruence Theorem. Justify your work.

BEAT THE TEST!

1. Consider the figure below.

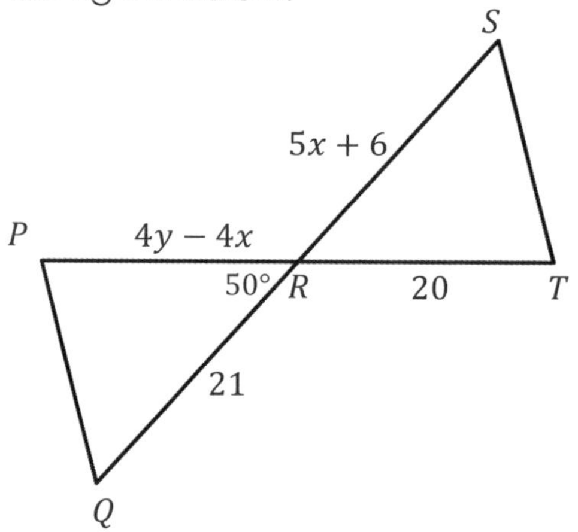

Part A: If $\overline{PQ} \cong \overline{TS}$ and $\overline{PQ} \parallel \overline{TS}$, which triangle congruency postulate can we use to determine $\Delta PRQ \cong \Delta TRS$ given the information on the figure? Select all that apply.

- ☐ AAS
- ☐ ASA
- ☐ SAS
- ☐ SSS
- ☐ SSA

Part B: What are the values of x and y?

Test Yourself! Practice Tool

Great job! You have reached the end of this section. Now it's time to try the "Test Yourself! Practice Tool," where you can practice all the skills and concepts you learned in this section. Log in to Math Nation and try out the "Test Yourself! Practice Tool" so you can see how well you know these topics!

Section 6: Triangles – Part 2

Topic 1: Triangle Similarity – Part 1 157
*Standards Covered:*G-SRT.3, G-SRT.5
- ☐ I can use triangle similarity criteria to prove two triangles are similar.
- ☐ I can use triangle similarity criteria to prove certain lengths of two triangles are similar.

Topic 2: Triangle Similarity – Part 2 160
*Standards Covered:*G-SRT.2, G-SRT.5
- ☐ I can use triangle similarity criteria to prove two triangles are similar.
- ☐ I can use triangle similarity criteria to prove certain lengths of two triangles are similar.

Topic 3: Triangle Midsegment Theorem – Part 1 163
*Standards Covered:*G-CO.10
- ☐ I can use the Triangle Midsegment Theorem to determine how midsegments of a triangle are related to the sides of a triangle.

Topic 4: Triangle Midsegment Theorem – Part 2 166
Standards Covered: G-CO.10
- ☐ I can use the Triangle Midsegment Theorem to find the missing side and angle measures of a triangle.

Topic 5: Triangle Inequalities 168
Standards Covered: G-CO.10
- ☐ I can apply inequalities in one triangle to draw conclusions about the measures of sides and angles of a triangle.

Topic 6: More Triangle Proofs 172
*Standards Covered:*G-GPE.5
- ☐ I can use triangle theorems to prove different features of a triangle.

Topic 7: Inscribed and Circumscribed Circles of Triangles 176
*Standards Covered:*G-C.3
- ☐ I can construct triangles.

Topic 8: Medians in a Triangle 179
*Standards Covered:*G-CO.10
- ☐ I can use medians of a triangle to solve problems.

Visit MathNation.com or search "Math Nation" in your phone or tablet's app store to watch the videos that go along with this workbook!

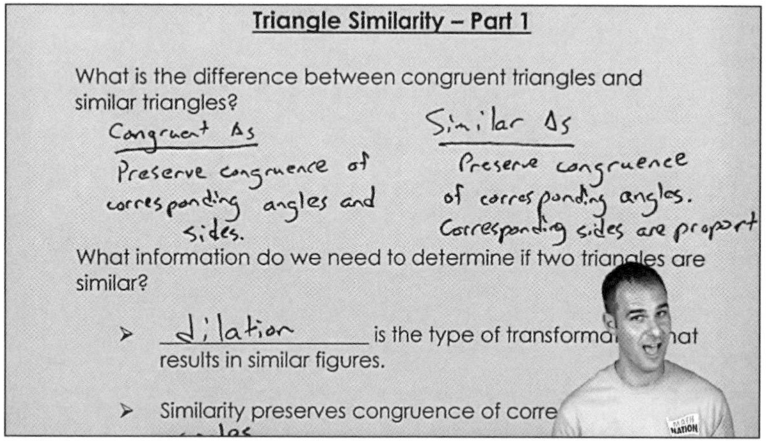
Triangle Similarity – Part 1
What is the difference between congruent triangles and similar triangles?
Congruent Δs
Preserve congruence of corresponding angles and sides.
Similar Δs
Preserve congruence of corresponding angles. Corresponding sides are proport
What information do we need to determine if two triangles are similar?
dilation is the type of transforma hat results in similar figures.
Similarity preserves congruence of corre

The following Michigan Mathematics Standards will be covered in this section:
G-C.3 - Construct the inscribed and circumscribed circles of a triangle and prove properties of angles for a quadrilateral inscribed in a circle.
G-CO.10 - Prove theorems about triangles; use theorems about triangles to solve problems.
G-GPE.5 - Prove the slope criteria for parallel and perpendicular lines and use them to solve geometric problems.
G-GPE.7 - Use coordinates to compute perimeters of polygons and areas of triangles and rectangles, e.g., using the distance formula.
G-SRT.2 - Given two figures, use the definition of similarity in terms of similarity transformations to decide if they are similar; explain using similarity transformations the meaning of similarity for triangles as the equality of all corresponding pairs of angles and the proportionality of all corresponding pairs of sides.
G-SRT.3 - Use the properties of similarity transformations to establish the AA criterion for two triangles to be similar.
G-SRT.5 - Use congruence and similarity criteria for triangles to solve problems and to prove relationships in geometric figures.

Section 6: Triangles – Part 2
Section 6 – Topic 1
Triangle Similarity – Part 1

What is the difference between congruent triangles and similar triangles?

What information do we need in order to determine if two triangles are similar?

- ____________________ is the type of transformation that results in similar figures.
- Similarity preserves congruence of corresponding ____________________.
- Similarity maintains the proportionality of corresponding ____________________.

Circle the best answer choice to complete the sentence below. Justify your answer.

Congruent triangles are always | sometimes | never similar triangles.

Circle the best answer choice to complete the sentence below. Justify your answer.

Similar triangles are always | sometimes | never congruent triangles.

Consider the diagram of ΔPHO and ΔYUM below, where $\Delta PHO \sim \Delta YUM$.

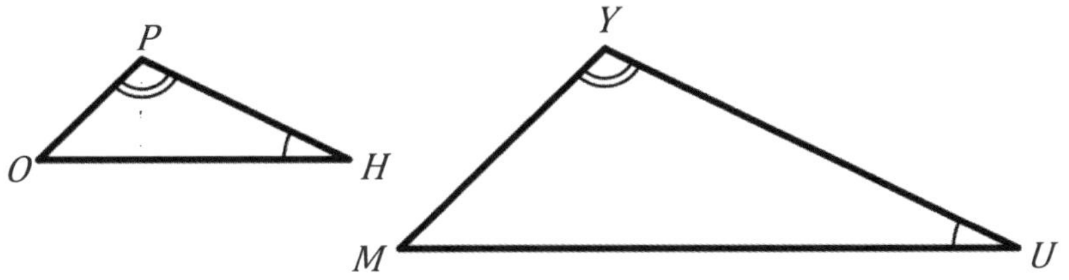

List the corresponding sides and angles of the triangles above.

Consider the diagrams of ΔMAN and ΔBOY below.

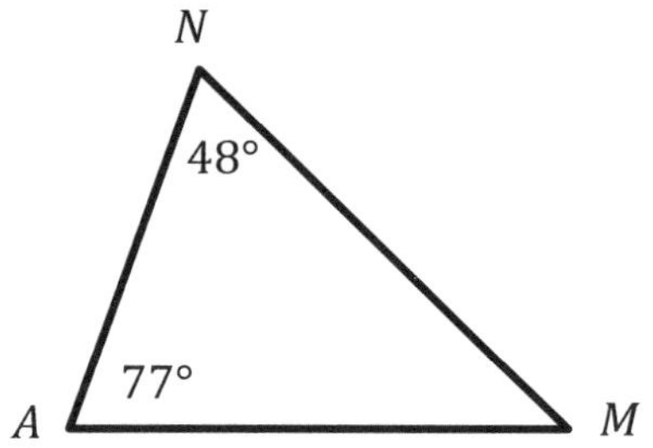

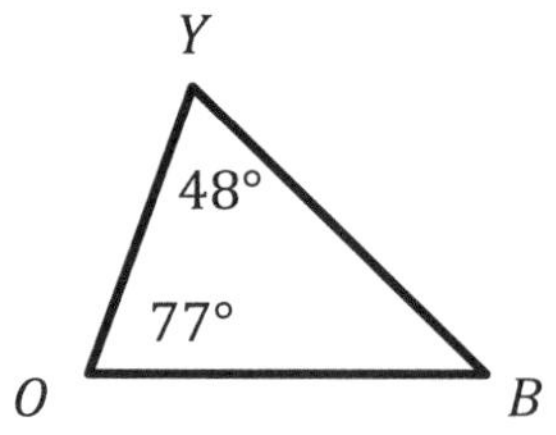

Determine $m\angle M$.

Determine $m\angle B$.

Compare the two angles.

If you know that two pairs of corresponding angles are congruent, what must be true of the third pair of angles?

> TAKE NOTE! *Postulates & Theorems*
> **Angle-Angle Similarity (AA~) Criterion**
> If two angles of one triangle are congruent to two angles of another triangle, then the two triangles are similar.

Consider the diagrams below.

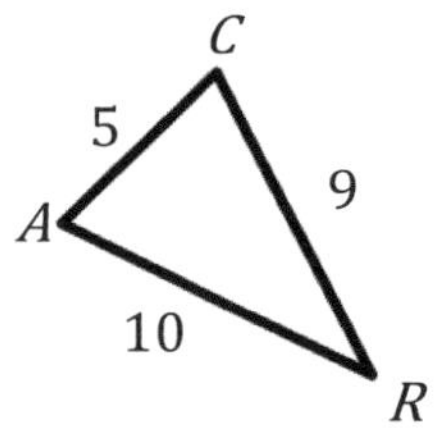

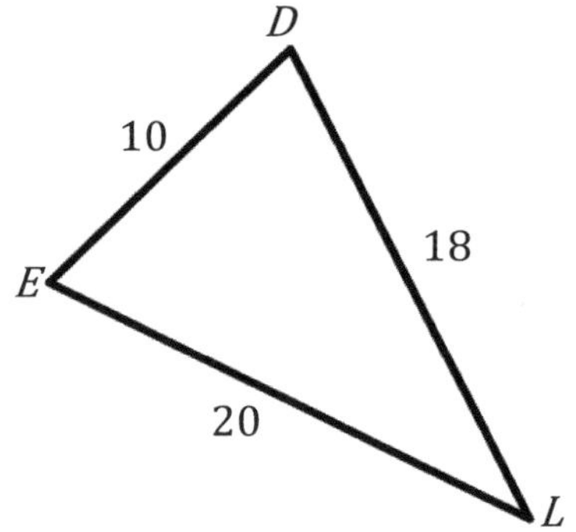

Prove that $\Delta CRA \sim \Delta DLE$.

> TAKE NOTE! *Postulates & Theorems*
> **Side-Side-Side Similarity (SSS~) Criterion**
> If the lengths of the corresponding sides of two triangles are proportional, then the triangles are similar.

Consider the diagram below.

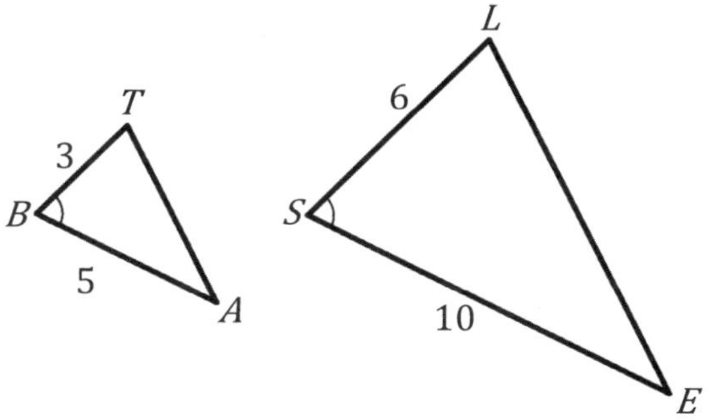

Prove that $\Delta TAB \sim \Delta LES$.

TAKE NOTE! *Postulates & Theorems*

Side-Angle-Side Similarity (SAS~) Criterion

If the lengths of two sides are proportional and their included angles are congruent on two different triangles, then the triangles are similar.

Suppose that you have ΔTRA and ΔSED, and $\frac{TR}{SE} = \frac{AT}{DS}$. Identify the criterion that proves that the two triangles are similar given each additional statement.

$\angle R \cong \angle E$

$\frac{TR}{SE} = \frac{RA}{ED}$

Section 6 – Topic 2
Triangle Similarity – Part 2

Consider the diagram to the right.

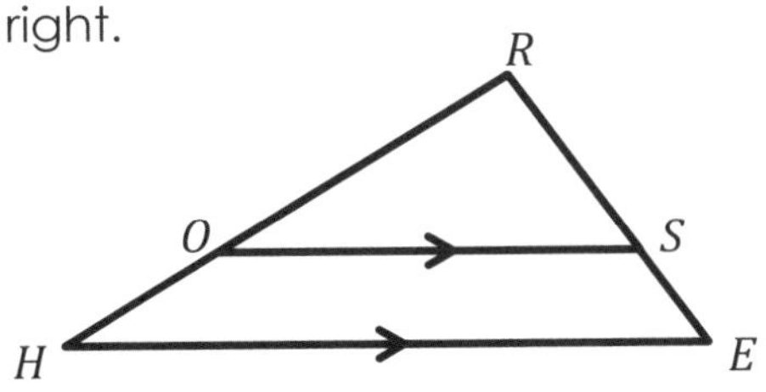

Given: $\overline{OS} \parallel \overline{HE}$

Prove: $\frac{OH}{OR} = \frac{SE}{RS}$

Complete the following two-column proof.

Statements	Reasons
1. $\overline{OS} \parallel \overline{HE}$	**1.**
2. $\angle ROS \cong \angle H$, $\angle RSO \cong \angle E$	**2.**
3.	**3.** AA Similarity Criterion
4. $\frac{HR}{OR} = \frac{RE}{RS}$	**4.**
5. $\frac{\_\_\_\_}{OR} = \frac{\_\_\_\_}{RS}$	**5.** Segment Addition Postulate
6. $\frac{OR}{OR} + \frac{HO}{OR} = \frac{RS}{RS} + \frac{SE}{RS}$	**6.**
7. $1 + \frac{HO}{OR} = 1 + \frac{SE}{RS}$	**7.**
8.	**8.** Subtraction Property of Equality

Let's Practice!

1. An artist is designing a sculpture for the town square that will contain two triangular solids. The artist wants the triangles in the bases of each solid to be similar.

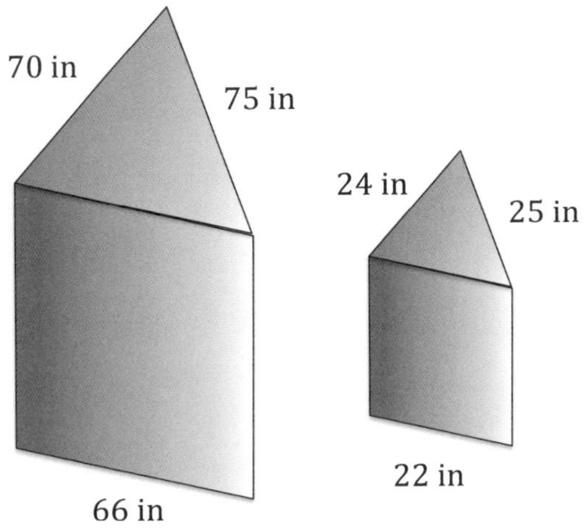

a. Are the triangles similar? Justify your answer.

b. If the triangles are not similar, what measurement(s) could be changed to make them similar? Justify your answer.

2. Consider the diagram to the right.

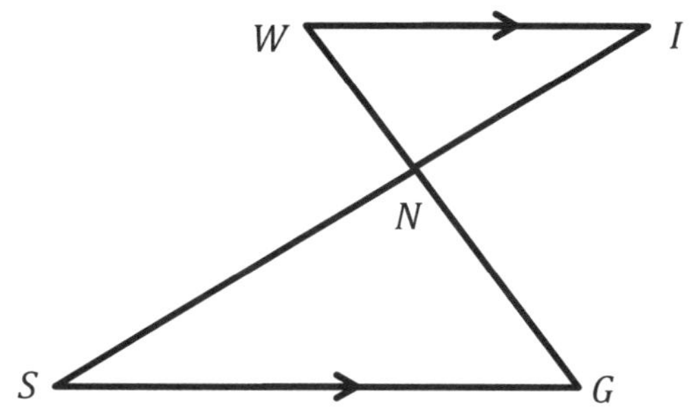

Given: $\overline{WI} \parallel \overline{SG}$

Prove: $\frac{WN}{NG} = \frac{WI}{SG}$

Complete the following two-column proof.

Statements	Reasons
1. $\overline{WI} \parallel \overline{SG}$	**1.** Given
2. $\angle WNI \cong \angle GNS$	**2.**
3.	**3.** Alternate Interior Angles Theorem
4.	**4.** AA~ Criterion
5. $\frac{WN}{NG} = \frac{WI}{SG}$	**5.**

Try It!

3. Consider the diagram below.

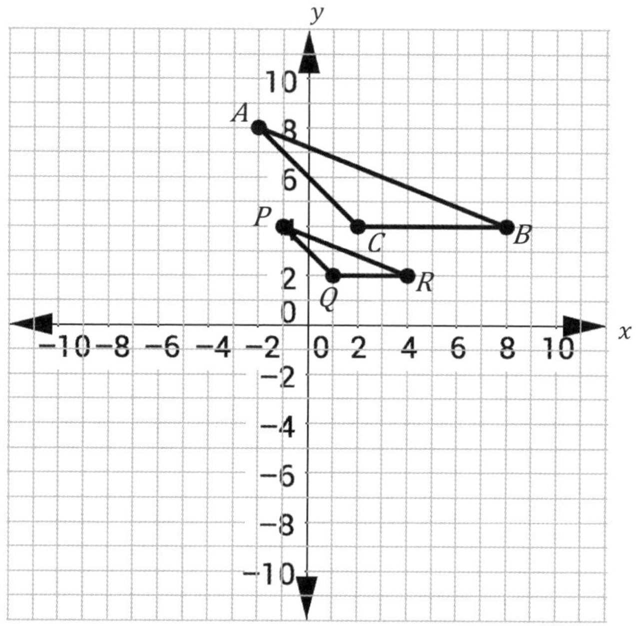

Prove $\Delta ACB \sim \Delta PQR$ by applying properties of transformations. Justify your steps.

4. A surveyor is measuring the width of a river for a future bridge.

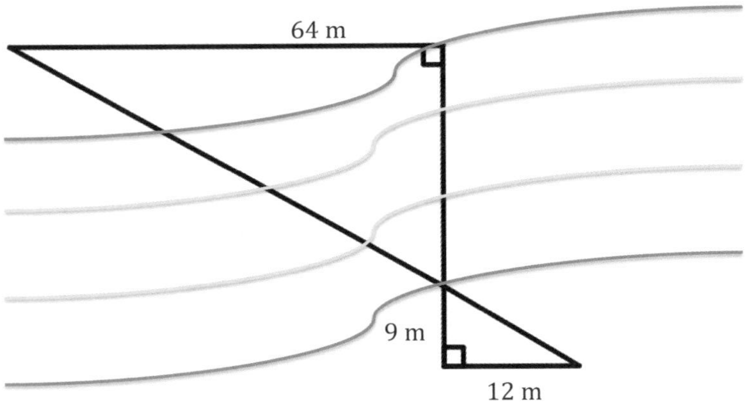

a. What similarity criterion can be used to prove that the triangles are similar?

b. Use the properties of similar triangles to set up a proportion and determine the width of the river.

BEAT THE TEST!

1. Consider the figure below.

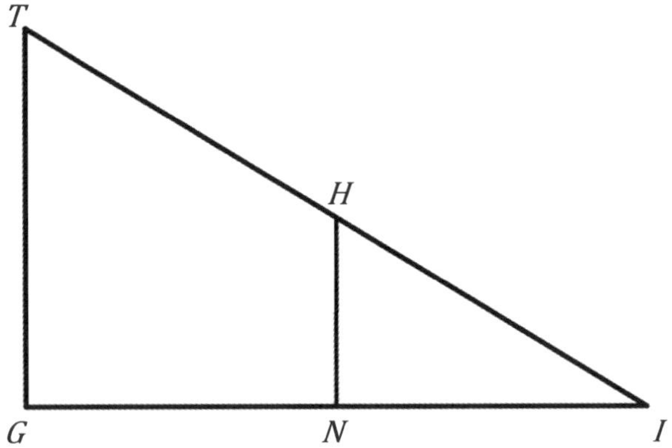

Which of the following could be used to prove that ΔHIN and ΔTIG are similar? Select all that apply.

- ☐ N is the midpoint of $\overline{GI}$
- ☐ $\overline{TG} \parallel \overline{HN}$
- ☐ $\angle T \cong \angle I$
- ☐ $\overline{TG} \perp \overline{IG}$
- ☐ $\overline{HN}$ bisects $\overline{IG}$ and $\overline{TI}$
- ☐ ΔTIG is dilated by a scale factor less than 1 centered at point I.

2. Mrs. Robinson assigned her class a project to find the height of the flagpole. The students could not easily measure the height, so they had to use their knowledge of similar triangles to determine the height of the flagpole. One student placed a mirror on the ground 21 feet from the base of the flagpole and backed up until the reflection of the top of the pole was centered in the mirror.

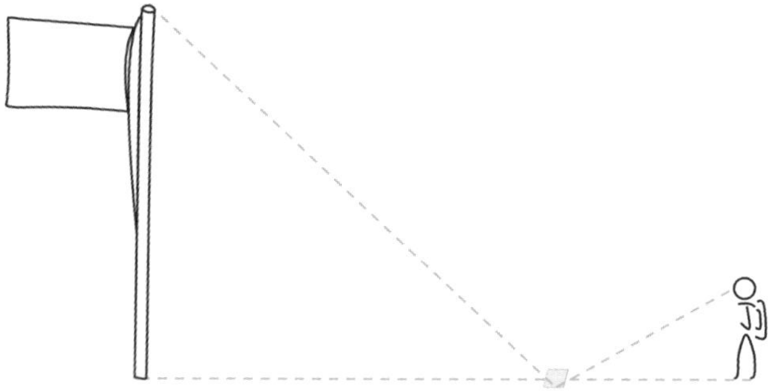

Part A: If the student is 5.4 feet tall and is standing 7.2 feet from the mirror, how tall is the flagpole?

Part B: Describe another way to use similarity of triangles to find the height of the flagpole.

Section 6 – Topic 3
Triangle Midsegment Theorem – Part 1

If the midpoint of a segment is the halfway point, then what is the midsegment of a triangle?

Construct the midsegment of triangle DEF below and label the midsegment $\overline{MP}$.

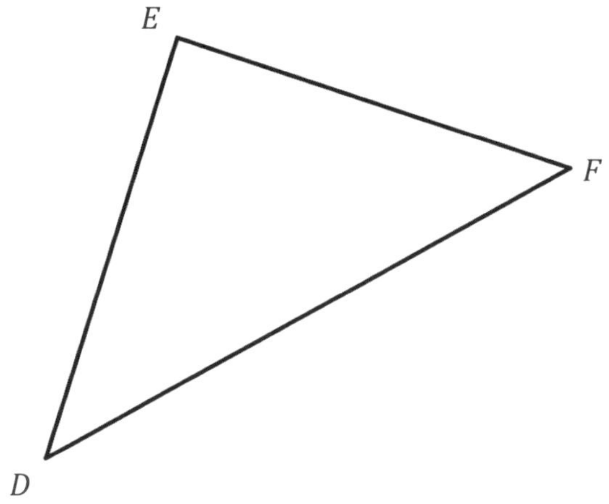

TAKE NOTE! *Postulates & Theorems*

Triangle Midsegment Theorem

The midsegment of a triangle joins the midpoints of two sides of a triangle such that its length is half the length of the third side of the triangle and it is parallel to the third side of the triangle.

Consider triangle DEF with midsegment $\overline{MP}$ below.

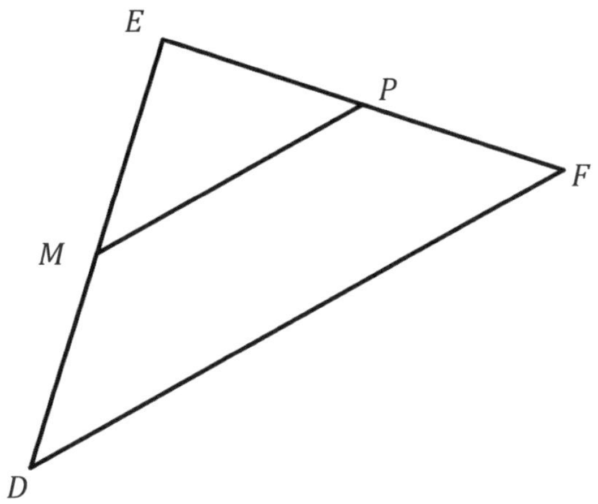

Describe the relationship between $\overline{MP}$ and $\overline{DF}$.

Describe the relationship between $\overline{DM}$ and $\overline{ME}$.

Describe the relationship between $\overline{FP}$ and $\overline{PE}$.

The area of the triangle MPE is what portion of the area of the triangle DFE?

Let's Practice!

1. In the diagram below, A is located at the origin, G is located at $(6, 15)$, H is located at $(6, 9)$ and I is located at $(12, 12)$. Assume that $D, E, F, G, H,$ and I are midpoints.

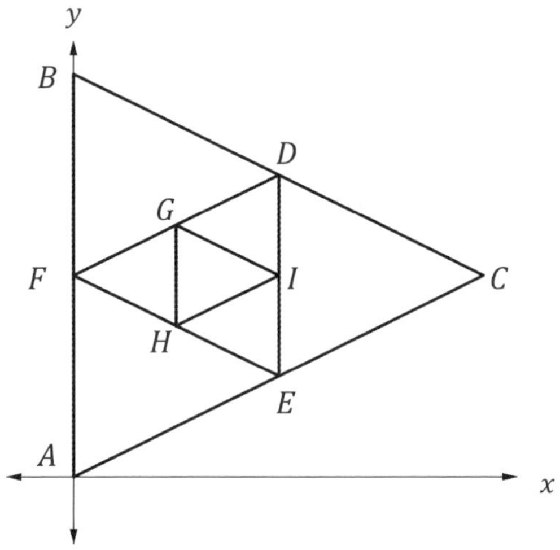

a. Complete the following table.

Vertex	B	C	D	E	F
Coordinates					

b. Which of the following statements about the previous diagram are correct? Select all that apply.

- ☐ Triangles ABC and GHI are isosceles.
- ☐ Triangle DEF is equilateral.
- ☐ $\overline{GH} \cong \overline{HI} \cong \overline{GI}$
- ☐ The area of triangle ABC is 16 times larger than the area of triangle GHI.
- ☐ The area of triangle GHI is one half the area of triangle DEF.
- ☐ $\overline{FE} > \overline{DE}$
- ☐ If triangle ABC is dilated by a scale factor of $\frac{1}{4}$ centered at C, then $\triangle A'B'C' \cong \triangle CDE$.

Try It!

2. If the midsegment of an isosceles triangle is 5 feet long and each of the congruent sides of the triangle are 6 feet long, what is the measure of the side parallel to the midsegment?

3. The Michigan Triangle is a region located in the middle of Lake Michigan. The triangle is bounded by Benton Harbor, MI; Ludington, MI; and Manitowoc, WI. If you draw their midsegments into the Michigan Triangle, how does the perimeter of the midsegment triangle compare to the perimeter of the Michigan Triangle?

Section 6 – Topic 4
Triangle Midsegment Theorem – Part 2

Let's Practice!

1. Consider the diagram below.

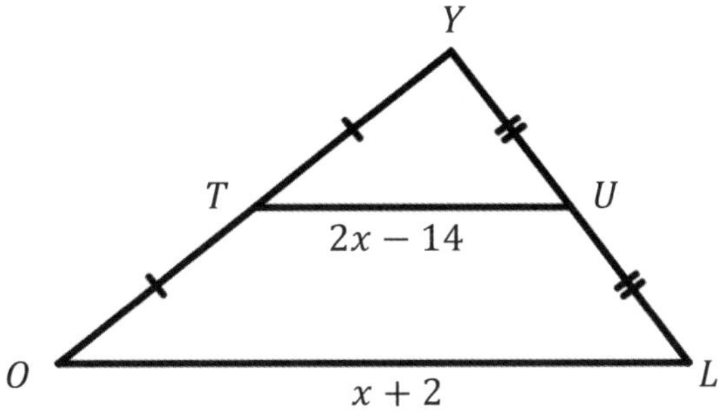

Find the sum of TU and OL.

Try It!

2. Consider the diagram below.

Given: $\overline{EK}, \overline{KO}$, and $\overline{OE}$ are midsegments of $\triangle MNY$.

Prove: The perimeter of $\triangle EKO = \frac{1}{2}(MN + NY + YM)$.

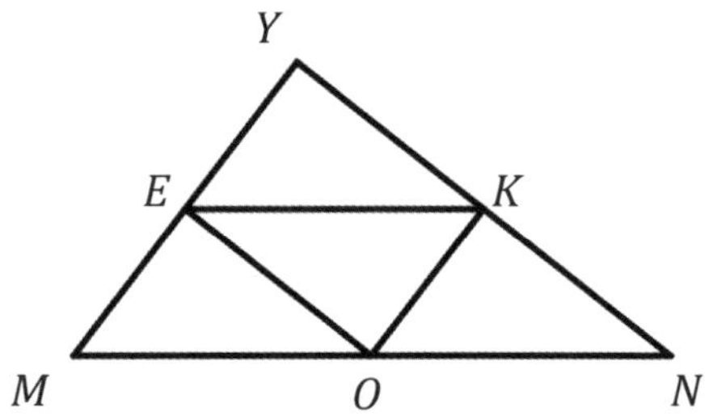

Complete the following two-column proof.

Statements	Reasons
1. $\overline{EK}, \overline{KO}$, and $\overline{OE}$ are midsegments of $\triangle MNY$.	**1.** Given
2.	**2.** Triangle Midsegment Theorem
3. The perimeter of $\triangle EKO = (EK + KO + OE)$.	**3.**
4.	**4.** Substitution
5. The perimeter of $\triangle EKO = \frac{1}{2}(MN + NY + YM)$.	**5.**

BEAT THE TEST!

1. Consider the figure below.

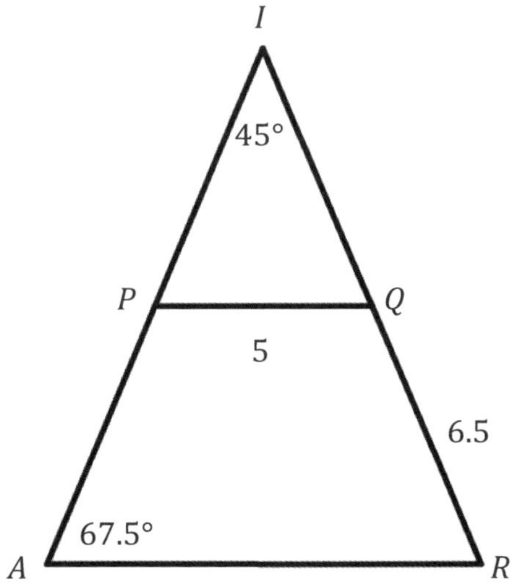

P and Q are the midpoints of $\overline{AI}$ and $\overline{IR}$, respectively. Use the properties of midsegments to find the perimeter of $\triangle AIR$.

2. In the following figure, $\overline{JK}$ is a midsegment of $\triangle COP$, $\overline{RS}$ is a midsegment of $\triangle PJK$, and $\overline{OK} \cong \overline{CJ}$.

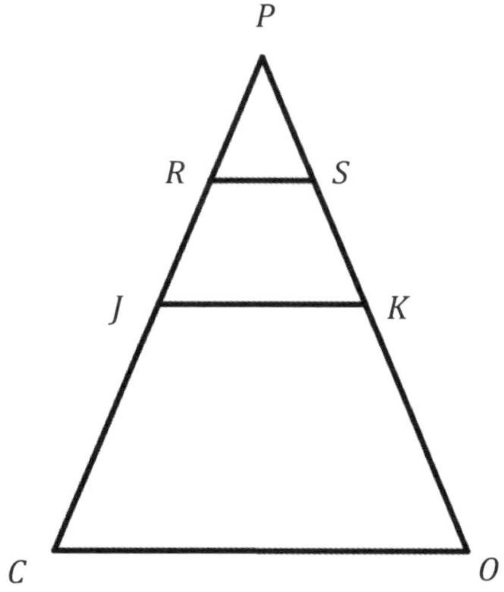

Part A: What can you conclude about $\angle C$ and $\angle O$? Justify your answer.

Part B: What is the relationship between the lengths $\overline{RS}$ and $\overline{CO}$?

Section 6 – Topic 5
Triangle Inequalities

Draw a triangle with sides measuring 2 centimeters and 4 centimeters. What is the length of the third side of this triangle?

Draw a triangle with sides 35 millimeters and 18 millimeters. What is the length of the third side of this triangle?

What relationship do you notice between the third side and the sum of the first two sides of the triangle you drew?

Is it possible to draw a triangle with a third side that is greater than the sum of the other two sides? Why or why not?

Consider the triangle and the information below.

$AB + BC > AC$
$BC + AC > AB$
$AC + AB > BC$

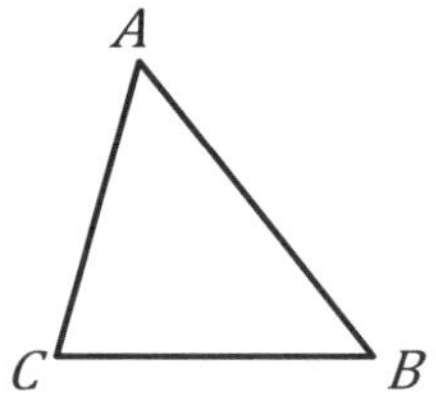

This is the **Triangle Inequality Theorem**.

> ***TAKE NOTE!*** *Postulates & Theorems*
>
> **Triangle Inequality Theorem**
> The sum of the lengths of any two sides of a triangle is greater than the length of the third side.

Let's Practice!

1. Consider the figure below.

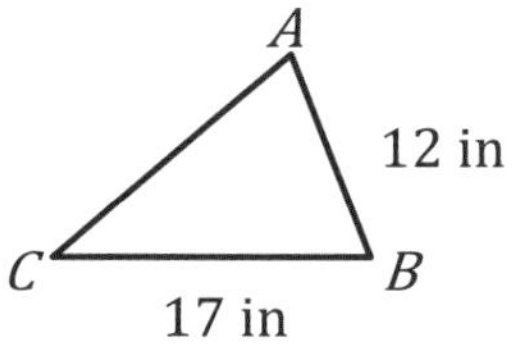

Find the range of possible sides lengths for the missing side of the triangle above.

Try It!

2. Consider the figure below.

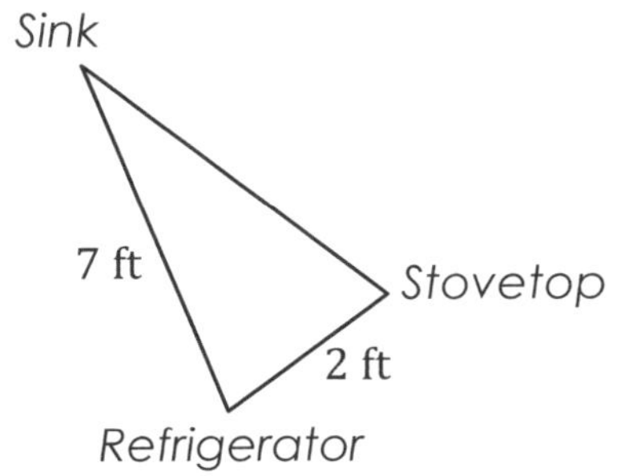

Darius is remodeling his kitchen. The "kitchen triangle" refers to the triangle formed by the sink, the refrigerator, and the stovetop. The above figure represents the remodeling plan.

Can the distance from his sink to stovetop be 9 feet long? Justify your answer.

TAKE NOTE! *Postulates & Theorems*

Hinge Theorem

If two sides of one triangle are congruent to two sides of another triangle, and the included angles are not congruent, then the longer third side is opposite the larger included angle.

Let's Practice!

3. Consider the figure below.

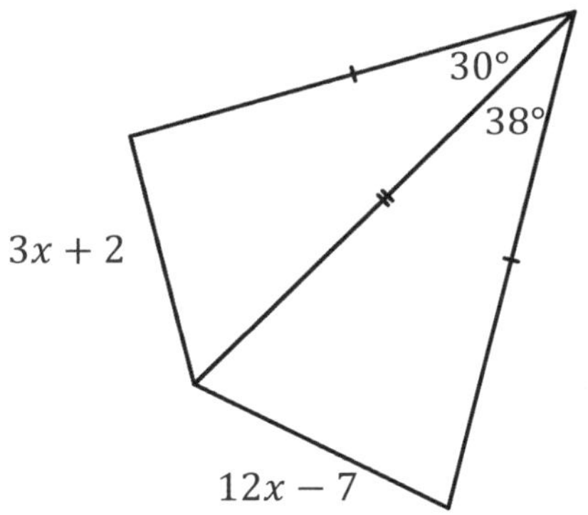

Use an inequality to describe a restriction on the value of x using the Hinge Theorem.

Try It!

4. Consider the figure below.

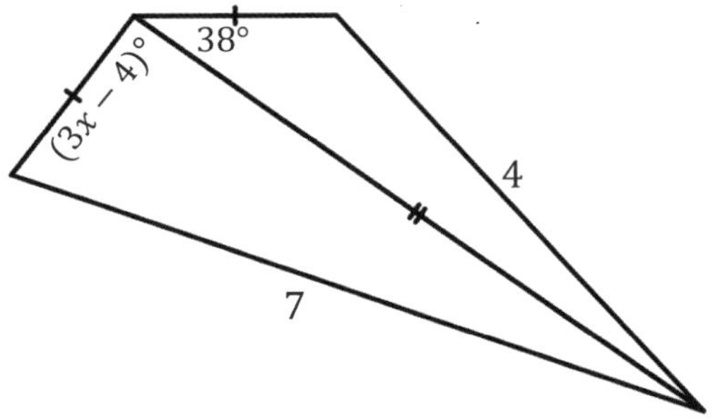

Use an inequality to describe a restriction on the value of x using the Hinge Theorem.

TAKE NOTE! *Postulates & Theorems*

Converse of the Hinge Theorem

If two sides of one triangle are congruent to two sides of another triangle, and the third side of the first triangle is greater than the third side of the second triangle, then the included angle of the first triangle is larger than the included angle of the second.

5. Consider the figure below.

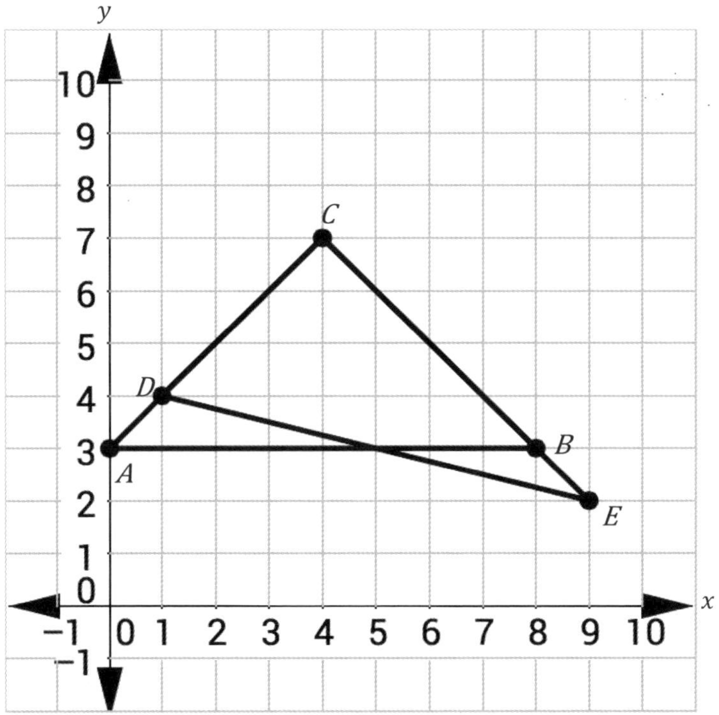

In the figure, $CA = CB$. D is a point on CA and E is a point on the prolonged line segment CB with $DA = BE$.
How would you prove $DE > BC$ by applying properties of transformations? Justify your steps.

BEAT THE TEST!

1. Consider the figure below.

Given: ΔABC with $\overline{AD} \perp \overline{BC}$

Prove: $\overline{BC} < \overline{AB} + \overline{AC}$

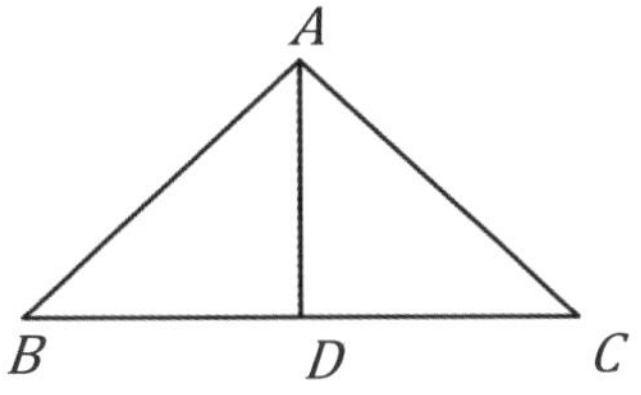

Use the options below to complete the flowchart to prove the triangle inequality theorem.

A. The shortest distance from a point q and a line r is the line perpendicular to r and passing through q.

B. If $a < b$ and $c < d$, then $a + c < b + d$.

C. Segment Addition Postulate

D. Given

E. Definition of perpendicular lines.

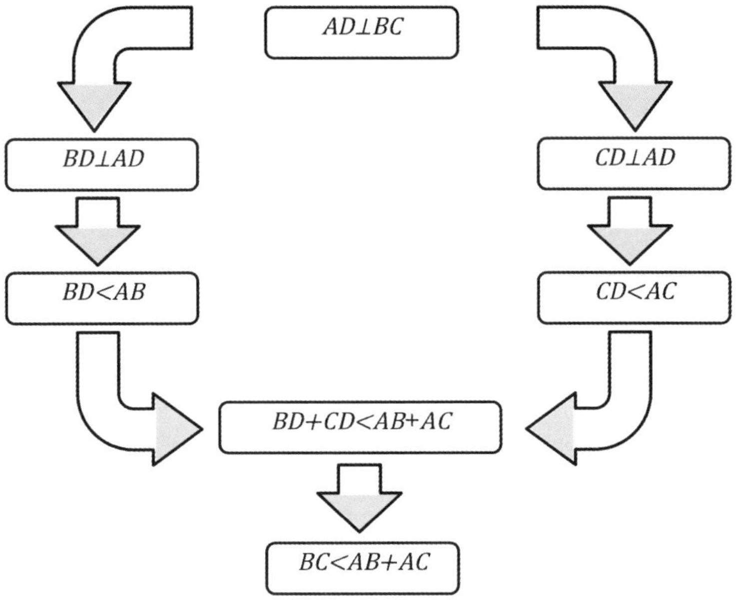

2. Which of the following could represent the lengths of the sides of a triangle? Select all that apply.

- ☐ $2\text{ m}, 4\text{ m}, 7\text{ m}$
- ☐ $3\text{ m}, 8\text{ m}, 10\text{ m}$
- ☐ $9\text{ m}, 10\text{ m}, 11\text{ m}$
- ☐ $4\text{ m}, 5\text{ m}, 9\text{ m}$
- ☐ $7\text{ m}, 13\text{ m}, 18\text{ m}$

Section 6 – Topic 6
More Triangle Proofs

Consider the figures below with $\Delta ABC \cong \Delta DEF$.

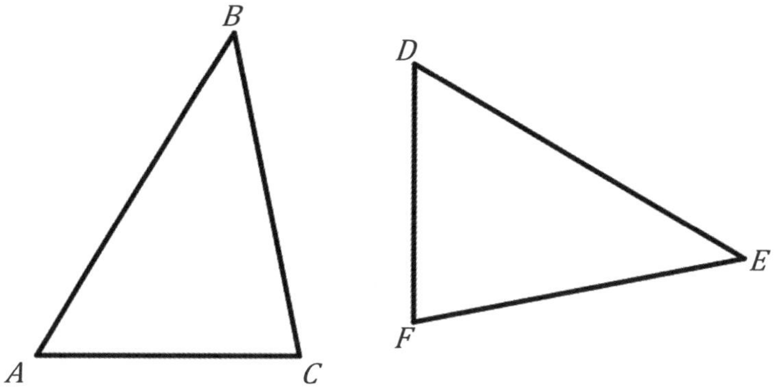

List the congruency statements about these triangles.

Now, consider the following theorem.

> **TAKE NOTE! Postulates & Theorems**
>
> **CPCTC**
> Corresponding parts of congruent triangles are congruent.

When given a congruence statement about two triangles, how can you use CPCTC?

We can use CPCTC to justify a congruence statement of angles or sides when two triangles are proven congruent.

Let's Practice

1. Consider the diagram to the right.

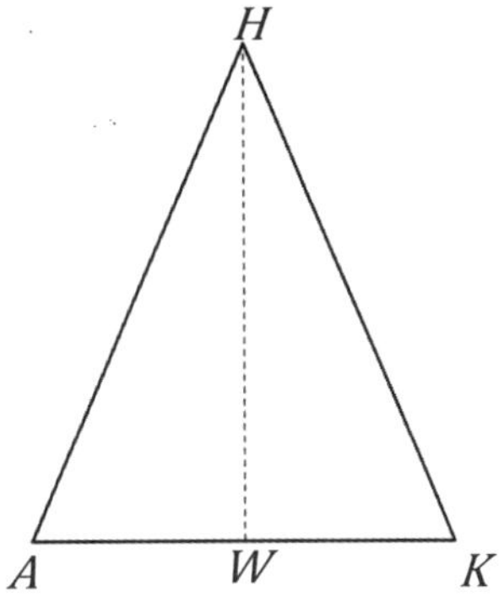

Given: $\overline{AH} \cong \overline{KH}$; $\overline{HW}$ bisects $\angle AHK$

Prove: $\angle A \cong \angle K$

Complete the following two-column proof.

Statements	Reasons
1. $\overline{AH} \cong \overline{HK}$	**1.** Given
2. $\overline{HW}$ bisects $\angle AHK$	**2.** Given
3. $\angle AHW \cong \angle KHW$	**3.** Definition of angle bisector
4. $\overline{HW} \cong \overline{HW}$	**4.** Reflexive Property
5. $\Delta AHW \cong \Delta KHW$	**5.**
6. $\angle A \cong \angle K$	**6.**

2. Consider the figure below.

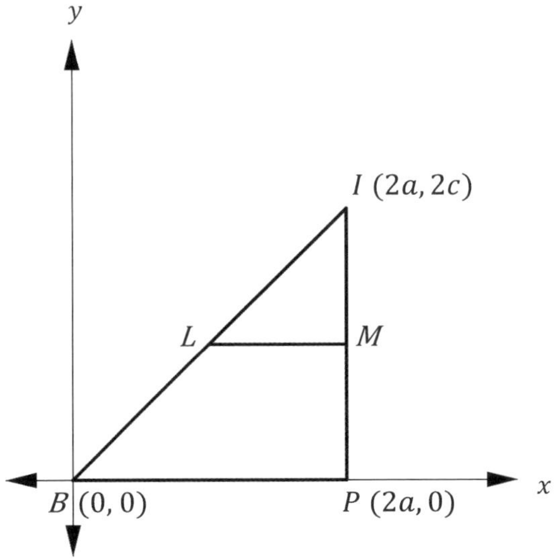

The above figure shows ΔBIP where L is the midpoint of $\overline{BI}$ and M is the midpoint of $\overline{IP}$.

Prove that $\overline{LM} \parallel \overline{BP}$ and $LM = \frac{1}{2}BP$.

Try It!

3. Consider the following diagram.

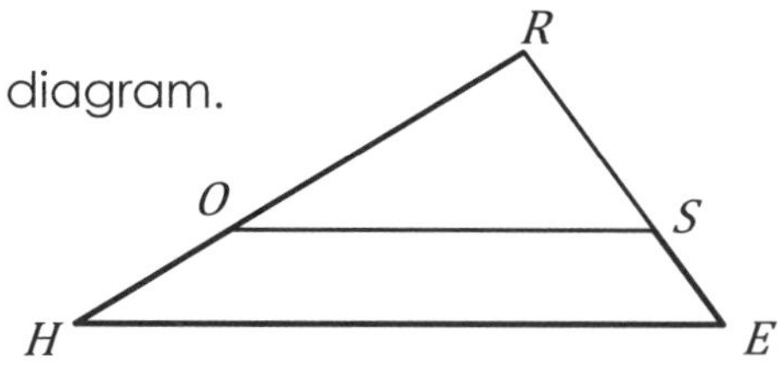

Given: $\frac{OH}{OR} = \frac{SE}{SR}$

Prove: $\overline{OS} \parallel \overline{EH}$

Complete the following two-column proof.

Statements	Reasons
1. $\frac{OH}{OR} = \frac{SE}{SR}$	**1.** Given
2. $1 + \frac{OH}{OR} = 1 + \frac{SE}{SR}$	**2.**
3. $\frac{OR}{OR} + \frac{OH}{OR} = \frac{SR}{SR} + \frac{SE}{SR}$	**3.** Substitution
4. $\frac{\qquad}{OR} = \frac{\qquad}{SR}$	**4.** Substitution
5. $\frac{HR}{OR} = \frac{RE}{RS}$	**5.**
6. $\angle R \cong \angle R$	**6.** Reflexive Property
7. $\Delta ORS \sim \Delta HRE$	**7.**
8. $\angle ROS \cong \angle H$ and $\angle RSO \cong \angle E$	**8.** Definition of Similar Triangles
9. $\overline{OS} \parallel \overline{EH}$	**9.**

4. Consider the figure below.

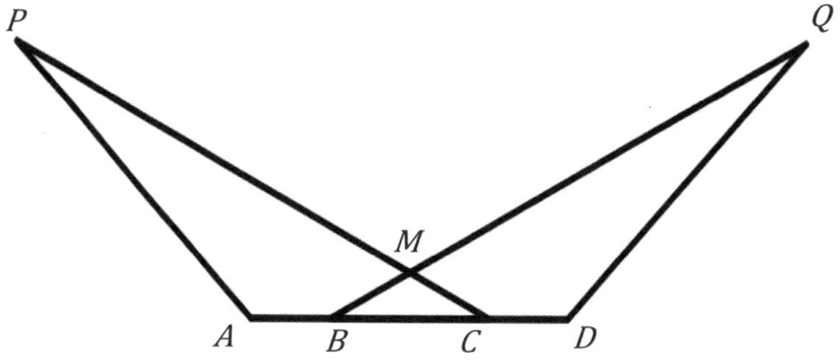

Given: $m\angle A = m\angle D,\ \overline{AP} \cong \overline{DQ},\ \overline{AB} \cong \overline{BC} \cong \overline{CD}$
Prove: $\overline{BM} \cong \overline{CM}$

a. Complete the following two-column proof.

Statements	Reasons
1. $m\angle A = m\angle D$	**1.** Given
2. $\overline{AP} \cong \overline{DQ},\ \overline{AB} \cong \overline{BC} \cong \overline{CD}$	**2.** Given
3.	**3.** Segment Addition Postulate
4. $AB + BC = DB$	**4.**
5.	**5.** Transitive Property
6. $\triangle CAP \cong \triangle BDQ$	**6.**
7.	**7.** CPCTC
8. $\overline{BM} \cong \overline{CM}$	**8.**

b. Prove $\overline{BM} \cong \overline{CM}$ by applying properties of transformations. Justify your steps.

5. Consider the figure below.

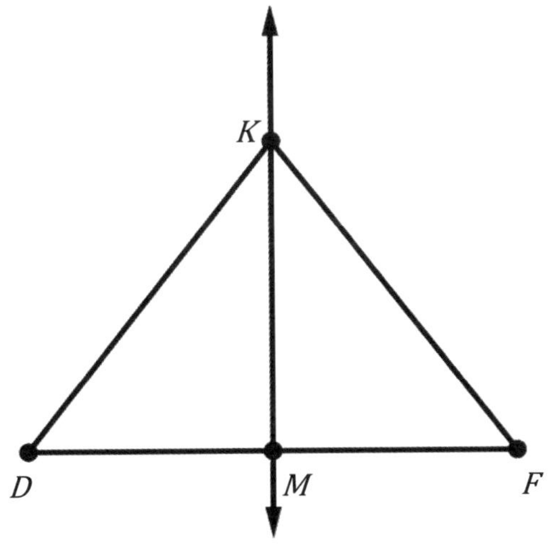

Given: $\overleftrightarrow{KM} \perp \overline{DF}$ and $\overleftrightarrow{KM}$ bisects $\overline{DF}$
Prove: $KD = KF$

Complete the following two-column proof.

Statements	Reasons
1. $\overleftrightarrow{KM} \perp \overline{DF}$, $\overleftrightarrow{KM}$ bisects $\overline{DF}$	**1.** Given
2. $\overline{DM} \cong \overline{FM}$	**2.**
3. $\angle DMK \cong \angle FMK$	**3.** Definition of Perpendicular Lines
4.	**4.** Reflexive Property
5. $\triangle DMK \cong \triangle FMK$	**5.**
6.	**6.** CPCTC
7. $KD = KF$	**7.**

BEAT THE TEST!

1. Consider the diagram and flow-proof below.

Given: $\angle PTS \cong \angle PLE$
$\overline{AP}$ bisects $\angle TAL$

Prove: $\overline{AL} \cong \overline{AT}$

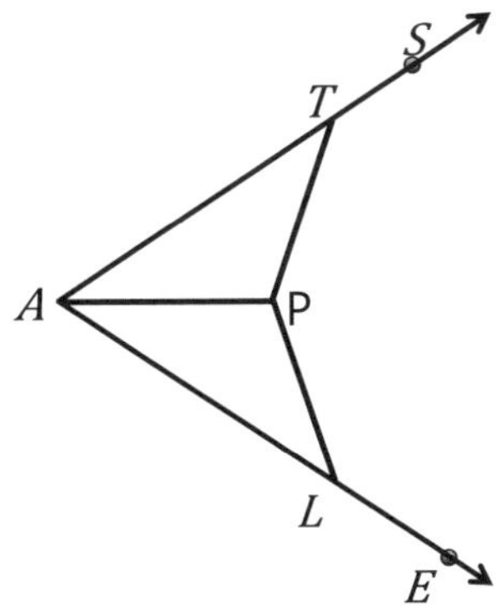

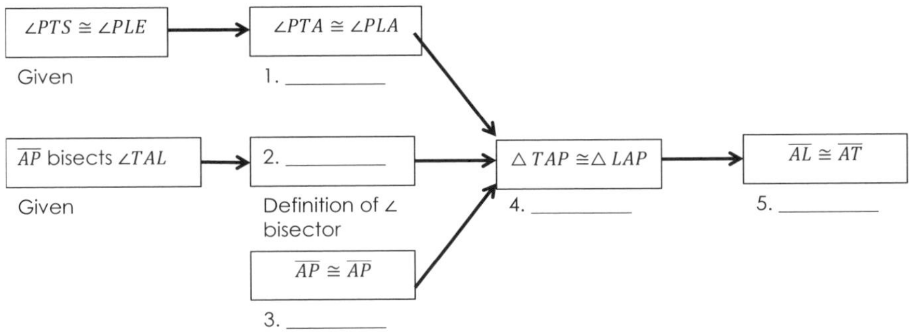

Use the choices below to complete the flow-proof.

A. $\angle TAP \cong \angle LAP$
B. CPCTC
C. AAS
D. Congruent Supplements Theorem
E. Reflexive Property

Section 6 – Topic 7
Inscribed and Circumscribed Circles of Triangles

Consider the figure below.

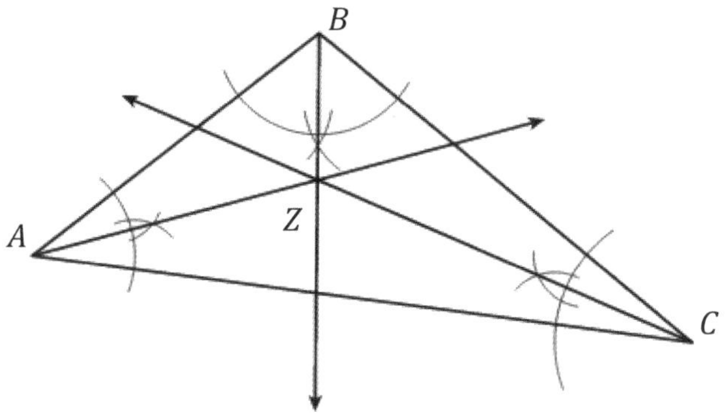

What observations can you make about $\overrightarrow{AZ}$?

What observations can you make about $\overrightarrow{BZ}$?

What observations can you make about $\overrightarrow{CZ}$?

Point Z is called the ________________ of the triangle. It is a point of concurrency formed by the intersection of the three angle bisectors.

Let's Practice!

1. Let $\triangle ABC$ be an arbitrary triangle with angle bisectors $\overline{AI}, \overline{BI}$, and $\overline{CI}$.

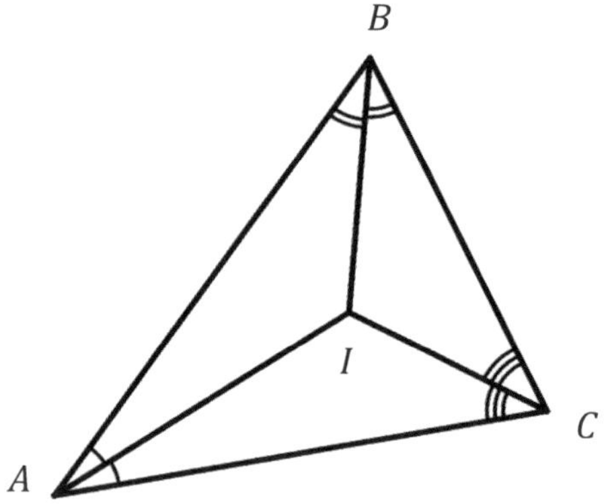

Complete the following paragraph that proves that the three angle bisectors of the internal angles of a triangle are concurrent.

Let's name the bisected angle in $\angle ABC$, $\angle 1$ and $\angle 2$. Then, since $\overline{BI}$ is the angle bisector of $\angle ABC$, ____≅____. Now, let's construct perpendicular lines segments from I to $\overline{AB}$, with the point of intersection labeled as M; from I to $\overline{BC}$, with the point of intersection labeled as N; and from I to $\overline{AC}$, with the point of intersection labeled as P. Notice that ______$\cong \triangle AIP$, ______$\cong \triangle BIN$, and ______$\cong \triangle CIP$, because of AAS. From these congruence statements, we can conclude that $\overline{IM} \cong \overline{IP}$, $\overline{IM} \cong \overline{IN}$, and $\overline{IN} \cong \overline{IP}$, because ____________. Finally, the ____________ Property of Congruence helps us prove that $\overline{IM} \cong \overline{IN} \cong \overline{IP}$. Therefore, the three angle bisectors of the internal angles of a triangle are ______________.

Try It!

2. Consider the figure below.

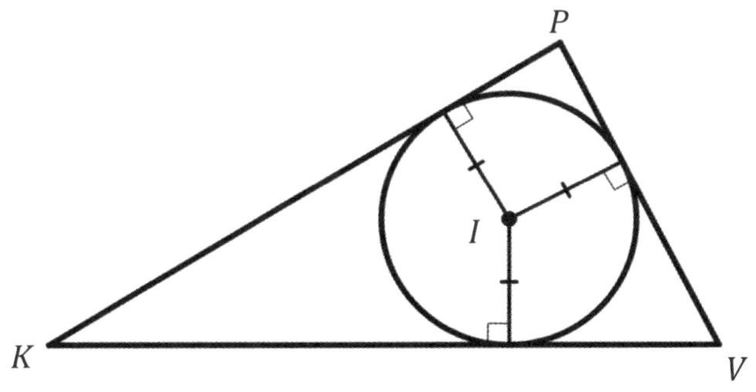

a. What observations can you make about the circle inside the triangle?

b. Complete the following statement.

Point I is the ____________ of both the triangle and the circle, and it is equidistant to the _____________ of the triangle.

Consider the figure below.

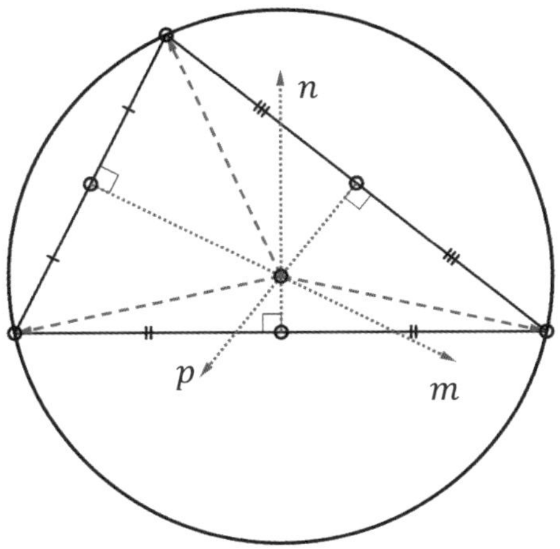

What observations can you make about the circle around the triangle?

What observations can you make about $m, n,$ and p?

Complete the following statements.

- A circle that is circumscribed about a triangle is called a _______________.
- The center of the circle is the point of concurrency of the perpendicular bisectors of the triangle and is called the ____________________. It is also equidistant to the _______________ of the triangle.

Let's Practice!

3. What is the location of the circumcenter of a right triangle?

4. Where is the circumcenter of an obtuse triangle?

Try It!

5. Tina is making part of a wind chime with a flat wooden triangular piece of wood. A wire that is anchored at a point equidistant from the sides of the triangle suspends the piece of wood. Where is the anchor point located?

BEAT THE TEST!

1. Three straight roads create the boundaries of a park as shown below.

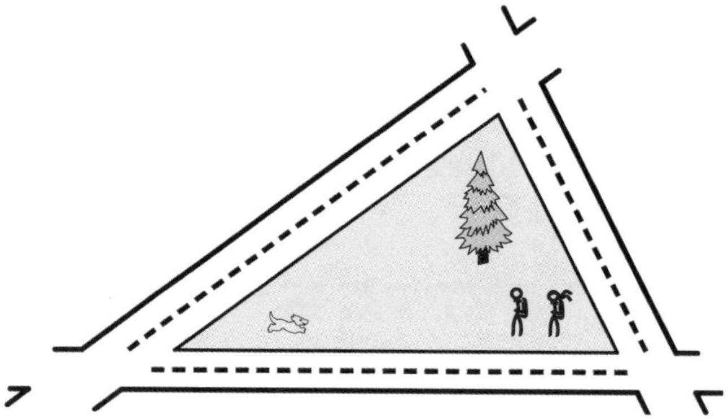

A developer wants to build sidewalks that are perpendicular bisectors of each road and to plant a maple tree where all three sidewalks meet inside the park.

Part A: At what point should the developer plant the maple tree?

Part B: Suppose the sidewalks are already built. Which of the following theorems, postulates, or properties help us prove that the three sidewalks are concurrent?

Ⓐ Hinge Theorem
Ⓑ Perpendicular Bisector Theorem
Ⓒ Transitive Property of Congruence
Ⓓ Triangle Midsegment Theorem

Section 6 – Topic 8
Medians in a Triangle

Consider the figure below.

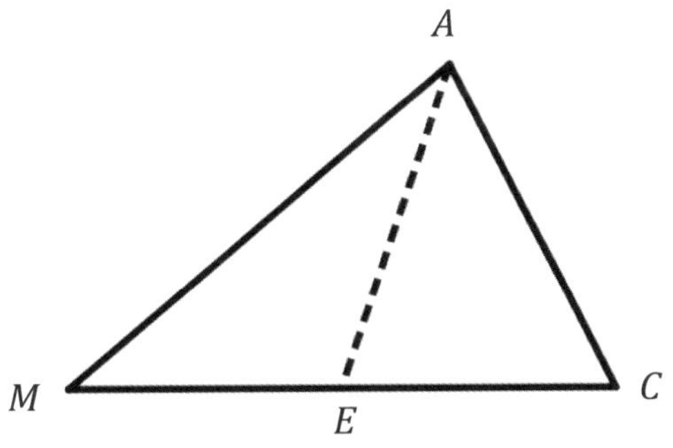

- A ______________ of a triangle is the segment from a vertex to the midpoint of the opposite side.
- Every triangle has ______ medians. Draw the other two medians in $\triangle MAC$.
- The intersection of the three medians is called the ______________, which is the point of concurrency for the medians of a triangle.
- Each median creates two ______________ triangles.
- The length from the vertex to the centroid is ______________ the length from the centroid to the midpoint of the side, which yields a ratio of ______.

Let's Practice!

1. Gretel is creating a logo for her company. She started her design as shown below.

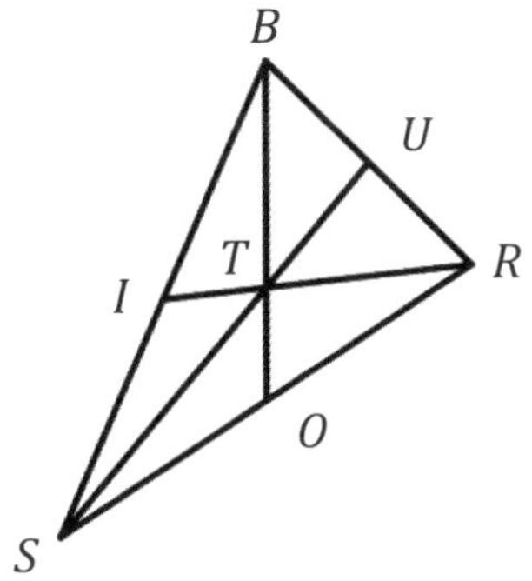

$\overline{IR}, \overline{US}$, and $\overline{OB}$ are all medians of $\triangle BRS$, and T is the centroid. $IR = 2.4$ in., $BT = 1$ in., $UT = 0.7$ in. Find RT, TI, OB, and US.

Try It!

2. Consider the figure below.

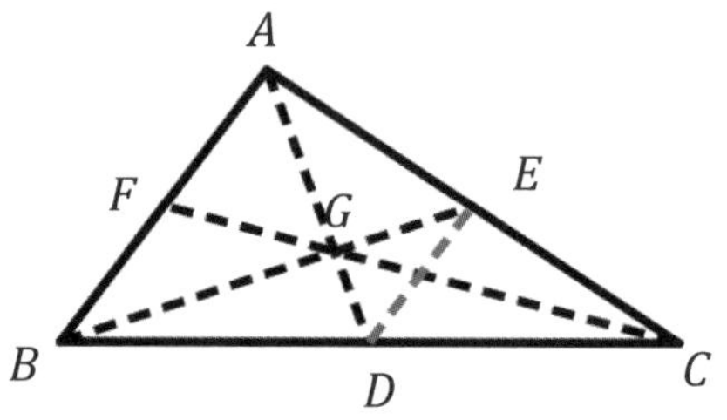

Given: D, E, and F are all midpoints of each of the sides of $\triangle ABC$, and G is the point where $\overline{AD}, \overline{BE}$, and $\overline{CF}$ meet.

Prove: $\overline{AD}, \overline{BE}$, and $\overline{CF}$ are all medians concurrent at G and G is one-third of the distance from the opposite side to the vertex along the median.

BEAT THE TEST!

1. Consider the triangle below.

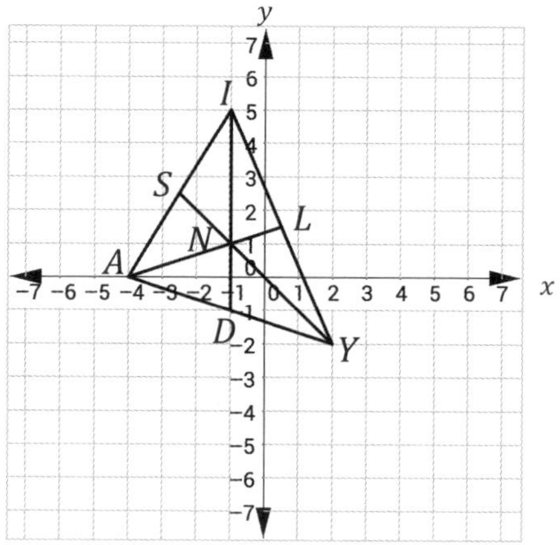

Prove that the ratio of the median from the point of concurrency is $2:1$ using the coordinate geometry of the medians and triangles similarity.

Test Yourself! Practice Tool

Great job! You have reached the end of this section. Now it's time to try the "Test Yourself! Practice Tool," where you can practice all the skills and concepts you learned in this section. Log in to Math Nation and try out the "Test Yourself! Practice Tool" so you can see how well you know these topics!

Section 7: Right Triangles and Trigonometry

Topic 1: The Pythagorean Theorem 183
*Standards Covered:*G-SRT.8, G-SRT.4
- ☐ I can use triangle similarity to prove the Pythagorean Theorem.

Topic 2: The Converse of the Pythagorean Theorem 185
Standards Covered: G-SRT.8
- ☐ I can determine the sides of a right triangle when given three values.

Topic 3: Proving Right Triangles Congruent 187
Standards Covered: G-SRT.5
- ☐ I can use the Hypotenuse-Leg Theorem to prove right triangles are congruent.

Topic 4: Special Right Triangles: 45°-45°-90° 190
Standards Covered: G-SRT.8
- ☐ I can use the features of a 45-45-90 triangle to solve problems.

Topic 5: Special Right Triangles: 30°-60°-90° 192
Standards Covered: G-SRT.8
- ☐ I can use the features of a 30-60-90 triangle to solve problems.

Topic 6: Right Triangles Similarity – Part 1 193
Standards Covered: G-SRT.5
- ☐ I can use the altitude of a triangle to identify similar triangles and determine the lengths of the non-adjacent legs of similar triangles.

Topic 7: Right Triangles Similarity – Part 2 196
Standards Covered: G-SRT.5
- ☐ I can use similarity in right triangles to find the lengths of adjacent sides.

Topic 8: Introduction to Trigonometry – Part 1 199
Standards Covered: G-SRT.7, G-SRT.6
- ☐ I can use trigonometric functions to find the value of missing sides.

Topic 9: Introduction to Trigonometry – Part 2 202
Standards Covered: G-SRT.8
- ☐ I can use trigonometric functions to find the value of missing angles.

Topic 10: Angles of Elevation and Depression 204
Standards Covered: G-SRT.8
- ☐ I can use trigonometric ratios to solve real-world problems.

Topic 11: Segments in Regular Polygons 207
Standards Covered: G-SRT.8
- ☐ I can compare diagonals, radii, and apothem within a polygon.

Topic 12: Area of Other Polygons 210
*Standards Covered:*G-MG.1
- ☐ I can calculate the area of a regular polygon given the perimeter and radius of a polygon.

Honors Topic 1: Proving and Applying the Law of Sines .... Available Online
Standards Covered: G-SRT.10 G-SRT.11
- ☐ I can use the Law of Sines to solve for a missing side or angle of a triangle.

Honors Topic 2: Proving and Applying the Law of Cosines .... Available Online
Standards Covered: G-SRT.10, G-SRT.11
- ☐ I can use the Law of Cosines to find unknown measurements in right and non-right triangles.

Visit MathNation.com or search "Math Nation" in your phone or tablet's app store to watch the videos that go along with this workbook!

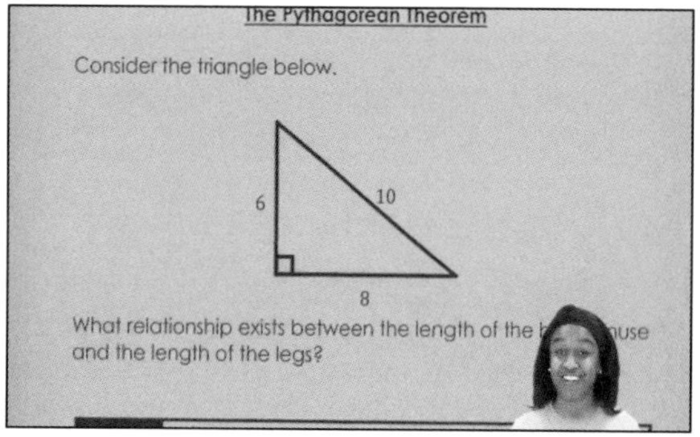

The following Michigan Mathematics Standards will be covered in this section:
G-MG.1 - Use geometric shapes. their measures, and their properties to describe objects.
G-SRT.10 - Prove the Laws of Sines and Cosines and use them to solve problems.
G-SRT.11- Understand and apply the Law of Sines and the Law of Cosines to find unknown measurements in right and non-right triangles (e.g., surveying problems, resultant forces).
G-SRT.4 - Prove theorems about triangles. *Theorems include: a line parallel to one side of a triangle divides the other two proportionally, and conversely; the Pythagorean Theorem proved using triangle similarity.*
G-SRT.5 - Use congruence and similarity criteria for triangles to solve problems and to prove relationships in geometric figures.
G-SRT.6 - Understand that by similarity, side ratios in right triangles are properties of the angles in the triangle, leading to definitions of trigonometric ratios for acute angles.
G-SRT.7 - Explain and use the relationship between the sine and cosine of complementary angles.
G-SRT.8 - Use trigonometric ratios and Pythagorean Theorem to solve right triangles in applied problems.

Section 7: Right Triangles and Trigonometry
Section 7 – Topic 1
The Pythagorean Theorem

Consider the triangle below.

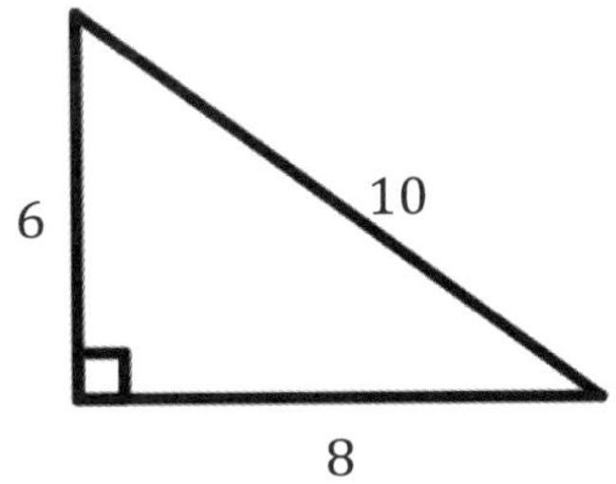

What relationship exists between the length of the hypotenuse and the length of the legs?

TAKE NOTE! *Postulates & Theorems*

Pythagorean Theorem
In a right triangle, the square of the hypotenuse (the side opposite to the right angle) is equal to the sum of the squares of the other two sides.

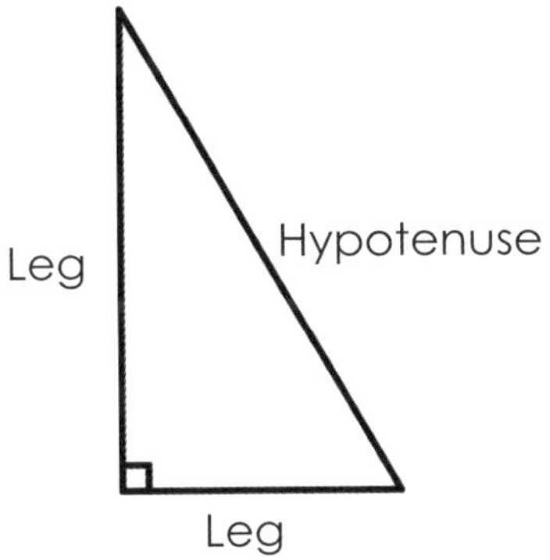

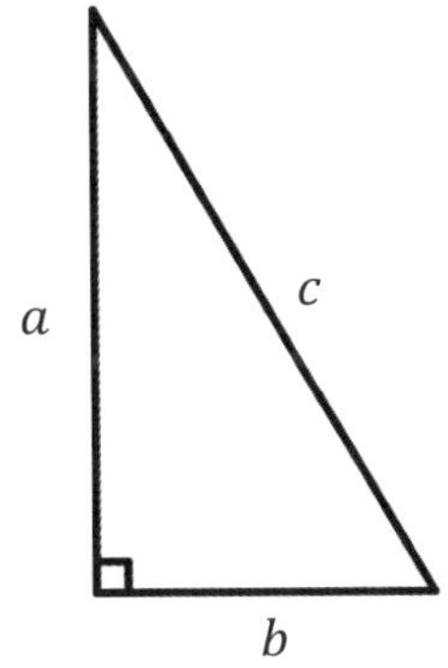

$$a^2 + b^2 = c^2$$

Consider the following diagram and complete the two-column proof below.

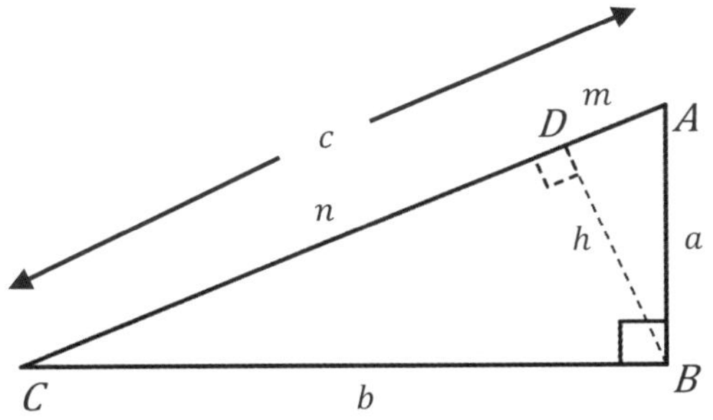

Given: $\triangle ABC \sim \triangle ADB \sim \triangle BDC$
Prove: $a^2 + b^2 = c^2$ using triangle similarity.

Statements	Reasons
1.	**1.** Given
2.	**2.** Corresponding sides of similar triangles are proportional
3.	**3.** Multiplication Property Of Equality
4. $a^2 + b^2 = cm + cn$	**4.**
5.	**5.** Distributive Property
6. $AD + DC = AC$ or $m + n = c$	**6.**
7. $a^2 + b^2 = c^2$	**7.**

Let's Practice!

1. A business building has several office spaces for rent. Each office is in the shape of a right triangle. If one side of the office is 11 feet long and the longest side is 15 feet long, what is the length of the other side?

Try It!

2. Mr. Roosevelt is leaning a ladder against the side of his son's tree house to repair the roof. The top of the ladder reaches the roof, which is 18 feet from the ground. The base of the ladder is 5 feet away from the tree. How long is the ladder?

BEAT THE TEST!

1. A baseball diamond is actually a square with sides of 90 feet.

   Part A: If a runner tries to steal second base, how far must the catcher, who is at home plate, throw the ball to get the runner out?

   Part B: Explain why runners try to steal second base more often than third base.

Section 7 – Topic 2
The Converse of the Pythagorean Theorem

Suppose you are given a triangle and the lengths of the sides. How can you determine if the triangle is a right triangle?

A Pythagorean triple is a set of positive integers a, b, and c that satisfy the Pythagorean Theorem, $a^2 + b^2 = c^2$.

The side lengths of a right triangle, 3, 4, and 5, form a Pythagorean triple. Prove that each set of numbers below is a Pythagorean triple.

- $5, 12, 13$

- $8, 15, 17$

- $7, 24, 25$

Hypothesize if multiples of Pythagorean triples are still Pythagorean triples. Justify your answer.

TAKE NOTE! Postulates & Theorems

Converse Pythagorean Theorem

If the square of one side of a triangle is equal to the sum of the squares of the other two sides, then the triangle is a right triangle.

Let's Practice!

1. Zully is designing a bird feeder that her husband will build for the little birds that come to eat in the mornings. The bird feeder must be a right triangle. The first draft of her design is displayed to the right.

   Does this design contain a right triangle? Justify your answer.

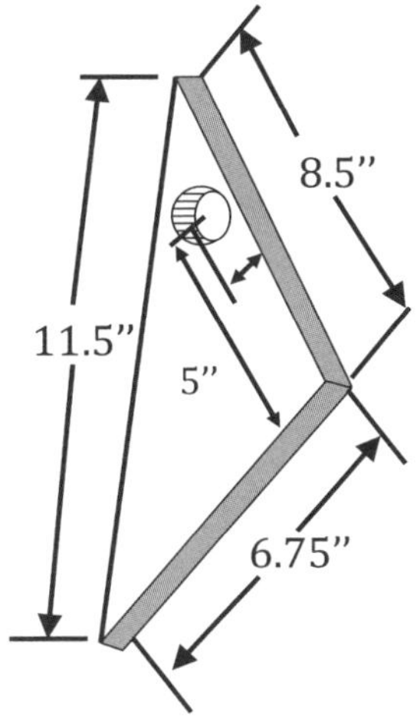

Try It!

2. Mr. Chris designed a Pratt Truss bridge with a structure that slanted towards the center of the bridge. In order to be a Pratt Truss bridge, the bridge has to contain right triangles in its design. However, his design was rejected by the construction firm. The firm said that Mr. Chris's design failed to meet the Pratt Truss requirements.

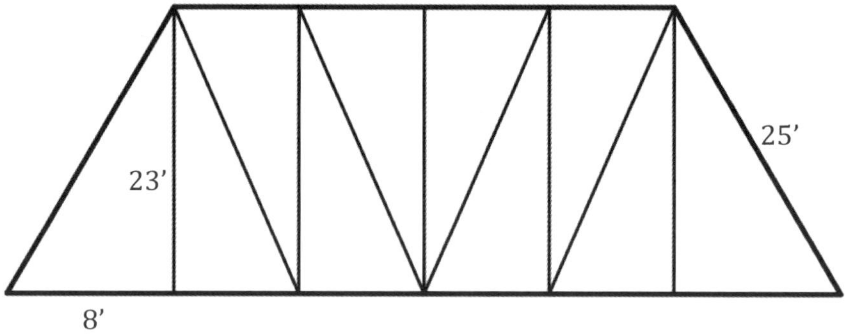

   a. Consider the above representation of the bridge Mr. Chris designed. Prove that the construction firm was correct in its rejection of Mr. Chris's design.

   b. What options does Mr. Chris have to fix the design? Justify your answer.

BEAT THE TEST!

1. Clay designs roofs that form 2 congruent right triangles. His designs are flawless. He submitted his latest design to a firm along with three other contractors, and the firm selected Clay's plan. Which of the following designs is Clay's design?

Ⓐ
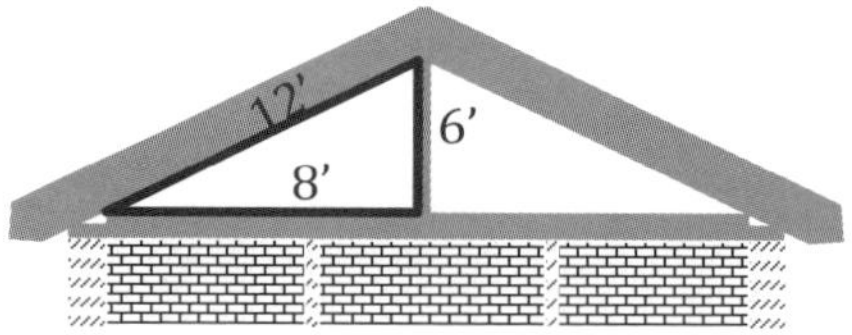

Ⓑ
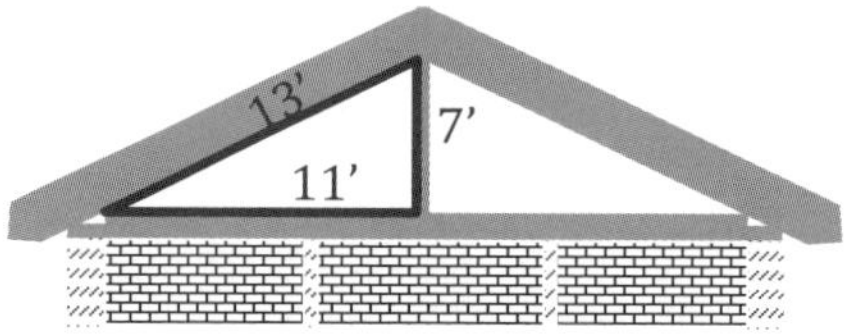

Ⓒ
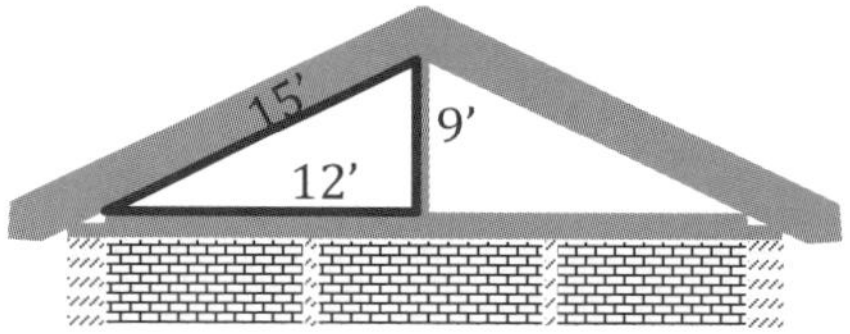

Ⓓ
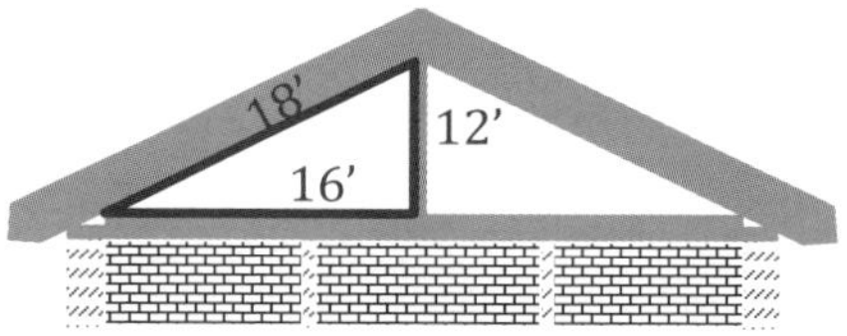

Section 7 – Topic 3
Proving Right Triangles Congruent

Let's review the four postulates that can be used to prove triangles are congruent.

Hypotenuse-Leg (HL) Theorem is another way to prove triangles are congruent.

> **TAKE NOTE! Postulates & Theorems**
> **The Hypotenuse-Leg (HL) Theorem**
> Two right triangles are said to be congruent if their corresponding hypotenuse and at least one of their legs are congruent.

Consider the diagram below.

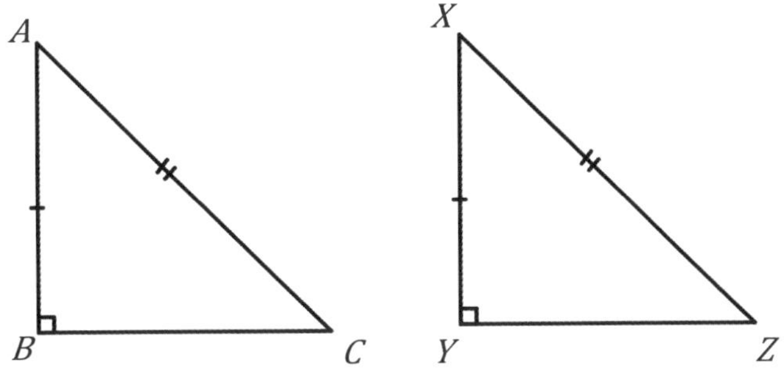

List three statements that prove the triangles are congruent by the HL Theorem.

Let's Practice

1. Consider ΔSQP and ΔRPQ in the diagram below. Complete the two column proof.

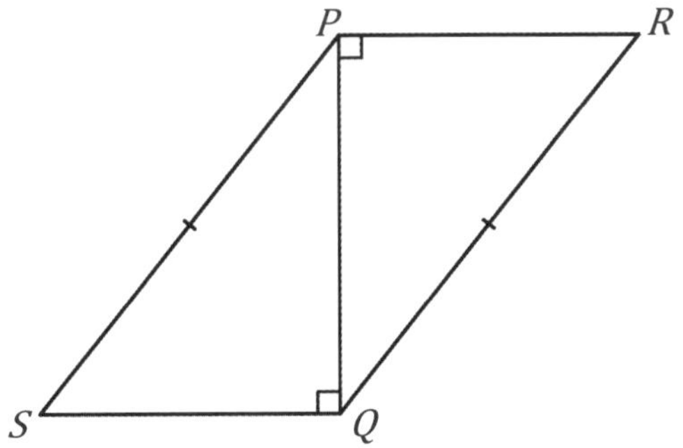

Given: ΔSQP and ΔRPQ are right triangles and $\overline{SP} \cong \overline{QR}$.
Prove: $\Delta SQP \cong \Delta RPQ$

Statements	Reasons
1. ΔSQP and ΔRPQ are right triangles.	**1.**
2.	**2.** Given
3.	**3.** Reflexive Property of Congruence
4. $\Delta SQP \cong \Delta RPQ$	**4.**

2. Consider the following diagrams.

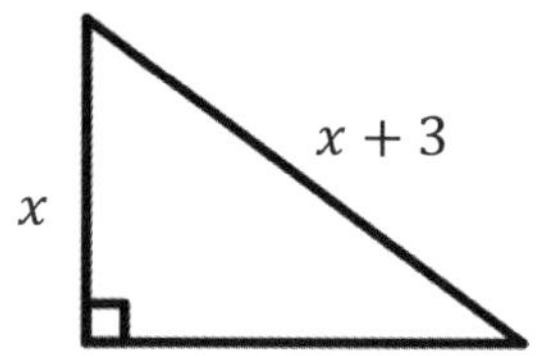

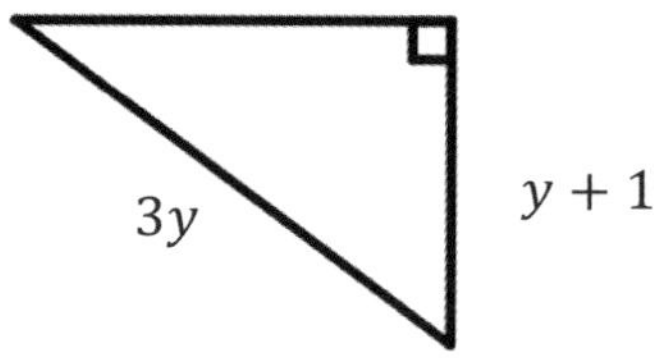

Find the values of x and y that prove the two triangles are congruent according to the HL Theorem.

Try It!

3. Consider ΔABC and ΔADC in the diagram below. Complete the two column proof.

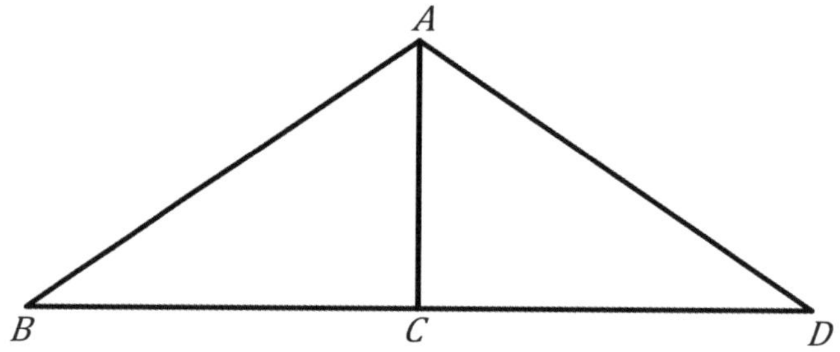

Given: $\overline{AC}$ is perpendicular to $\overline{BD}$; $\overline{AB} \cong \overline{AD}$

Prove: $\Delta ABC \cong \Delta ADC$

Statements	Reasons
1. $\overline{AC}$ is perpendicular to $\overline{BD}$.	**1.** Given
2. $\angle ACB$ and $\angle ACD$ are right angles.	**2.**
3. $\overline{AB} \cong \overline{AD}$	**3.** Given
4. $\overline{AC} \cong \overline{AC}$	**4.**
5. $\Delta ABC \cong \Delta ADC$	**5.**

4. Consider the diagrams below.

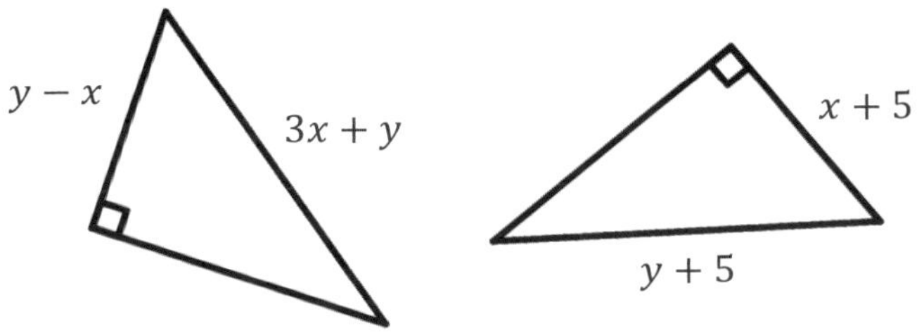

Find the values of x and y that make the right triangles congruent.

BEAT THE TEST!

1. Engineers are designing a new bridge to cross the Intracoastal Waterway. Below is a diagram that represents a partial side view of the bridge. The bridge must be designed so that $\Delta ABC \cong \Delta EDC$. Engineers have measured the support beams, represented by $\overline{AC}$ and $\overline{EC}$ in the diagram, and found they are both $120\ ft$ long. The engineers also determined that beams $\overline{AB}$ and $\overline{ED}$ are perpendicular to the bridge, $\overline{BD}$. Point C represents the midpoint of $\overline{BD}$.

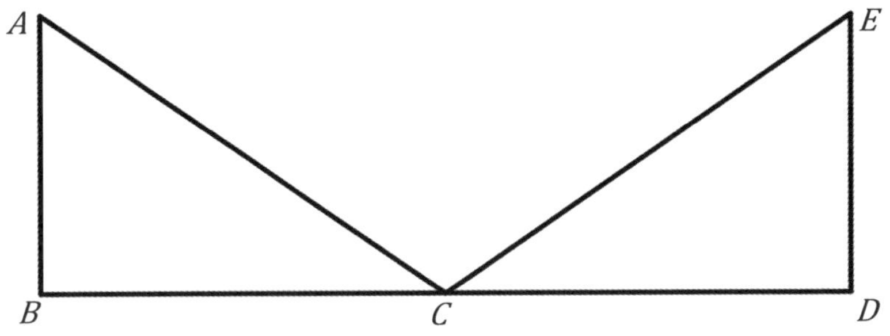

Complete the two-column proof on the next page to prove $\Delta ABC \cong \Delta EDC$.

Statements	Reasons
1.	**1.** Given
2. $\overline{AB} \perp \overline{BD}$ and $\overline{ED} \perp \overline{BD}$	**2.**
3.	**3.** Definition of a midpoint
4. $\angle ABC$ and $\angle EDC$ are right angles.	**4.**
5. $\Delta ABC \cong \Delta EDC$	**5.**

Section 7 – Topic 4
Special Right Triangles: $45° - 45° - 90°$

Use the Pythagorean Theorem to find the missing lengths of the following triangles.

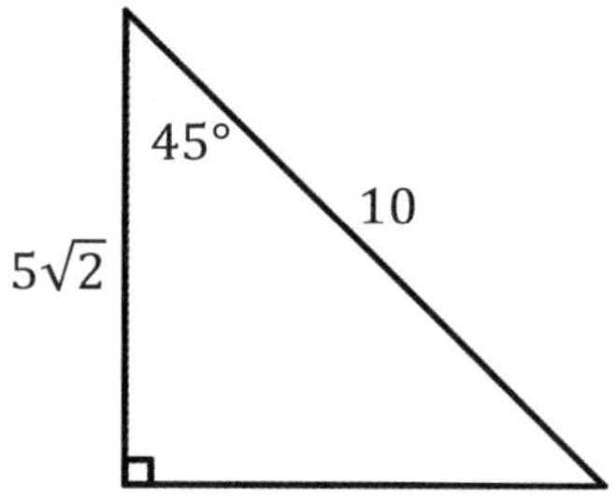

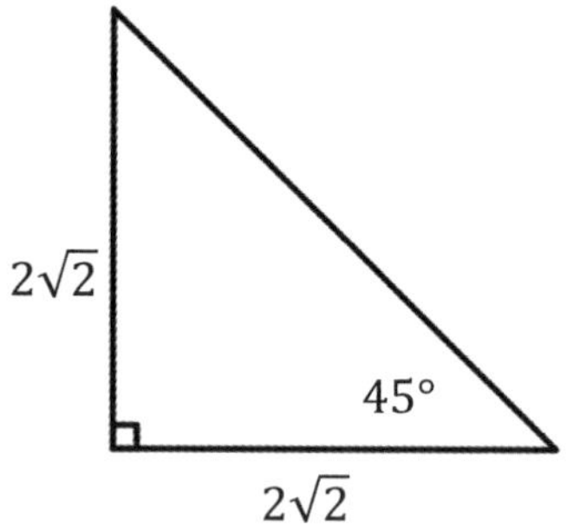

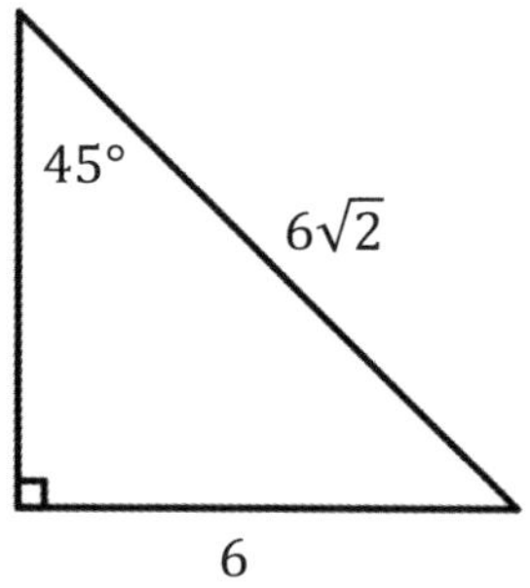

Choose three patterns that you observe in the three right triangles and list them below.

Let's Practice!

1. Consider the following $45° - 45° - 90°$ triangle. Prove that the ratio of the hypotenuse to one of the legs is $\sqrt{2}:1$.

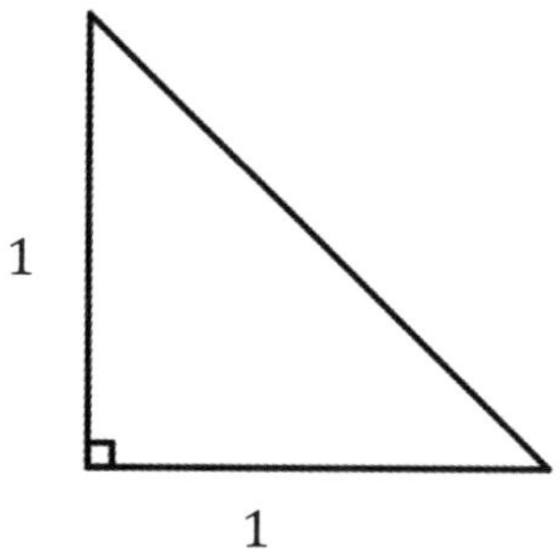

2. Find the hypotenuse of a $45° - 45° - 90°$ triangle with legs equal to 5 cm.

Try It!

3. Find the length of the sides of a square with a diagonal of $25\frac{2}{3}$ meters.

4. The Tilley household wants to build a patio deck in the shape of a $45° - 45° - 90°$ triangle in a nice corner section of their backyard. They have enough room for a triangular deck with a leg measuring 36 feet. What will the length of the longest side be?

BEAT THE TEST!

1. Consider the drawing below.

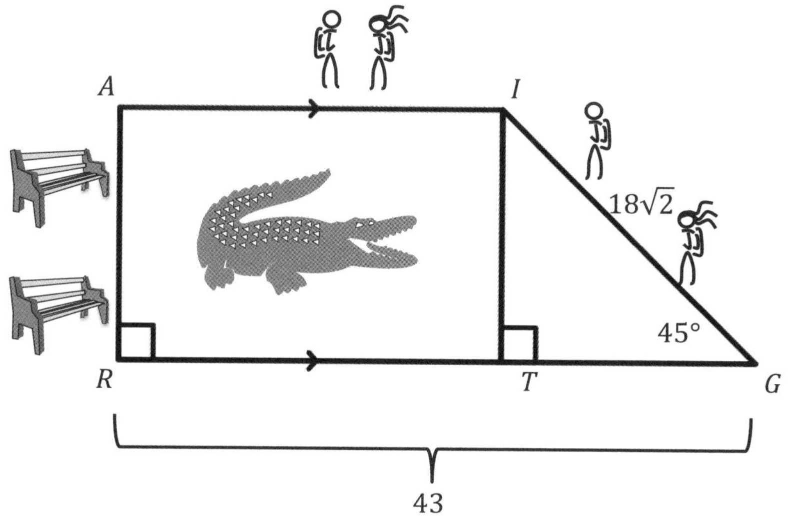

Part A: What is the perimeter of the figure?

Part B: Write a 3 – sentence long short story about the drawing and the calculations made in *Part A*.

Section 7 – Topic 5
Special Right Triangles: $30° - 60° - 90°$

Use the Pythagorean Theorem to find the missing lengths of the following triangles.

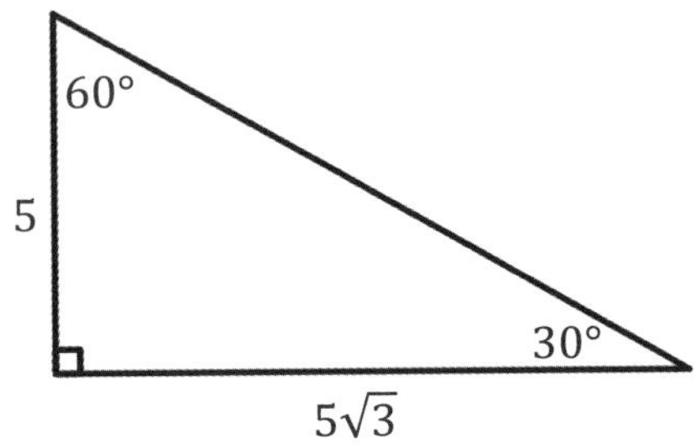

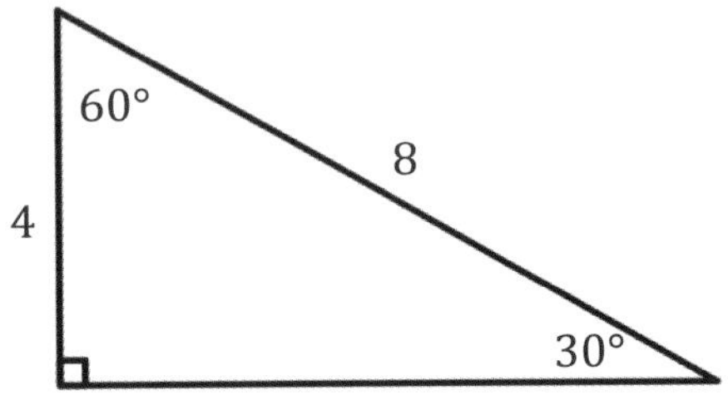

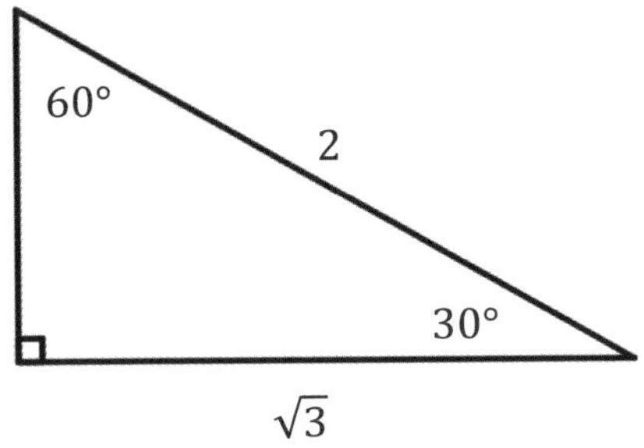

Choose three patterns that you observe in the three right triangles and list them below.

Let's Practice!

1. The length of a hypotenuse of a $30° - 60° - 90°$ right triangle is 17 yards. Find the other two lengths.

Try It!

2. A right triangle has a leg with a length of 34 inches and a hypotenuse with a length of 68 inches. A student notices that the hypotenuse is twice the length of the given leg and says that this means it is a $30° - 60° - 90°$ triangle. If the student is correct, what should the length of the remaining leg be? Explain your answer. Confirm your answer using the Pythagorean Theorem.

BEAT THE TEST!

1. The base of the engineering building at Lenovo Tech Industries is approximately a $30° - 60° - 90°$ triangle with a hypotenuse of about 294 feet. The base of the engineering building at Asus Tech Industries is approximately an isosceles right triangle with a side about $144.5\sqrt{2}$ feet.

   What is the difference between the perimeters of the two buildings? Round your answer to the nearest hundredth.

Section 7 – Topic 6
Right Triangles Similarity – Part 1

Make observations about the following triangles.

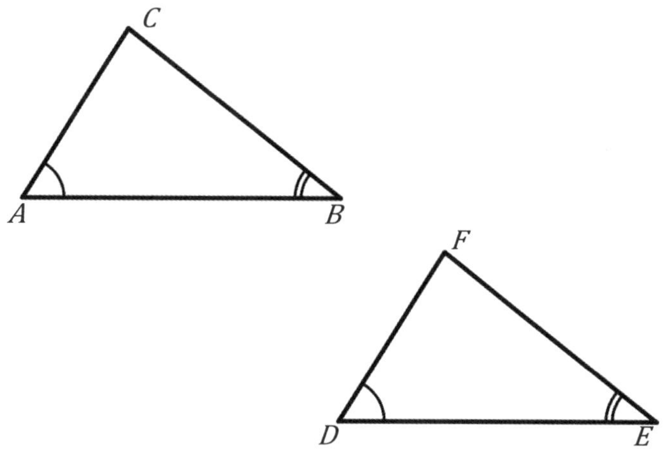

These triangles are similar by the ____________________.

Consider the diagrams below.

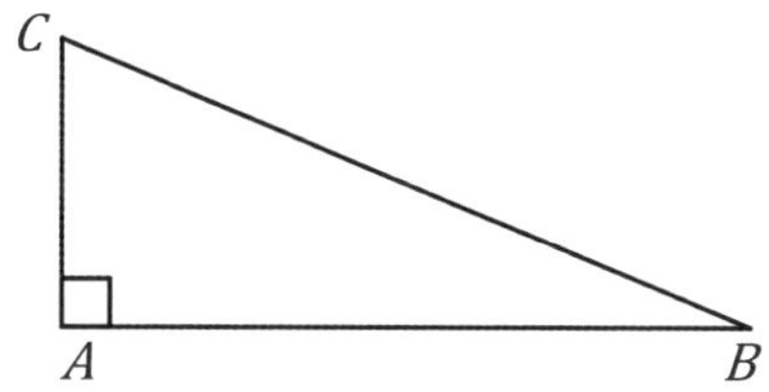

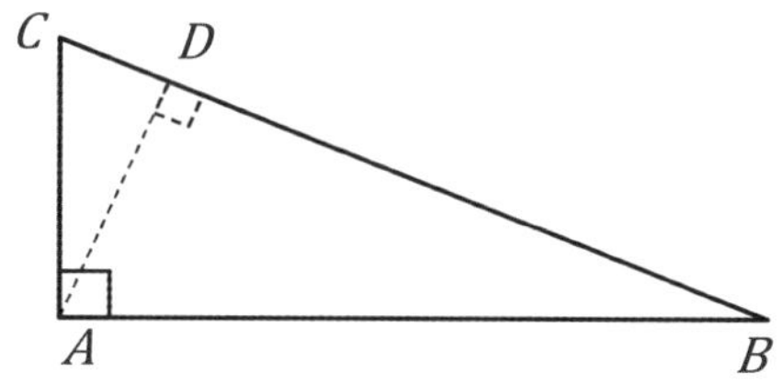

Make observations about ΔABD and ΔACD.

TAKE NOTE! *Postulates & Theorems*

Right Triangle Altitude Theorem

If the altitude is drawn to the hypotenuse of a right triangle, then the two triangles formed are similar to the original triangle and to each other.

Let's Practice!

1. Consider the following diagram.

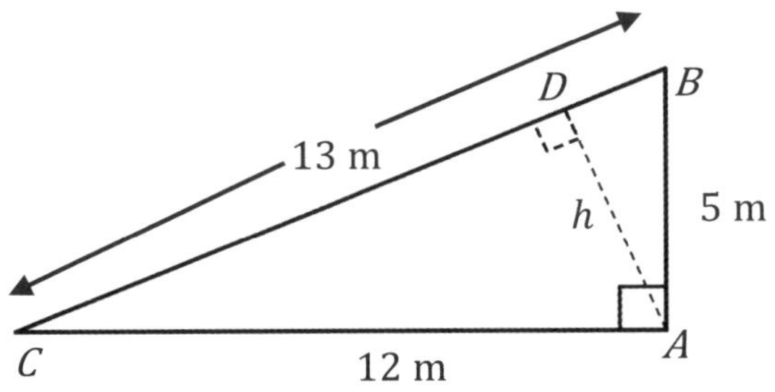

a. Identify the similar triangles in the above diagram.

b. Find h in the above diagram.

Try It!

2. A roof's cross section forms a right angle. Consider the diagram below that shows the approximate dimensions of this cross section.

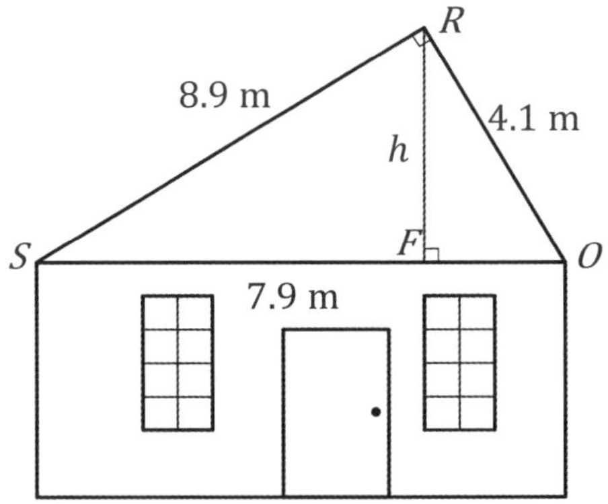

a. Identify the similar triangles represented in the above figure.

b. Find the height h of the roof represented above.

TAKE NOTE! *Postulates & Theorems*

Geometric Mean Theorem: Altitude Rule

In a right triangle, the altitude from the right angle to the hypotenuse divides the hypotenuse into two segments. The length of the altitude is the geometric mean of the lengths of the two segments.

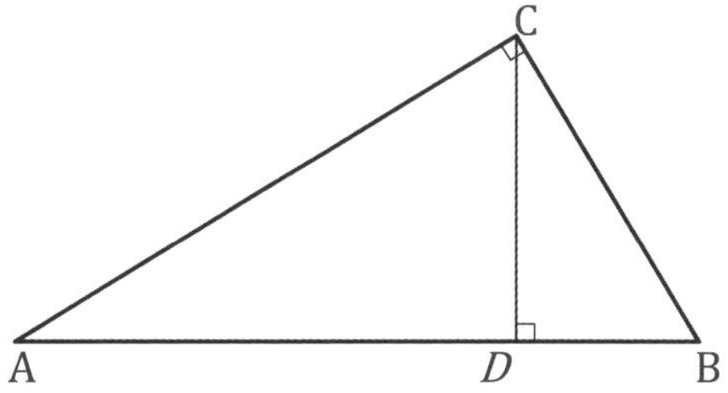

$\frac{AD}{\square} = \frac{\square}{DB}$

TAKE NOTE! *Postulates & Theorems*

Geometric Mean Theorem: Leg Rule

In a right triangle, the altitude from the right angle to the hypotenuse divides the hypotenuse into two segments. The length of each leg of the right triangle is the geometric mean of the lengths of the hypotenuse and the segment of the hypotenuse that is adjacent to the leg.

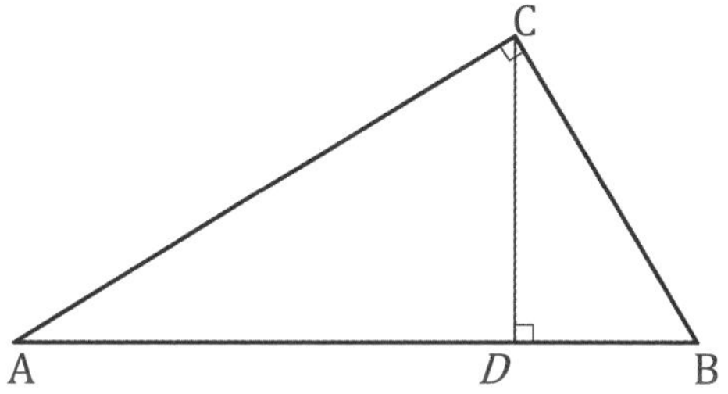

$\frac{AB}{\square} = \frac{\square}{DB}$

or

$\frac{AB}{\square} = \frac{\square}{AD}$

Consider the following diagram.

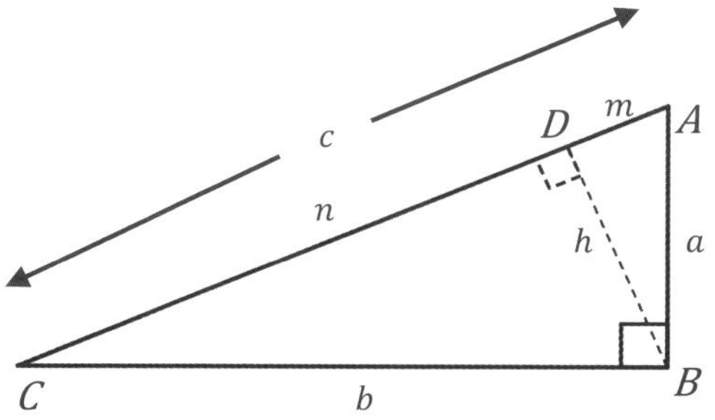

Can we accept $\triangle ADB \sim \triangle BDC$ as a given statement? Justify your answer.

Complete the following two-column proof to prove that $h = \sqrt{mn}$.

Statements	Reasons
1.	**1.** Given
2. $\frac{m}{h} = \frac{h}{n}$	**2.**
3.	**3.** Multiplication Property of Equality
4. $h = \sqrt{mn}$	**4.**

Section 7 – Topic 7
Right Triangles Similarity – Part 2

Let's Practice!

1. Consider the diagram below and find the value of x.

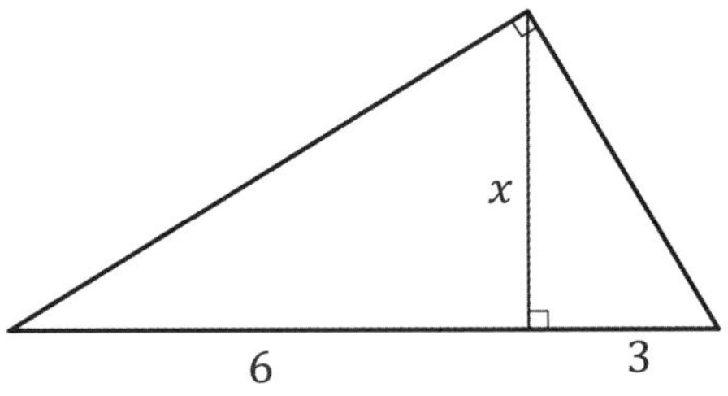

2. Consider the diagram below and find the value of y.

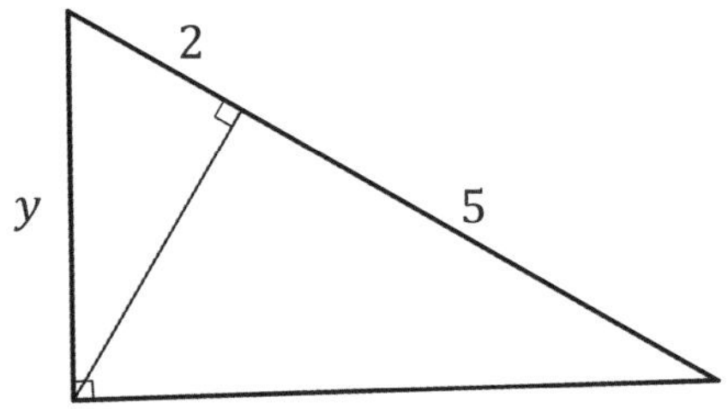

3. Consider the diagram below.

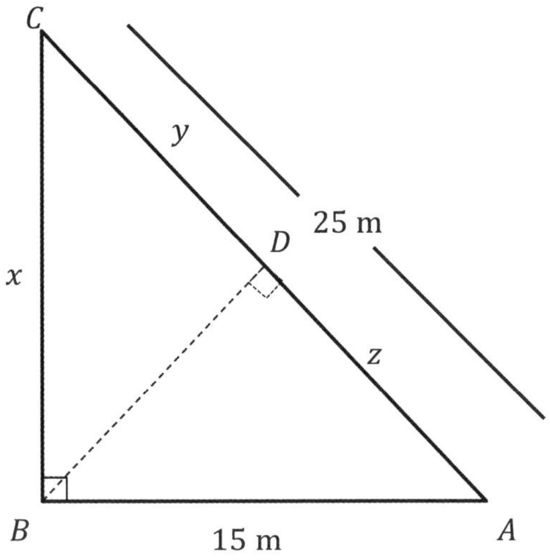

Given: $\Delta CDB \sim \Delta ADB$

Prove: $x = 20\ m$
$y = 16\ m$
$z = 9\ m$

Try It!

4. Consider the diagram below.

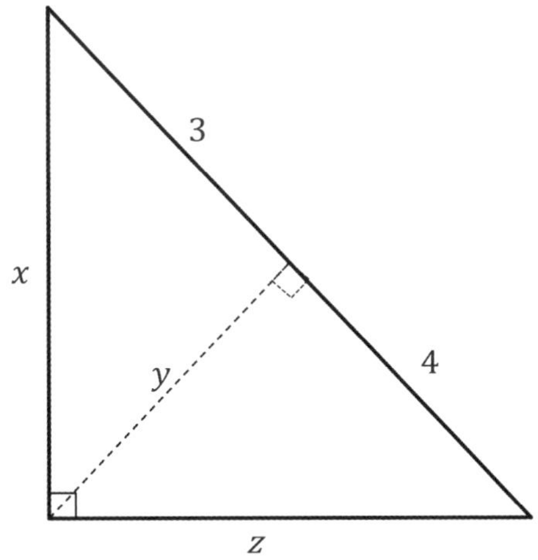

Find the values of x, y, and z to the nearest tenth.

5. A cruise port, a business park, and a federally protected forest are located at the vertices of a right triangle formed by three highways. The port and business park are 6.0 miles apart. The distance between the port and the forest is 3.6 miles, and the distance between the business park and the forest is 4.8 miles.

   A service road will be constructed from the main entrance of the forest to the highway that connects the port and business park. What is the shortest possible length for the service road? Round your answer to the nearest tenth.

BEAT THE TEST!

1. Consider the statement below.

   In a right triangle, the altitude from the right angle to the hypotenuse divides the hypotenuse into two segments. The length of the altitude is the geometric mean of the lengths of the two segments.

   Which of the following figures is a counterexample of the statement above?

Ⓐ

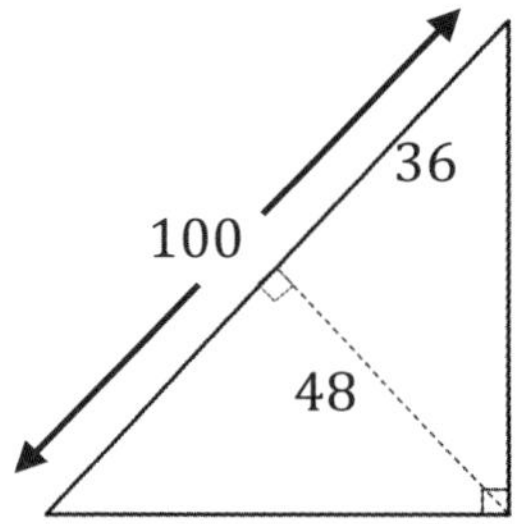

Ⓑ

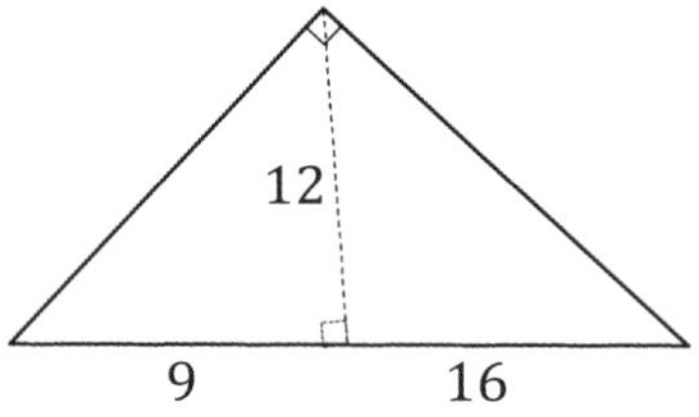

Ⓒ

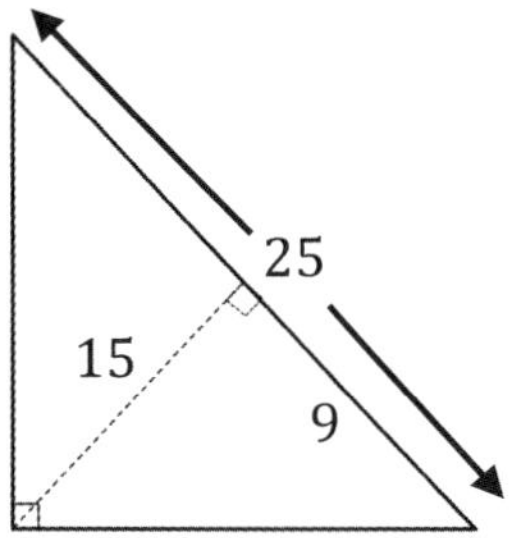

Ⓓ

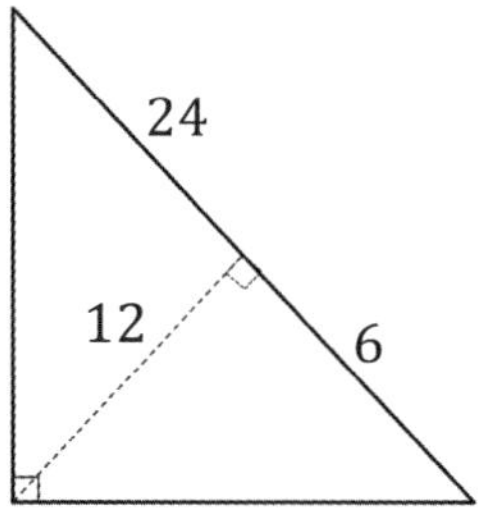

2. A shopping center has the shape of a right triangle with sides measuring $600\sqrt{3}$ meters, 600 meters, and $1{,}200$ meters. During the holidays and busy seasons, the shopping center is so crowded that it needs another walkway. The owners will construct the walkway from the right angle to the hypotenuse. They want to use the shortest possible length for the walkway.

   a. Determine the length of the segment of the hypotenuse adjacent to the shorter leg.

   ☐ meters.

   b. Determine the length of the new walkway.

   ☐ meters.

Section 7 – Topic 8
Introduction to Trigonometry – Part 1

In previous lessons, we learned that the lengths of the sides of a right triangle have a certain relationship, which allows us to use the ____________________________________.

Consider the following right triangles.

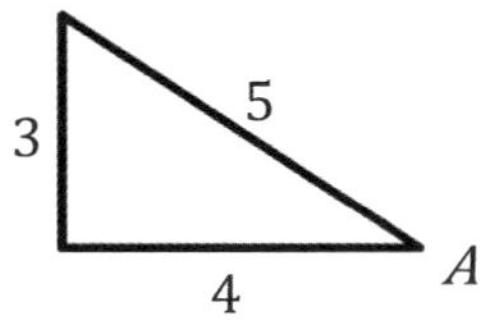

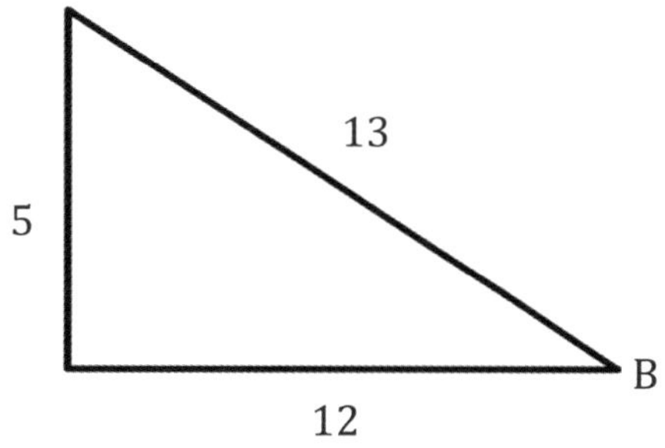

For angle A, find the ratio of the opposite leg to the hypotenuse.

$$\frac{Opposite}{Hypotenuse} = \_\_\_\_$$

Find the same ratio for angle B. ______ = ______

The ratio of the lengths of any 2 sides of a right triangle is a ________________________ ________________________.

Let's examine the three main trigonometric ratios. Complete the statements below.

$$\_\_\_\_\_\_\_ = \frac{leg\ opposite\ to\ the\ angle}{hypotenuse}$$

$$\_\_\_\_\_\_\_ = \frac{leg\ adjacent\ to\ the\ angle}{hypotenuse}$$

$$\_\_\_\_\_\_\_ = \frac{leg\ opposite\ to\ the\ angle}{leg\ adjacent\ to\ the\ angle}$$

Let's Practice!

1. Consider the figure below.

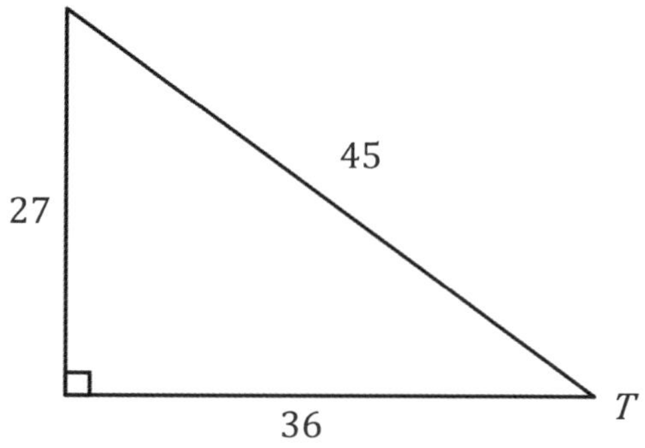

Find the sine, cosine, and tangent of $\angle T$ for the figure.

Try It!

2. Consider the figure below.

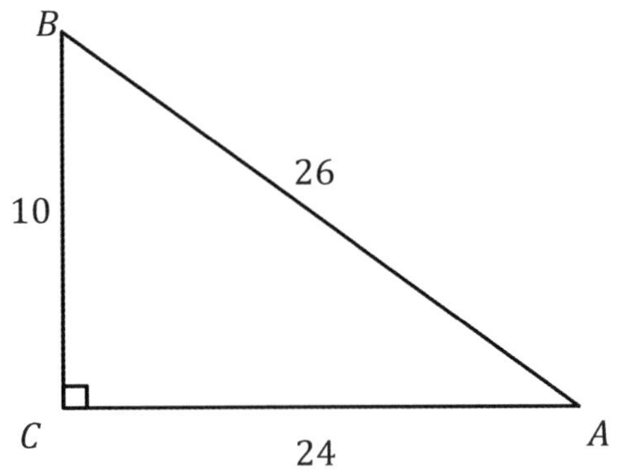

a. Find $\sin A$ for the above triangle.

b. Find $\cos B$ for the above triangle.

c. What do you notice about the values of $\sin A$ and $\cos B$?

Now, let's consider the figure below.

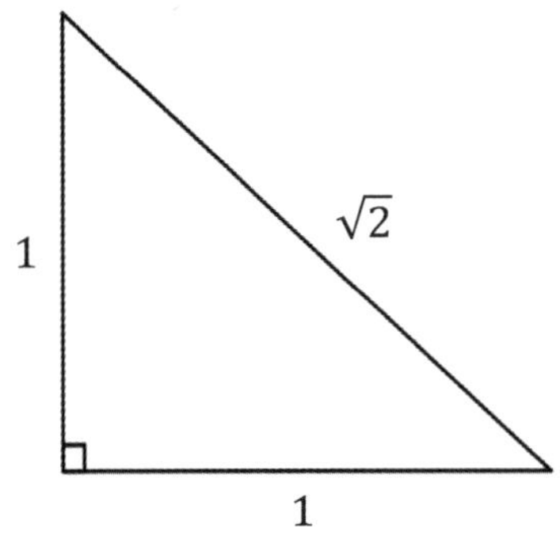

The triangle above is a special right triangle known as the ______ ______ ______ triangle. We know that the two non-right angles measure ______.

Write proportions for $\sin$, $\cos$, and $\tan$ of the acute angles of the triangle.

Use a calculator to verify the proportions.

If there is an unknown length, we can set up an equation to find it.

Let's Practice!

3. Consider the following figure.

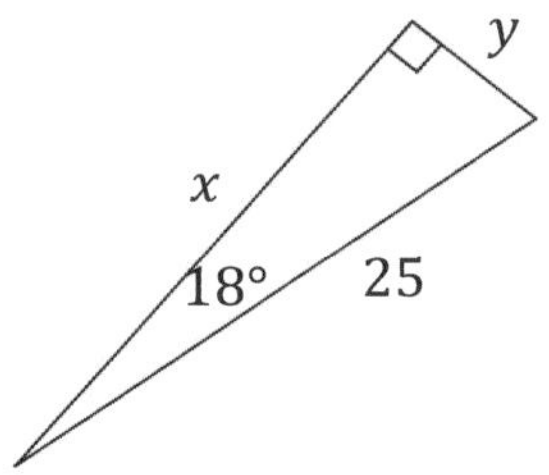

a. Which trigonometric function should you use to find the value of x?

b. Write an equation to find x in the above figure.

c. Find the value of x in the above figure.

Try It!

4. Consider the figure below.

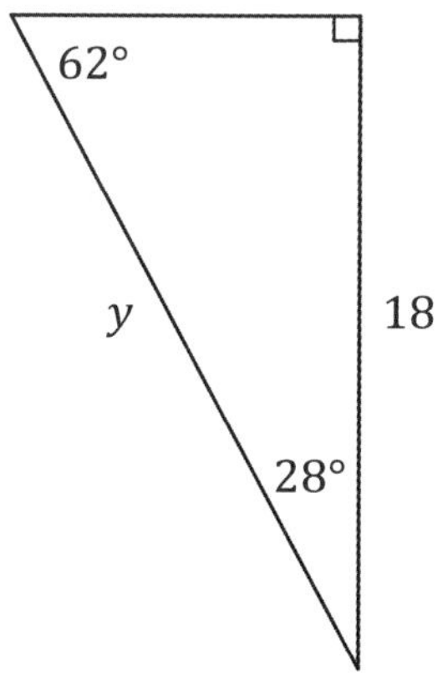

Determine the value of y.

Section 7 – Topic 9
Introduction to Trigonometry – Part 2

Given the lengths of sides, we can use "trig" functions to find missing angles by using their inverses: $\sin^{-1}$, $\cos^{-1}$, and $\tan^{-1}$.

Let's Practice!

1. Consider the triangle below.

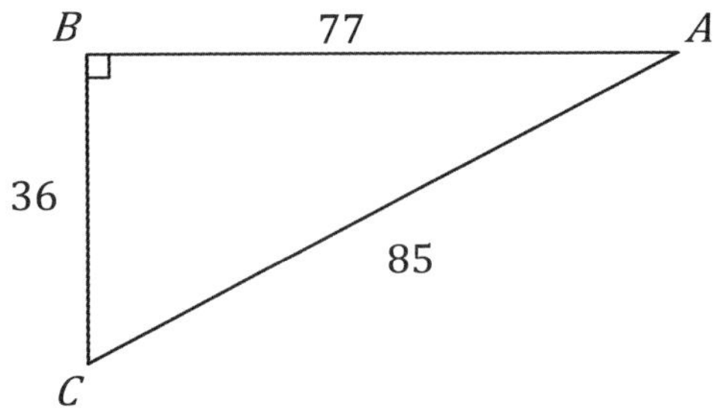

Find $\cos C$, $\sin A$, $m\angle A$, and $m\angle C$ for the triangle.

Try It!

2. Consider the triangle below.

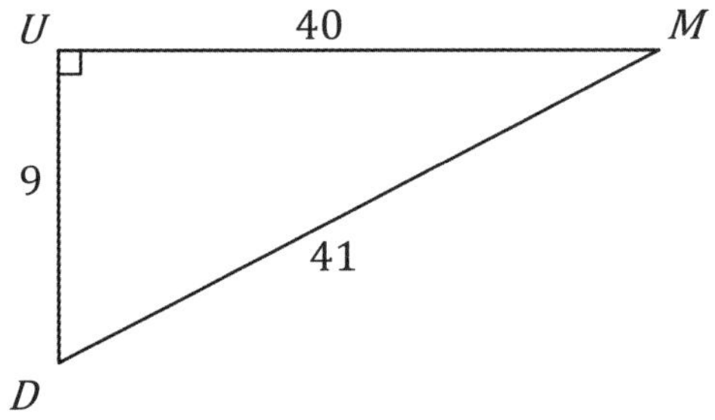

Find $\tan M$, $\cos D$, $m\angle D$, and $\sin M$ for the triangle.

BEAT THE TEST!

1. The picture below shows the path that Puppy Liz is running. The electrical post is 40 feet tall. Puppy Liz usually starts at the bench post and runs until she gets to the fire hydrant, rests, and then she runs back to the bench. How far does Puppy Liz run to get to the fire hydrant?

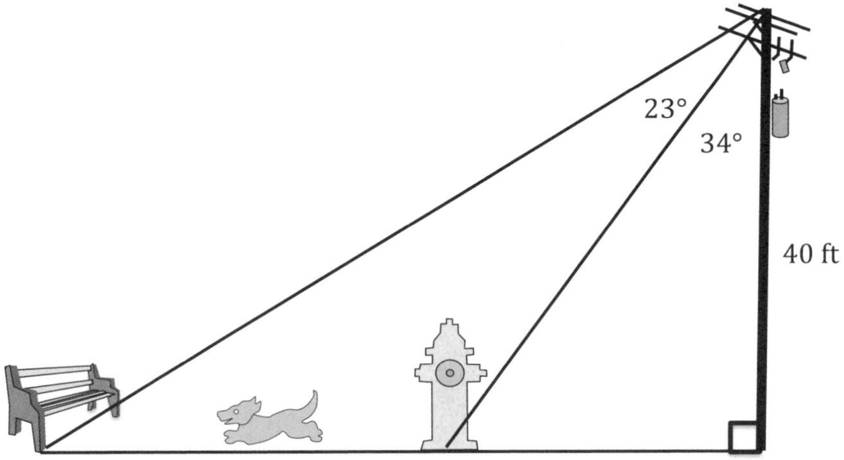

Puppy Liz runs [ ] feet.

2. Consider the triangle below.

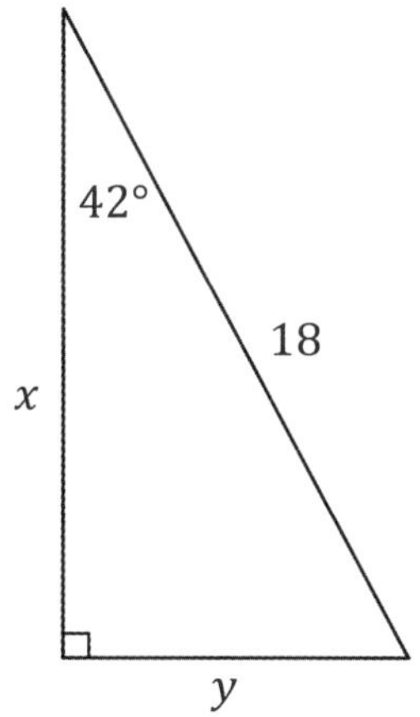

Which of the following measurements represents the perimeter and area of the triangle above?

Ⓐ Perimeter: 80.55 units
Area: 43.42 square units

Ⓑ Perimeter: 43.42 units
Area: 80.55 square units

Ⓒ Perimeter: 21.71 units
Area: 161.03 square units

Ⓓ Perimeter: 161.03 units
Area: 21.71 square units

3. Yandel will place a ramp over a set of stairs at the backyard entrance so that one end is 5 feet off the ground. The other end is at a point that is a horizontal distance of 40 feet away, as shown in the diagram. The angle of elevation of the ramp is represented by $e°$. Each step of the stairs is one foot long.

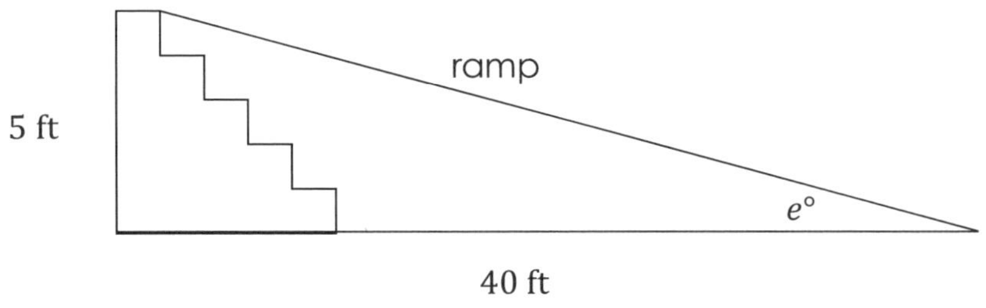

What is the angle of elevation to the nearest tenth of a degree?

Section 7 – Topic 10
Angles of Elevation and Depression

Angles of elevation are angles ____________ the horizon.

Angles of depression are angles ____________ the horizon.

In your own words, explain what are angles of elevation and angles of depression.

Explain how the properties of a right triangle fit into the properties of angles of elevation or depression.

Describe a situation where you would deal with angles of elevation.

Describe a situation where you would deal with angles of depression.

Label the angles of elevation with an E and angles of depression with a D in the appropriate spaces provided below.

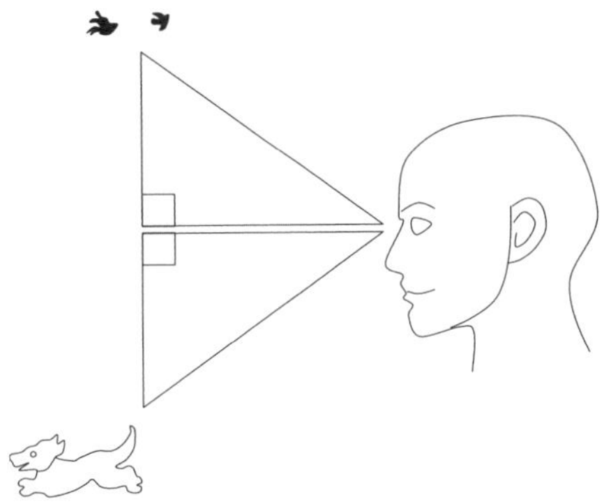

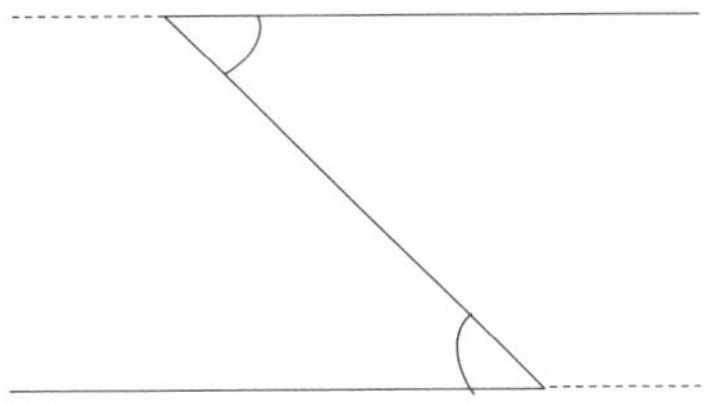

Suppose that you see a flock of birds at an angle of elevation of $32°$.

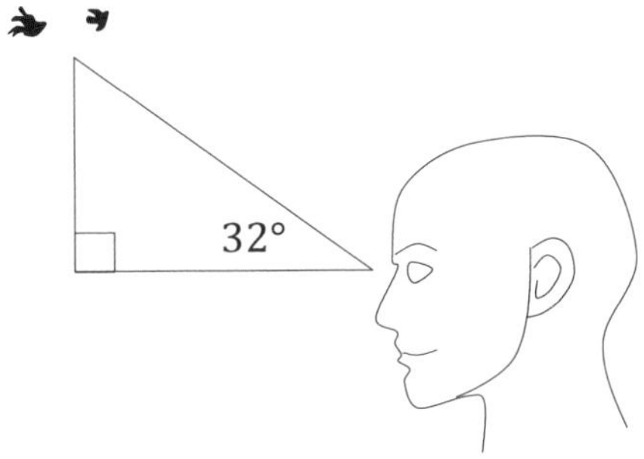

If the birds are at an altitude of $12{,}000$ feet, then what does this mean with regards to angles of elevation or depression?

If your eye level is 6 feet above the ground, then what is the vertical distance from your eyes to the birds?

How can you use this information to find your horizontal distance from the birds?

Let's Practice!

1. Suppose that an airplane is currently flying at an altitude of $39{,}000$ feet and will be landing on a tarmac 128 miles away. Find the average angle at which the airplane must descend for landing. Round your answer to the nearest tenth of a unit.

2. Consider the diagram below that represents someone's eye level as he looks at his dog. Find the value of x, and round to the nearest hundredth of a foot.

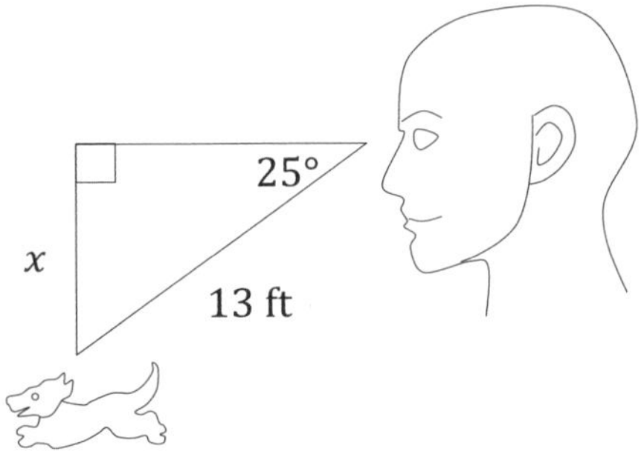

Try It!

3. If Lionel has an eye level of 5 feet above the ground and he is standing 40 feet from a flagpole that is 32 feet tall, then what is the angle of elevation?

4. Suppose that you are standing on a hill that is 59.5 feet tall looking down on a lake at an angle of depression of $48°$. How far are you from the lake? Round your answer to the nearest foot.

BEAT THE TEST!

1. A man is 6 feet 3 inches tall. The tip of his shadow touches a fire hydrant that is 13 feet 6 inches away. What is the angle of elevation from the base of the fire hydrant to the top of the man's head? Round to the nearest tenth of a degree.

   Ⓐ $24.8°$
   Ⓑ $34.5°$
   Ⓒ $42.6°$
   Ⓓ $65.2°$

Section 7 – Topic 11
Segments in Regular Polygons

Understanding how to work with interior angles, exterior angles, and regular polygons will help us find the length of certain segments such as a side, radius, apothem, and diagonals, among others.

Consider the following regular polygons, and use them to answer the questions below.

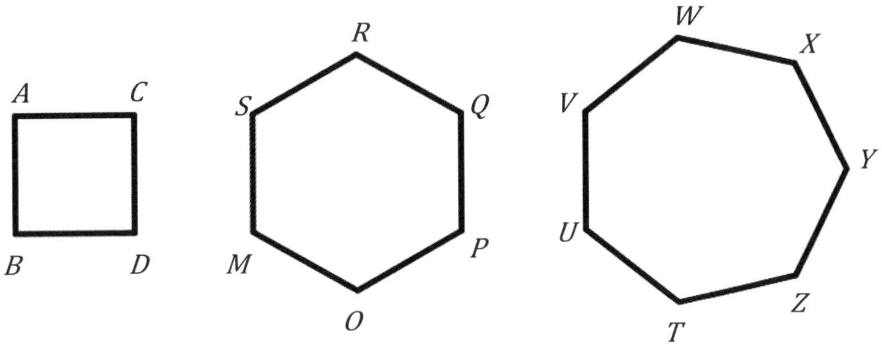

How many diagonals does each regular polygon have?

What connections can you make about the number of diagonals in regular polygons and the number of sides of those regular polygons?

STUDY EDGE TIP

A polygon's ***diagonals*** are line segments from one vertex to another nonconsecutive vertex. The number of diagonals of an n-sided polygon is $\frac{n(n-3)}{2}$.

Let's Practice!

1. Consider the following regular polygon and use it to answer the questions below.

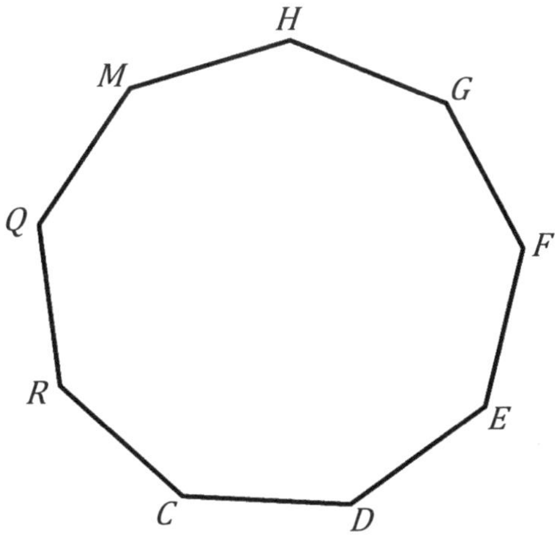

   a. How many diagonals does the regular polygon have?

   b. Diagonal $\overline{CM}$ forms quadrilateral $CRQM$. What type of quadrilateral is $CRQM$?

   c. What are the measures of its interior angles?

2. Consider the regular polygons with centers Z and Q that are shown below.

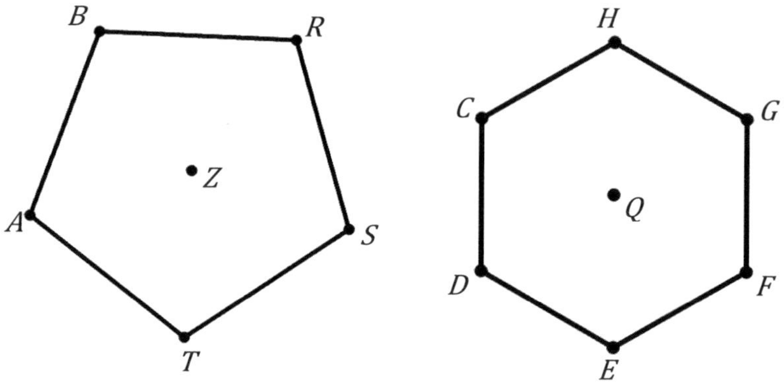

a. Which of the following statements is correct?

Ⓐ The length of the radius of $ABRST$ will be half of the length of the diagonal that passes through Z.
Ⓑ The length of the radius of $CDEFGH$ will be half of the length of the diagonal that passes through Q.
Ⓒ In regular polygons with an odd number of sides, the diagonals start at a vertex and end at a side.
Ⓓ In regular polygons with an even number of sides, the diagonals never pass through the center.

b. How can you find the length of the radius, the length of the apothem, and the length of each side of $ABRST$ and $CDEFGH$?

Try It!

3. A regular pentagon with center Z has a radius that is two units long. Determine the length of the apothem and each side of the pentagon.

4. An engineer is designing a roof for a gazebo in the shape of a regular polygon with a 10-foot diagonal that passes through the center of the polygon. The measure of each interior angle of the regular polygon is three times the measure of each exterior angle.

a. How many sides does the polygon described above have?

b. What is the length of each side in the polygon described above?

c. What is the length of the radius of this polygon?

d. What is the length of the apothem of this polygon?

BEAT THE TEST!

1. In the United States, stop signs are regular red octagons with a length of 750 millimeters from side to side and a 20-millimeter wide border.

How much longer is the radius of the stop sign when compared to a side?

[ ] [ ] millimeters

2. The diameter of the circumcircle of the Pentagon building located in Arlington, VA measures 483.28 meters approximately.

Which of the following is the approximate measure of one of the sides of the Pentagon?

Ⓐ 142.03 meters
Ⓑ 223.25 meters
Ⓒ 284.06 meters
Ⓓ 369.89 meters

Section 7 – Topic 12
Area of Other Polygons

How can you use your knowledge of regular polygons to calculate their area?

Let's Practice!

1. Use the regular polygon with center G to answer the questions below.

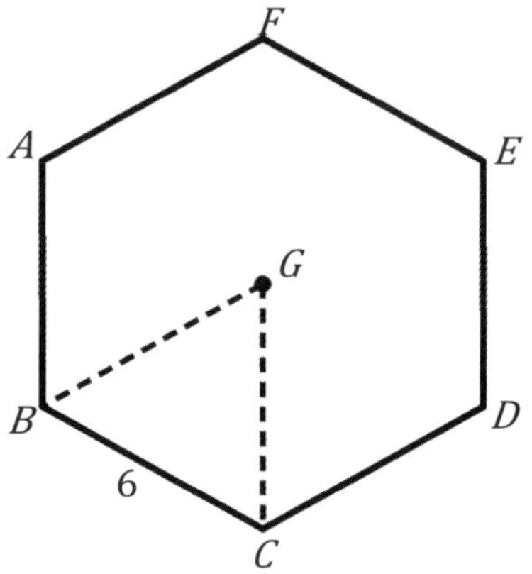

   a. What is the area of ΔBGC?

   b. How can we use the area of ΔBGC to find the area of the regular polygon?

   c. What is the area of the regular polygon?

Try It!

2. What is the area of this regular polygon with center R?

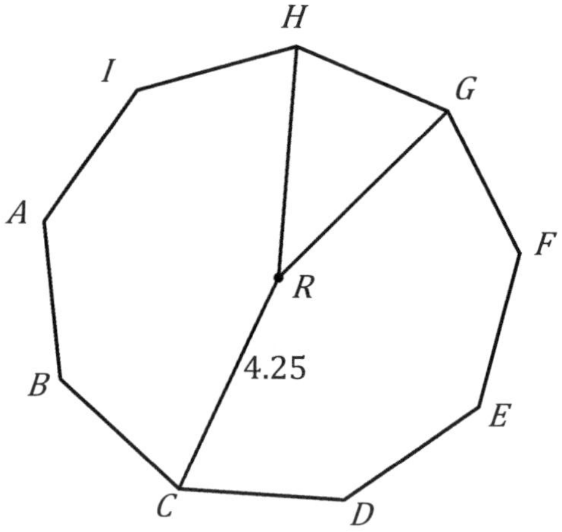

The area of a regular polygon can also be calculated by first finding the perimeter p and the apothem a, then calculating $\frac{ap}{2}$.

Let's investigate why this formula works.

What is the formula used to find the area of one isosceles triangle in a regular polygon?

How can you use that to write a formula for the area of the polygon?

Rewrite this formula in terms of the apothem and the perimeter of the polygon.

Let's Practice!

3. Find the area of a regular dodecagon with a perimeter of 84 inches and a radius of 13.523 inches.

Try It!

4. Pete and Bella each have a poster in the shape of a regular polygon. Pete's poster has an apothem of 14.4 inches and an area of 756.56 square inches. Bella's poster has an apothem of 16.5 inches and an area of 891 square inches.

   Which regular polygon has the largest perimeter? Justify your answer.

BEAT THE TEST!

1. *J.Russel Flooring* is putting in a new floor for an intramural basketball court. Gymnasium flooring costs $2.00 per square foot. Consider the available options for designing and installing the floor.

   ➢ Court Option 1 is a regular octagon with a side length of 50 feet and a distance of 65 feet from the center to a vertex.

   ➢ Court Option 2 is a regular decagon with a side length of 42 feet.

   Which of the following statements are true? Select all that apply.

   - ☐ Court Option 2 costs $13,572.58 for floor installation.
   - ☐ Court Option 1 costs $26,000.00 for floor installation.
   - ☐ Court Option 2 is approximately 572 square feet larger than Court Option 1.
   - ☐ Court Option 2 costs more for floor installation.
   - ☐ Court Option 2 has a longer distance from the center of the floor to a vertex.
   - ☐ The area of Court Option 1 is 13,000 square feet.

Test Yourself! Practice Tool

Great job! You have reached the end of this section. Now it's time to try the "Test Yourself! Practice Tool," where you can practice all the skills and concepts you learned in this section. Log in to Math Nation and try out the "Test Yourself! Practice Tool" so you can see how well you know these topics!

THIS PAGE WAS INTENTIONALLY LEFT BLANK

Section 8: Quadrilaterals

Topic 1: Introduction to Quadrilaterals – Part 1 215
Standards Covered: G-CO.1
- ☐ I can use diagonals to determine a type of quadrilateral.

Topic 2: Introduction to Quadrilaterals – Part 2 217
Standards Covered: G-GPE.4
- ☐ I can use characteristics to define a shape that is not a quadrilateral.

Topic 3: Introduction to Quadrilaterals – Part 3 218
Standards Covered: G-GPE.4
- ☐ I can use diagonals to bisect vertex angles when determining a type of quadrilateral.

Topic 4: Parallelograms – Part 1 220
Standards Covered: G-CO.11
- ☐ I can define the properties of a parallelogram.

Topic 5: Parallelograms – Part 2 221
Standards Covered: G-CO.11
- ☐ I can prove that a given quadrilateral is a parallelogram.

Topic 6: Rectangles 222
Standards Covered: G-CO.11
- ☐ I can use the properties and theorems of rectangles to prove certain characteristics or relationships in quadrilaterals.

Topic 7: Rhombi 224
Standards Covered: G-CO.11
- ☐ I can use properties and theorems of rhombi to prove certain characteristics or relationships in quadrilaterals.

Topic 8: Squares 227
Standards Covered: G-CO.11
- ☐ I can use properties and theorems of squares and rhombi to prove certain characteristics or relationships in quadrilaterals.

Topic 9: Kites 231
Standards Covered: G-CO.1
- ☐ I can use properties and theorems of kites to prove certain characteristics or relationships in quadrilaterals.

Topic 10: Trapezoids 234
Standards Covered: G-CO.1
- ☐ I can use properties and theorems of trapezoids to prove certain characteristics or relationships in quadrilaterals.

Topic 11: Quadrilaterals in Coordinate Geometry – Part 1 237
Standards Covered: G-GPE.4
- ☐ I can use the distance, midpoint, and slope formulas when developing coordinate geometry proofs for quadrilaterals.

Topic 12: Quadrilaterals in Coordinate Geometry – Part 2 240
Standards Covered: G-GPE.4
- ☐ I can use the distance, midpoint, and slope formulas when developing coordinate geometry proofs for quadrilaterals.

Honors Topic 1: Midsegment of Trapezoids .... Available Online
Standards Covered: G-GPE.4
☐ I can use the Midsegment Theorem for trapezoids to solve problems or prove certain characteristics or relationships in quadrilaterals.

Visit MathNation.com or search "Math Nation" in your phone or tablet's app store to watch the videos that go along with this workbook!

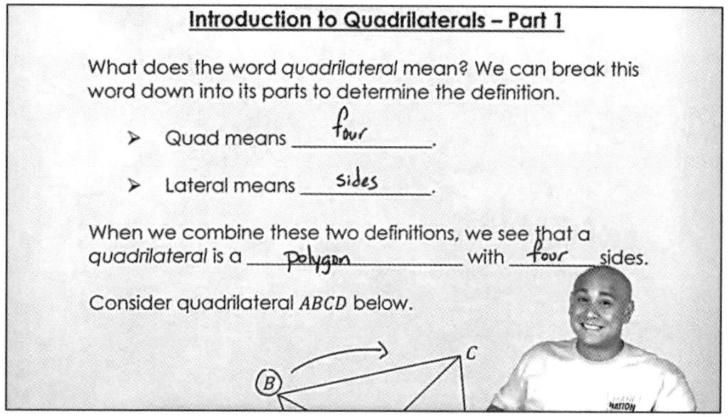

The following Michigan Mathematics Standards will be covered in this section:
G-CO.1 - Know precise definitions of angle, circle, perpendicular line, parallel line, and line segment, based on the undefined notions of point, line, distance along a line, and distance around a circular arc.
G-CO.11 - Prove theorems about parallelograms; use theorems about parallelograms to solve problems.
G-GPE.4 - Use coordinates to prove simple geometric theorems algebraically. *For example, prove or disprove that a figure defined by four given points in the coordinate plane is a rectangle; prove or disprove that the point* $(1, \sqrt{3})$ *lies on the circle centered at the origin and containing the point* $(0, 2)$.

Section 8: Quadrilaterals
Section 8 – Topic 1
Introduction to Quadrilaterals – Part 1

What does the word ***quadrilateral*** mean? We can break this word down into its parts to determine the definition.

- Quad means ______________.
- Lateral means _____________.

When we combine these two meanings, we see that a quadrilateral is a _____________________ with ________ sides.

Consider quadrilateral $ABCD$ below.

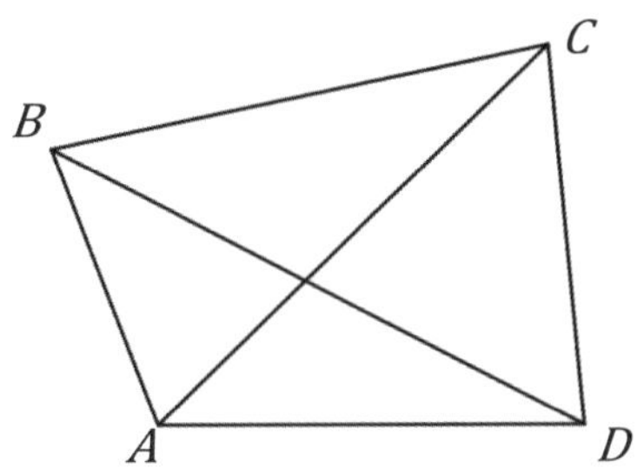

- ***Consecutive vertices*** or ***adjacent vertices*** of a quadrilateral are vertices that have endpoints of the same side.

Name four sets of consecutive or adjacent vertices in the quadrilateral $ABCD$ above.

- ***Consecutive sides*** or ***adjacent sides*** of a quadrilateral are sides that have a common endpoint.

Name four sets of consecutive or adjacent sides in the previous quadrilateral $ABCD$.

- ***Opposite sides*** of a quadrilateral are sides that do not have a common endpoint.

Name two sets of opposite sides in the previous quadrilateral $ABCD$.

- ***Consecutive angles*** of a quadrilateral are angles with vertices that are consecutive.

Name four sets of consecutive angles in the previous quadrilateral $ABCD$.

- ***Opposite angles*** of a quadrilateral are angles with vertices that are not consecutive.

Name two sets of opposite angles in the previous quadrilateral $ABCD$.

- A ***diagonal*** of a quadrilateral is a line segment with endpoints that are two nonadjacent vertices of the quadrilateral.

Name two diagonals in the previous quadrilateral $ABCD$.

- The sum of the measures of the angles of a quadrilateral is ________ degrees.

Name the specific quadrilaterals in the Venn Diagram below.

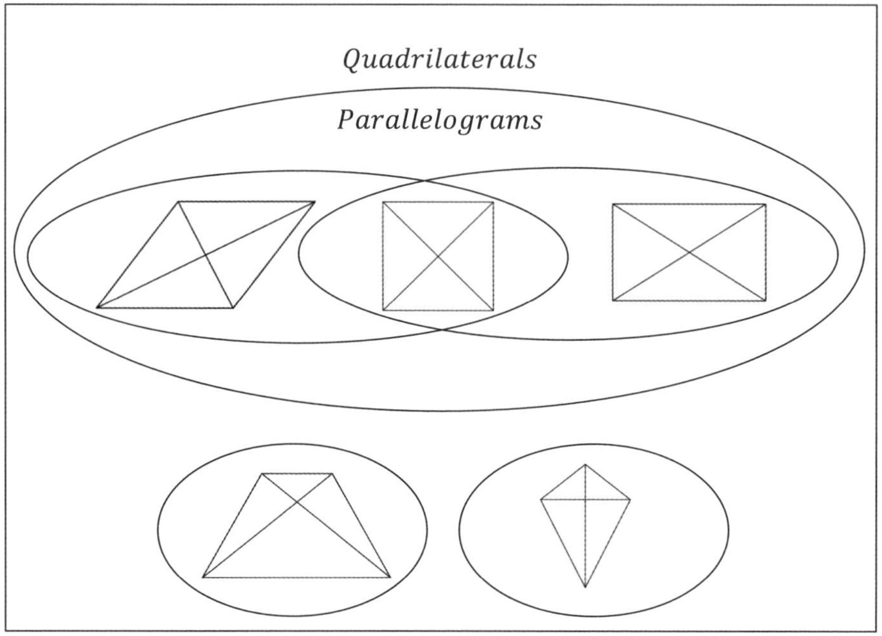

In each empty square, write the most appropriate description for the quadrilateral.

Characteristics of Quadrilaterals				
Polygon	**Opposite Sides**	**Adjacent Sides**	**Angles**	**Diagonals**
Parallelogram				
Rhombus				
Square				
Rectangle				
Isosceles Trapezoid				
Kite				

Section 8 – Topic 2
Introduction to Quadrilaterals – Part 2

Let's Practice!

1. The quadrilateral $ABCD$ has the following characteristics.

   $\overline{AD}$ can be represented by the equation $y = -2x$ where $-1 \leq x \leq 0$.

   $\overline{BC}$ can be represented by the equation $y = -2x + 4$ where $-0.5 \leq x \leq 1.5$.

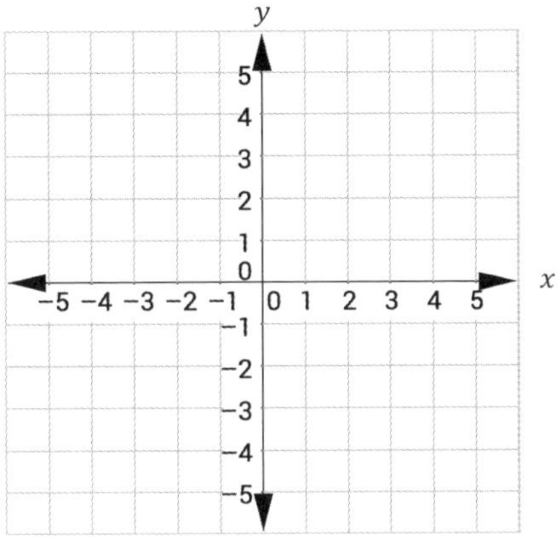

   a. On the coordinate plane above, graph the figure represented by the information given.

   b. Describe the type of quadrilateral represented above.

Try It!

2. Find the measure of each interior angle.

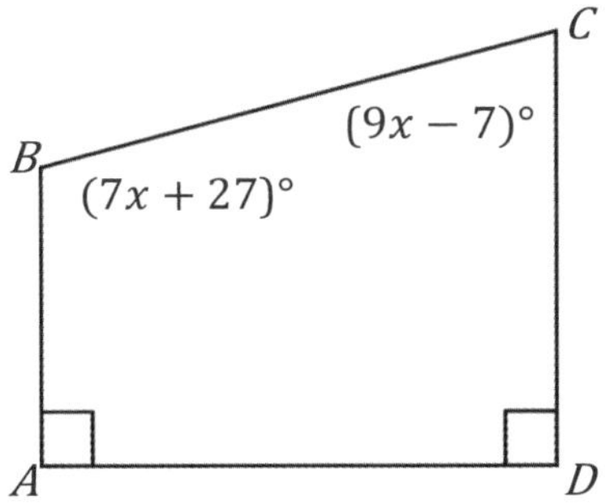

3. Classify the following descriptive statements as quadrilaterals or non-quadrilaterals. If the statements describe a non-quadrilateral, explain why.

   a. A figure with $m\angle a = 91, m\angle b = 72, m\angle c = 86$, and $m\angle d = 93$.

      o Quadrilateral　　　o Non-quadrilateral

   b. A figure with two diagonals, $\overline{RT}$ and $\overline{PS}$, with endpoints that are two nonadjacent vertices.

      o Quadrilateral　　　o Non-quadrilateral

   c. A figure with only three consecutive sides.

      o Quadrilateral　　　o Non-quadrilateral

Identify the most appropriate way to find the area of each type of quadrilateral and fill in the table below with your answers.

Polygon	Area
Parallelogram	
Rhombus	
Square	
Rectangle	
Isosceles Trapezoid	
Kite	

Section 8 – Topic 3
Introduction to Quadrilaterals – Part 3

Let's Practice!

1. Determine the area and perimeter of each quadrilateral.

a.

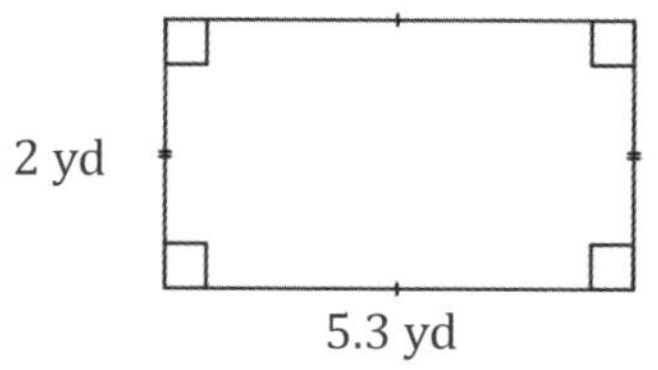

b.

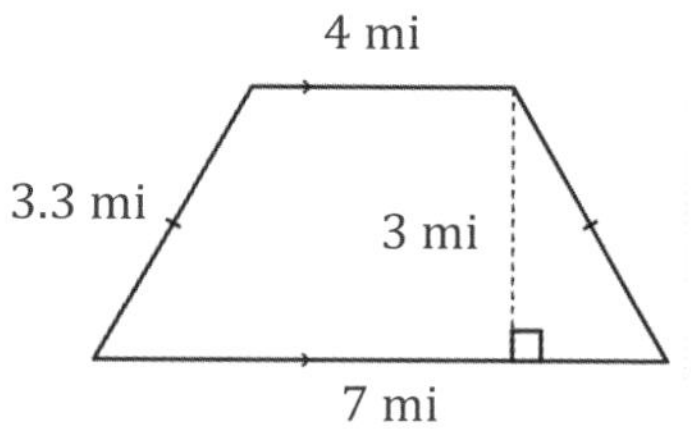

Try It!

2. Determine the measure of each interior angle below.

a. Parallelogram $TUVW$ with $m\angle T = 10x$ and $m\angle U = 20x$

b. Isosceles trapezoid $MNPQ$ with $\angle P \cong \angle Q$, $m\angle Q = 30x$, $\angle M \cong \angle N$, and $m\angle M = 20x$

3. Determine the area and perimeter of the following quadrilaterals.

a.

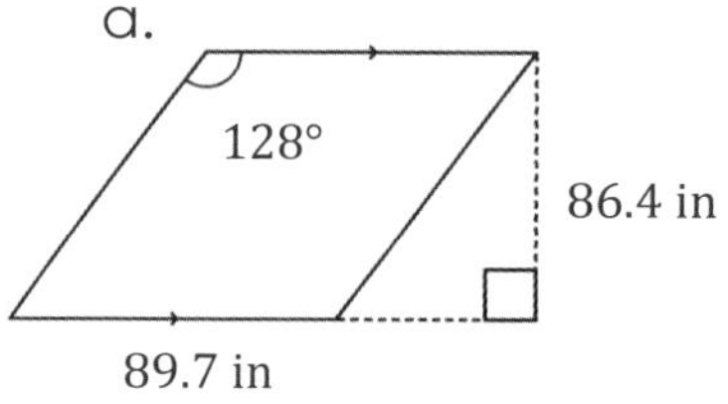

b.

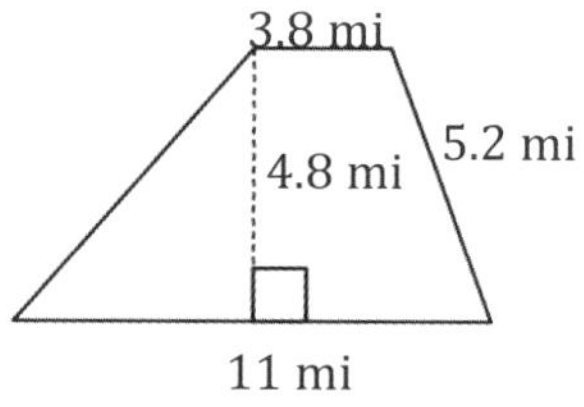

BEAT THE TEST!

1. Identify which quadrilateral(s) meet the following criteria.

Criteria	Trapezoid	Parallelogram	Kite	Rhombus	Rectangle	Square
No parallel sides	☐	☐	☐	☐	☐	☐
Exactly one pair of parallel sides	☐	☐	☐	☐	☐	☐
Two pairs of opposite sides are congruent	☐	☐	☐	☐	☐	☐
Two pairs of opposite angles are congruent	☐	☐	☐	☐	☐	☐
Consecutive angles are supplementary	☐	☐	☐	☐	☐	☐
Diagonals bisect the vertex angles	☐	☐	☐	☐	☐	☐

2. Sabrina would like her fiancé to buy her an engagement ring fitted with an exclusive diamond in it. She wants the diamond to have a cross section in the shape of a kite. She also wants the diamond to be a perfect cut, with diagonals of 4 millimeters and 7 millimeters. What would the area of the diamond's cross section be?

   Ⓐ 7 square millimeters
   Ⓑ 10.5 square millimeters
   Ⓒ 14 square millimeters
   Ⓓ 28 square millimeters

Section 8 – Topic 4
Parallelograms – Part 1

A parallelogram is a quadrilateral in which two pairs of opposite sides are ________________ and congruent, and two pairs of ________________ angles are congruent.

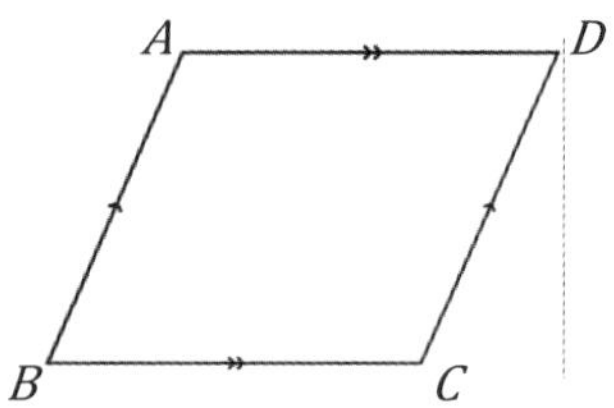

Is quadrilateral $ABCD$ a parallelogram? Justify your answer.

TAKE NOTE! Postulates & Theorems

Parallelogram Theorems

- A diagonal divides a parallelogram into two congruent triangles.
- Two consecutive angles of a parallelogram are supplementary.
- The diagonals of a parallelogram bisect each other.

Let's Practice!

1. Consider $PQRS$.

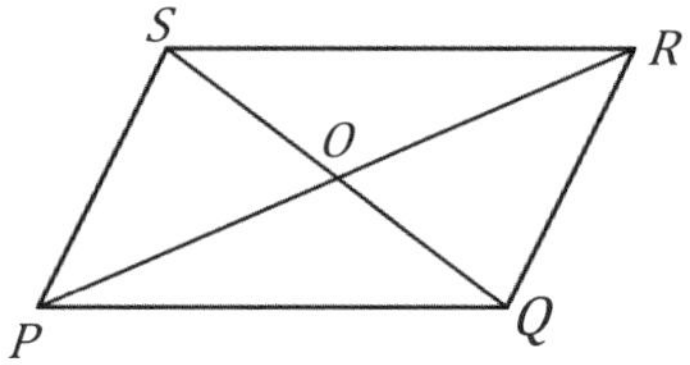

Given: Parallelogram $PQRS$ with diagonals $\overline{PR}$ and $\overline{SQ}$

Prove: $\Delta PQR \cong \Delta RSP$

Complete the two-column proof on the next page.

Statements	Reasons
1.	**1.** Given
2. $\overline{RQ} \cong \overline{PS}$	**2.**
3.	**3.** Property of parallelogram
4.	**4.**
5. $\Delta PQR \cong \Delta RSP$	**5.**

Try It!

2. Consider parallelogram $PQRS$ again.

If $m\angle SPQ = 11x + 2$ and $m\angle PQR = 15x - 4$, find $m\angle QRS$ and $m\angle RSP$.

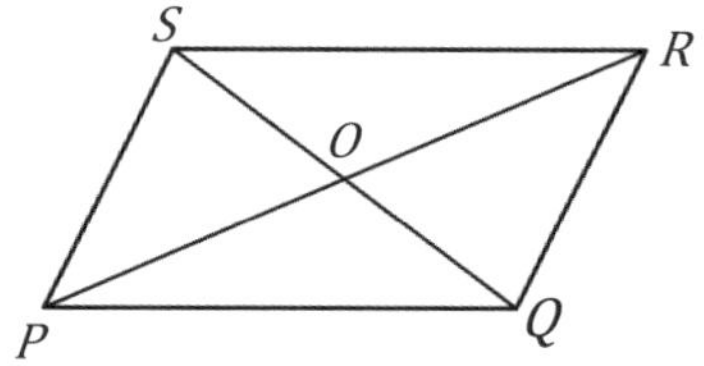

3. Suppose you have parallelogram $FGHI$, where the $m\angle G$ exceeds the $m\angle F$ by 46 degrees. Find $m\angle I$.

Section 8 – Topic 5
Parallelograms – Part 2

Consider $PQRS$ on the right.

Given: Parallelogram $PQRS$ with diagonals $\overline{PR}$ and $\overline{SQ}$ intersecting at O.

Prove: $\overline{PR}$ and $\overline{SQ}$ bisect each other.

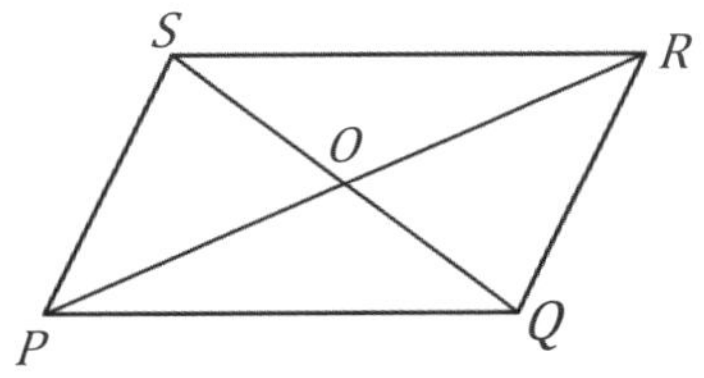

Complete the following two-column proof.

Statements	Reasons
1.	**1.** Given
2. $\overline{RQ} \cong \overline{SP}$; $\overline{SR} \cong \overline{PQ}$	**2.**
3.	**3.** Alternate Interior Angles Theorem
4. $\Delta POQ \cong \Delta ROS$	**4.**
5.	**5.** CPCTC
6. O is the midpoint of $\overline{SQ}$. O is the midpoint of $\overline{PR}$	**6.**
7.	**7.** Definition of segment bisector

BEAT THE TEST!

1. If two opposite angles of a quadrilateral are supplementary, is the quadrilateral a parallelogram?

   Ⓐ No, because in parallelograms, angles are supplementary if and only if they are consecutive.
   Ⓑ No, because opposite angles in a parallelogram are never congruent.
   Ⓒ Yes, but only when the angles of the quadrilateral are right angles. Otherwise, it will be a trapezoid rather than a parallelogram.
   Ⓓ Yes, because only squares have that property, and squares are both parallelograms and quadrilaterals.

2. The deck that Kenneth is building is in the shape of a parallelogram, $ABCD$. The measure of $\angle C$ is one-third the measure of $\angle B$. Find the measure of each angle of the deck.

   $m\angle A =$

   $m\angle B =$

   $m\angle C =$

   $m\angle D =$

3. Complete the following proof.

Given: $JKLM$ is a parallelogram
$\overline{PX} \cong \overline{QX}$

Prove: $JPLQ$ is a parallelogram.

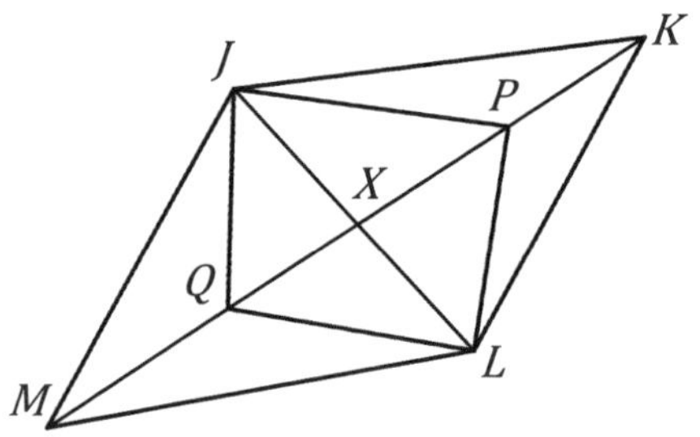

Statements	Reasons
1. $JKLM$ is a parallelogram $\overline{PX} \cong \overline{QX}$	**1.** Given
2. $\overline{JX} \cong \overline{XL}$	**2.**
3. X is the midpoint of $\overline{JL}$. X is the midpoint of $\overline{QP}$	**3.**
4.	**4.** Definition of segment bisector
5. $JPLQ$ is a parallelogram.	**5.**

Section 8 – Topic 6
Rectangles

What do you know about rectangles?

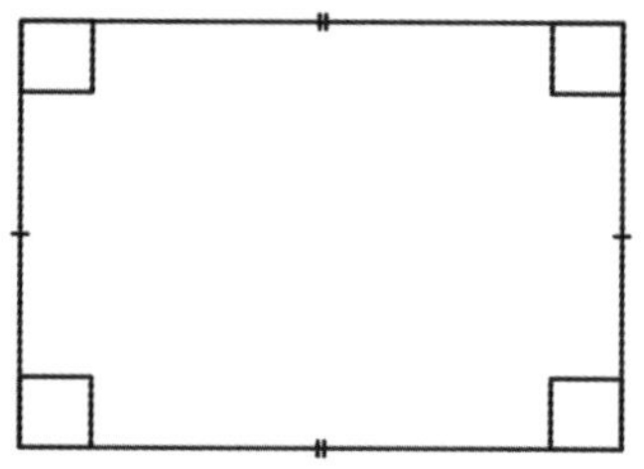

- A rectangle is a parallelogram with four __________ angles.

TAKE NOTE! *Postulates & Theorems*

Theorems about Rectangles

- All angles of a rectangle are right angles.
- The opposite sides of a rectangle are parallel and congruent.
- The diagonals of a rectangle are congruent.
- If a quadrilateral is equiangular, then it is a rectangle.
- If the diagonals of a parallelogram are congruent, the parallelogram is a rectangle.

Let's Practice!

1. Complete the following flow chart proof.

   Given: $CUPS$ is a rectangle
   Prove: $\overline{PC} \cong \overline{US}$

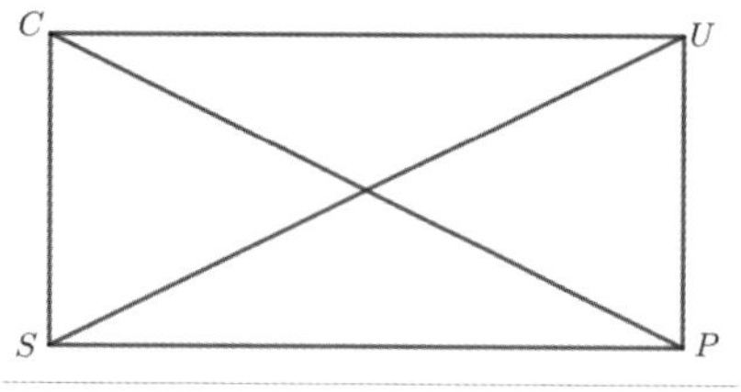

Reasons Bank		
A. CPCTC	**B.** SAS	**C.** AAS
D. Theorem about rectangles	**E.** Definition of a rectangle	**F.** All right angles congruent
G. Reflexive Property of Congruence	**H.** ASA	**I.** Opposite sides of a parallelogram are congruent

Note: You may use the reasons more than once or not at all.

Flow chart:
- $CUPS$ is a rectangle (Given) → $CUPS$ is a Parallelogram → $\overline{CS} \cong \overline{UP}$
- $CUPS$ is a rectangle → $\overline{PS} \cong \overline{PS}$ → $\triangle CSP \cong \triangle UPS$ → $\overline{PC} \cong \overline{US}$
- $CUPS$ is a rectangle → $\angle CSP$ and $\angle UPS$ are right angles → $\angle CSP \cong \angle UPS$

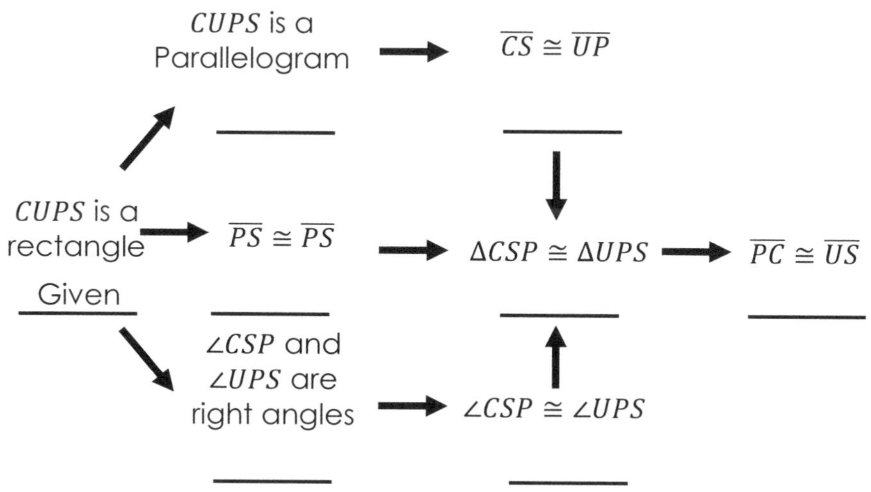

2. The lengths of diagonals of a rectangle are represented by $5x$ yards and $7x - 18$ yards. Find the length of each diagonal.

Try It!

3. Rectangle $JKLM$ has diagonals intersecting at P. If $m\angle LJK = 35°$, find $m\angle LJM$, $m\angle JLK$, $m\angle JPK$, and $m\angle JPM$.

4. Complete the following proof.

   Given: $ABCD$ is a rectangle and Q is the midpoint of $\overline{CD}$.
   Prove: $\overline{AQ} \cong \overline{BQ}$

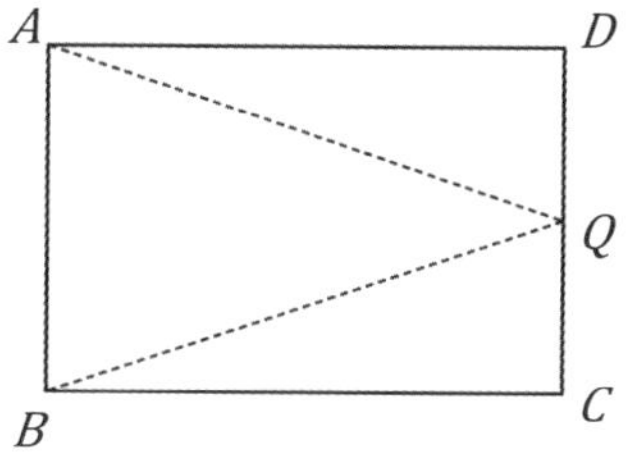

Statements	Reasons
1. $ABCD$ is a rectangle and Q is the midpoint of $\overline{CD}$.	1. Given
2. $\overline{DQ} \cong \overline{QC}$	2.
3.	3. In a rectangle, opposite sides are congruent.
4. $\angle D \cong \angle C$	4.
5.	5. SAS
6. $\overline{AQ} \cong \overline{BQ}$	6.

BEAT THE TEST!

1. A rectangular beach volleyball court measures 16 meters by 8 meters. Winston serves the ball from point S to point E. How far did the ball travel in his serve? Round your answer to the nearest hundredth.

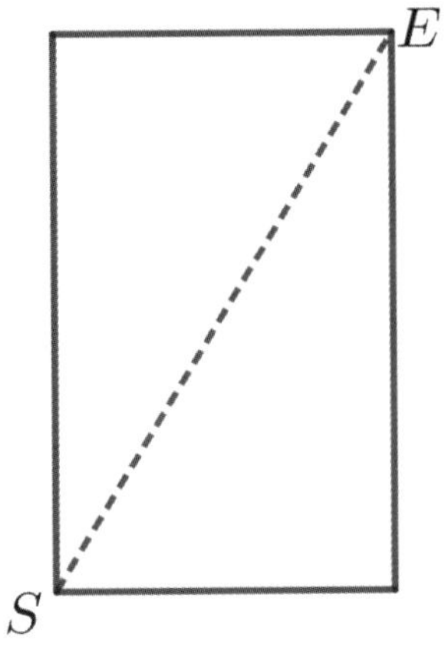

Section 8 – Topic 7
Rhombi

A rhombus is a ***parallelogram*** that has _______ congruent consecutive sides and ___________ sides; the angles of a rhombus do NOT all have to be congruent or right angles.

TAKE NOTE! *Postulates & Theorems*

Theorems About the Rhombus

- All sides of a rhombus are congruent.
- The diagonals of a rhombus are perpendicular to each other.
- The diagonals of a rhombus bisect its angles.
- If a quadrilateral is equilateral, then it is a rhombus.
- If the diagonals of a parallelogram are perpendicular to each other, the parallelogram is a rhombus.

Illustrate the theorems about the rhombus in the figure below.

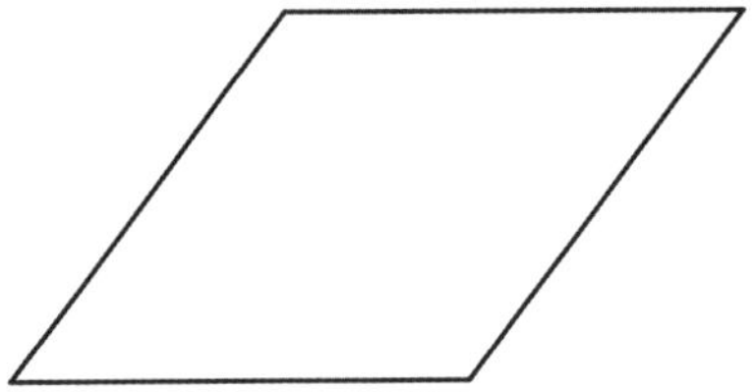

STUDY EDGE TIP

Recall that the rhombus method was used for the construction of parallel lines. Since the opposite sides of a rhombus are parallel, the construction of a rhombus creates the desired parallel lines.

Let's Practice!

1. A diagonal of a rhombus that is on the coordinate plane can be modeled by the equation $6x + y = 13$. What is the slope of the other diagonal?

2. In rhombus $HIJK$, $m\angle H$ is $120°$. Does the diagonal $\overline{HJ}$ divide the rhombus into two equilateral triangles? Justify your answer.

3. The size of the acute angle of a rhombus is half the size of its obtuse angle. The side length of the rhombus is equal to 20 feet. Find the lengths of the diagonals of the rhombus.

Try It!

4. Complete the following proof.

Given: $ABCD$ is a parallelogram with $AB = 4x + 3$, $DC = 7x - 6$, and $AD = 5x$.

Prove: $ABCD$ is a rhombus.

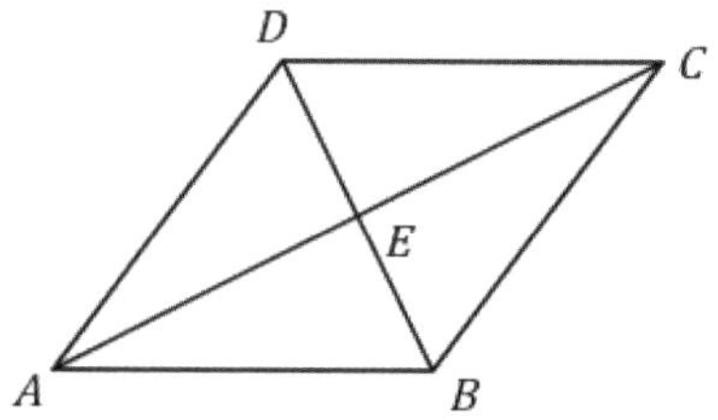

We are given that $ABCD$ is a parallelogram with $AB = 4x + 3$, $DC = 7x - 6$ and $AD = 5x$. Because the ______________ sides of a parallelogram are ____________________, $7x - 6 = 4x + 3$.

Using the Addition Property of Equality, we can conclude that _________. Further, the Multiplication Property of Equality tells us that $x = 3$.

By substitution, ________________________________ and $BC = 15$ since ______________ sides of a parallelogram are ____________________.

Therefore, $ABCD$ is a rhombus, since all sides of the parallelogram are congruent.

5. Complete following proof.

Given: $ABCD$ is a rhombus.

Prove: $\overline{AC}$ bisects $\angle DCB$ of the rhombus.

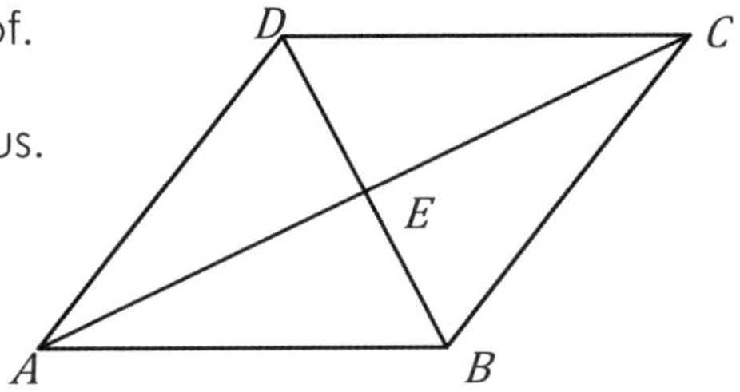

Statements	**Reasons**
1. $ABCD$ is a rhombus.	**1.** Given
2.	**2.** Diagonals of a rhombus are perpendicular
3.	**3.** Definition of perpendicular lines
4. $\angle DEC \cong \angle BEC$	**4.**
5. $\overline{DE} \cong \overline{BE}$	**5.**
6.	**6.** Reflexive Property
7. $\Delta DEC \cong \Delta BEC$	**7.**
8.	**8.** CPCTC
9. $\overline{AC}$ bisects $\angle DCB$ of the rhombus.	**9.** Definition of an angle bisector

BEAT THE TEST!

1. Complete the two-column proof below.

Given: Parallelogram $ABCD$
$\angle CBD \cong \angle ABD, \angle BDC \cong \angle BDA.$

Prove: $ABCD$ is a rhombus.

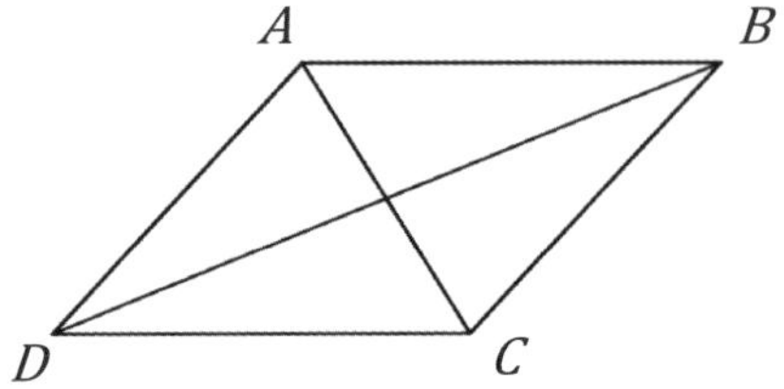

Statements	**Reasons**
1. $ABCD$ is a parallelogram.	**1.** Given
2. $\angle CBD \cong \angle ABD$, $\angle BDC \cong \angle BDA$	**2.** Given
3. $\overline{BD} \cong \overline{BD}$	**3.** Reflexive Property
4. $\Delta DBA \cong \Delta DBC$	**4.** ASA congruence theorem
5. $\overline{CD} \cong \overline{AD}$	**5.** CPCTC
6. $\overline{AB} \cong \overline{BC}$	**6.** CPCTC
7. $\overline{CD} \cong \overline{AB}$, $\overline{AD} \cong \overline{BC}$	**7.** Opposite sides of a parallelogram are ≅
8.	**8.**
9. $ABCD$ is a rhombus.	**9.** If a quadrilateral is equilateral, then it is a rhombus.

2. The perimeter of a rhombus is 120 feet and one of its diagonals has a length of 40 feet. Find the area of the rhombus.

The area is ☐ square feet.

3. Consider the following statement.

All squares are rhombi.

Is the converse of the above statement also true? Justify your answer.

Section 8 – Topic 8
Squares

Use the descriptions to identify and label each quadrilateral in the diagram below.

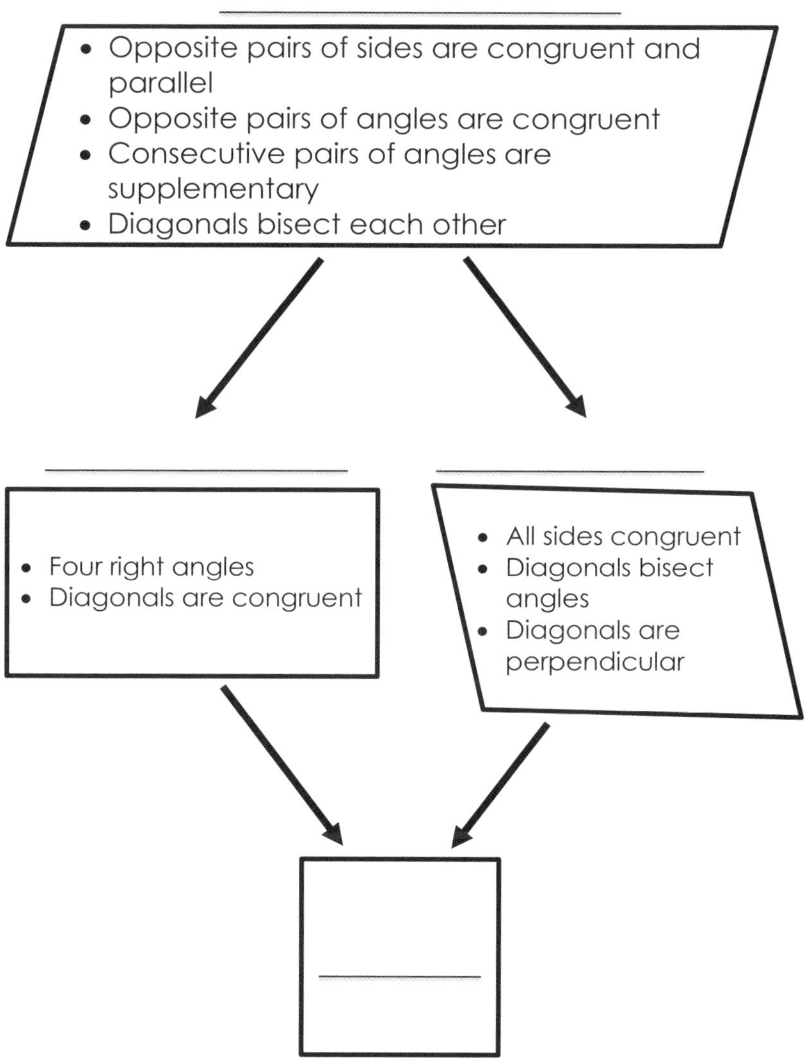

Opposite pairs of sides are congruent and parallel
Opposite pairs of angles are congruent
Consecutive pairs of angles are supplementary
Diagonals bisect each other
Four right angles
Diagonals are congruent
All sides congruent
Diagonals bisect angles
Diagonals are perpendicular

A ***square*** has all the characteristics of a parallelogram, rectangle, and rhombus.

TAKE NOTE! *Postulates & Theorems*

Theorems about Squares

- A square is a rhombus and a rectangle.
- If one of the angles of a rhombus is a right angle, then the rhombus is a square.

Let's Practice!

1. State whether you agree or disagree with the following statements. Justify your answers.

   a. The diagonals of a square separate the square into four congruent isosceles right triangles.

   b. If the midpoints of the sides of a square are connected in order, another square is formed.

2. Complete the following proof.

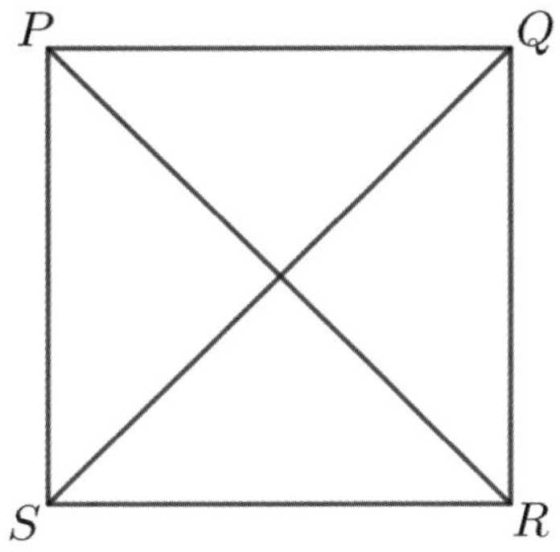

Given: $PQRS$ is a square.

Prove: $\overline{PR} \cong \overline{QS}$

Statements	Reasons
1. $PQRS$ is a square.	**1.** Given
2.	**2.** Definition of a square: All sides are congruent
3. $\angle P \cong \angle Q \cong \angle R \cong \angle S$	**3.**
4. $m\angle P = m\angle Q = m\angle R = m\angle S$	**4.** Definition of congruence
5.	**5.** SAS
6. $\overline{PR} \cong \overline{QS}$	**6.**

Try It!

3. Complete the following proof.

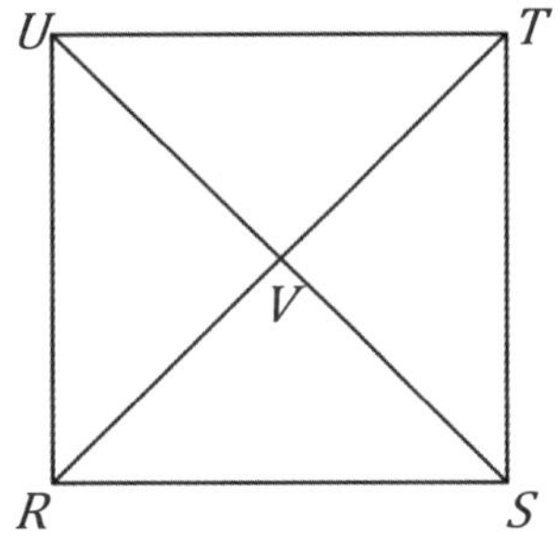

Given: $\overline{RT} \cong \overline{SU}$
$\overline{US}$ is the perpendicular bisector of $\overline{RT}$.
$\overline{RT}$ is the perpendicular bisector of $\overline{US}$.

Prove: $RSTU$ is a square.

Statements	Reasons
1. $\overline{RT} \cong \overline{SU}$ $\overline{US}$ is the perpendicular bisector of $\overline{RT}$. $\overline{RT}$ is the perpendicular bisector of $\overline{US}$.	**1.** Given
2.	**2.** Definition of perpendicular bisector
3. $m\angle UVR = m\angle RVS = m\angle SVT = m\angle TVU = 90°$	**3.**
4. $\angle UVR \cong \angle RVS \cong \angle SVT \cong \angle TVU$	**4.**
5.	**5.** SAS
6. $\overline{UT} \cong \overline{TS} \cong \overline{RS} \cong \overline{RU}$	**6.** CPCTC
7. $RSTU$ is a square.	**7.**

4. Jerome and Claire cut up a rectangle and reassembled it into a square as shown in the figure below. Let x represent the side length of the square. Jerome thinks the rectangle has the greater perimeter and Claire thinks the square has the greater perimeter. Who is correct? Explain your reasoning.

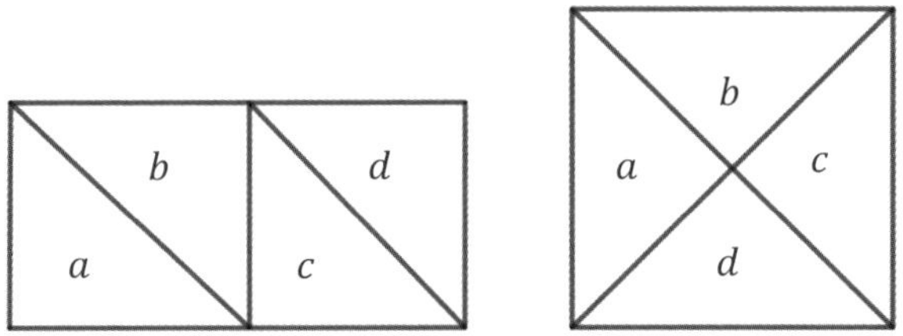

BEAT THE TEST!

1. In square $ABCD$, the diagonals intersect at G.

   If $m\angle AGD = a + 2b$ and $m\angle ABC = 2a - b$, find the values of a and b.

2. Consider the two-column proof below. Put the statements and reasons in the correct order by writing the correct number in the left column.

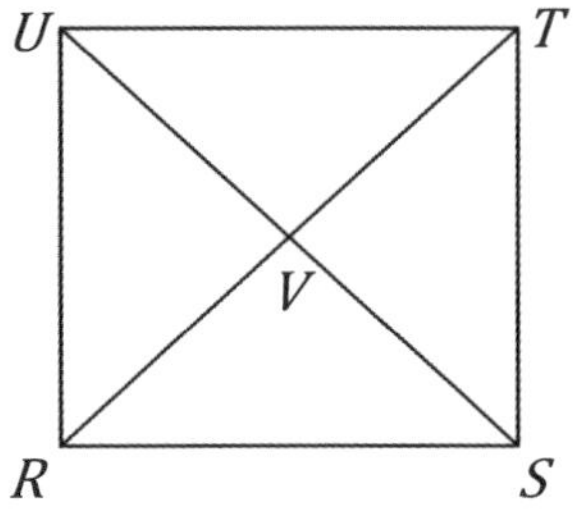

Given: $RSTU$ is a square.

Prove: $\overline{RT} \perp \overline{SU}$

	Statements	Reasons
	$\overline{UV} \cong \overline{SV} \cong \overline{RV} \cong \overline{TV}$	In a square, diagonals are congruent and bisect each other.
	$\overline{RT} \perp \overline{SU}$	Diagonals of a square bisect each other and are perpendicular.
	$m\angle UVR + m\angle TVU = 180°$ $m\angle RVS + m\angle TVS = 180°$	Linear Pairs
	$\overline{UT} \cong \overline{TS} \cong \overline{RS} \cong \overline{UR}$	Definition of a square
	$m\angle UVR = m\angle TVU = m\angle RVS = m\angle TVS = 90°$	Substitution
	$\Delta UVR \cong \Delta RVS \cong \Delta SVT \cong \Delta TVU$	SSS
	$RSTU$ is a square.	Given
	$\angle UVR \cong \angle TVU \cong \angle RVS \cong \angle TVS$	CPCTC
	$\angle UVT$ and $\angle TVS$ are right angles.	If two angles are congruent and supplementary, then they are right angles.

Section 8 – Topic 9
Kites

A kite is a quadrilateral that has two pairs of ______________ congruent sides, but the opposite sides are not congruent.

TAKE NOTE! *Postulates & Theorems*

Theorems About Kites

If a quadrilateral is a kite:

- Its diagonals are perpendicular.
- It has one pair of congruent opposite angles.
- One of its diagonals forms two isosceles triangles, and the other forms two congruent triangles.
- It has one diagonal that bisects a pair of opposite angles.
- It has one diagonal that bisects the other diagonal.
- If one of the diagonals of a quadrilateral is the perpendicular bisector of the other, the quadrilateral is a kite.

Illustrate the theorems about kites in the figure below.

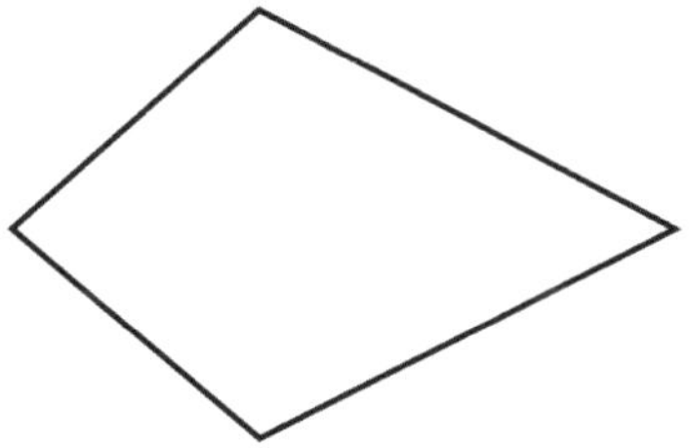

Let's Practice!

1. Consider kite $WXYZ$ below.

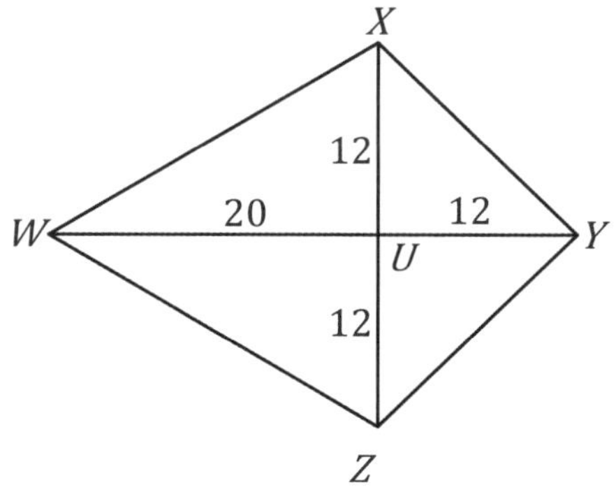

a. Determine the lengths of each side of kite $WXYZ$.

b. Which diagonal bisects a pair of opposite angles?

2. Complete the following proof.

Given: $ABCD$ is a kite.
Prove: $\Delta BCM \cong \Delta DCM$.

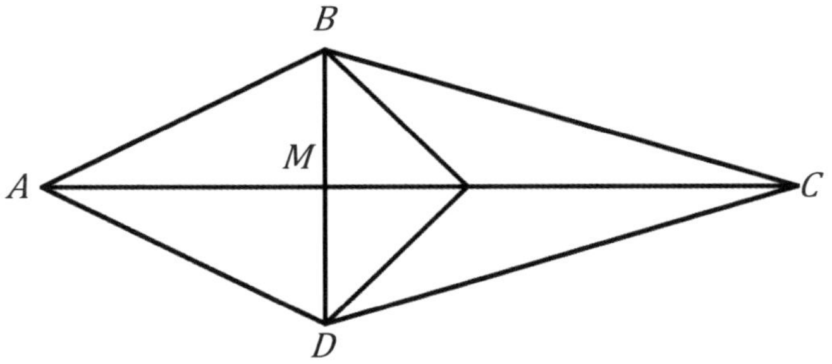

Statements	Reasons
1. $ABCD$ is a kite.	**1.** Given
2. $\angle BMC, \angle BMA, \angle DMA,$ and $\angle DMC$ are right angles	**2.** Diagonals of a kite are perpendicular
3. $m\angle BMC = m\angle BMA = m\angle DMA = m\angle DMC = 90°$	**3.**
4.	**4.** Right angles are congruent
5. $\overline{CM} \cong \overline{CM}$	**5.** Reflexive Property
6.	**6.** One diagonal bisects the other
7. $\Delta BCM \cong \Delta DCM$	**7.**

Try It!

3. Complete the following proof.

Given: $ABCD$ is a kite.
Prove: $\overline{AC}$ bisects $\angle BCD$.

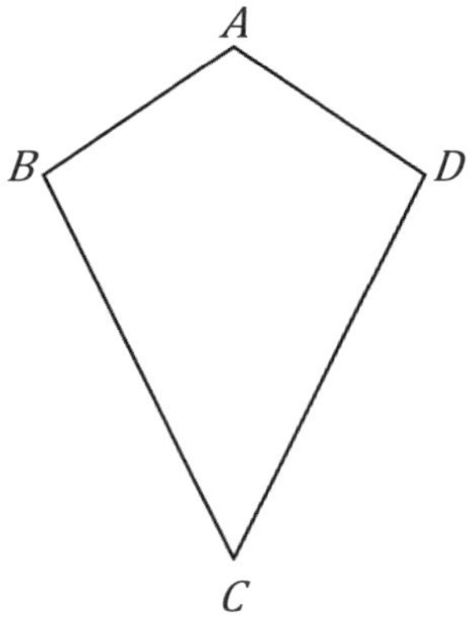

We are given that $ABCD$ is a kite. Using the properties of a kite, we can say that $\overline{AC}$ is a diagonal of the kite, ________________, and $\overline{DC} \cong \overline{BC}$.

The statement $\overline{AC} \cong \overline{AC}$ is true, because of the Reflexive Property, and using ____________, we know that $\Delta ABC \cong \Delta ADC$.

The statement $\angle ABC \cong \angle ADC$ is true because of ____________. Therefore, ________________________________ by the definition of angle bisector.

4. Consider kite $WXYZ$. If $m\angle WZT = 55°$ and $m\angle WXY = 30°$, find $m\angle ZWX$.

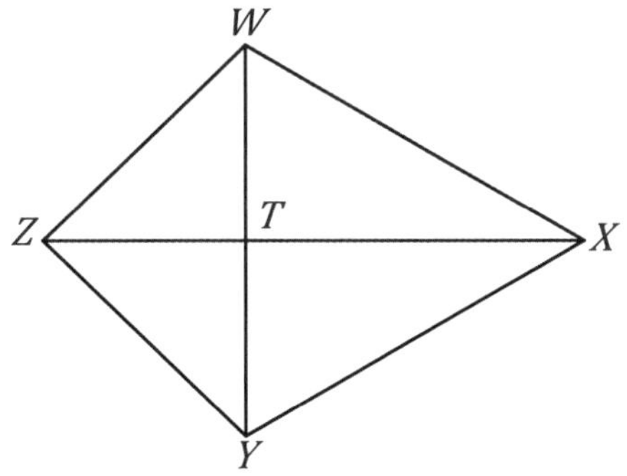

5. Consider kite $HIJK$. If $HK = 8$ and $HP = 5$, find KP.

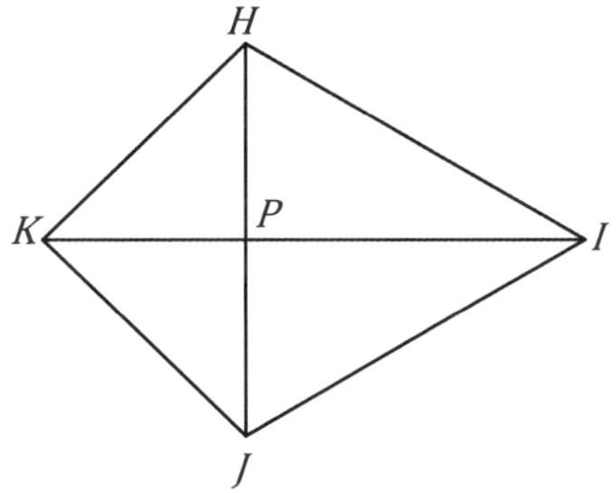

BEAT THE TEST!

1. Complete the two-column proof below.

Given: $ABCD$ is a quadrilateral.
$\overline{AC}$ is the perpendicular bisector of $\overline{BD}$.
Prove: $ABCD$ is a kite.

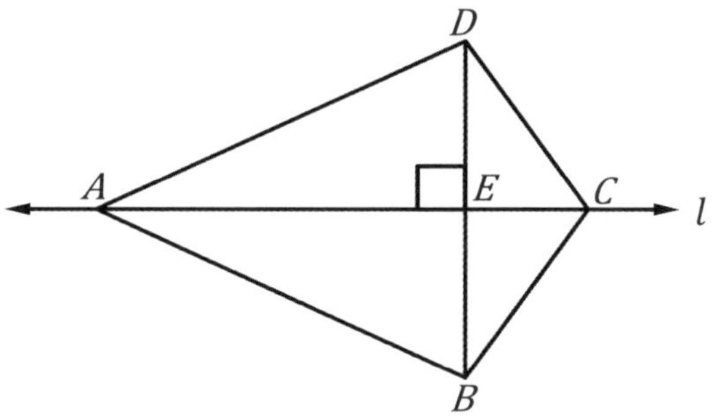

Statements	Reasons
1. $ABCD$ is a quadrilateral. $\overline{AC}$ is the perpendicular bisector of $\overline{BD}$.	**1.** Given
2. $\overline{DE} \cong \overline{EB}$	**2.**
3. $m\angle DEA = m\angle BEA = m\angle CED = m\angle CEB = 90°$	**3.** Perpendicular lines form right angles
4. $\angle DEA \cong \angle BEA \cong \angle CED \cong \angle CEB$	**4.** All right angles are congruent
5. $\overline{AE} \cong \overline{AE}$; $\overline{CE} \cong \overline{CE}$	**5.** Reflexive Property
6.	**6.** SAS
7. $\overline{AB} \cong \overline{AD}$, $\overline{DC} \cong \overline{BC}$	**7.**
8. $ABCD$ is a kite.	**8.** Definition of a kite

2. Consider kite $WXYZ$.

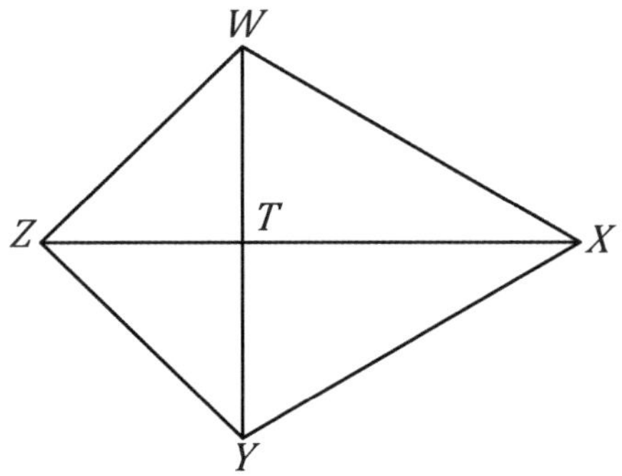

If $WT = 12$ yards, $TZ = 5$ yards, and $TX = 40$ yards, the perimeter of $WXYZ$ is [   ] yards.

Section 8 – Topic 10
Trapezoids

Consider the following trapezoid.

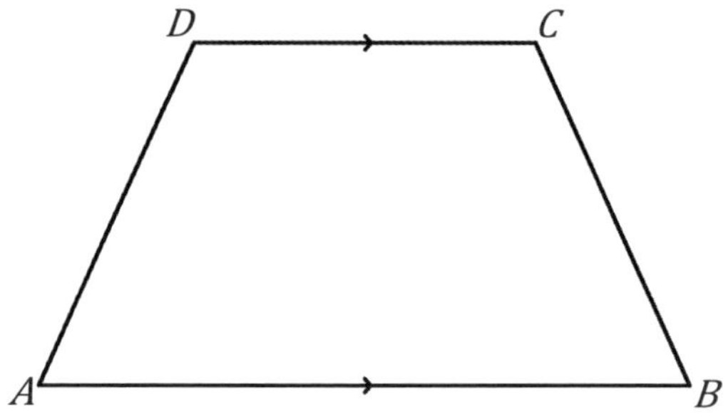

- A trapezoid is a quadrilateral with exactly one pair of opposite sides that are ____________________.
- The parallel sides are called the _____________ of the trapezoid.
- The non-parallel sides are called the ________.
- A trapezoid has two ____________ of base angles.
- A trapezoid is isosceles if it has one pair of non-consecutive congruent sides, congruent base angles, and _____________________ opposite angles.

> **TAKE NOTE!** *Postulates & Theorems*
>
> **<u>Theorems About Trapezoids</u>**
>
> If a quadrilateral is an isosceles trapezoid,
>
> - its pairs of base angles are congruent.
> - its diagonals are congruent.

Let's Practice!

1. Consider isosceles trapezoids $ABCD$ and $PQRS$ below.

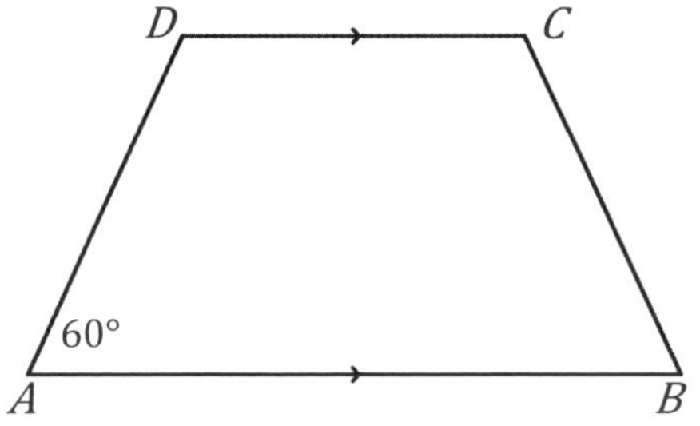

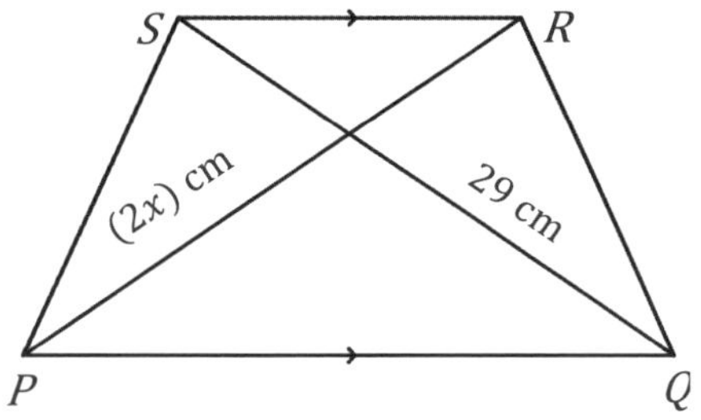

Find x, $m\angle DCB$, and PR.

2. Consider the figure below.

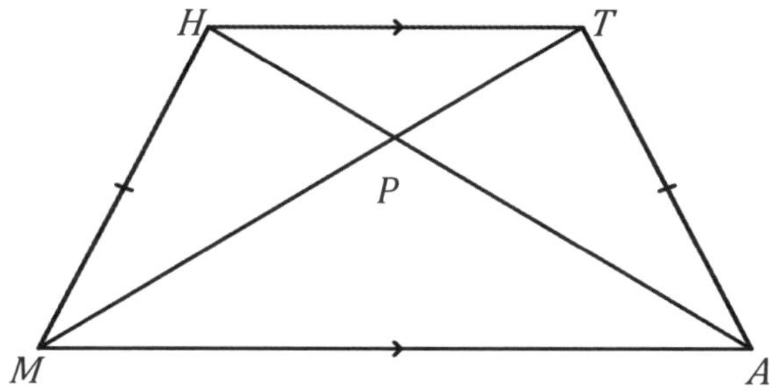

Given: $MATH$ is an isosceles trapezoid with bases $\overline{MA}$ and $\overline{TH}$.
Prove: $\overline{PH} \cong \overline{PT}$.

Complete the following two-column proof.

Statements	Reasons
1. $MATH$ is an isosceles trapezoid with bases $\overline{MA}$ and $\overline{HT}$.	**1.** Given
2.	**2.** Legs are congruent in isosceles trapezoids.
3. $\angle MHT \cong \angle ATH$	**3.**
4.	**4.** Reflexive Property
5. $\Delta THM \cong \Delta HTA$	**5.**
6.	**6.** CPCTC
7. $\angle HPM \cong \angle TPA$	**7.**
8.	**8.** AAS
9. $\overline{PH} \cong \overline{PT}$	**9.**

Try It!

3. Consider the figure below.

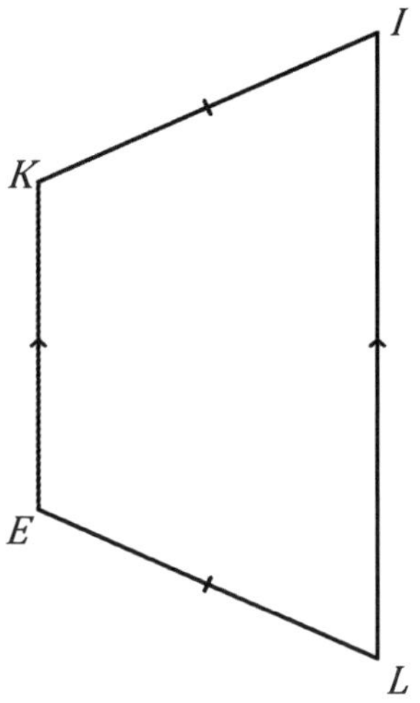

Given: $LIKE$ is a quadrilateral with $\overline{LI} \parallel \overline{EK}$ and $\overline{LE} \cong \overline{IK}$.
Prove: $\angle ELI \cong \angle KIL$.

Write a paragraph proof.

4. Consider isosceles trapezoids $TRAP$ and $FRED$.

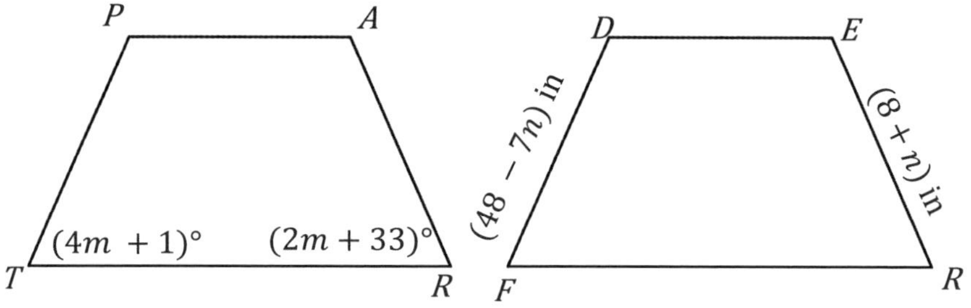

Find m, n, $m\angle PTR$, $m\angle PAR$, and FD.

BEAT THE TEST!

1. Complete the following proof.

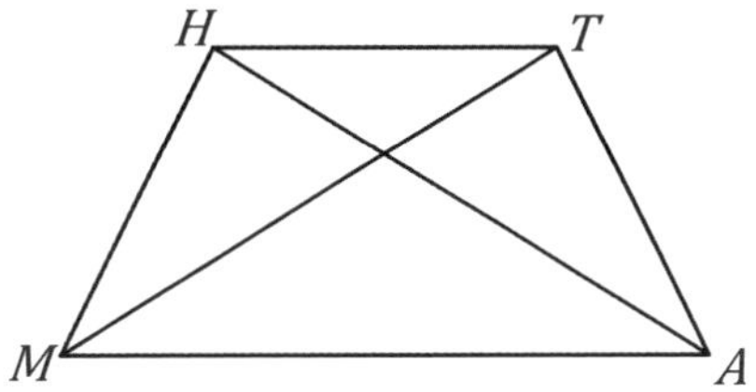

Given: $MATH$ is an isosceles trapezoid.
Prove: $\angle MHA \cong \angle ATM$

Complete the paragraph proof using the bank of terms below.

It is given that $MATH$ is an isosceles trapezoid. We can prove that $\overline{MH} \cong \overline{AT}$ ______. Then, $\overline{MA} \cong \overline{MA}$ by the ______. We can state that $\overline{AH} \cong \overline{MT}$ by using the ______. Now, we have triangles $\Delta HMA \cong \Delta TAM$ by ______. Finally, by using ______, we can prove that $\angle MHA \cong \angle ATM$.

Reflexive Property	Midsegment Theorem for Trapezoids
Trapezoid Base Angles Theorem	Definition of Isosceles Trapezoid
ASA	SSS
Trapezoid Diagonals Theorem	Transitive Property
Alternate Interior Angles	CPCTC

Section 8 – Topic 11
Quadrilaterals in Coordinate Geometry - Part 1

Let's discuss writing proofs using Coordinate Geometry.

- Coordinate geometry involves placing geometric figures in a ______ ______.
- Coordinate geometry proofs use several kinds of formulas.

Distance Formula	Slope Formula	Midpoint Formula

When developing a coordinate geometry proof, we should complete the following steps:

- Draw and label the graph (or identify a graph in a plane).
- Decide which formula(s) are needed to prove the type of quadrilateral.
- Develop a two-column, paragraph, or flow map proof.

Let's Practice!

1. Consider the information and figure below.

Given:
$PINE$ is a quadrilateral with vertices at $P(-5, 2), I(4, 9)$, $N(3, 10)$, and $E(-6, 3)$.

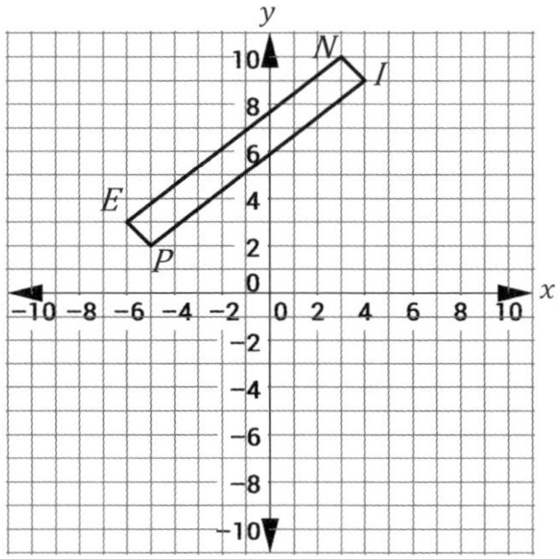

Prove:
$PINE$ is a parallelogram.

Write a paragraph proof based on the above information and diagram.

2. Consider the information below.

Given: $J(2, 2), U(0, 10), M(8, 8), P(10, 0)$.
Prove: $JUMP$ is a rhombus

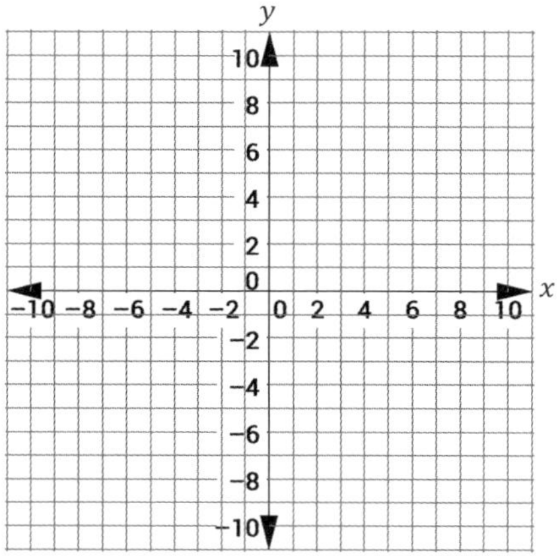

Write a paragraph proof.

3. Consider the quadrilateral $JUMP$ from the previous exercise. The midpoint of $\overline{JU}$ is $(1,6)$, called W. The midpoint of $\overline{UM}$ is $(4,9)$, called A. The midpoint of $\overline{MP}$ is $(9,4)$, called L. The midpoint of $\overline{PJ}$ is $(6,1)$, called K.

Use the information above to prove that the line segments joining the midpoints of the consecutive sides of a rhombus form a rectangle. Complete the following two-column proof.

Statements	Reasons
1. $JUMP$ is a rhombus where the midpoint of $\overline{JU}$ is $(1,6)$,the midpoint of $\overline{UM}$ is $(4,9)$, the midpoint of $\overline{MP}$ is $(9,4)$, and the midpoint of $\overline{PJ}$ is $(6,1)$.	**1.** Given
2.	**2.** Slope Formula, because opposite sides of a rectangle are parallel
3.	**3.** Perpendicular lines have slopes that are opposite reciprocals.
4.	**4.** Distance Formula, because opposite sides of a rectangle are congruent
5.	**5.** Definition of rectangle

Try It!

4. Graph $COLD$ and complete the following paragraph proof.

Given: $COLD$ is a quadrilateral with vertices at $C(1,1), O(2,5), L(5,7)$, and $D(7,5)$.

Prove: $COLD$ is a trapezoid, but is *NOT* an isosceles trapezoid.

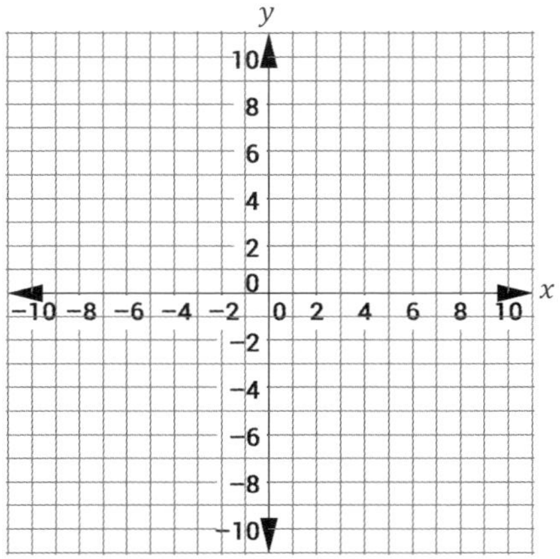

Given that $COLD$ is a quadrilateral with vertices at $C(1,1), O(2,5), L(5,7)$, and $D(7,5)$, the slope of $\overline{OL}$ is _____________ and the slope of $\overline{CD}$ is _____________, so _____________ because their slopes are equal. However, the slopes of $\overline{CO}$ and $\overline{LD}$ are not _________________, so these lines are not parallel. Therefore, $COLD$ is a trapezoid by definition.

$\overline{CO}$ is _____________ units long and $\overline{LD}$ is _____________ units long, by the distance formula. Since, _____________ and _____________, trapezoid $COLD$ is not isosceles. Their _____________ are not congruent.

Section 8 – Topic 12
Quadrilaterals in Coordinate Geometry – Part 2

Let's Practice!

1. Consider quadrilateral $JKLM$ with the following coordinates: $J(1,-2), K(-1,-4), L(-3,-2), M(-1,10)$. What kind of quadrilateral is $JKLM$? Remember to justify your answer!

2. Which of the following conclusions cannot always be drawn using coordinate geometry?

   Ⓐ Two sides are congruent.
   Ⓑ A segment bisects another segment.
   Ⓒ Two angles are congruent.
   Ⓓ A quadrilateral is a trapezoid with a midsegment.

3. Quinn graphs parallelogram $GRIT$ with the coordinates $G(10,8)$, $R(10,20), I(18,20), T(18,8)$.

   The diagonals meet at point ☐.

Try It!

4. Quadrilateral $ABCD$ has the following coordinates: $A(0,0), B(0,3), C(5,5), D(5,2)$. What kind of quadrilateral is $ABCD$? Prove your answer.

5. Quadrilateral $GRIT$ has coordinates $G(10,8), R(10,20)$, $I(18,20)$, and $T(18,8)$.

   Part A: Circle the correct answer that completes the statement below.

   $GRIT$ is a rectangle | rhombus | isosceles trapezoid.

   Part B: Which of the following statements is enough to justify your answer?

   Ⓐ $GRIT$ has four right angles and two pairs of congruent sides.

   Ⓑ $GRIT$ has opposite angles that are congruent but not right angles.

   Ⓒ $GRIT$ has diagonals that intersect at $90°$.

   Ⓓ $GRIT$ has one pair of parallel opposite sides and one pair of non-parallel but congruent sides.

BEAT THE TEST!

1. Consider quadrilateral $MATH$ below.

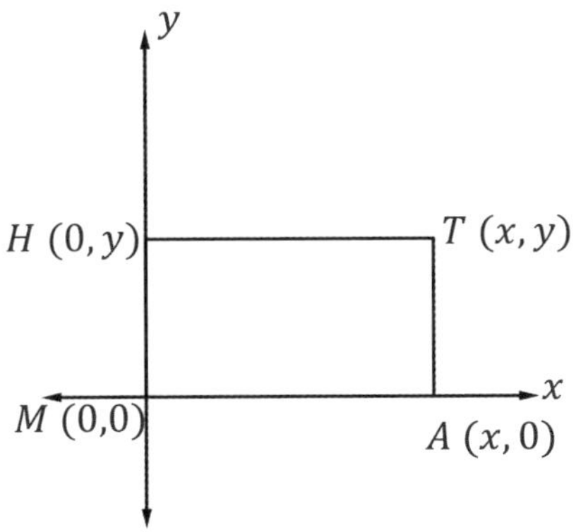

We can prove that $MATH$ is a rectangle by calculating the length of each diagonal.

Write the algebraic expression for the length of each diagonal.

2. Prove that quadrilateral $LEAP$ with vertices $L(-3,1), E(3,3)$, $A(5,7)$, and $P(-1,5)$ is a parallelogram.

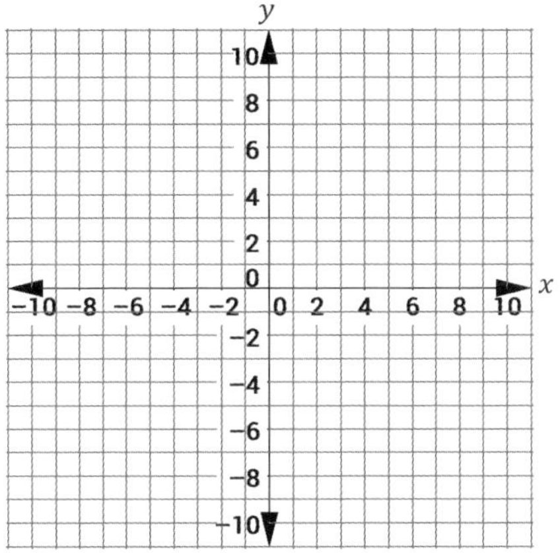

Which of the following statements help to prove that $LEAP$ is a parallelogram? Select all that apply.

- ☐ $LE = 2\sqrt{10}$, $EA = 2\sqrt{5}$, $AP = 2\sqrt{10}$, $LP = 2\sqrt{5}$, so $\overline{LE} \cong \overline{AP}$ and $\overline{EA} \cong \overline{LP}$. Opposite sides of a parallelogram are congruent.
- ☐ $LE = EA = AP = LP = 2\sqrt{10}$, so $\overline{LE} \cong \overline{EA} \cong \overline{AP} \cong \overline{LP}$. All sides are congruent, depicting a square, which is a type of parallelogram.
- ☐ The slope of $\overline{LE}$ and $\overline{AP}$ is $\frac{1}{3}$. The slope of $\overline{EA}$ and $\overline{LP}$ is 2. Since $\overline{LE} \parallel \overline{AP}$ and $\overline{EA} \parallel \overline{LP}$, opposite sides of a parallelogram are parallel.
- ☐ The slope of $\overline{LE}$ and $\overline{AP}$ is $\frac{1}{3}$. Since $\overline{LE} \parallel \overline{AP}$, parallelograms have one pair of parallel sides.
- ☐ The slope of $\overline{LE}$ and $\overline{AP}$ is $\frac{1}{3}$, while the slope of $\overline{EA}$ and $\overline{LP}$ is -3. These slopes are opposite reciprocals of each other, so $LEAP$ is a rectangle, which is a type of parallelogram.

Test Yourself! Practice Tool

Great job! You have reached the end of this section. Now it's time to try the "Test Yourself! Practice Tool," where you can practice all the skills and concepts you learned in this section. Log in to Math Nation and try out the "Test Yourself! Practice Tool" so you can see how well you know these topics!

Section 9: Circles – Part 1

Topic 1: Introduction to Circles 244
Standards Covered: G-GMD.1
- ☐ I can use the circumference of a circle to solve problems.

Topic 2: Arcs and Circumference of a Circle 247
Standards Covered: G-C.5
- ☐ I can calculate and use the circumference of a circle to solve problems.

Topic 3: Area of a Circle 249
Standards Covered: G-C.2, G-GMD.1
- ☐ I can calculate and use area of a circle to solve problems

Topic 4: Sectors of a Circle 251
Standards Covered: G-C.2
- ☐ I can calculate and use area of a circle and sectors to solve problems.

Topic 5: Circles in the Coordinate Plane: Standard Form 253
Standards Covered: G-GPE.1
- ☐ I can derive and apply the equation of a circle in standard form on a coordinate plane.

Topic 6: Circles in the Coordinate Plane: General Form 257
Standards Covered: G-GPE.1
- ☐ I can derive and apply the equation of a circle in general form on a coordinate plane.

Topic 7: Deriving the Equation of a Parabola Given a Focus and Directrix 259
Standards Covered: G-GPE.2
- ☐ I can define and represent points, lines, line segments, planes, rays, and angles.

Topic 8: Circle Transformations 262
Standards Covered: G-C.1
- ☐ I can transform circles, especially dilating a circle centered at the origin or on another point.

Topic 9: Radians and Degrees 265
Standards Covered: G-C.5
- ☐ I can convert from radians to degrees, and from degrees to radians.

Visit MathNation.com or search "Math Nation" in your phone or tablet's app store to watch the videos that go along with this workbook!

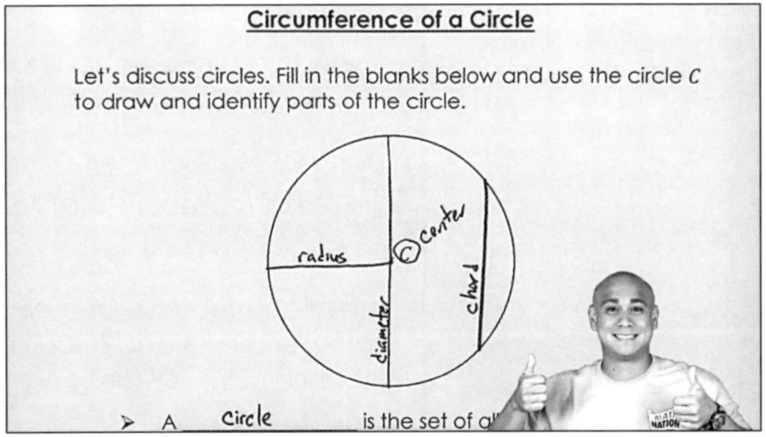

Circumference of a Circle
Let's discuss circles. Fill in the blanks below and use the circle C to draw and identify parts of the circle.
radius
C
center
diameter
chord
➢ A circle is the set of a

The following Michigan Mathematics Standards will be covered in this section:
G-C.1 - Prove that all circles are similar.
G-C.2 - Identify and describe relationships among inscribed angles, radii, and chords. *Include the relationships between central, inscribed, and circumscribed angles; inscribed angles on a diameter are right angles; the radius of a circle is perpendicular to the tangent where the radius intersects the circle.*
G-C.5 - Derive using similarity the fact that the length of the arc intercepted by an angle is proportional to the radius, and define the radian measure of the angle as the constant of proportionality; derive the formula for the area of a sector.
G-GMD.1 - Give an informal argument for the formulas for the circumference of a circle, area of a circle, volume of a circle, pyramid and cone.
G-GPE.1 - Derive the equation of a circle of given center and radius using the Pythagorean Theorem; complete the square to find the center and radius of a circle given by an equation.
G-GPE.2 - Derive the equation of a parabola given a focus and directrix.

Section 9: Circles – Part 1

Section 9 – Topic 1

Introduction to Circles

Solimar was designing a quilt that had a circle on it. To create a circle pattern she used a pin, string, and a pencil.

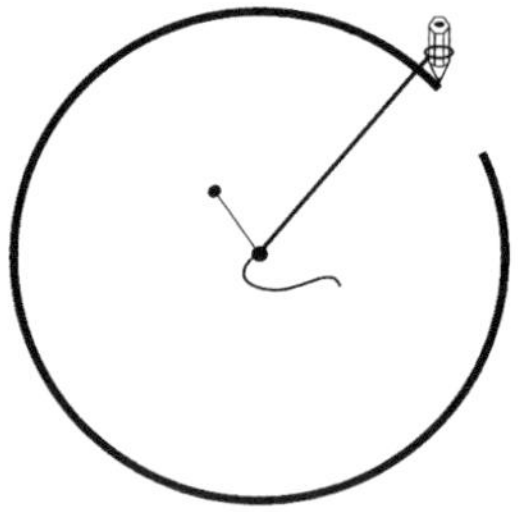

Solimar placed a pin on a sheet of paper then attached a string to the pin and a pencil. She then drew the circle.

What part of Solimar's drawing is the center of the circle?

What part of the circle is the string?

What part of the circle is drawn by the pencil?

What do all of the points on Solimar's circle have in common?

Here is one precise definition of a circle.

The set of all points in a plane that are equidistant from a fixed point (the center).

Below are some definitions of a circle that are not precise.

Draw a counterexample for each one.

- A round plane figure
- A two-dimensional shape made by drawing a curve that is always the same distance from a center
- All of the points that lie a distance from a center point

The circumference of a circle is a special case of perimeter. Both perimeter and circumference describe the total distance around a two-dimensional shape.

The diagram below shows circle C. The circumference of the circle is the string. Below the circle is the same piece of string displayed as a straight line.

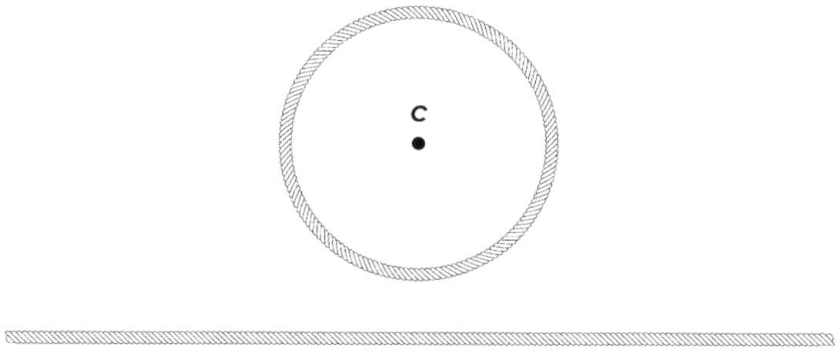

Draw the radius for circle C.

Estimate the number of radii that are the same length as the length of the circumference.

How does this illustrate the formula for circumference, $C = 2\pi r$, where r is the radius?

Let's Practice!

1. The diagram below shows different polygons inscribed in a circle.

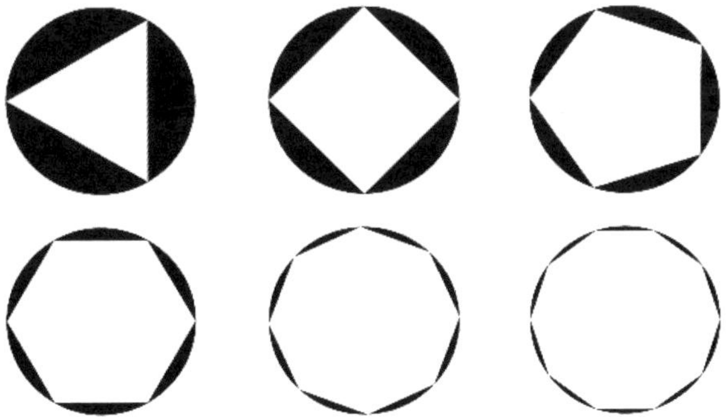

As the number of sides in the polygon increases, the ________________ of the polygon approximates the _______________ of the circle.

2. The diagram below shows point, W and a line segment $\overline{PK}$. Mark seven points that are a distance of $\overline{PK}$ from W.

3. Use the precise definition of a circle to explain why the seven points you drew are on the circumference of circle W.

Try It!

4. The diagram shows a hexagon inscribed in a circle. The hexagon is partitioned into six equilateral triangles. The triangles in the hexagon are decomposed and lined up by joining vertices.

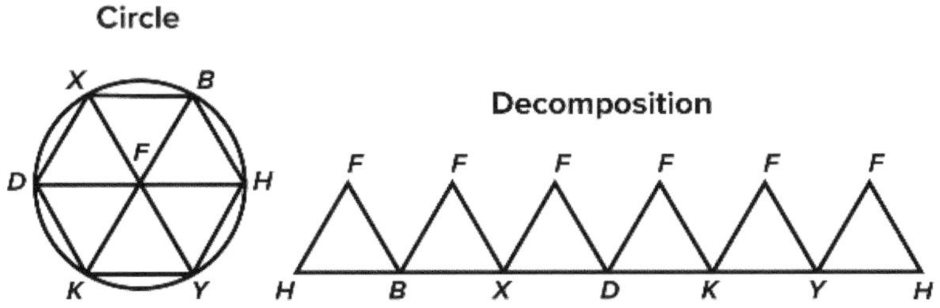

The decomposition of the hexagon goes counterclockwise around the circle. The H on the left of the decomposition represents the starting point and the H on the right represents the ending point.

a. What part of the circle does $\overline{FX}$ represent?

b. In the decomposition, how is the distance from the H on the left to B related to the circle?

c. Explain how the distance between the H on the left of the decomposition to the H on the right approximates the formula $C = 2\pi r$.

d. What part of the circle is $\overline{DH}$?

e. In the decomposition, how do you know that the distance from the H on the left to X is the same as the length of $\overline{DH}$ in the circle?

f. Explain how using the distance from the H on the left to X, from X to K, and from K to the H on the right approximates the formula $C = \pi d$.

BEAT THE TEST!

1. Three geometry students wrote the given definitions of a circle.

   Brian: A circle is the set of all points that are a given distance from a specific point.

   Yolanda: A circle is all of the points in a plane that are the same distance from the endpoints of a line segment.

   Eric: A circle is the collection of all of the points in a plane that are equidistant from a line segment.

   Part A: Match each definition with a diagram that represents a counterexample of the definition given by the student.

Definition	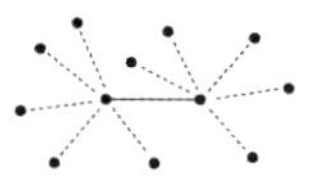	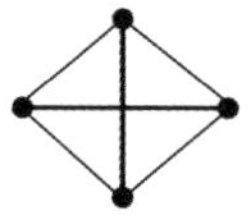		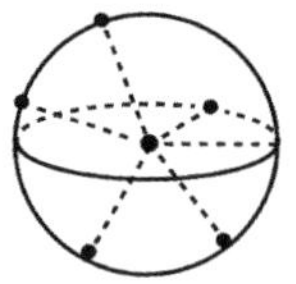
Brian	○	○	○	○
Yolanda	○	○	○	○
Eric	○	○	○	○

Part B: Complete the sentence so that it is a precise definition of a circle.

A circle is the set of all
- o points in a plane
- o line segments rotated around a point

that are equidistant from a(n)
- o point.
- o line segment.
- o endpoint of the radius.

Section 9 – Topic 2
Arcs and Circumference of a Circle

What is an arc of a circle? How can you find the length of an arc?

Given two points on a circle:

- An arc length is a portion of the ________________ of a circle.
- The _________ arc is the shortest arc linking both points. The _________ arc is the longest and often defined using another point on the arc, and use all three points to define it.
- The ratio of the length of an arc to the ________________ is equal to the ratio of the measure of the arc to _______.

Consider circle H below and solve for arc length of $\widehat{XY}$.

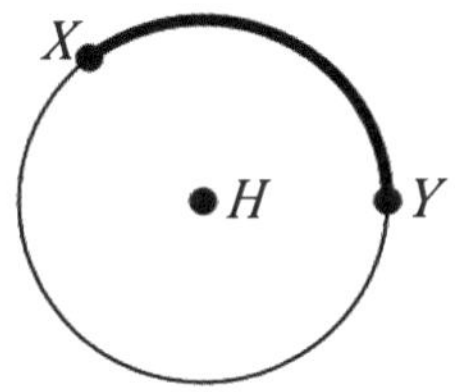

$$\frac{\widehat{XY}}{2\pi r} = \frac{m\widehat{XY}}{360^\circ}$$

Let's Practice!

1. Suppose circles O and P have the same center with radii of 4 and 6 centimeters, respectively. $\widehat{RE}$ is a minor arc in circle O and $\widehat{MI}$ is a minor arc in circle P. Both arcs have an angle measure of $36°$. Are their arc lengths the same? Justify your answer.

Try It!

2. Estimate the length of $\widehat{FN}$ if $m\angle FAN = 120°$. Use 3.14 for π.

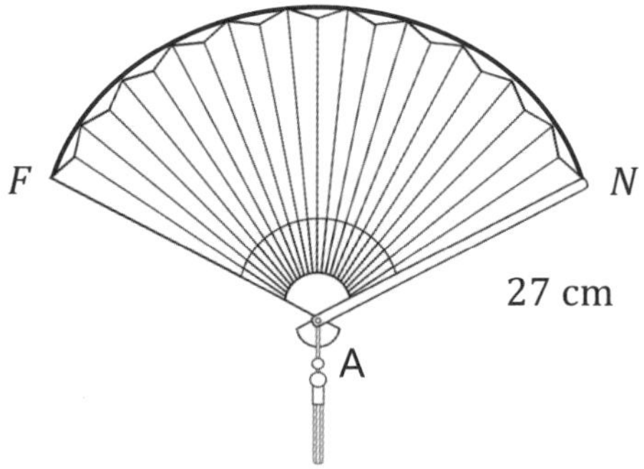

BEAT THE TEST!

1. Dominic is riding the Ferris wheel at the county fair. The Ferris wheel has a radius of 60 ft and rotates counter-clockwise. Seats are equidistant from each other.

a. After the ride begins from point A, it pauses at point B. How many feet has Dominic traveled when his seat pauses at point B?

☐ ☐ π or ☐ feet

b. About how many feet has Dominic traveled if the full ride is 4 revolutions?

☐ ☐ π or ☐ feet

Section 9 – Topic 3
Area of a Circle

What is the term for the amount of space occupied by any shape?

How can we find the area of a circle? Explain how the same elements used to find the circumference of a circle can be used to find its area.

Consider the regular hexagon shown on the right.

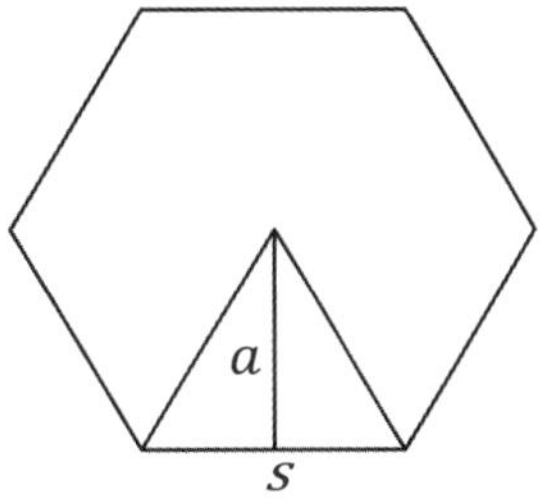

One way to find the area of the hexagon is to find the area of one triangle formed by the radii and multiply by six. Why six?

$A =$ ______________

The perimeter of the hexagon is equal to ____________. Using substitution, we can replace this value with P for perimeter.

$A = \frac{1}{2} \cdot a \cdot$ _________

Consider the circle shown here.

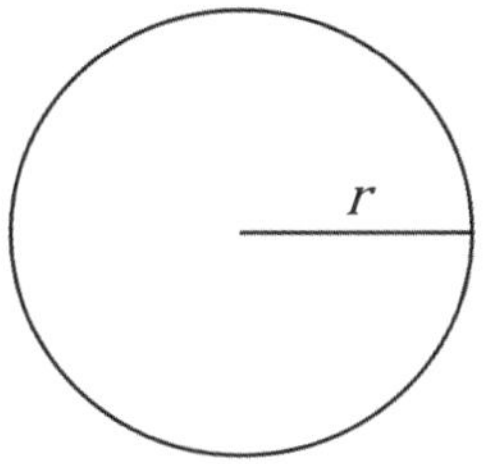

The apothem (a) in a polygon is the distance from the center to a side (or to a point in the incircle).

In a circle, this is known as the _____________.

$$A = \frac{1}{2} \cdot \text{\_\_\_\_} \cdot P$$

In addition, the perimeter of a circle is known as the ***circumference***. The circumference can be calculated using the equation ___________________.

Substitute into the formula and simplify.

$$A = \frac{1}{2} \cdot r \cdot \text{\_\_\_\_\_\_\_\_\_}$$

$$A = \text{\_\_\_\_\_\_\_\_\_\_\_\_\_\_}$$

Let's Practice!

1. A circle has a diameter of 18 inches. Find the exact area (using π) and an approximate area rounded to the nearest hundredth.

2. Dale is spreading grass seed over the putting green on a golf course. The circular green has a radius of 30 feet. If each bag of grass seed covers an area of 315 ft^2, how many bag(s) of grass seed does Dale need?

Try It!

3. A sidewalk bounds a circular playground at *GeoCity Park*. Parents can exercise by walking around on the sidewalk, while watching their children play. If the inner edge of the sidewalk is $1{,}256.64$ meters around, approximate the area of the playground inside the circular path.

4. Most road and racing bicycles today use $3{,}038.58$ square centimeter rims, though $2{,}560.52$ square centimeter rims are popular with smaller riders and triathletes. What is the difference between the diameters of the rims?

BEAT THE TEST!

1. A sprinkler rotates in a circular pattern and sprays water over a distance of 25 feet.

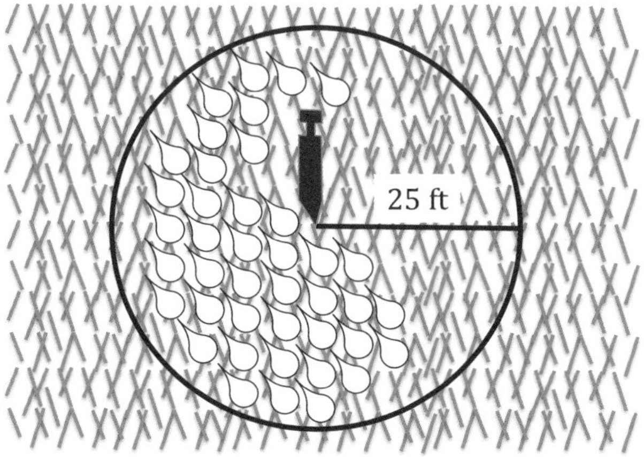

What is the approximate area of the circular region covered by the sprinkler?

Ⓐ 490.9 square feet
Ⓑ 1,963.5 square feet
Ⓒ 4,417.9 square feet
Ⓓ 7,853.9 square feet

Section 9 – Topic 4
Sectors of a Circle

Let's consider the area of a sector in the figure below.

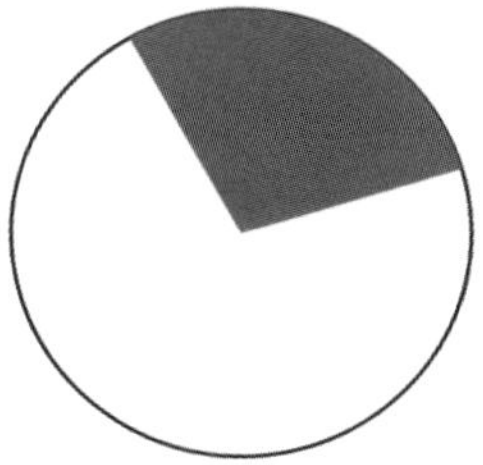

➢ A ***sector*** is the region bounded by two ________ of a circle and their intercepted arc.

What can we use to calculate the area of the sector?

The ratio of the area, A, of a sector to the area of the circle is equal to the ratio of the measure of the intercepted arc to $360°$.

$$\frac{A}{\pi r^2} = \frac{m\angle XHY}{360°}$$

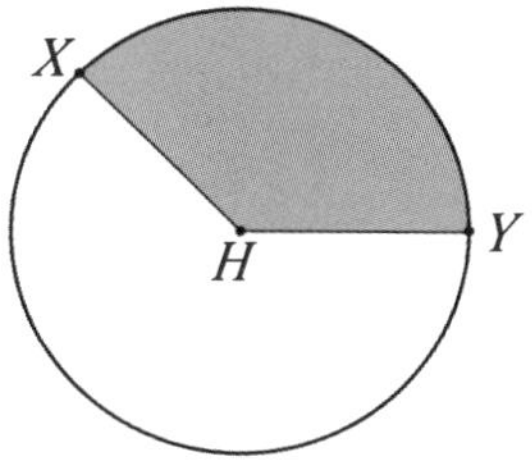

Solve for the area, A, of shaded sector of circle H to the right.

Let's Practice!

1. A circle has a 6 centimeter radius and a shaded sector with a central angle of $60°$. Determine the area of the shaded sector.

2. The area of a sector with a radius of 8 inches is 74.84 square inches. Calculate the approximate angle of the sector.

Try It!

3. A lighthouse is situated on the northern tip of an island. Determine the area of water that the light of the lighthouse can cover.

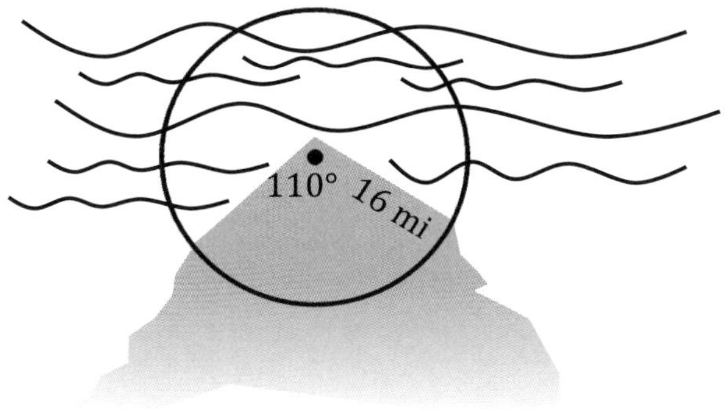

BEAT THE TEST!

1. In Sarah's family, the birthday person always gets to cut the first piece of cake. Sarah is celebrating her birthday with both of her parents, her two brothers, and her best friend. She cuts her piece of birthday cake as shown by the sector below.

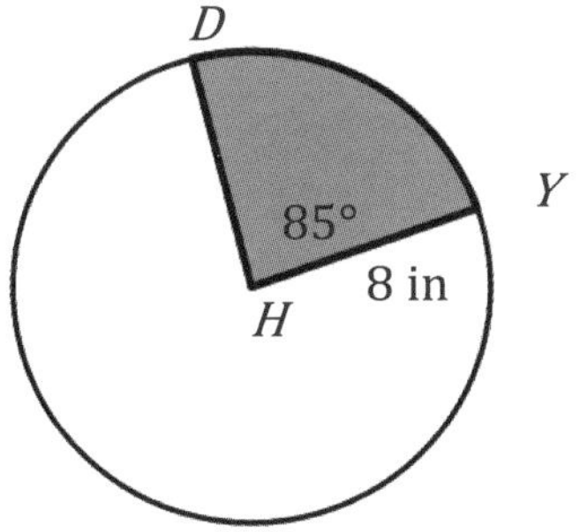

If the rest of the party equally shares the remaining portion of the cake, what is the approximate area that each one receives?

Ⓐ 30.718 in^2
Ⓑ 47.473 in^2
Ⓒ 153.589 in^2
Ⓓ 201.062 in^2

Section 9 – Topic 5
Circles in the Coordinate Plane: Standard Form

Determine what is required to create a circle on a coordinate plane.

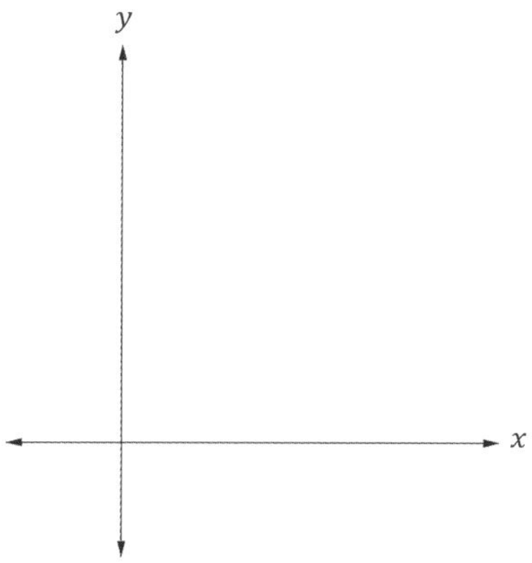

Consider the figure below.

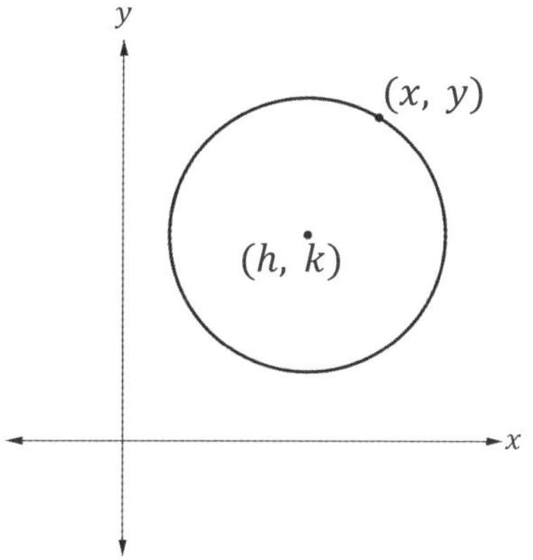

How would you derive the equation of a circle? Justify your answer.

Consider the graph of the circle below.

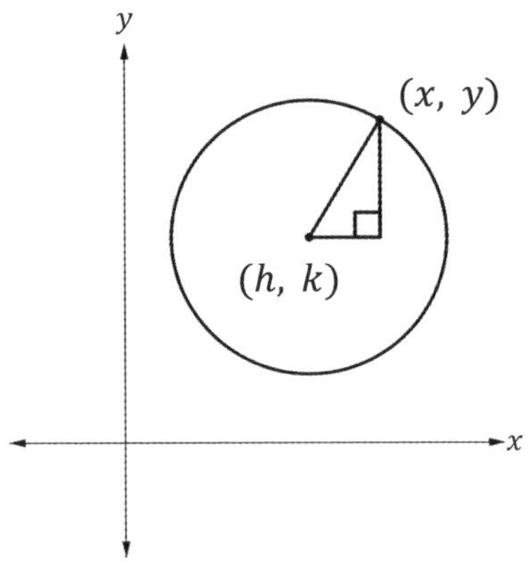

To find the radius, you can use the ***distance formula***.

Now, we find the length of the hypotenuse and the horizontal and vertical legs of the triangle.

- Horizontal Leg Length: ____________________
- Vertical Leg Length: ____________________
- Hypotenuse Length: ____________________

Substitute these lengths into the Pythagorean Theorem.

(________)^2 + (________)^2 = ______^{2}

This is the ***standard form*** for the equation of a circle with center ____________ and radius _________.

Let's Practice!

1. Graph the equation $x^2 + y^2 = 36$.

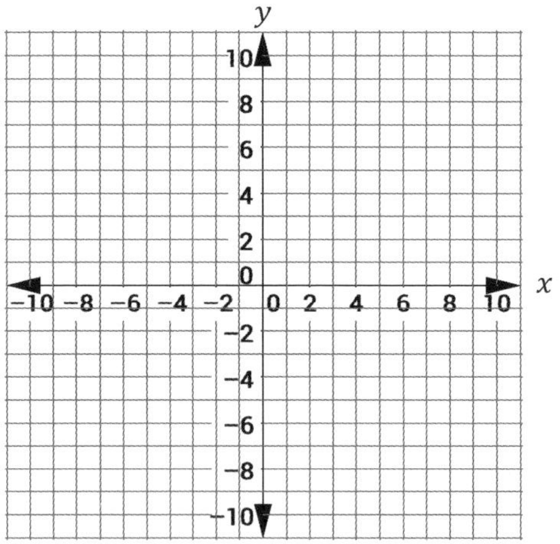

2. Write the equation of the graphed circle.

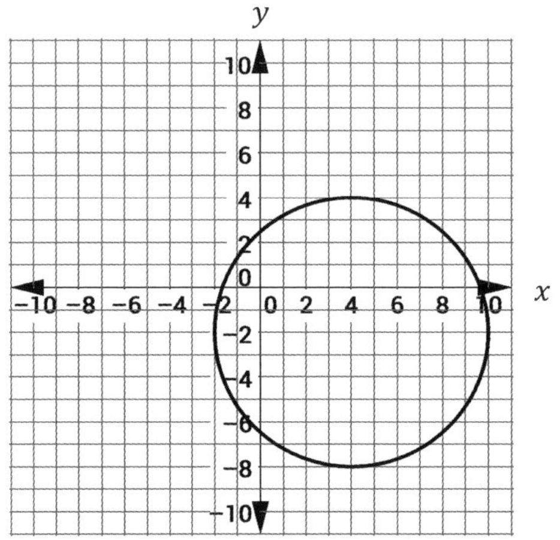

3. Leonard states that if $A, B,$ and C are points on a circle where the line $\overline{AC}$ is a diameter of the circle, then $\angle ABC$ is a right angle. Use coordinate geometry on the plane provided to prove Leonard's statement.

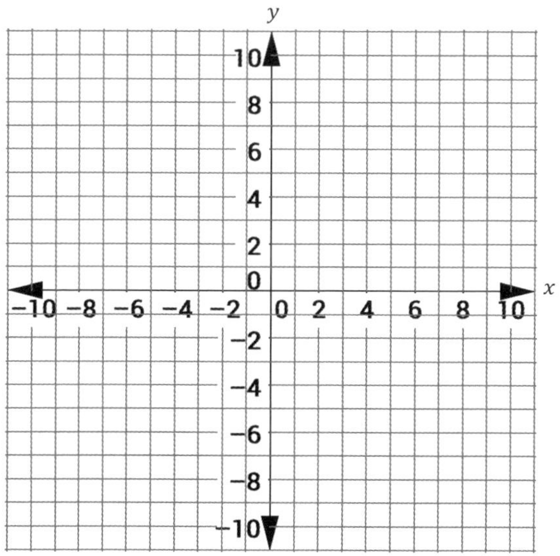

Try It!

4. Graph each equation.

a. $(x+1)^2 + (y-4)^2 = 9$

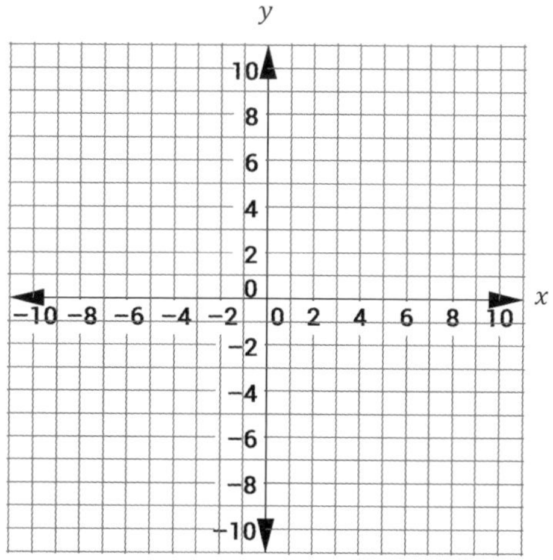

b. $x^2 + (y-3)^2 = 25$

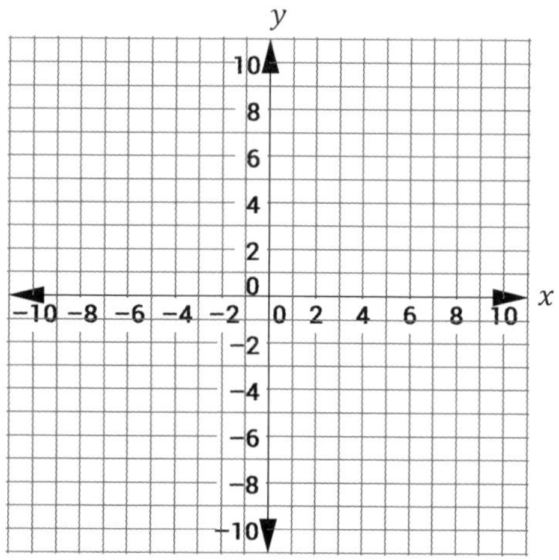

5. Write the equation of the graphed circle.

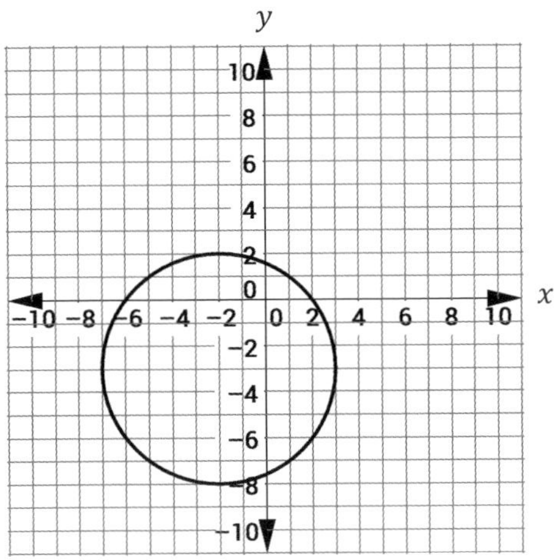

6. The local ABC broadcast tower services a 30–mile radius. Suppose you live in an apartment located 25 miles east and 21 miles north of the tower. Will you be able to receive TV waves from the tower? Justify your answer.

BEAT THE TEST!

1. A licensed gardener wants to position a tree 4 meters east and 7 meters north of his house in a garden. When the tree is fully grown, its branches will be roughly circular with a diameter of about 8 meters.

   Part A: Write an equation representing the outside of the grown tree's branches relative to his house.

   Part B: Will the house be covered by any of the branches of the tree? Justify your answer.

2. Ms. Arsolino showed the following exit ticket on the projector.

Find the equation of a circle with center (5, -7) and radius of 4. Justify your answer without the use of a coordinate plane.

Florence got the correct answer and her argument is shown on the next page. Choose the correct expression to complete each sentence in the argument.

Let $(5, -7)$ be the center of the circle and (x, y) be any point on the circle. Then, the horizontal distance from (x, y) to the center is

- o $|x - 5|$.
- o $|x + 5|$.
- o $|x - 7|$.
- o $|x + 7|$.

The vertical distance from (x, y) to the center is

- o $|y - 5|$.
- o $|y + 5|$.
- o $|y - 7|$.
- o $|y + 7|$.

The distance from (x, y) to the center is

- o 2.
- o 4.
- o 12.
- o 16.

Finally, the

- o perimeter formula
- o Pythagorean Theorem
- o quadratic formula
- o slope formula

can now be used to create an equation that shows the relationship between the horizontal distance, vertical distance, and distance of (x, y) to the center of the circle.

Section 9 – Topic 6
Circles in the Coordinate Plane: General Form

How could we solve the trinomial $x^2 + 6x - 8 = 0$ by completing the square?

Consider the equation written in ***general form***, $x^2 + y^2 - 10y = 119$. How can we use completing the square to show that the equation resembles a circle?

Let's Practice!

1. Complete the square to transform the equation to standard form. What is the center and radius of the circle?

   $x^2 + y^2 - 10y = 119$

2. Complete the square to transform the equation to standard form. Then, graph it on the coordinate plane.

$x^2 + y^2 - 6x + 4y - 12 = 0$

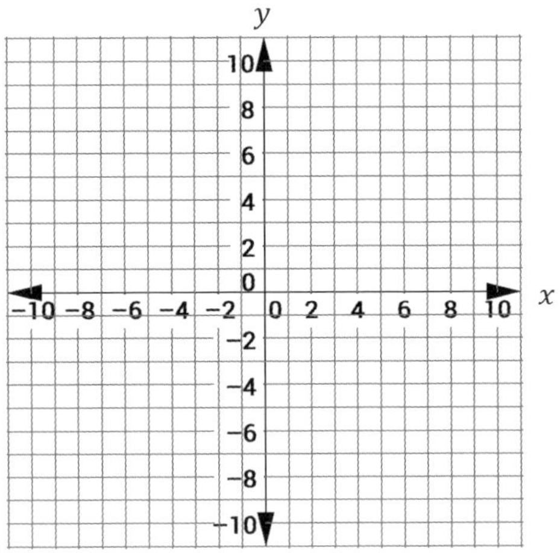

Try It!

3. Complete the square to transform the equation to standard form. Then, graph it on the coordinate plane.

$x^2 + y^2 - 8x - 12y = -36$

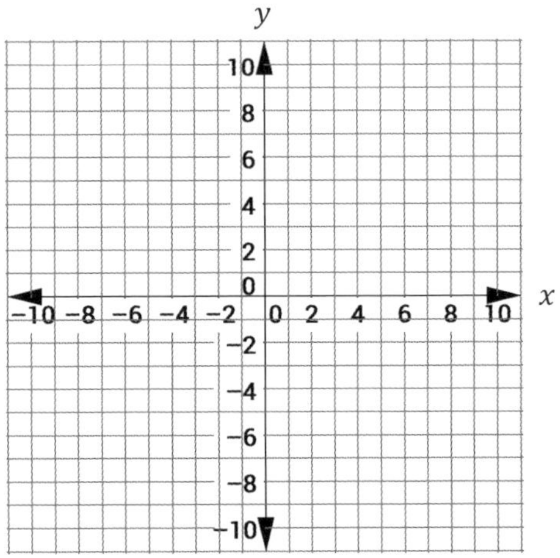

BEAT THE TEST!

1. Graph the following equation on the coordinate plane provided.

$x^2 + y^2 - 10x - 12y + 45 = 0$

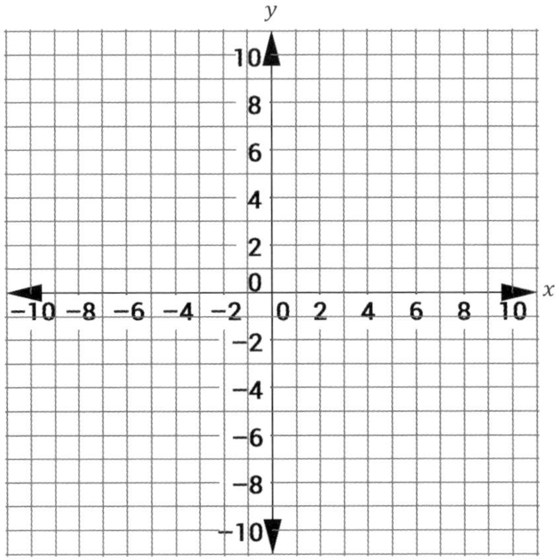

2. WXRT radio has a tower that is 30 miles east and 38 miles south of Donatello's apartment. The tower emits a signal that reaches all receivers within 45 miles of its location.

Part A: Write an equation in general form that describes the locations within the receiving distance of the tower.

Part B: Determine if Donatello is within the receiving distance of the signal.

Section 9 – Topic 7
Deriving the Equation of a Parabola Given a Focus and Directrix

The following parabola represents quadratic function $f(x)$, given the focus at $(0, p)$ and the directrix represented by line $y = -p$, where $p < 0$.

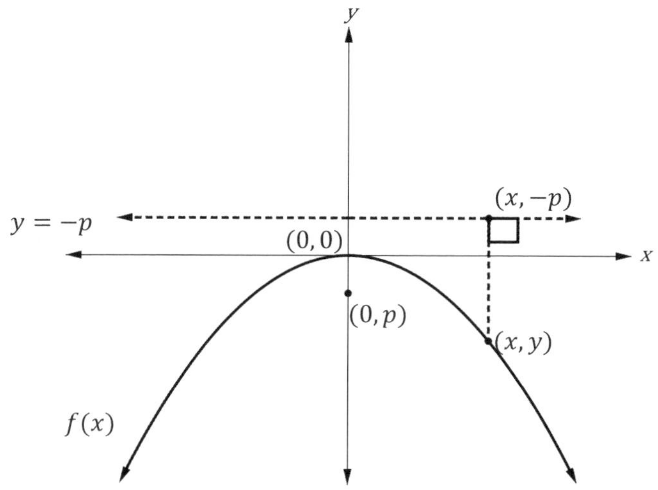

A ***parabola*** is a set of points in the plane equidistant from a fixed line (the __________) and a fixed point (the __________) not on the line.

The vertex of this parabola is ____________. For an arbitrary point (x, y) on the parabola the distance to the directrix is the distance from (x, y) to ____________. The distance to the focus is the distance between (x, y) and ____________.

Let's find an equation of a parabola with directrix $y = -p$ and focus $(0, p)$, where $p < 0$.

Statement	Reason
	Definition of a parabola
	Square both sides
	Equivalent Equation
	Addition Property of Equality
	Equivalent Equation
	Multiplication Property of Equality
	Equivalent Equation
	Reflective Property

Since a curve that satisfies the geometric definition of parabola has an equation of the form ____________________, let $a = \frac{1}{4p}$ and then, $y = ax^2$.

If the focus at $(0, p)$ with $p > 0$ and the directrix is $y = -p$, then, the parabola opens ____________.

Deriving the equation from the distances (as was done for $p < 0$) again yields $y = \frac{1}{4p}x^2$, which is of the form $y = ax^2$ for $a = \frac{1}{4p}$.

Note that a and p have the same sign because $a = \frac{1}{4p}$.

Let's Practice!

1. Based on the derivation of the equation of a parabola with directrix $y = p$ and focus $(0, -p)$, write a general equation in vertex form of $f(x)$ of any parabola with a horizontal directrix and vertex (h, k).

Statement	Reason
$(x - h)^2 = 4p(y - k)$	Given
	Square both sides
	Equivalent Equation
	Addition Property of Equality
	Equivalent Equation
	Equivalent Equation

2. Derive the equation of a parabola with directrix $y = -5$ and focus $(3, 1)$.

Try It!

3. The graph below shows a focus and directrix for a specific parabola.

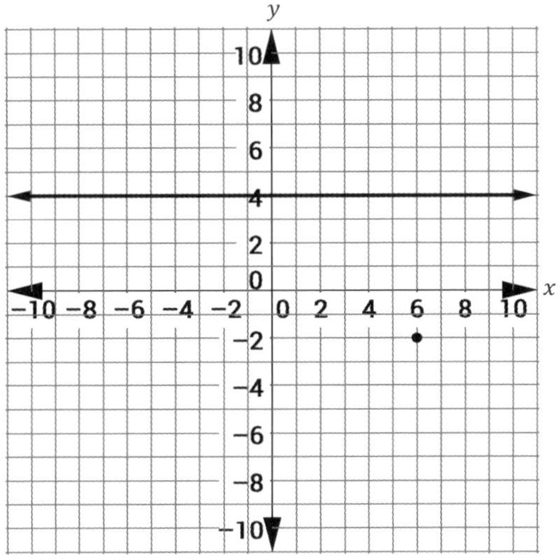

Derive the equation of the parabola and sketch the parabola on the graph.

BEAT THE TEST!

1. Mario is given the following information for two parabolas:

Parabola 1	**Parabola 2**
Focus: $(0, 8)$	Focus: $(1, 4)$
Directrix: $y = -2$	Directrix: $y = 1$

Which of the following are true? Select all that apply.

- ☐ The equation of Parabola 1 is $y = \frac{x^2}{20} + 3$.
- ☐ The equation of Parabola 2 is $y = \frac{x^2}{6} + \frac{5}{6}$.
- ☐ Both parabolas open upward.
- ☐ Both parabolas open downward.
- ☐ The coefficient on x^2 is $\frac{1}{6}$ for both parabolas.
- ☐ The y-value of the vertex for Parabola 1 is greater than the y-value of the vertex for Parabola 2.

Section 9 – Topic 8
Circle Transformations

Understanding how to transform circles is critical to success in real-world fields such as architecture or farming.

Let's review key points related to circle transformations.

- How can you determine if two circles are congruent?

- How can you determine if two circles are similar?

- How is the equation of a circle affected by a rigid transformation?

- How is the equation of a circle affected by a non-rigid transformation?

Consider the two circles on the coordinate plane below.

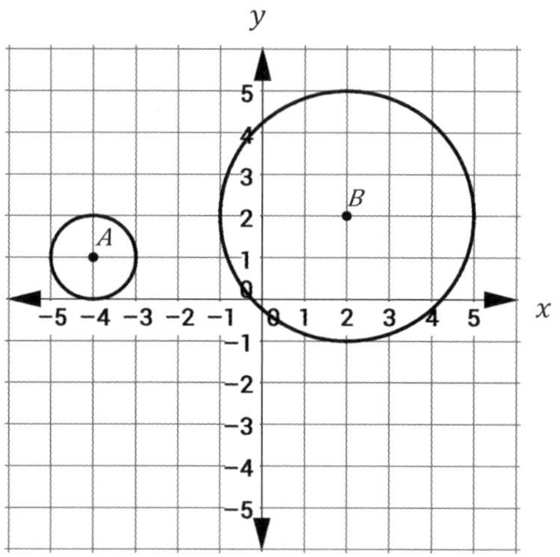

What is the key feature of a circle when dealing with transformations?

Evaluate which transformation will map circle A onto circle B.

What transformation could be applied to match circle A's radius to that of circle B?

Use the definition of similarity and transformations to justify that all circles are similar.

Let's Practice!

1. Consider the two circles on the coordinate plane below.

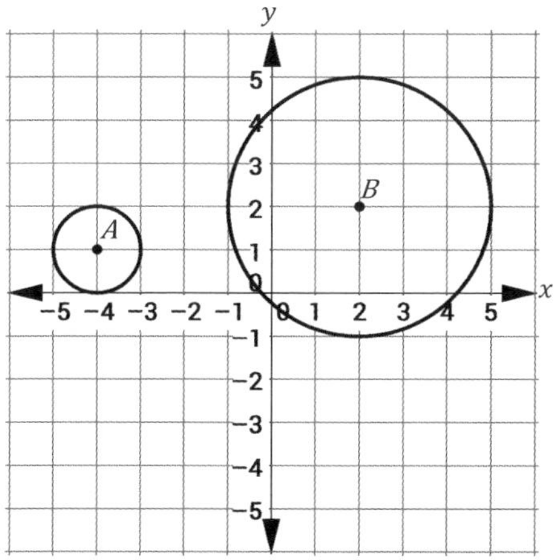

   a. Which transformation(s) will map circle A onto itself? Which transformation(s) will map circle B onto itself? Justify your answer.

   b. Graph the result of a transformation of circle A using the rule $(x, y) \rightarrow (x + 1, y + 1)$ followed by a dilation of scale factor two centered at point A'.

   c. Describe where A'' will be located if circle A' is dilated by scale factor two centered at the origin instead of centered at point A'?

Try It!

2. Graph the result of a transformation using the rule $(x, y) \rightarrow (x - 3, y + 2)$ followed by a dilation of scale factor $\frac{2}{3}$ centered on point O' on the coordinate plane below.

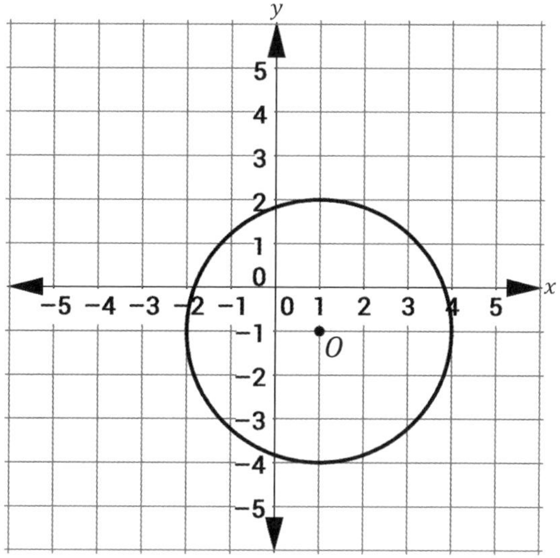

3. Consider the following diagram.

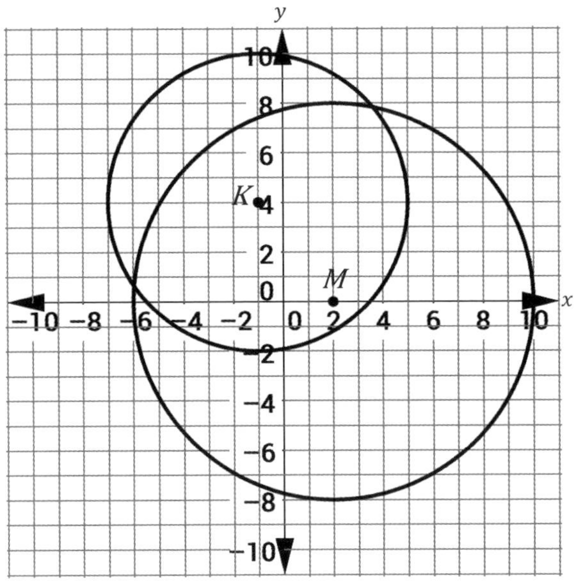

Describe the sequence of transformations that carry circle K onto circle M.

BEAT THE TEST!

1. Tom is building a new corral for his horse farm. He wants a corral with half the diameter of his current one. The schematic of his land is shown below. Circle C is the current corral. The rectangles represent barns. Select the series of transformations that would result in a corral that has the dimensions that Tom wants but would not interfere with any other structures.

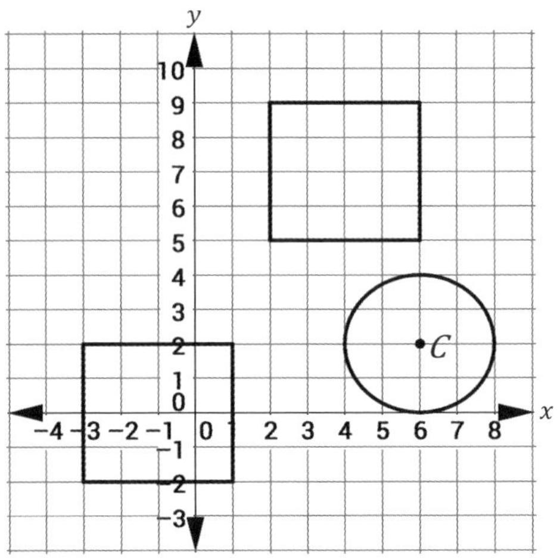

Ⓐ First, dilate the circle centered at point C. Then, $(x, y) \to (x - 9, y)$.

Ⓑ First, $(x, y) \to (x - 6, y + 1)$. Then, $(x, y) \to \left(\frac{3}{2}x, \frac{1}{2}y\right)$.

Ⓒ First, $(x, y) \to \left(\frac{1}{2}x, \frac{1}{2}y\right)$. Then, $(x, y) \to (x + 2, y + 5)$.

Ⓓ First, $(x - 2, y + 1)$. Then, $(x, y) \to \left(\frac{1}{2}x, \frac{1}{2}y\right)$ centered at point C'.

2. Let C be a circle in the coordinate plane that passes though the points $(0,0)$, $(0,6)$, and $(8,0)$.

Describe a sequence of transformations that would map circle C to a circle with radius of 1, centered at the origin.

Section 9 – Topic 9
Radians and Degrees

Consider the figure below.

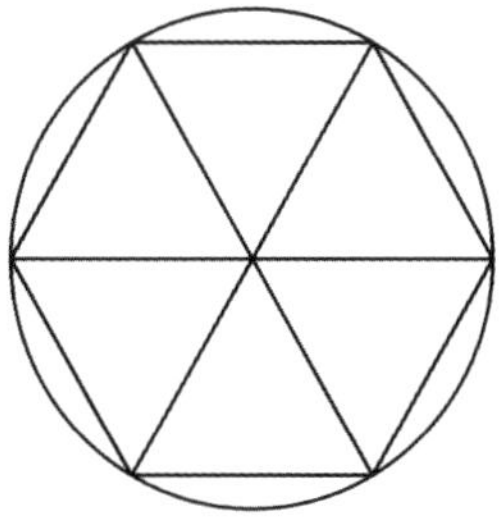

For one complete revolution of a circle, we have the circumference, $C = 2\pi r$.

- ***Radius*** is the size of the circle and determines the arc ____________.
- ***Radians*** represent the number of times the radius goes around a ______________.
  - Radian is defined by an arc of a circle.
- _______________ represents the $360°$ needed to complete one revolution.

Therefore, in radians, the angle around the circle is:

$$Radians = \frac{Circumference}{Radius} = \frac{2\pi r}{r} = \_\_\_\_\_\_$$

What would the angle be in radians for half a revolution?

To convert from **degrees to radians**, multiply the angle by $\frac{\pi}{180°}$.

To convert from **radians to degrees**, multiply the angle by $\frac{180°}{\pi}$.

Let's Practice!

1. Perform the following conversions.

   a. Convert $160°$ to radians.

   b. Convert $\frac{11\pi}{6}$ radians to degrees.

2. What is the length of an arc with a measure of $60°$ in a circle with a 10-centimeter radius?

Try It!

3. Perform the following conversions.

   a. Convert $315°$ to radians.

   b. Convert $\frac{7\pi}{4}$ radians to degrees.

4. An arc with a measure of $120°$ has an arc length of 10π inches. What is the radius of the circle on which the arc sits?

5. An arc has a length of 4π units and a radius of 6 units. What is the angle of the sector in radians?

Consider the diagram below depicting three concentric circles, with radius one unit, two units and three units.

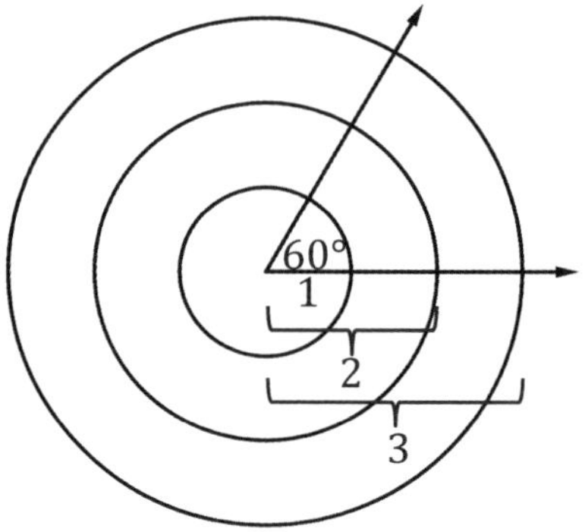

Does the angle change by increasing the radius?

Determine the length of the arcs formed by the $60°$ angle for each circle.

- Circle with 1-unit radius:

- Circle with 2-unit radius:

- Circle with 3-unit radius:

What is the ratio of arc length to radius for each circle?

Now, consider the following diagram.

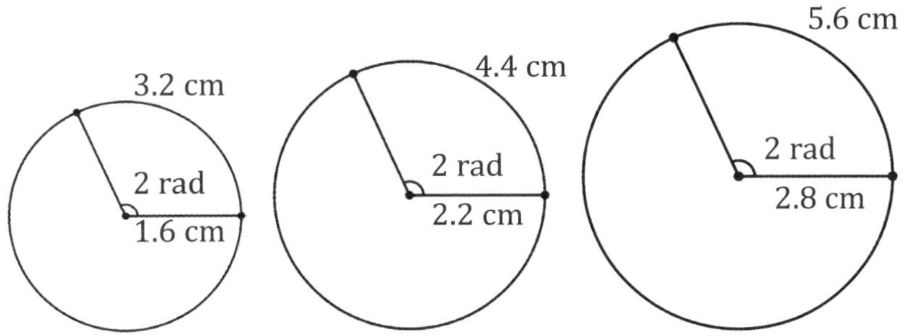

What is the relationship between an angle measure in radians, the radius, and the intercepted arc?

Now, consider the following diagram and determine the length of the arc intercepted by the 1.2-rad angle.

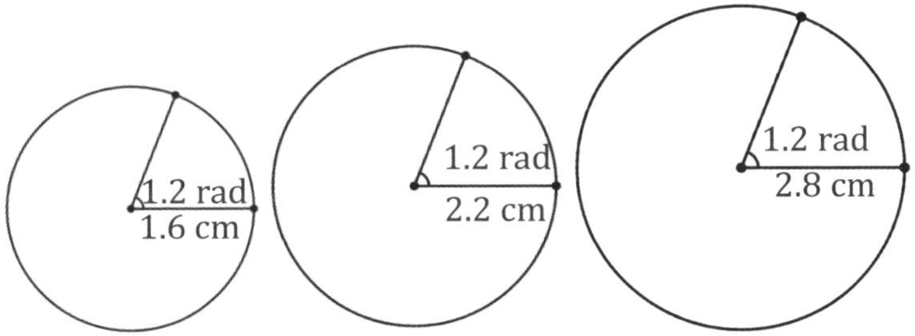

STUDY EDGE TIP

The length of the arc intercepted by an angle is proportional to the radius, with the radian measure of the angle being the constant of proportionality.

Let's Practice!

6. Given any circle with a radius of r units, write an expression in terms of r to describe the arc length for a central angle measure of $30°$.

7. Suppose a circle with an 11.4-inch arc is intercepted by the central angle and a radius that is 3 inches long. Determine the measure of the central angle in radians.

Try It!

8. Write an expression in terms of r to describe the arc length for a central angle measure of $120°$.

9. Choose the correct measure that completes the following statement.

   The length of the arc intercepted by a central angle that measures 0.5 radians is 2.2 feet long. Therefore, the radius is 1.1 | 2.2 | 4.4 feet long.

BEAT THE TEST!

1. Given the concentric circles with center P and with $m\angle P = 60°$, calculate the arc length intercepted by $\angle P$ on each circle. The inner circle has a radius of 15 meters and each circle has a radius 15 units greater than the previous circle.

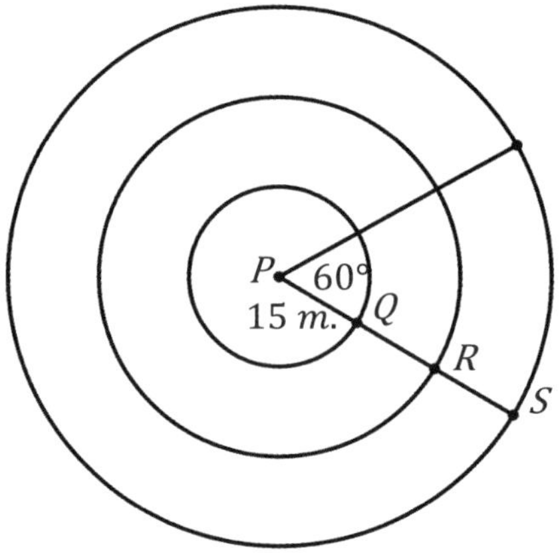

The arc length intercepted by $\angle P$ on each circle is:

Arc length of circle with radius $\overline{PQ}$: ☐ .

Arc length of circle with radius $\overline{PR}$: ☐ .

Arc length of circle with radius $\overline{PS}$: ☐ .

Test Yourself! Practice Tool

Great job! You have reached the end of this section. Now it's time to try the "Test Yourself! Practice Tool," where you can practice all the skills and concepts you learned in this section. Log in to Math Nation and try out the "Test Yourself! Practice Tool" so you can see how well you know these topics!

THIS PAGE WAS INTENTIONALLY LEFT BLANK

Section 10: Circles – Part 2

Topic 1: Arcs and Inscribed Angles – Part 1 271
Standards Covered: G-C.2
- ☐ I can apply properties of inscribed angles to solve a problem.

Topic 2: Arcs and Inscribed Angles – Part 2 273
Standards Covered: G-C.2
- ☐ I can determine the role of an isosceles triangle when determining the measure of an inscribed angle.

Topic 3: Inscribed Polygons in a Circle 276
Standards Covered: G-C.3
- ☐ I can use properties of a cyclic quadrilateral and other polygons to determine the measure of an angle.

Topic 4: Constructing Polygons Inscribed in a Circle 279
Standards Covered: G-C0.13
- ☐ I can construct an equilateral triangle, a square, and a regular hexagon inscribed in a circle.

Topic 5: Tangent Lines, Secants, and Chords – Part 1 283
Standards Covered: G-C.2
- ☐ I can prove and apply properties and theorems about tangent lines, secants, and chords.

Topic 6: Tangent Lines, Secants, and Chords – Part 2 286
Standards Covered: G-C.2
- ☐ I can prove and apply properties and theorems about tangent lines, secants, and chords.

Topic 7: Circumscribed Angles and Beyond – Part 1 290
Standards Covered: G-C.2
- ☐ I can identify and calculate tangent-chord angles and circumscribed angles.

Topic 8: Circumscribed Angles and Beyond – Part 2 292
Standards Covered: G-C.2
- ☐ I can identify and calculate tangent-chord angles and circumscribed angles.

Topic 9: Constructing Inscribed and Circumscribed Circles of Triangles 295
Standards Covered: G-C.3
- ☐ I can construct inscribed and circumscribed circles on a triangle.

Honors Topic 1: Tangent Lines Through an External Point of a Circle .... Available Online
Standards Covered: G-C.4
- ☐ I can construct a tangent line from an external point.

Visit MathNation.com or search "Math Nation" in your phone or tablet's app store to watch the videos that go along with this workbook!

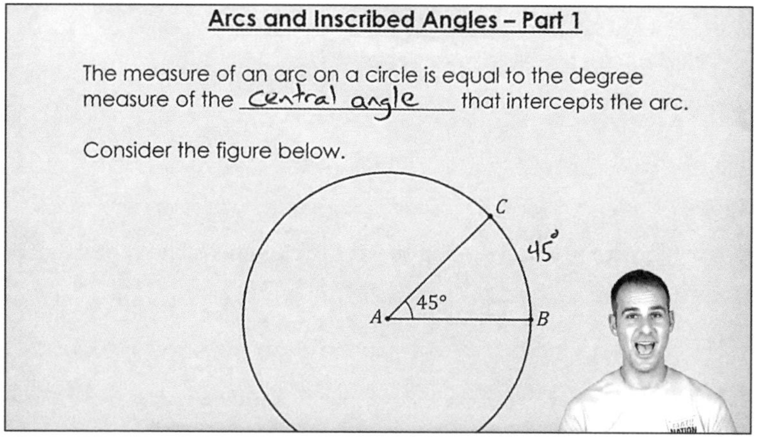
Arcs and Inscribed Angles – Part 1
The measure of an arc on a circle is equal to the degree measure of the central angle that intercepts the arc.
Consider the figure below.
C
45°
45°
A
B

The following Michigan Mathematics Standards will be covered in this section:
G-C.2 - Identify and describe relationships among inscribed angles, radii, and chords. *Include the relationships between central, inscribed, and circumscribed angles; inscribed angles on a diameter are right angles; the radius of a circle is perpendicular to the tangent where the radius intersects the circle.*
G-C.3 - Construct the inscribed and circumscribed circles of a triangle, and prove properties of angles for a quadrilateral inscribed in a circle.
G-C.4 - Construct a tangent line from a point outside a given circle to the circle.
G-CO.13 - Construct an equilateral triangle, a square, and a regular hexagon inscribed in a circle.

Section 10: Circles – Part 2
Section 10 – Topic 1
Arcs and Inscribed Angles – Part 1

The measure of an arc on a circle is equal to the degree measure of the ____________________ that intercepts the arc.

Consider the figure below.

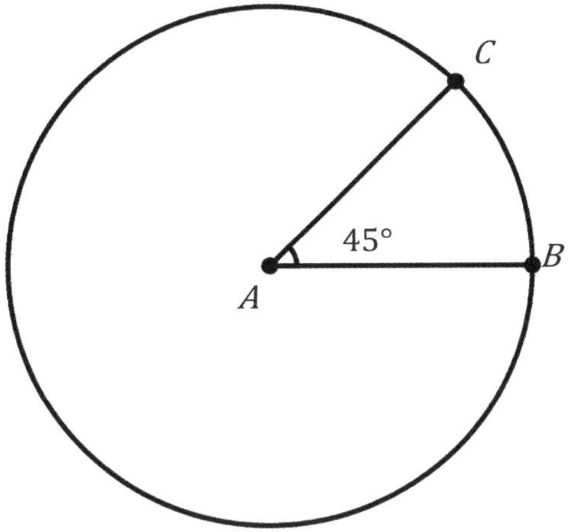

What is $m\widehat{BC}$?

Consider the figure below. $\angle E$ is an inscribed angle. $\widehat{BC}$ is an intercepted arc by both the central angle, $\angle A$, and the inscribed angle.

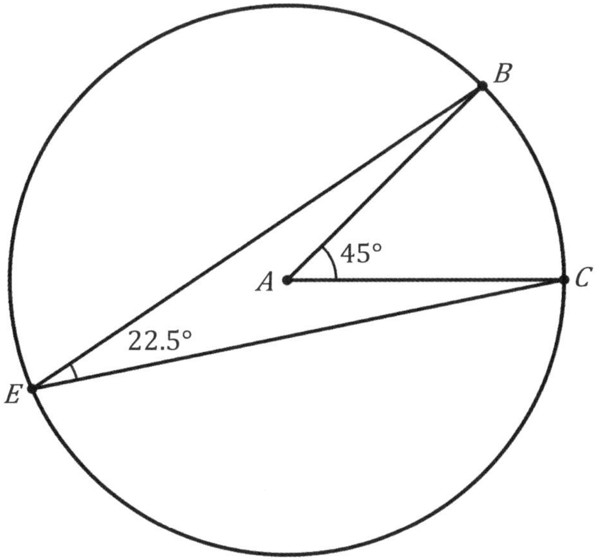

Based on the above figure, define an inscribed angle. Justify your answer.

Based on the above figure, compare and contrast the inscribed angle and the central angle. Justify your answer.

TAKE NOTE! *Postulates & Theorems*

Inscribed Angles Conjectures

- In a circle, the measure of an inscribed angle is half the measure of the central angle with the same intercepted arc.
- In a circle, two inscribed angles with the same intercepted arc are congruent.
- Any angle inscribed in a semi-circle is a right angle.

Let's Practice!

1. Consider circle A in the following figure, and find $m\angle BED$, $m\angle BCD$, and $m\widehat{CD}$. Justify your answer.

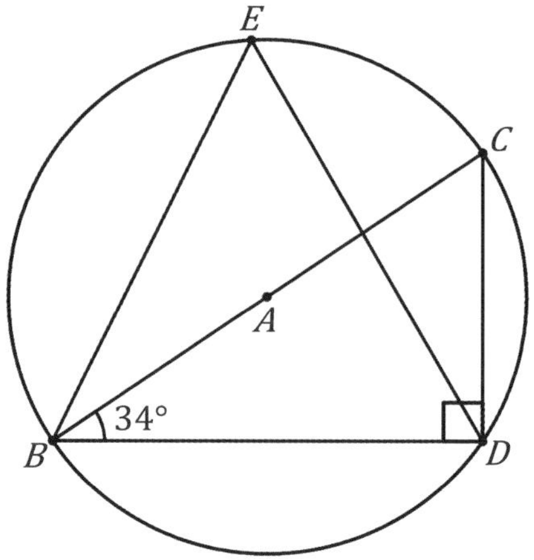

$m\widehat{BD} = 112°$

Try It!

2. Consider circle A in the following figure, and find $m\angle BCF$, $m\angle BED$, and $m\widehat{DB}$. Justify your answer.

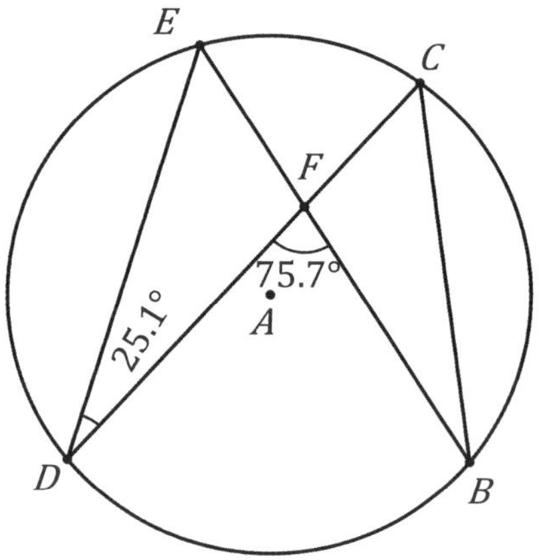

Sometimes, two chords do not intersect "on" the circle, but "in" the circle.

These chords cannot be called inscribed angles.

When two chords intersect "inside" a circle, two sets of ______________ angles are formed.

Consider the figure below.

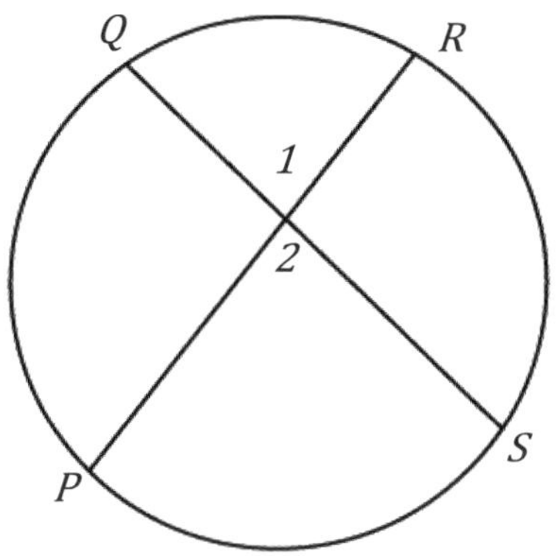

The angle formed inside of a circle by two intersecting chords is _______________ of the sum of the chords' intercepted arcs.

Using the above circle as an example, angles 1 and 2 can be found using the function __________________________.

Section 10 – Topic 2
Arcs and Inscribed Angles – Part 2

Let's Practice!

1. Consider the figure below, and determine $m\angle AQC$.

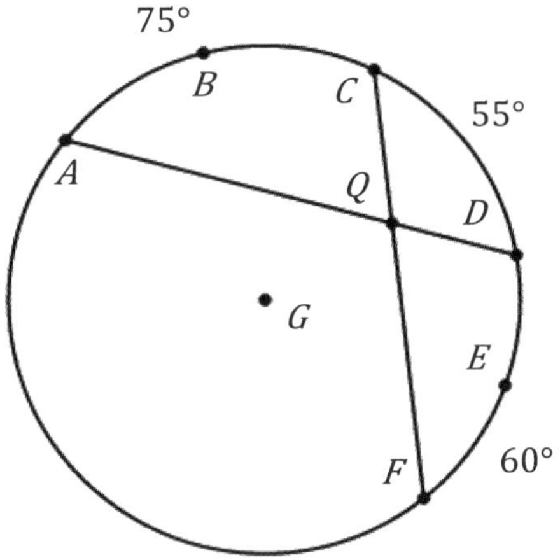

Try It!

2. Consider the diagram below and find $m\angle CFD$. Justify your answer.

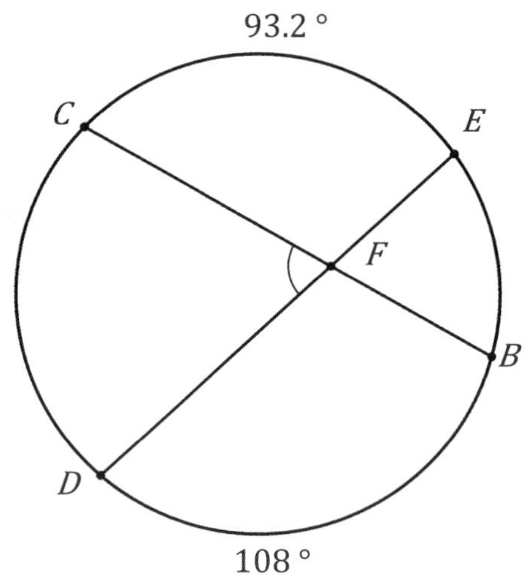

3. Consider the statements and figure below.

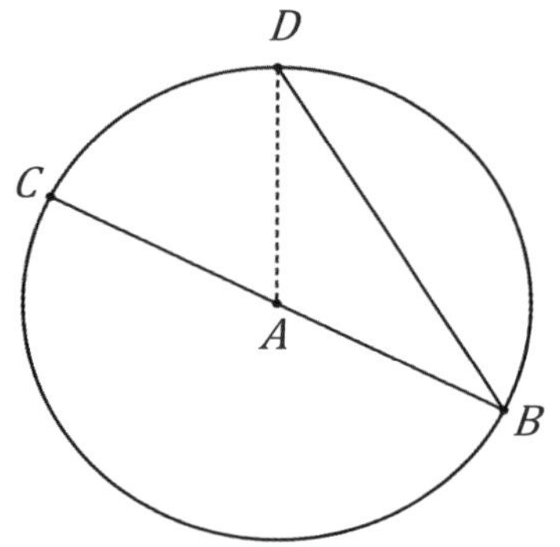

Given: $\angle DBC$ is inscribed in circle A and $\overline{BC}$ is the diameter of circle A.

Prove: $m\angle DBC = \frac{1}{2}m\widehat{CD}$.

Complete the following proof.

Statements	Reasons
1. $\angle DBC$ is inscribed in circle A. $\overline{BC}$ is the diameter of circle A.	**1.** Given
2. $\overline{AB} \cong \overline{AD}$	**2.**
3. ΔABD is isosceles $\angle D \cong \angle B$	**3.** Definition of Isosceles Triangle
4. $m\angle DAC = m\angle D + m\angle B$	**4.** Exterior Angle Theorem
5. Let $x = m\angle DBA = m\angle BDA$, so that $m\angle DAC = (2x)°$	**5.** Substitution
6. $m\widehat{CD} = m\angle DAC = (2x)°$	**6.**
7. $m\widehat{CD} = 2(m\angle DBC)$	**7.** Substitution
8. $m\angle DBC = \frac{1}{2}m\widehat{CD}$	**8.** Multiplication Property of Equality

BEAT THE TEST!

1. Consider the figure below.

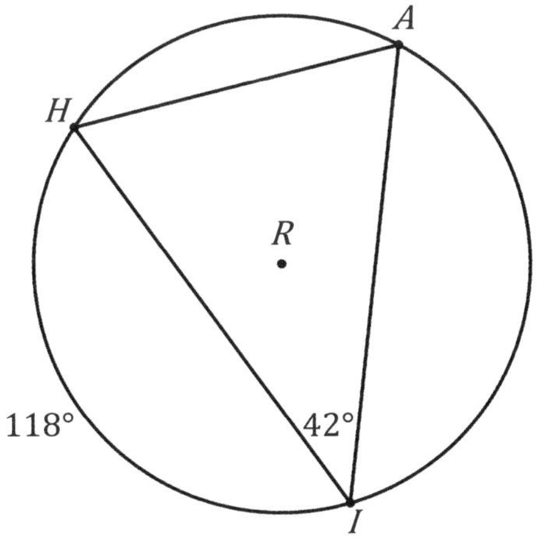

Which of the following is the measure of $\widehat{AI}$?

- Ⓐ $118°$
- Ⓑ $158°$
- Ⓒ $160°$
- Ⓓ $202°$

2. Consider the figure below.

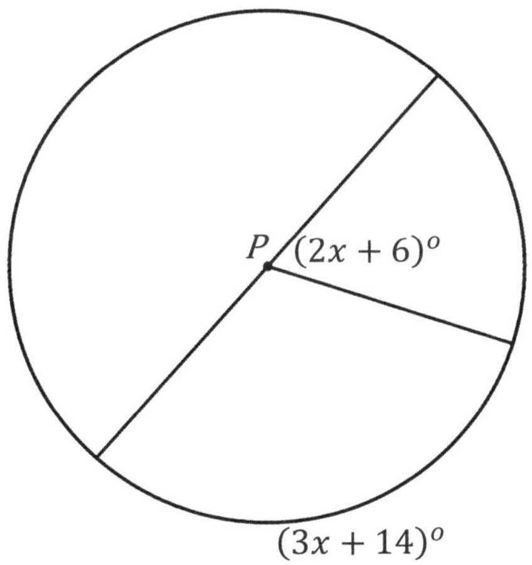

To find the measure of x in circle P above, Karina set up the following equation: $(2x + 6) + (3x + 14) = 90$. Her teacher disagreed with Karina.

Part A: Why did Karina's teacher disagree with her equation to find x? Justify your answer.

Part B: Write the correct equation and solve for x.

3. Mr. Fadhil gave the daily exit ticket shown in the diagram to his Geometry students.

Mr. Fadhil's Geometry 3rd Block
Exit Ticket:
Find $m\widehat{DF}$

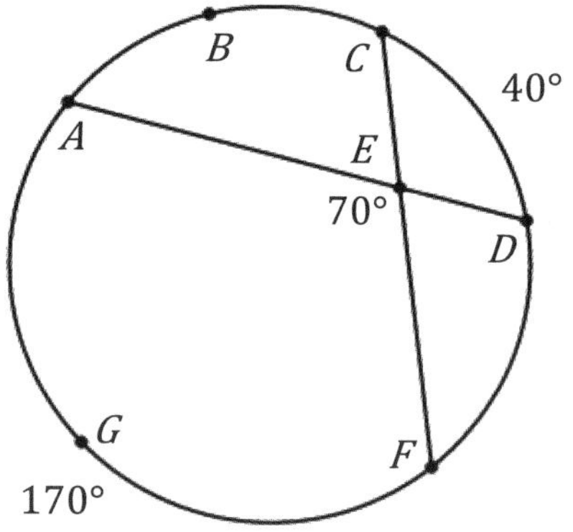

One of Mr. Fadhil's students argued that there was something wrong with this problem, based on the above diagram and the measurements.

What is the error in this problem? Justify your answer.

Section 10 – Topic 3
Inscribed Polygons in a Circle

Consider the figure below that represents an inscribed polygon.

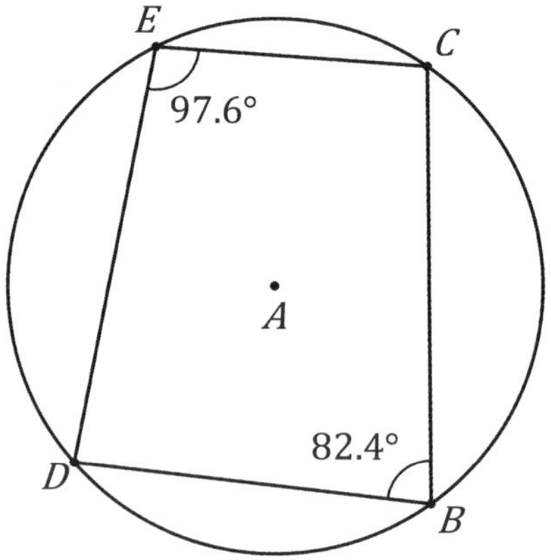

What figure is inscribed in the circle?

What do you notice about the angles?

A polygon is inscribed in a circle when all vertices of the polygon lie on the ______________. The circle is circumscribed about the ___________.

STUDY EDGE TIP

In a ***cyclic quadrilateral*** every vertex is on the circumference of a circle, and the opposite angles of the quadrilateral are supplementary.

Let's Practice!

1. Consider the figure below and find the pair(s) of angles that are supplementary.

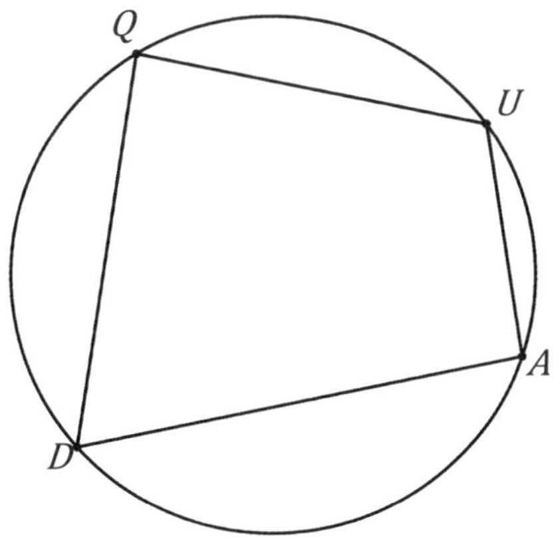

2. Consider circle A below and find $m\angle CBD$ and $m\widehat{CD}$.

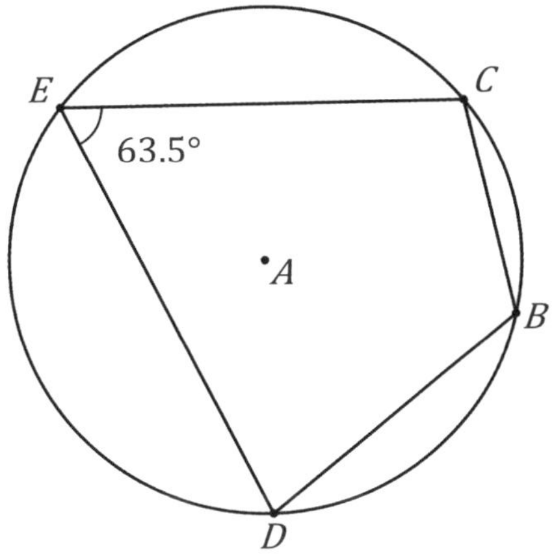

Try It!

3. Consider the following diagrams and find the value of each variable.

a.

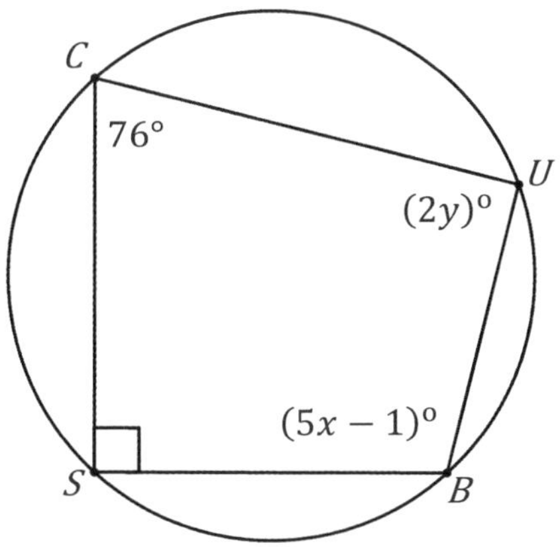

b.

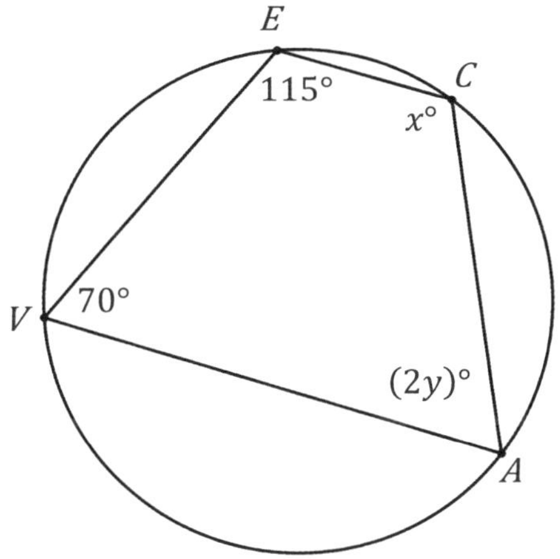

4. Complete the two-column proof with the given information.

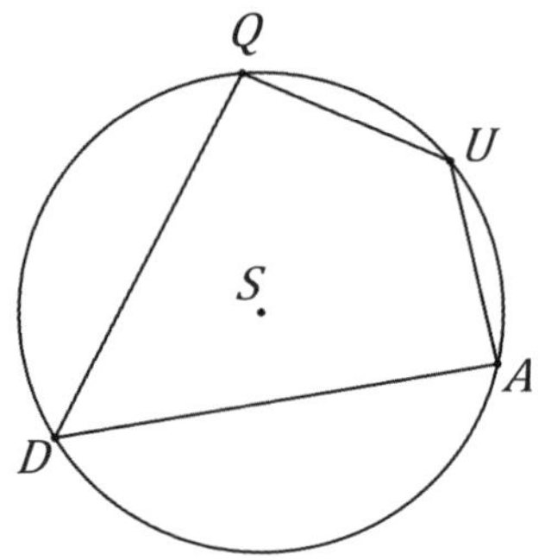

Given: $QUAD$ is inscribed in circle S.

Prove: $m\angle Q + m\angle A = 180°$

Statements	Reasons
1. $QUAD$ is inscribed in circle S.	**1.**
2. $m\widehat{DQU} = 2 \cdot m\angle A$	**2.**
3. $m\widehat{DAU} = 2 \cdot m\angle Q$	**3.**
4. $m\widehat{DQU} + m\widehat{DAU} = 360°$	**4.**
5. $2 \cdot m\angle A + m\widehat{DAU} = 360°$	**5.**
6. $2 \cdot m\angle A + 2 \cdot m\angle Q = 360°$	**6.**
7. $2(m\angle A + m\angle Q) = 360°$	**7.**
8. $m\angle Q + m\angle A = 180°$	**8.**

BEAT THE TEST!

1. Quadrilateral $BCDE$ is inscribed in circle A. Diagonals $\overline{BD}$ and $\overline{EC}$ intersect at point F.

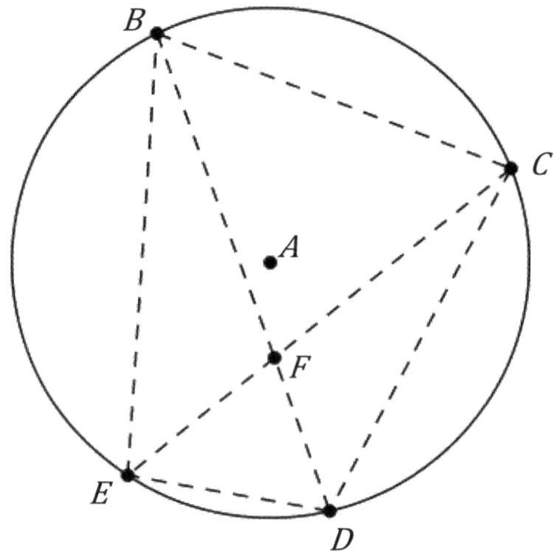

Select the angles and value that would make the statement true about quadrilateral $BCDE$.

$m\angle$ [ ] $=$ [ ] $- m\angle$ [ ]

First blank	Second blank	Third blank
EBF	$90°$	EBC
EDC	$180°$	EBF
EDF		EDF
CFB		CFB
FED		FED

2. Consider the following diagram, and find the value of each variable. Justify your answer.

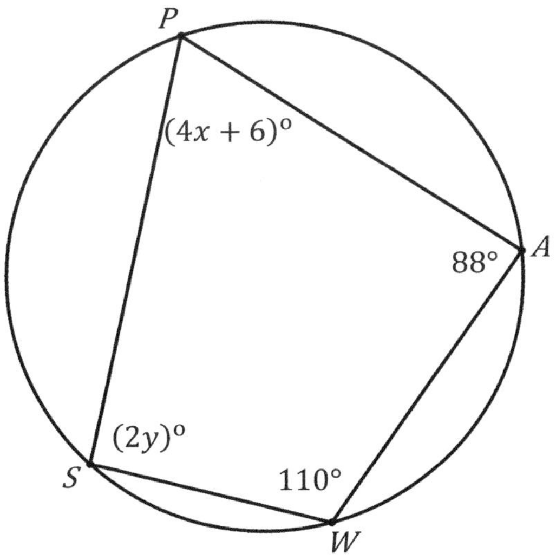

Section 10 – Topic 4
Constructing Polygons Inscribed in a Circle

Consider the circle and steps below to construct an equilateral triangle inscribed in a circle.

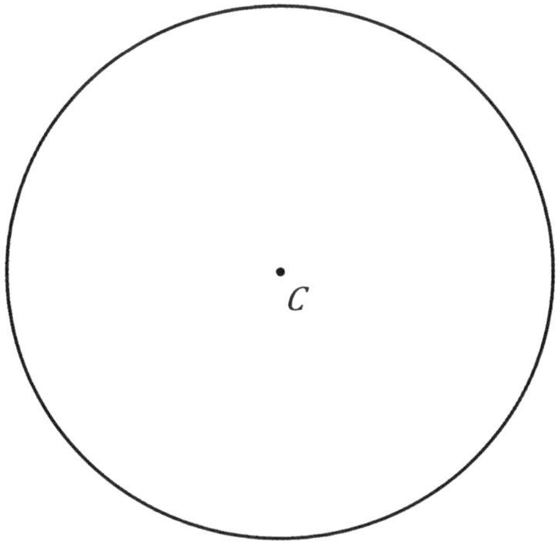

Step 1. Use a straightedge to construct the diameter of the circle (passing through center C).

Step 2. Use the compass to measure the radius. Keeping the same setting, place the point of the compass at an endpoint of the diameter. Make two arcs that intersect the circle at two different points (on both sides of the diameter).

Step 3. Construct the sides of the equilateral triangle by connecting these two points to the far endpoint of the diameter.

Let's Practice!

1. Consider the following construction.

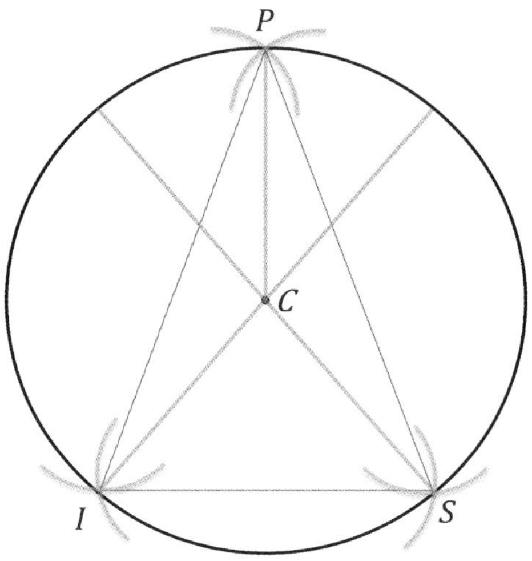

   a. Is $\triangle ISP$ an equilateral triangle inscribed in circle C? Justify your answer.

   b. What steps were followed for the construction above? What are some corrections you would suggest in order to make it better?

2. Consider the diagram below that presents a regular hexagon inscribed within a circle.

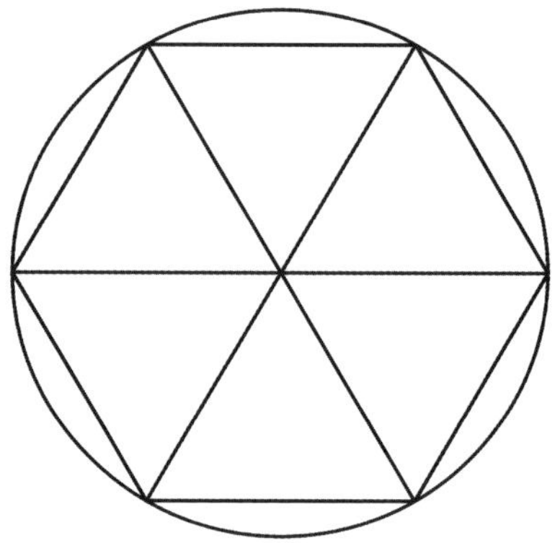

   a. What is the relationship between the radius of the circle and a side of one of the triangles?

   b. How would we use the construction skills we have acquired so far to construct an inscribed regular hexagon?

Try It!

3. Consider the circle below.

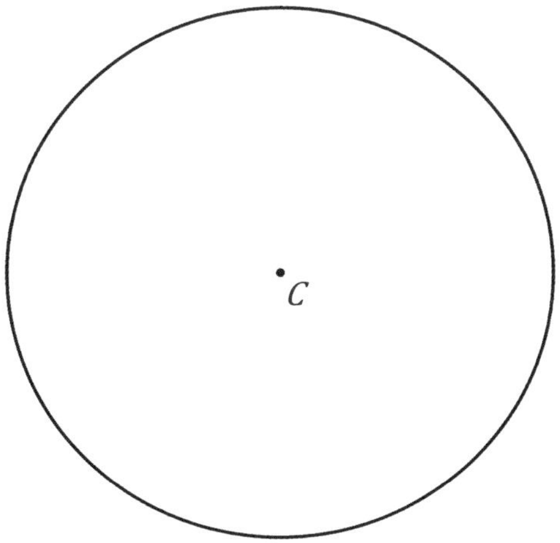

   a. Draw a diameter of circle C above.

   b. Draw a perpendicular bisector of the diameter.

   c. What inscribed polygon can you construct based on what you did in parts a and b above? Justify your answer.

4. Sahel starts the construction of an inscribed polygon in the circle below.

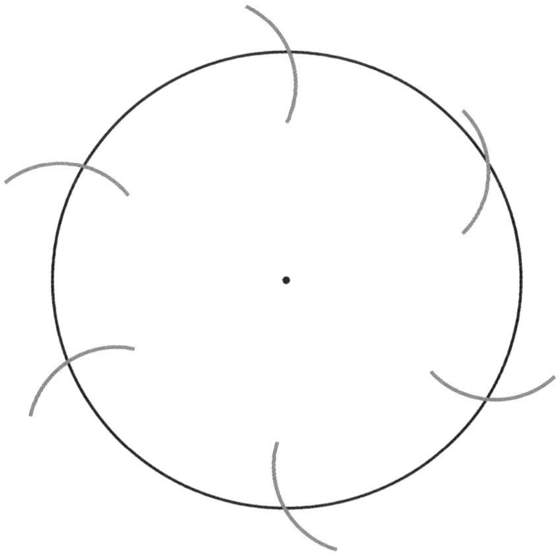

Sahel's brothers, Nil and Ravi, are trying to figure out what inscribed polygon Sahel is constructing. Nil claims it is an equilateral triangle. Ravi claims it is a regular hexagon. Which brother is correct?

Ⓐ Nil

Ⓑ Ravi

Ⓒ Both Nil and Ravi

Ⓓ Neither of them

BEAT THE TEST!

1. Which of the following are strategies for constructing an equilateral triangle in a circle? Select all that apply.

   - ☐ Draw a diameter and a perpendicular bisector of the diameter, and then connect the endpoints of the diameters that are on the circle.
   - ☐ Use a compass to measure the radius of a circle and draw consecutive $60°$ arcs on the circle to connect every other arc.
   - ☐ Use an endpoint of a diameter to construct two arcs on the circle and connect the arcs with the far endpoint of the diameter.
   - ☐ Use a compass to measure the radius of a circle and draw consecutive $60°$ arcs on the circle and connect every arc.
   - ☐ Draw a diameter and a perpendicular bisector of the diameter, and then connect the endpoints of one of the diameters with one of the endpoints of the other diameter.

2. The diagram below displays Hazel's construction of an inscribed square in a circle.

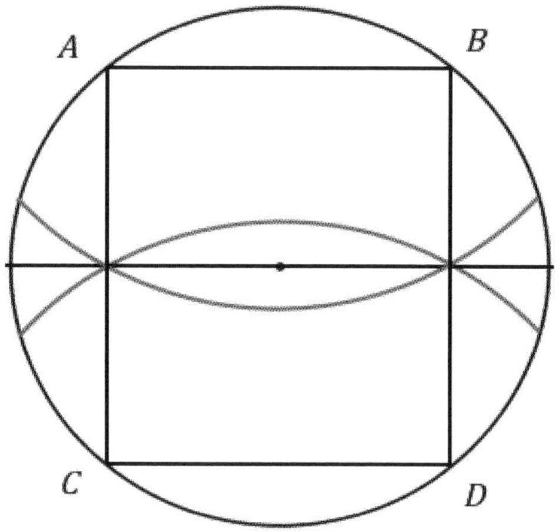

Determine if Hazel's construction is correct and how to fix it (if needed).

Section 10 – Topic 5
Tangent Lines, Secants, and Chords – Part 1

Let's examine the following figures.

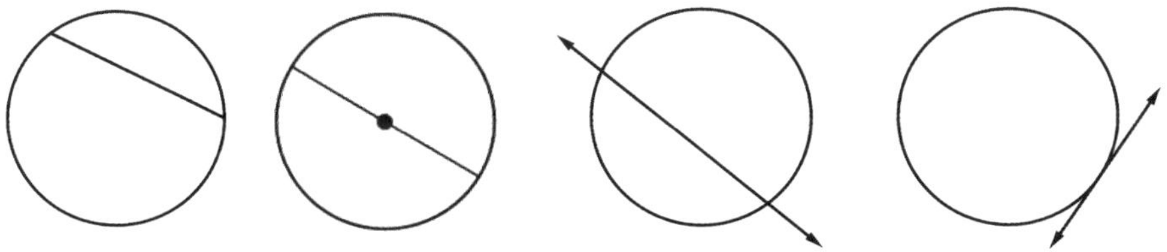

What differences do you see among these figures?

Which of these figure(s) have you not seen yet?

A ***secant*** is a line that intersects a circle at ________ points.

A ***tangent*** is a line in the plane of a circle that intersects the circle at exactly _______ point.

Let's Practice!

1. Classify each of the following segments as a radius, chord, secant, tangent, or diameter.

$\overline{IB}$ is a _______________.
$\overline{AN}$ is a _______________.
$\overline{WR}$ is a _______________.
$\overline{RS}$ is a _______________.
$\overline{IO}$ is a _______________.

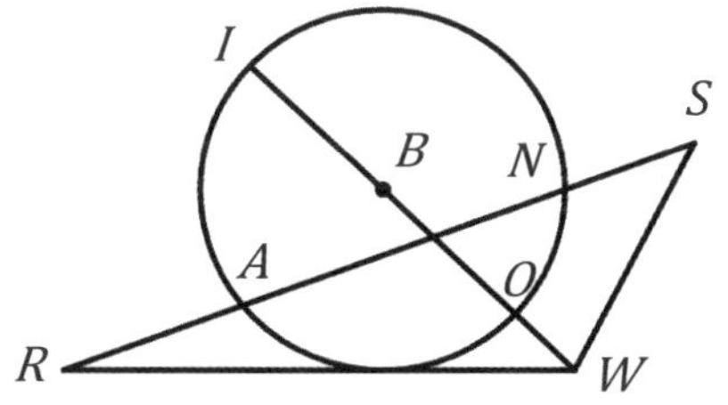

Try It!

2. Mark the most appropriate answer for each statement in the table below.

Statements	Always	Sometimes	Never
A chord is part of a secant.	o	o	o
A diameter is a tangent.	o	o	o
A tangent is a ray.	o	o	o
A tangent has exactly one point in common with a circle.	o	o	o
A secant to a circle contains the diameter.	o	o	o
A chord in a circle contains a radius.	o	o	o

TAKE NOTE! Postulates & Theorems

Tangent Theorem

If a line is tangent to a circle, then the line is perpendicular to the radius at the point of tangency.

The converse is also true: If a line in the plane of a circle is perpendicular to a radius at its endpoint on the circle, then the line is tangent to the circle.

How could we prove the Tangent Theorem using the figure below?

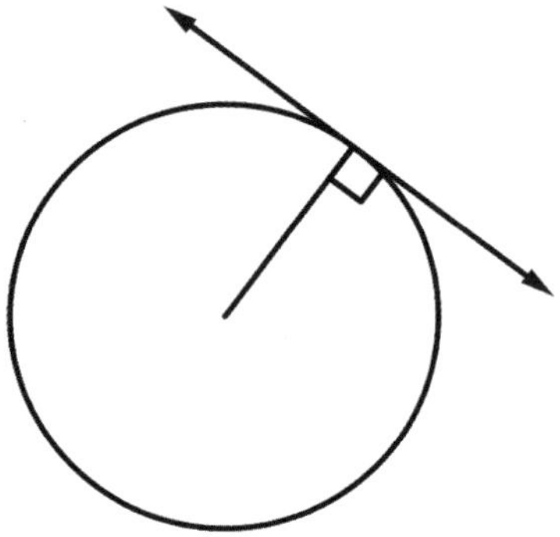

TAKE NOTE! Postulates & Theorems

Tangent Segments Theorem

If two segments are tangent to a circle from the same exterior point, they are congruent.

How could we prove the Tangent Segments Theorem using the figure below?

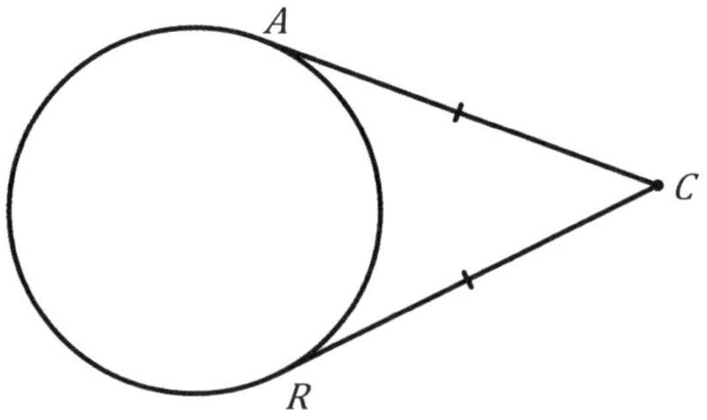

Let's Practice!

3. Albert the Alligator is sunning himself next to his favorite, perfectly circular pond. He is 25 feet from the bank and 45 feet from the point of tangency. Determine the radius of Albert's favorite pond using the given information.

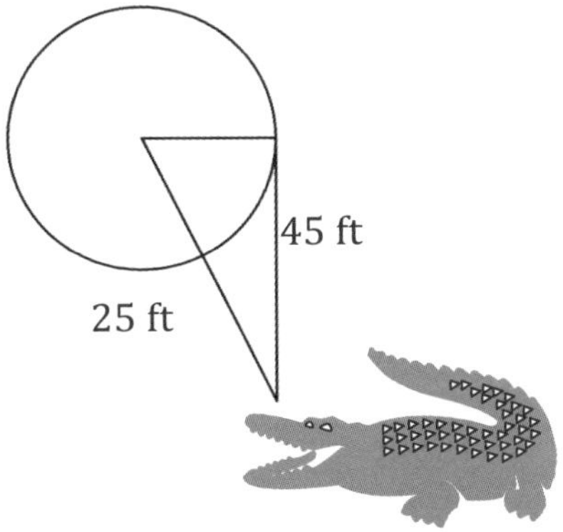

4. George is standing in front of a silo and can only see as far as the diagram shows. Determine the value of x. Support your conclusion with a theorem.

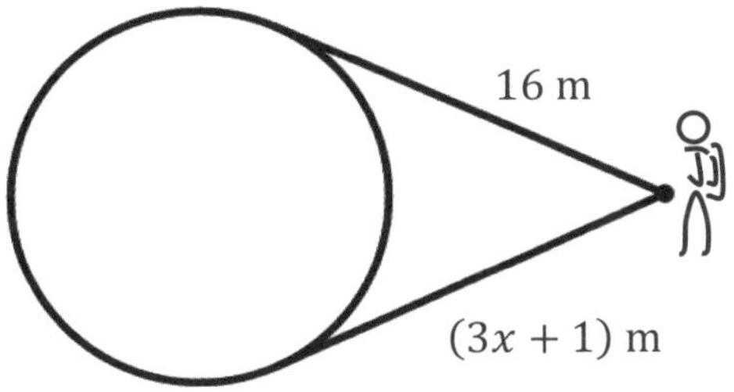

Try It!

5. Three teammates from a local soccer club are practicing passing in triangular pattern as shown in the diagram below.

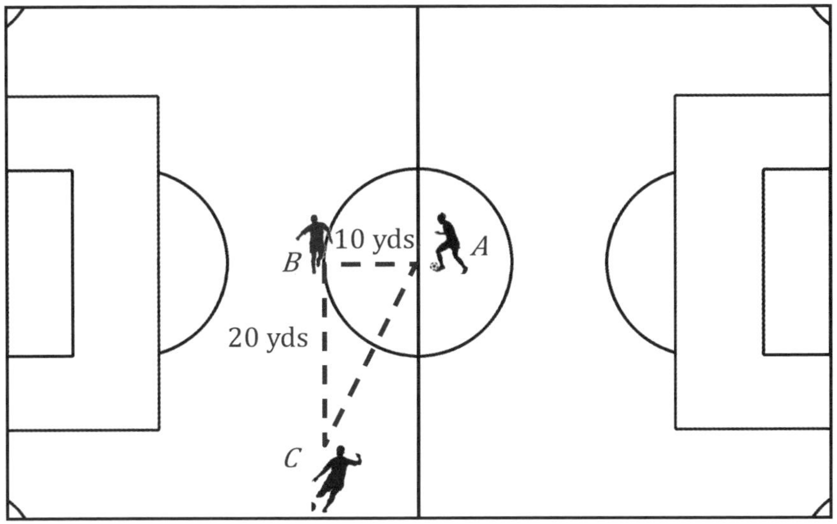

Player A has the ball and is 10 yards from Player B, who is 20 yards from Player C. How far would the ball travel if Player A decides to pass the ball to Player C? Justify your answer.

6. Jasmyn is standing at the point of tangency to a wishing well, 27 feet from a bench. Her friend Willard is at the other point of tangency. Determine the value of x.

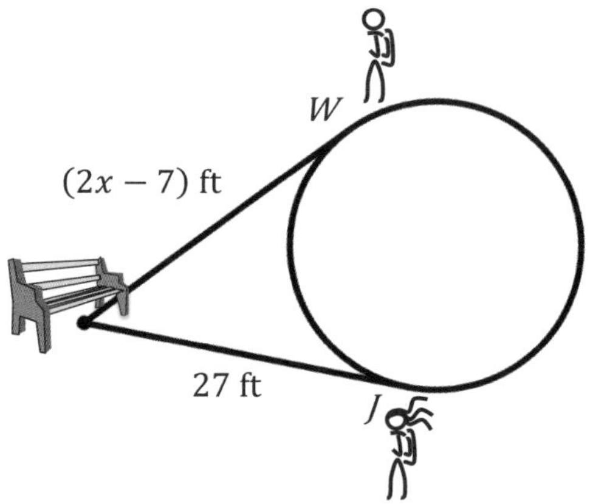

7. Find the perimeter of the ΔNET in the diagram below. Points A, R, and G are points of tangency. Justify your answer.

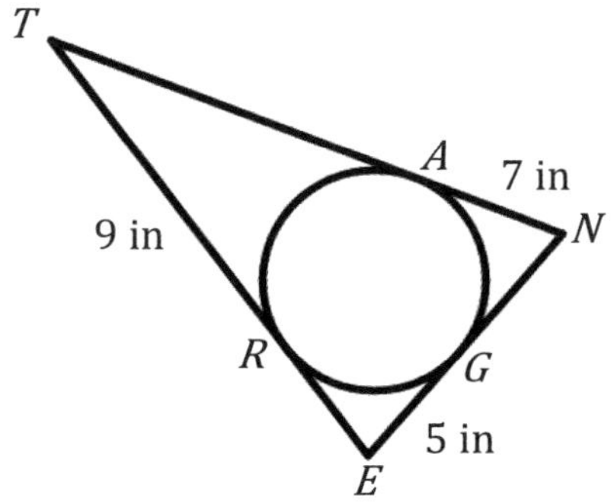

Section 10 – Topic 6
Tangent Lines, Secants, and Chords – Part 2

> **TAKE NOTE!** *Postulates & Theorems*
>
> **Perpendicular to a Chord Theorem**
>
> If the diameter of a circle is perpendicular to a chord, then the diameter bisects the chord.

How could we prove the Perpendicular to a Chord Theorem using the figure below?

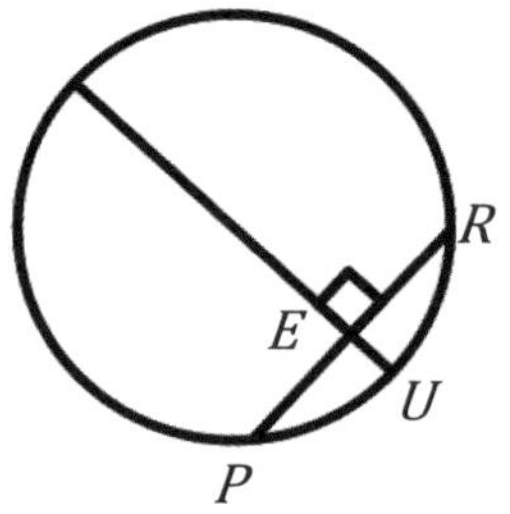

TAKE NOTE! *Postulates & Theorems*

Chords Distance to Center Theorem

In congruent circles or the same circle, chords are congruent if and only if they are equidistant from the center.

How could we prove the Chords Distance to Center Theorem using the figure below, where $\overline{EW} \cong \overline{PO}$ if and only if $\overline{UR} \cong \overline{US}$?

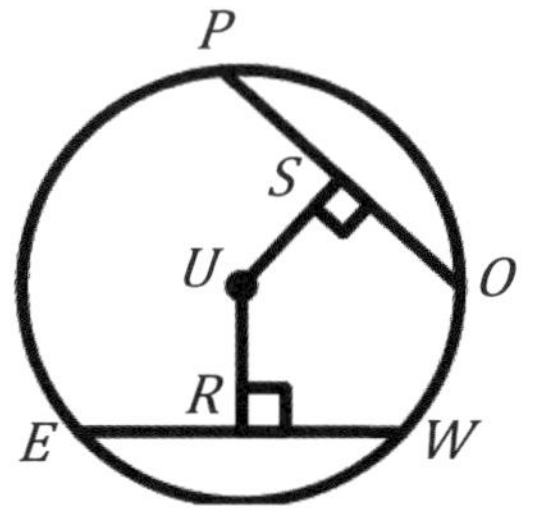

TAKE NOTE! *Postulates & Theorems*

Intersecting Chords Theorem

If two chords intersect on the interior of a circle, then the product of the lengths of the segments of one chord is equal to the product of the lengths of the segments of the other chord.

How could we prove the Intersecting Chords Theorem using the figure below?

$$BT \cdot AT = ST \cdot ET$$

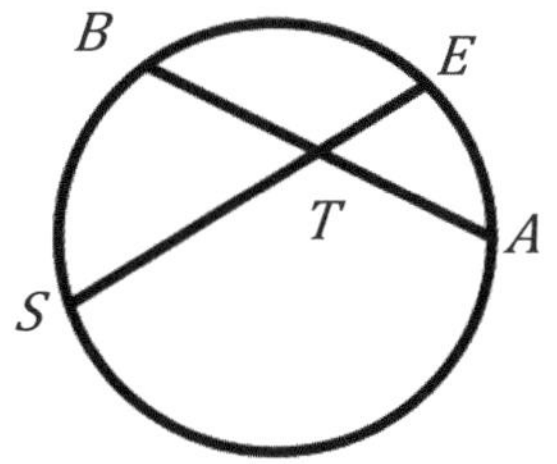

Let's Practice!

1. Complete the following two-column proof.

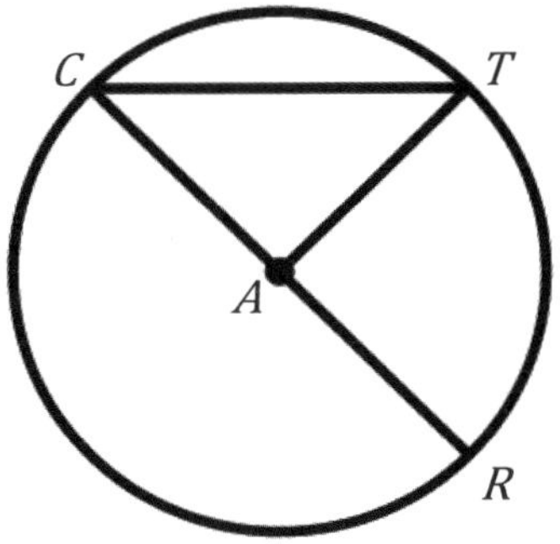

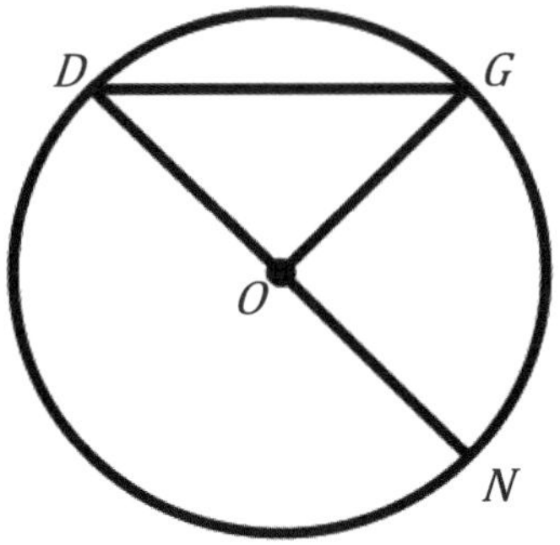

Given: Circle $A \cong$ Circle O
$\angle ACT \cong \angle ODG$

Prove: $\angle CAT \cong \angle DOG$
$\overline{CT} \cong \overline{DG}$

Statements	Reasons
1.	**1.** Given
2.	**2.** Congruent circles have congruent radii.
3. $\angle ACT \cong \angle ATC$ and $\angle ODG \cong \angle OGD$	**3.**
4. $\angle ACT \cong \angle ODG$	**4.**
5.	**5.** Transitive Property
6.	**6.** AAS
7. $\angle CAT \cong \angle DOG$	**7.**
8. $\overline{CT} \cong \overline{DG}$	**8.**

Try It!

2. Determine the radius of the circle shown below.

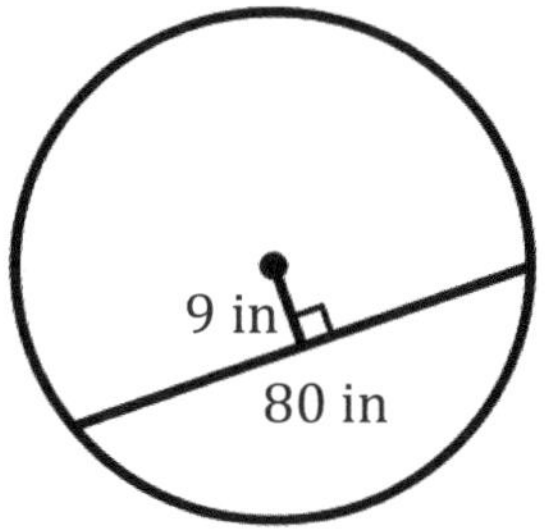

3. A chord of a circular clock is 48 inches long and has a midpoint that is 7 inches from the center of the circle. Determine the radius of the clock. Justify your answer.

BEAT THE TEST!

1. Scientists from around the world watch the International Space Station (ISS). A scientist in California (C) observes the ISS at the exact time that the ISS is 249 miles above Moscow, Russia (M). If the Earth's radius is 3,959 miles long, determine how far the International Space Station is from the scientist in California. Round to the nearest hundredth of a mile.

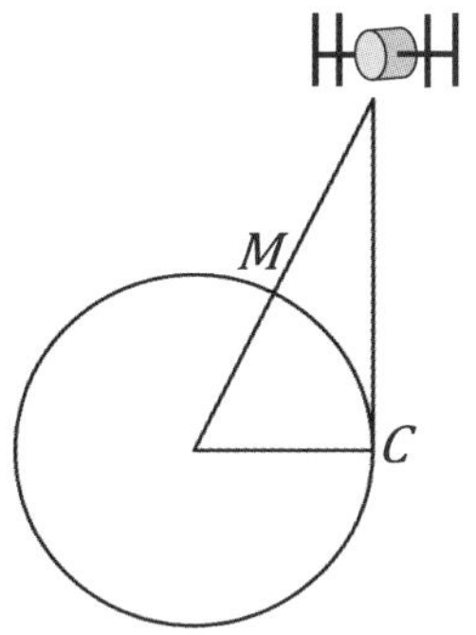

☐ miles

2. You are making a set of curved stairs for an upcoming chorus production. The diagram shows the top view of your plans and the dimensions of the stairs. To design the curvature correctly, you need to know the radius of the circle. Determine the radius of the circle.

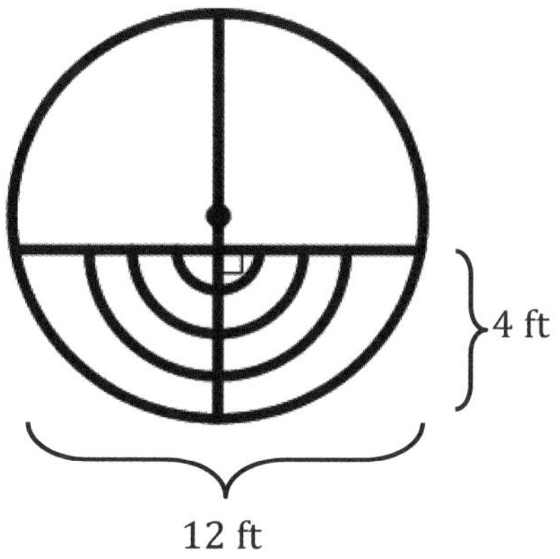

☐ feet

Section 10 – Topic 7
Circumscribed Angles and Beyond – Part 1

Points B, C, and D are on the circle A. Line WY is tangent to circle A at point C. Circle A has chord $\overline{BC}$. The chord intersects $\overleftrightarrow{WY}$ at point C.

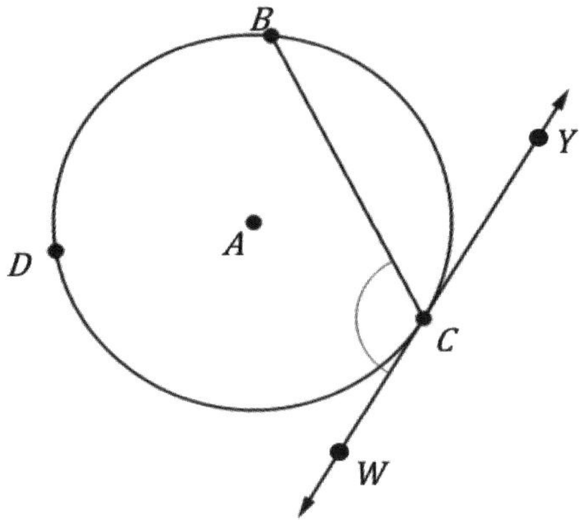

What do you know is true about the sum of $m\angle BCW$ and $m\angle BCY$?

What do you know is true about the sum of $m\widehat{CDB}$ and $m\widehat{BC}$?

How do you think $m\angle BCW$ is related to $m\widehat{CDB}$?

TAKE NOTE! *Postulates & Theorems*

Tangent-Secant Angle Theorem

The measure of an angle formed by a secant and a tangent line is one-half the measure of the intercepted arc.

Let's Practice!

1. Points G, K, and T are on the circle X. Line $\overleftrightarrow{WB}$ is tangent to circle X at point G.

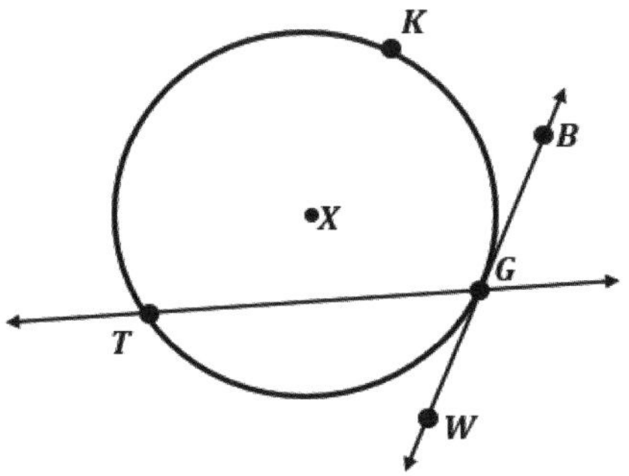

a. If $m\widehat{TKG} = 277^\circ$, find $m\angle BGT$.

b. If $m\angle WGT = (4x - 2)^\circ$ and $m\angle TGB = (7x - 5)^\circ$, find $m\widehat{TKG}$.

c. If $m\widehat{TKG} = (18x + 2)^\circ$ and $m\widehat{TG} = (10x - 6)^\circ$, find $m\angle TGW$.

Try It!

2. Points G, B, K, and W are on the circle P. Point X is the intersection of $\overleftrightarrow{GK}$ and $\overleftrightarrow{FB}$. Line FH is tangent to circle P at point K.

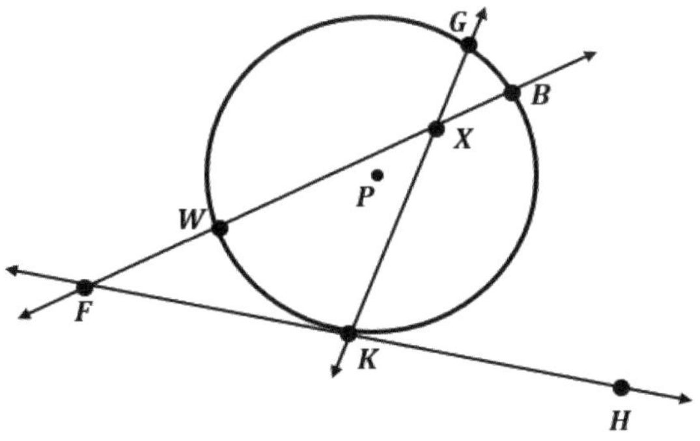

not to scale

a. If $m\widehat{BK} = (3x)^{\circ}$, $m\widehat{KW} = (x)^{\circ}$, $m\widehat{BG} = 24^{\circ}$, and $m\widehat{WGB} = 160^{\circ}$, find $m\angle XKH$.

b. If $m\widehat{WK} = 96^{\circ}$, $m\widehat{BG} = 32^{\circ}$, $m\angle XKH = (12x + 6)^{\circ}$, and $m\angle WFK = (x + 8)^{\circ}$,

i. find x.
ii. $m\angle WFK =$ ________.
iii. $m\widehat{BK} =$ __________.

Let's Practice!

3. For circle C, $\angle AEP$ is created by two tangent lines to circle C. $\angle AEP$ is known as a circumscribed angle.

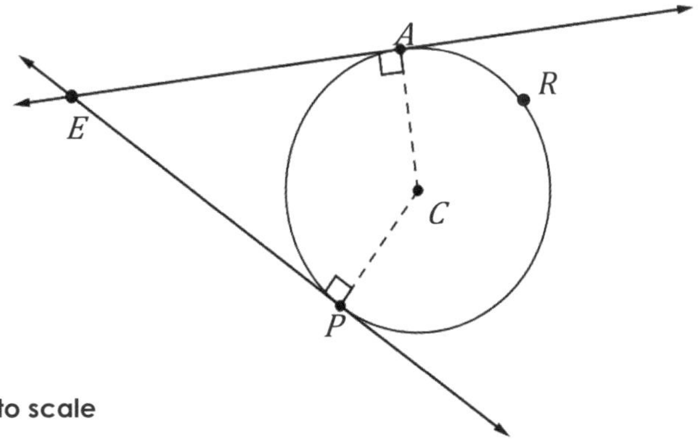

not to scale

Because $\overline{AC}$ and $\overline{PC}$ are radii, they are perpendicular to the tangent lines. Quadrilateral $ACPE$ can be used to find $m\angle AEP$ since the sum of $m\angle CAE$ and $m\angle CPE$ is 180°. Then $m\angle AEP = 180^{\circ} - m\angle ACP$.

a. If $m\widehat{AP} = 113^{\circ}$, find $m\angle AEP$.

b. Fill in the blanks to discover another way to find $m\angle AEP$.

Since $m\widehat{AP} = 113^{\circ}$, then $m\widehat{ARP} =$ _______$^{\circ}$.
Next, find $m\widehat{ARP} - m\widehat{AP} =$ _______$^{\circ}$.
How is your answer to part a related to $m\widehat{ARP} - m\widehat{AP}$?

TAKE NOTE! *Postulates & Theorems*

Circumscribed Angle Theorem
The measure of a circumscribed angle formed by two tangent lines is one-half of the difference of the measure of the two intercepted arcs.

Try It!

4. Points Y, H, and W are on the circle K. Line DL is tangent to circle K at point Y. Chords YW and FH intersects at point T.

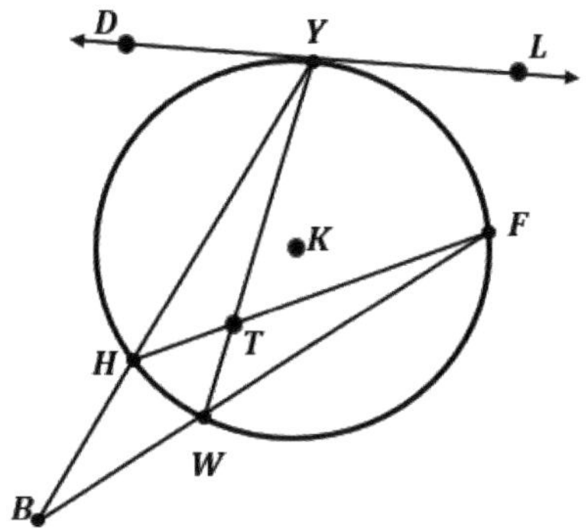

Given that $m\angle HYW = 12^{\circ}$, $m\,\widehat{HW} = (3x-3)^{\circ}$, $m\,\widehat{YF} = (8x)^{\circ}$, and $m\,\widehat{FW} = (14x+2)^{\circ}$, find each.

a. $m\angle YWF=$________

b. $m\angle YTH=$________

c. $m\angle LYT=$________

d. $m\angle YBF=$________

Section 10 – Topic 8
Circumscribed Angles and Beyond – Part 2

Consider the diagram below where $\angle RSC$ is formed by two secants intersecting outside of circle Q.

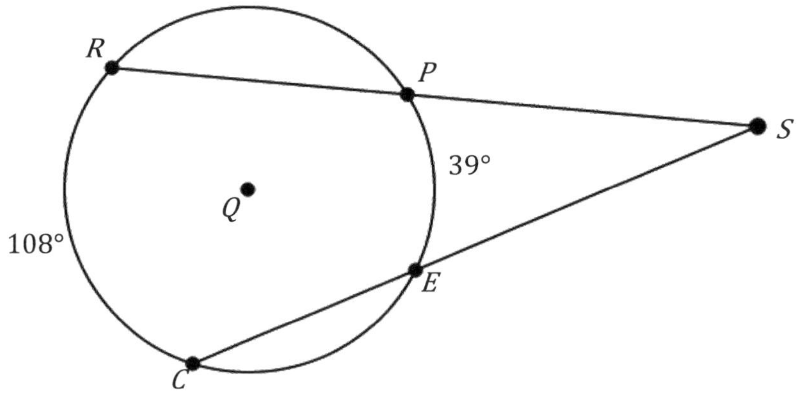

Identify the intercepted arcs.

Determine $m\angle RSC$.

Explain why the relationship between the angle formed by the secants and the intercepted arcs is valid.

Let's Practice!

1. Consider the diagram below, where $\angle ASC$ is formed by a tangent line and a secant line intersecting outside of circle Q.

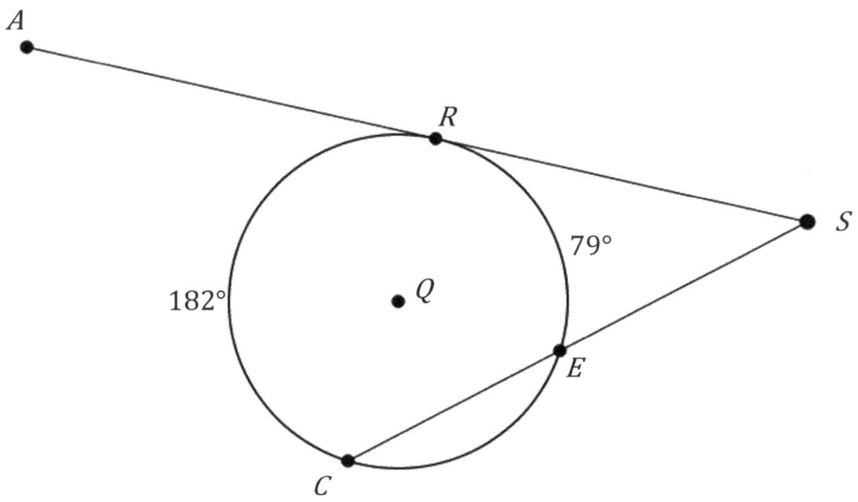

   a. What are the intercepted arcs in the above diagram?

   b. Determine $m\angle ASC$.

Try It!

2. Angle S is formed by the secant and the tangent in the following diagram.

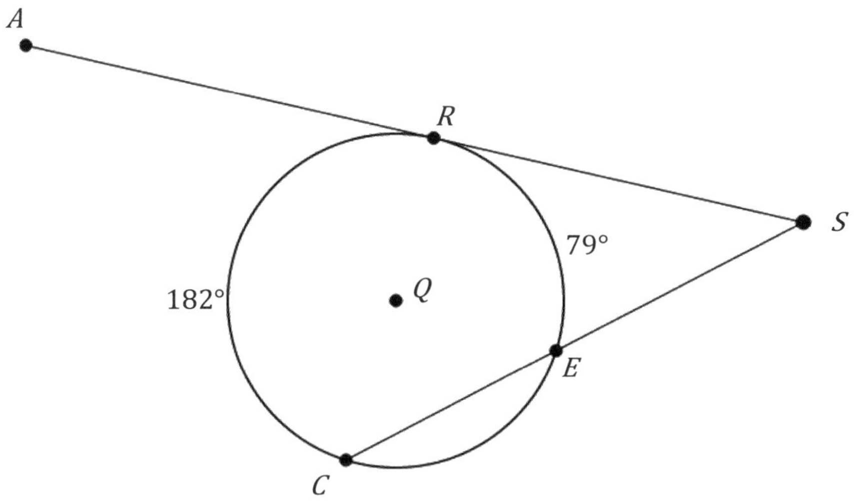

   Explain why this relationship between angle S and the intercepted arcs is valid.

BEAT THE TEST!

1. Consider the diagram below.

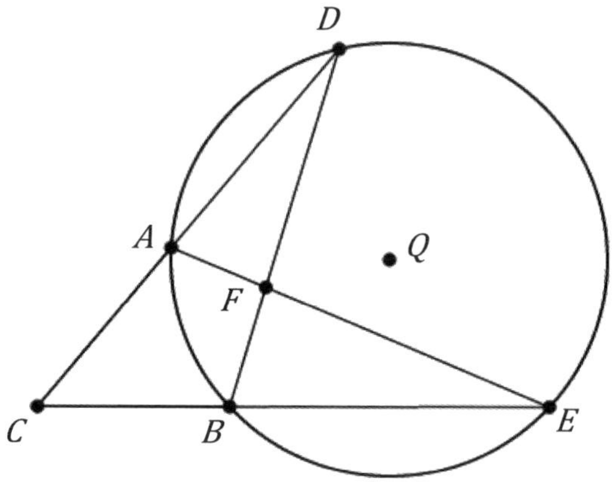

Which of the following statements is correct?

Ⓐ $\Delta DCB \sim \Delta ECA$ by Angle-Angle Similarity.

Ⓑ $\angle ACB \cong \angle BFA$ by definition of an angle formed by two secants intersecting outside of a circle.

Ⓒ $\angle DAF \cong \angle CBF$ by Alternate Interior Angles Theorem.

Ⓓ $m\angle BFE = m\widehat{BE}$ by definitions of central angles and inscribed angles.

2. Consider the diagram below.

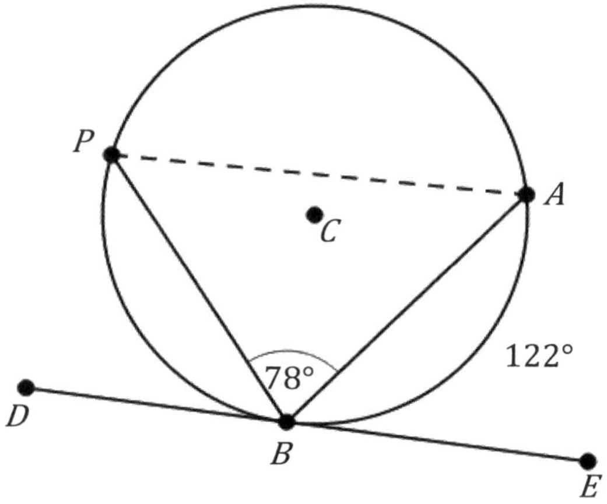

If triangles PCB and ACB are constructed, what are the measures of $\angle PCB$ and $\angle CAB$?

$m\angle PCB =$ ☐

$m\angle CAB =$ ☐

Section 10 – Topic 9
Constructing Inscribed and Circumscribed Circles of Triangles

Consider the following triangle.

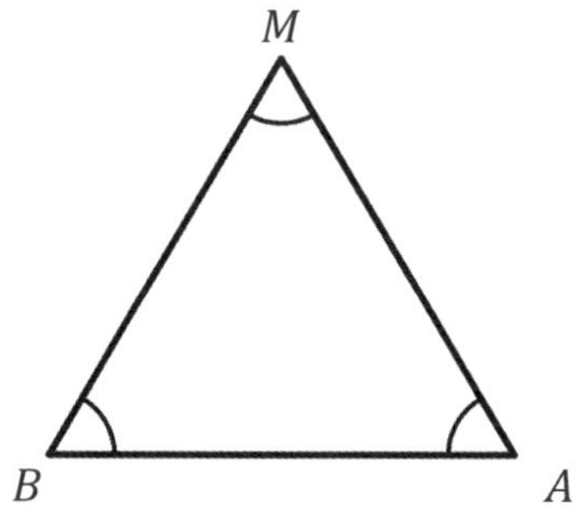

What's the difference between the ***inscribed circle*** of the triangle and the ***circumscribed circle*** of the triangle?

Given the above triangle MBA, a(n) ______________ __________ is the largest circle contained within the triangle.

- The inscribed circle will touch each of the three sides of the triangle at ____________ _______ point.
- The center of the circle inscribed in a triangle is the ______________ of the triangle.

Given the previous triangle MBA, a(n) ______________ __________ is the circle drawn on the outside that contains a given triangle.

- The circumscribed circle passes through all three ______________ of the triangle.
- The center of the circle circumscribed in a triangle is the ________________ of the triangle.

To construct the inscribed circle:

Step 1. Use your compass and straightedge to construct the angle bisectors of all the angles. The point of intersection of the angle bisectors is the incenter.

Step 2. Use your compass and straightedge to construct a line perpendicular to one side of the triangle that passes through the incenter, which creates the radius of the incircle.

Step 3. Use your compass to construct a circle centered at the incenter that passes through the point of intersection of the side of the triangle and the perpendicular line.

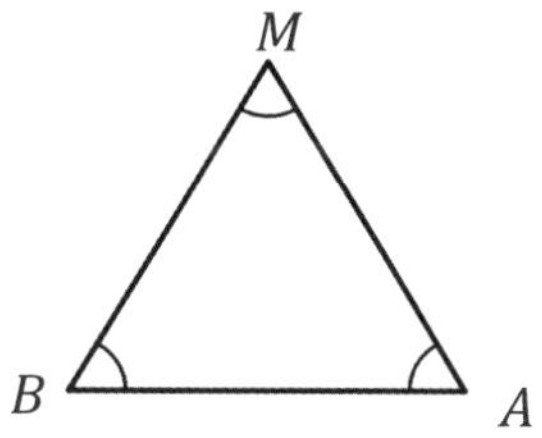

To construct the circumscribed circle:

Step 1. Use your compass and straightedge to construct the perpendicular bisectors of two of the sides of the triangle, which creates the circumcenter.

Step 2. Use your compass to construct a circle centered at the circumcenter that passes through all of the vertices of the triangle.

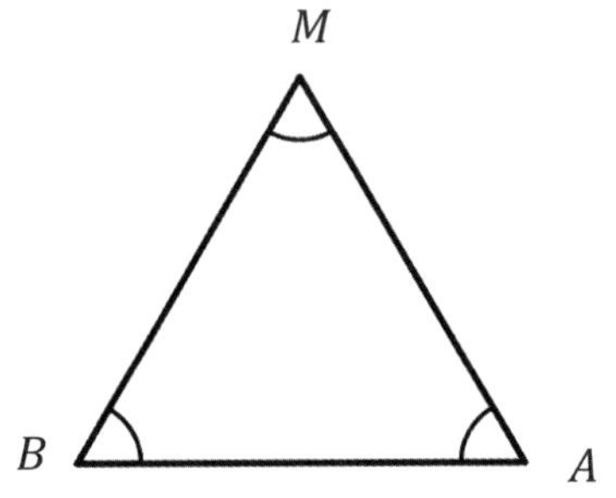

Let's Practice!

1. Construct an inscribed circle in $\triangle TRI$.

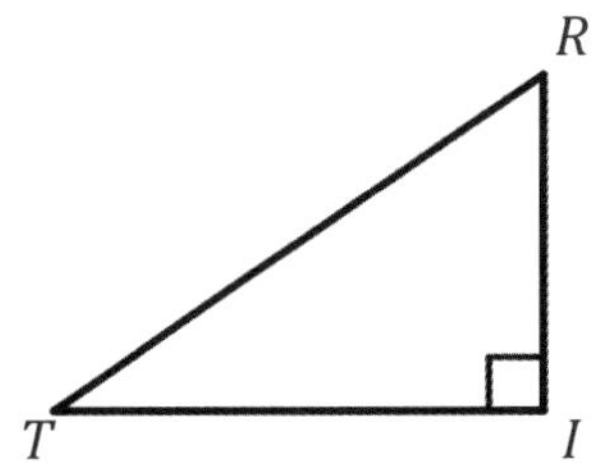

2. Construct a circumscribed circle in $\triangle TRI$.

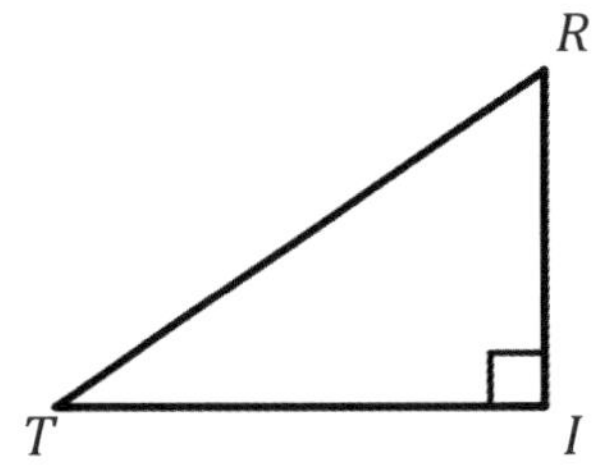

Try It!

3. Consider the following dialogue amongst the math cheerleaders.

Are they correct?
Did you know that an inscribed triangle is the largest circle contained within the triangle?
I totally did! And the circumscribed circle creates the smallest circle that contains the triangle!

Is there a mistake in any of the information exchanged by the above cheerleaders? Explain. If you think there is a mistake, give a counterexample.

BEAT THE TEST!

1. Consider the triangle below.

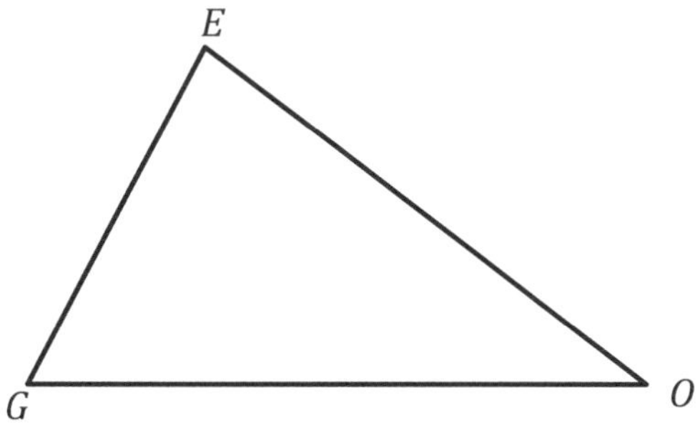

Reorder the following steps to describe how to construct an incircle. Write the letter of the most appropriate answer beside each step below.

A. Construct line p through point M so that p is perpendicular to $\overline{GO}$. Use T to label the intersection of p and $\overline{GO}$.
B. Bisect $\angle G$. Use l to label the bisector.
C. Construct circle M using M as the center and $\overline{MT}$ as the radius.
D. Find the intersection of l and n. Label the point M.
E. Bisect $\angle O$. Use n to label the bisector.

Step 1: __________
Step 2: __________
Step 3: __________
Step 4: __________
Step 5: __________

2. A teacher gave out the following warm-up exercise.

   1. *Is it true that the hypotenuse of a right triangle will be a diameter of the circumscribed circle of the triangle? Why?*

   2. *Circle the word that completes the sentence correctly. Justify your answer.*

      The diameter of any circumscribed circle of any triangle will ALWAYS | SOMETIMES | NEVER be one of the sides the triangle.

   How would you answer the above warm-up questions?

Test Yourself! Practice Tool

Great job! You have reached the end of this section. Now it's time to try the "Test Yourself! Practice Tool," where you can practice all the skills and concepts you learned in this section. Log in to Math Nation and try out the "Test Yourself! Practice Tool" so you can see how well you know these topics!

THIS PAGE WAS INTENTIONALLY LEFT BLANK

Section 11: Three-Dimensional Geometry

Topic 1: Geometry Nets and Three-Dimensional Figures 302
Standards Covered: This topic covers supporting knowledge
- ☐ I can unfold a geometric solid into a net.

Topic 2: Cavalieri's Principle for Area 305
Standards Covered: G-MG.1
- ☐ I can use Cavalieri's Principle to estimate area of a 2-dimensional and 3-dimensional case.

Topic 3: Cavalieri's Principle for Volume 309
Standards Covered: G-GMD.1
- ☐ I can use Cavalieri's Principle to estimate volume of a 3-dimensional case.

Topic 4: Cross Sections and Plane Rotations 313
Standards Covered: G-GMD.4
- ☐ I can rotate a 2-dimensional or 3-dimensional figure on a plane.

Topic 5: Volume of Prisms and Cylinders 317
Standards Covered: G-MG.3
- ☐ I can understand, calculate and apply the volume of prisms and cylinders.

Topic 6: Surface Area of Prisms and Cylinders 321
Standards Covered: G-MG.1
- ☐ I can understand, calculate and apply the lateral area and surface area of prisms and cylinders.

Topic 7: Volume of Pyramids and Cones 324
Standards Covered: G-GMD.3
- ☐ I can understand, calculate and apply the volume of pyramids and cones.

Topic 8: Surface Area of Pyramids and Cones 328
Standards Covered: G-MG.1
- ☐ I can understand, calculate and apply the lateral area and surface area of pyramids and cones.

Topic 9: Spheres 331
Standards Covered: G-MG.3
- ☐ I can understand, calculate and apply the surface area and volume of spheres and hemispheres.

Topic 10: Area in Real-World Contexts 334
Standards Covered: G-MG.1, G-MG.3
- ☐ I can apply the concept of 2-dimensional areas and 3-dimensional lateral and surface areas to solve real world problems.

Topic 11: Geometric Design 336
Standards Covered: G-MG.3
- ☐ I can apply geometric methods to real world modeling situations such as minimizing cost or maximizing profit or area.
- ☐ I can apply geometric methods to solve design problems when working with typographic grid systems based on ratios.

Topic 12: Volume in Real-World Contexts 340
Standards Covered: G-MG.3
- ☐ I can apply the concept of volume to solve real world problems.

Topic 13: Density 342
Standards Covered: G-MG.2
- ☐ I can apply concepts of density, based on area and volume in real world modeling situations.

Topic 14: Similar Shapes 345
Standards Covered: G-MG.1
- ☐ I can use characteristics of similar solids and use those characteristics to find lateral area, surface area, volume or missing segments.

Honors Topic 1: Deriving the Ellipse Formula .... Available Online
Standards Covered: G-GPE.2, G-GPE.3
- ☐ I can use graphic and analytic methods to write the equation of an ellipse given the foci and directrices.

Honors Topic 2: Deriving the Equation of a Hyperbola .... Available Online
Standards Covered: G-GPE.2, G-GPE.3
- ☐ I can derive the equation of a hyperbola given the foci and directrices.

Visit MathNation.com or search "Math Nation" in your phone or tablet's app store to watch the videos that go along with this workbook!

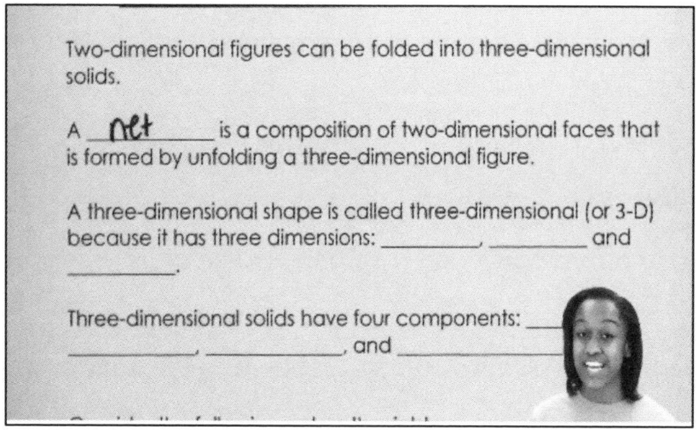

The following Michigan Mathematics Standards will be covered in this section:
G-GMD.1 - Give an informal argument for the formulas for the circumference of a circle, area of a circle, volume of a cylinder, pyramid, and cone.
G-GMD.3 - Use volume for cylinders, pyramids, cones, and spheres to solve problems.
G-GMD.4 - Identify the shapes of two-dimensional cross-sections of three-dimensional objects and identify three-dimensional objects generated by rotations of two-dimensional objects.
G-GPE.2 - Derive the equation of a parabola given a focus and directrix.
G-GPE.3 - Derive the equations of ellipses and hyperbolas given the foci and directrices.
G-MG.1 - Use geometric shapes, their measures, and their properties to describe objects.
G-MG.2 - Apply concepts of density based on area and volume in modeling situations.
G-MG.3 - Apply geometric methods to solve design problems.

Section 11: Three-Dimensional Geometry

Section 11 – Topic 1
Geometry Nets and Three-Dimensional Figures

Two-dimensional figures can be folded into three-dimensional solids.

A ____________ is a composition of two-dimensional faces that is formed by unfolding a three-dimensional figure.

A three-dimensional shape is called three-dimensional (or 3-D) because it has three dimensions: __________, __________ and __________.

Three-dimensional solids have four components: __________, ____________, _____________, and ________________.

Consider the following net on the right.

Identify the base(s) and face(s).

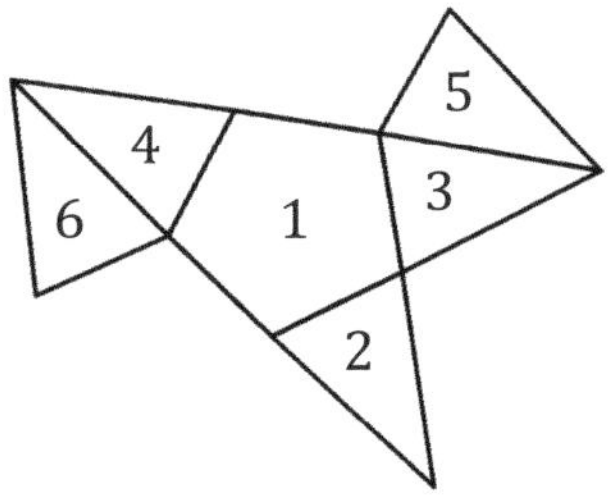

What type of three-dimensional shape is constructed when the net is folded?

How many edges and vertices does the solid have when folded?

Consider the following quartet of nets and determine which figures can fold into a cube.

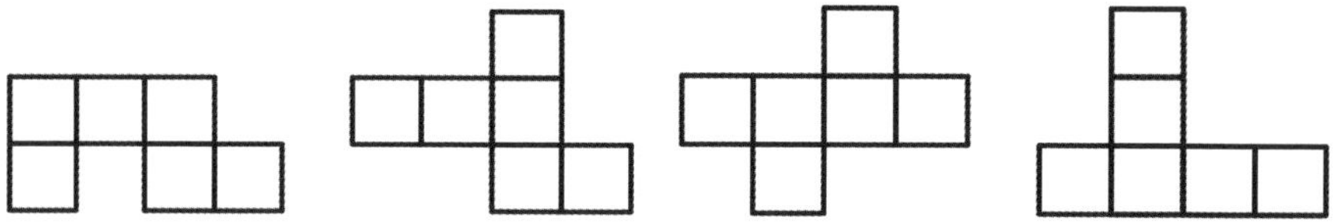

How do we distinguish the faces from the bases in a cube?

How many edges and vertices does a cube have?

If all the faces of a three-dimensional solid are polygonal, then the solid is in the form of a ____________________.

Fill in the blanks below and draw an example of a net for each solid geometric figure.

Geometric Solid	Geometry Net
A ____________ is a solid geometric figure that has two parallel congruent bases that are connected by lateral faces that are parallelograms.	
A ____________ is a solid geometric figure formed by connecting a polygonal base with a point forming triangular lateral faces.	
A ____________ is a solid geometric figure that is composed of two parallel congruent circles (bases) and a rectangle as a lateral face.	
A ____________ is a solid geometric figure that has a flat base (frequently, though not necessarily, a circle) and tapers to a point called the apex or vertex.	

Let's Practice!

1. Consider the following triplet of nets.

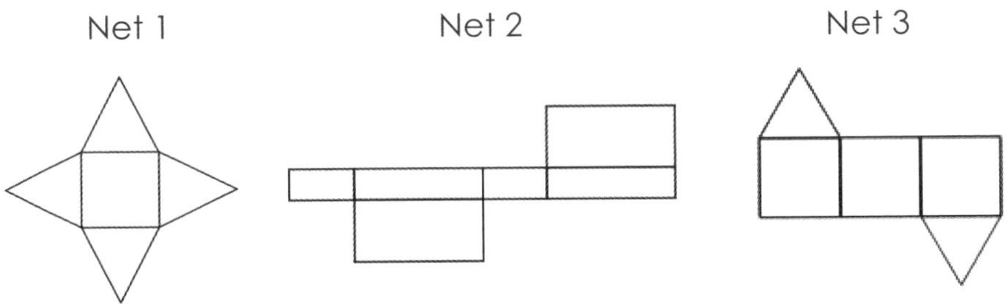

Complete the table below by using your knowledge of nets and create a conjecture to determine surface area and volume.

Net	Solid	Conjectures	
		Surface Area	Volume
1			
2			
3			

Try It!

2. Consider the following triplet of nets.

Net 1

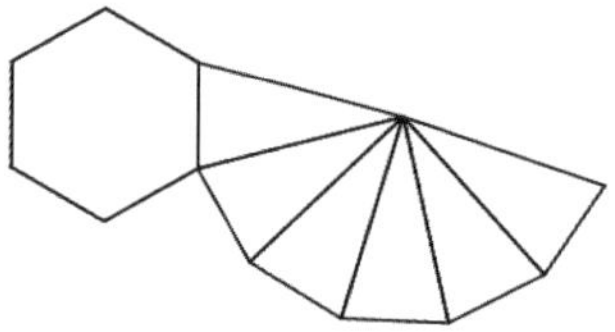

Net 2

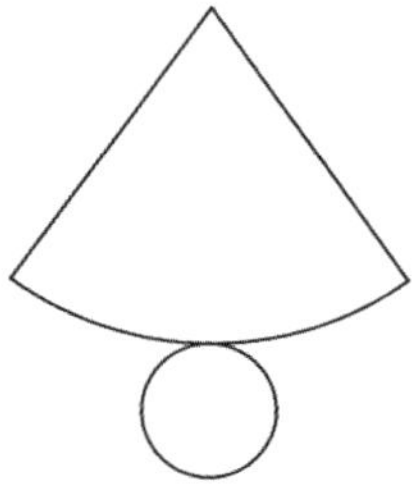

Net 3

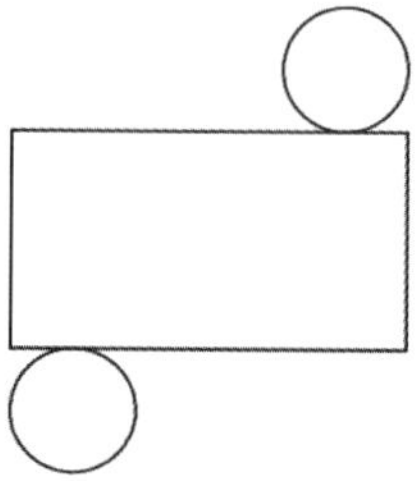

Complete the table below. Use your knowledge of nets to create conjectures to determine surface area and volume.

Net	Solid	Conjectures	
		Surface Area	Volume
1			
2			
3			

BEAT THE TEST!

1. Alberto unfolded a three-dimensional solid to create the two-dimensional figure below.

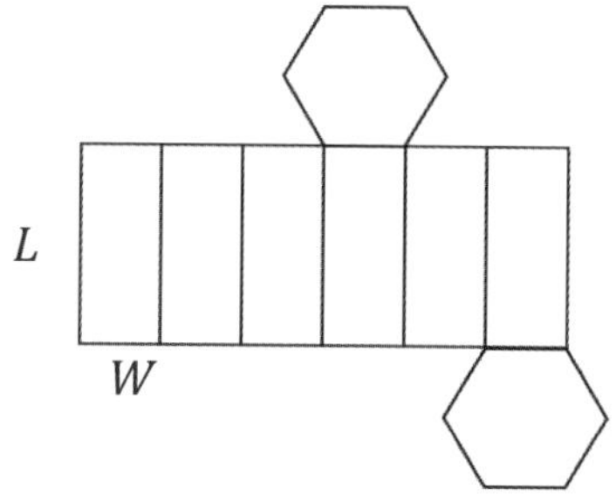

Select all the statements that apply to the figure.

- ☐ The figure shows a net for a hexagonal prism.
- ☐ The areas of each two-dimensional section of the figure add up to the surface area of the hexagonal prism.
- ☐ The height of the solid equals the length of any of the 6 rectangles in the figure.
- ☐ The volume of the solid equals the sum of the areas of each rectangle.
- ☐ The figure shows a net for a solid that has 8 faces, 12 vertices, and 18 edges.

2. Which of the nets below can be folded to form a triangular prism?

Figure 1 Figure 2 Figure 3

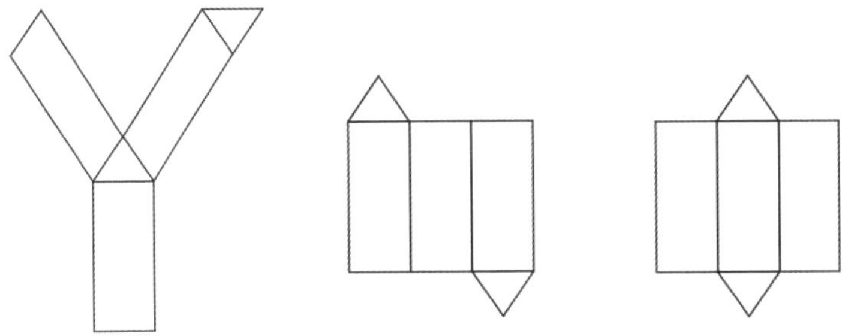

Ⓐ Figure 1
Ⓑ Figure 2
Ⓒ Figures 2 and 3
Ⓓ Figures $1, 2,$ and 3

Section 11 – Topic 2
Cavalieri's Principle for Area

The ***Cavalieri's Principle*** is a strategy that can be used for approximating the ____________ and ______________ of an irregularly shaped figure.

> STUDY EDGE TIP
>
> To use the **Cavalieri's Principle**, we divide a figure into familiar shapes to determine the total area or volume of the original shape.

Consider rectangle $ABCD$ and parallelogram $EFGH$ below.

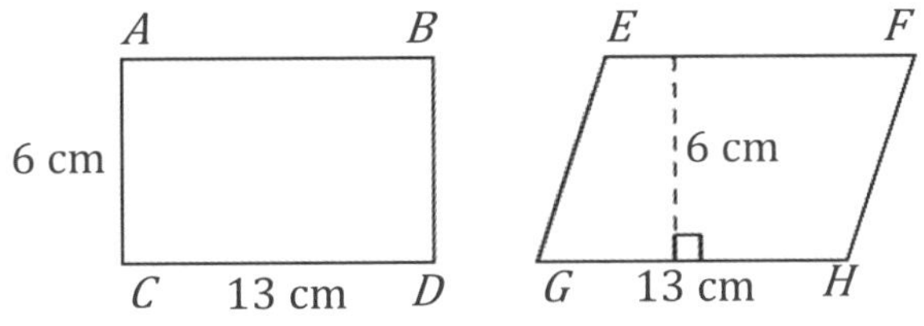

What is the length of every line segment drawn in the interior of $ABCD$ and parallel to $\overline{AB}$ and $\overline{CD}$?

What is the length of every line segment drawn in the interior of $EFGH$ and parallel to $\overline{EF}$ and $\overline{GH}$?

Compare the area of $ABCD$ to the area of $EFGH$.

Divide the irregular shape below into 10 congruent rectangles and approximate the length, height, and area of each congruent rectangle.

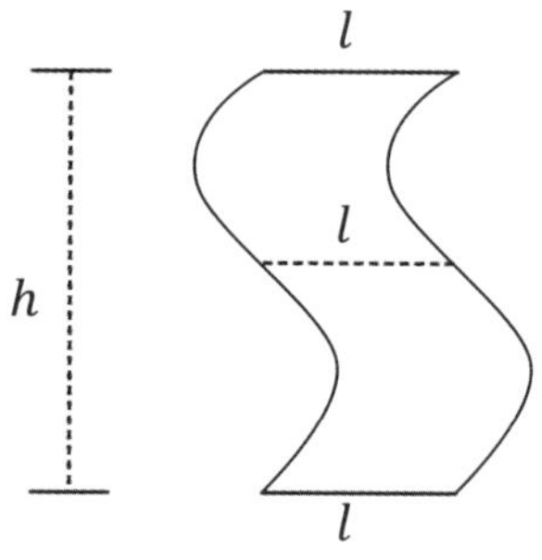

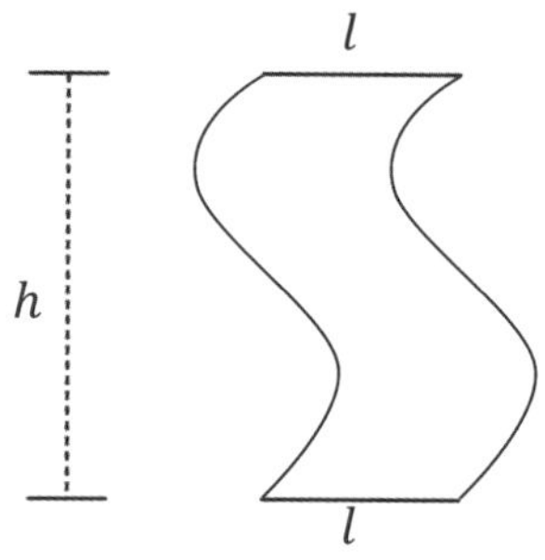

Length: ________________

Height: ________________

Area: ________________

What is the approximate area of the irregularly shaped figure?

Let's Practice!

1. Consider the figure below.

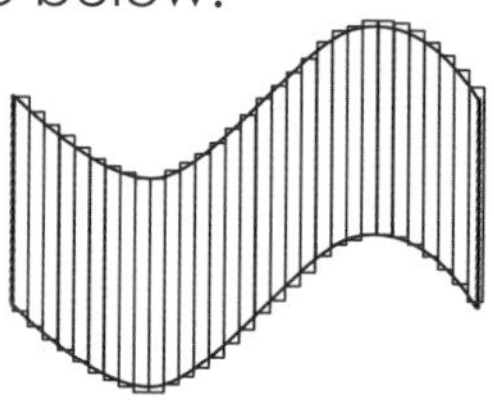

If each rectangle has a height of 12 yards and a width of 2.5 yards, estimate the approximate area of the irregular figure. Round to the nearest tenth, if necessary.

Try It!

2. Consider the stack of credit cards below.

One credit card is 3.375 inches long, 2.125 inches wide, and 0.03 inches thick. Estimate the approximate surface area of the stack of 11 credit cards. Round your answer to the nearest tenth.

3. Music used to be stored on things called compact disks (CDs). A stack of CDs is below.

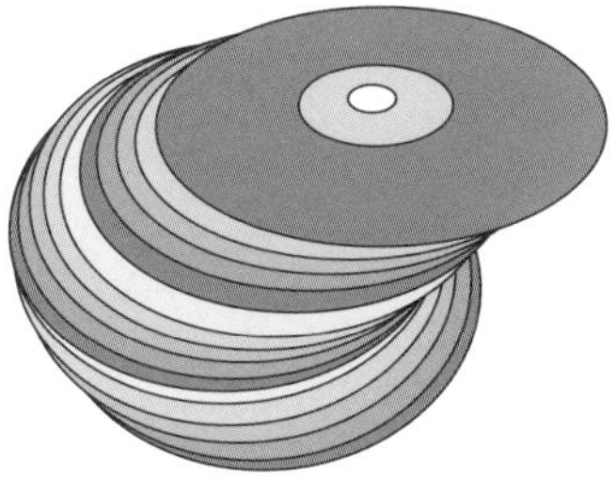

Write a plan to show how you will find the surface area of the stack using Cavalieri's Principle.

BEAT THE TEST!

1. Consider the roll of quarters below.

If the diameter of a quarter is 24.26 millimeters and the width of each quarter is 1.75 millimeters, what is the approximate surface area of the roll of quarters? Round your answer to the nearest tenth.

[ ] mm

2. Jaime cut a circle with circumference C and radius r into 8 congruent sectors and used the pieces to make the following figure.

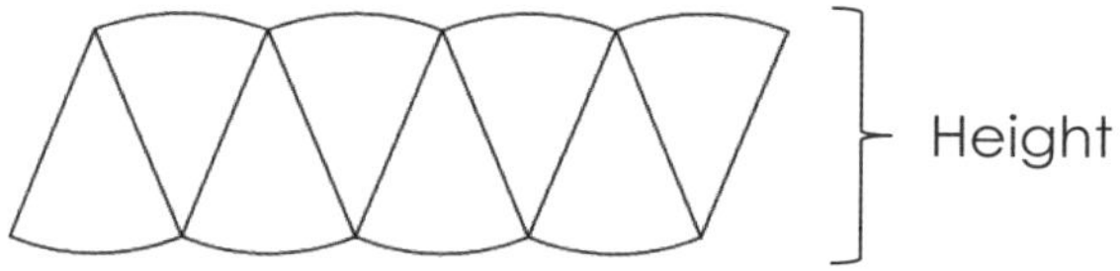

The above figure created by Jaime is very close to the shape of a(n) ______________.

Complete this statement by marking the most appropriate answer below.

Ⓐ Octagon
Ⓑ Parallelogram
Ⓒ Semicircle
Ⓓ Trapezoid

Section 11 – Topic 3
Cavalieri's Principle for Volume

If two solids have equal ____________, and each cross-section is ____________, then the volumes of the two solids are equal.

STUDY EDGE TIP The **Cavalieri's Principle** for volume is based on the idea that a plane figure can be made up of infinite parallelograms with equal areas.

How can we represent the Cavalieri's Principle for volume using the figure below?

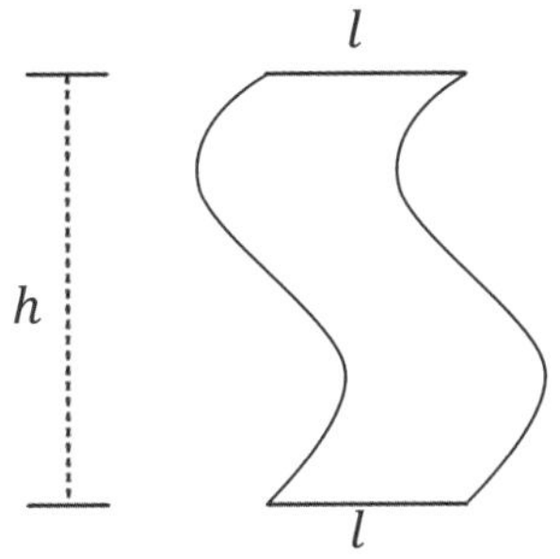

Consider the right rectangular prism and the oblique rectangular prism shown below.

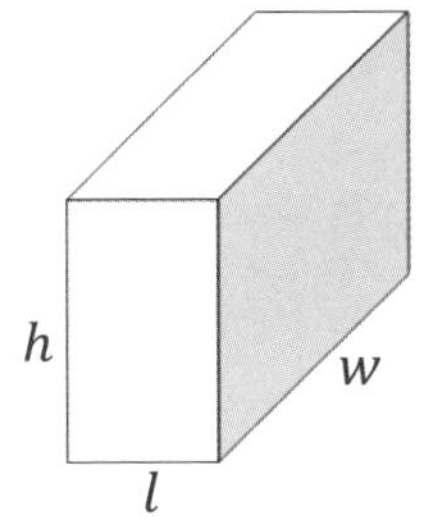

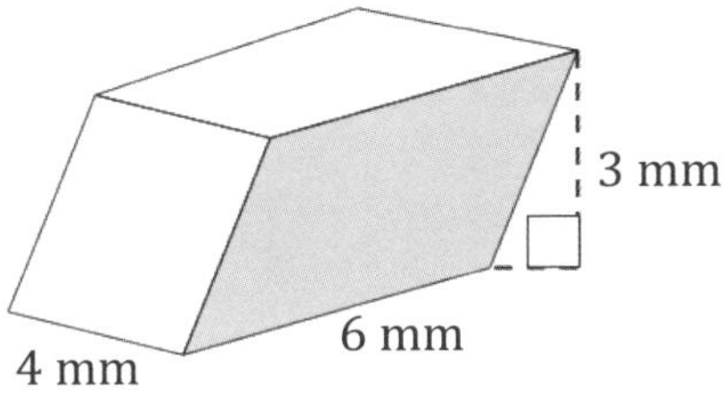

What geometric figure represents a cross section of each figure that is perpendicular to the base of each figure?

What are the dimensions of one cross section?

What is the volume of the right rectangular prism?

Approximate the volume of the oblique rectangular prism by dividing the prism into ten congruent right prisms.

Consider the figure below.

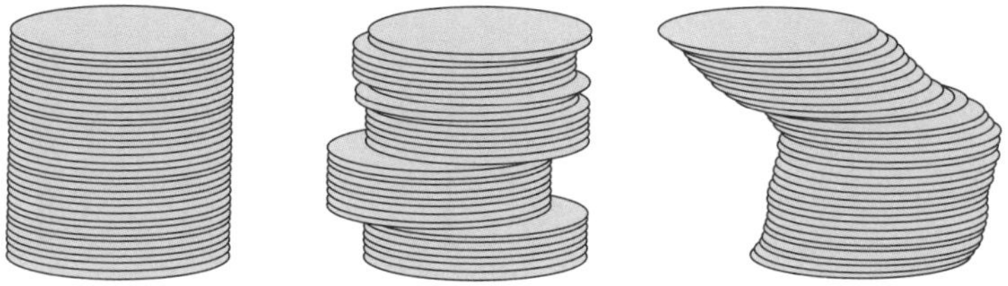

Compare and contrast the characteristics of the three stacks of pennies.

Do the three stacks of pennies have the same volume? Justify your answer.

Consider the stacks shown below.

Do the above stacks have the same volume? Justify your answer.

Cavalieri's Principle on Pyramids

If two pyramids have the same base area and the same height, then they must have the same volume.

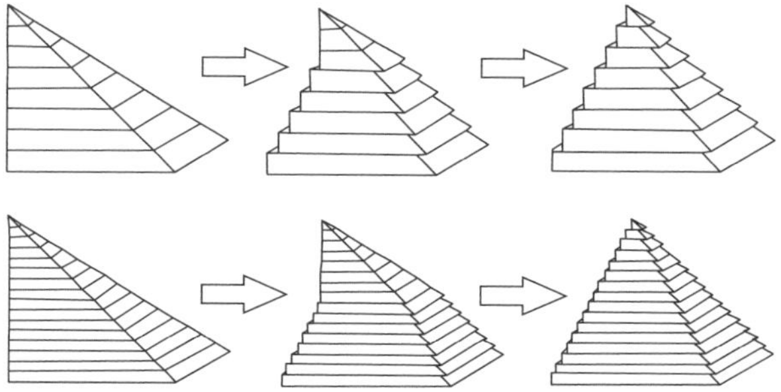

Let's Practice!

1. Consider the figure of the Leaning Tower of Pisa below. There is a vertical distance of about 180 feet from the top of the tower to the ground. The base of the tower has a diameter of 50 feet. What additional information do we need to estimate the volume of the tower using Cavalieri's Principle?

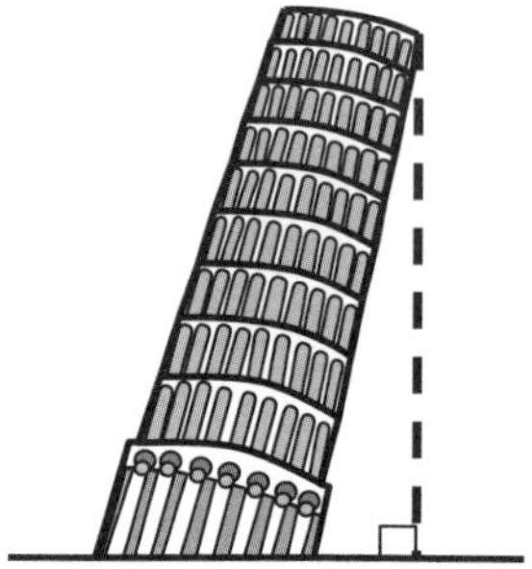

Try It!

2. Approximate the volume of the stack of CDs below. Round to the nearest tenth.

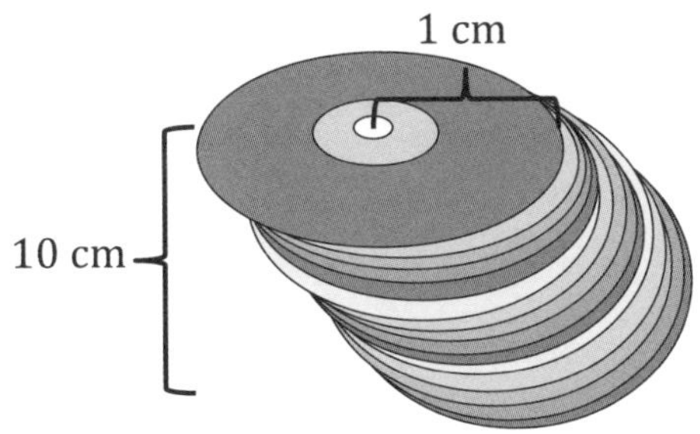

3. Given the following figure made of stacked disks with congruent heights, describe the steps to determine its volume.

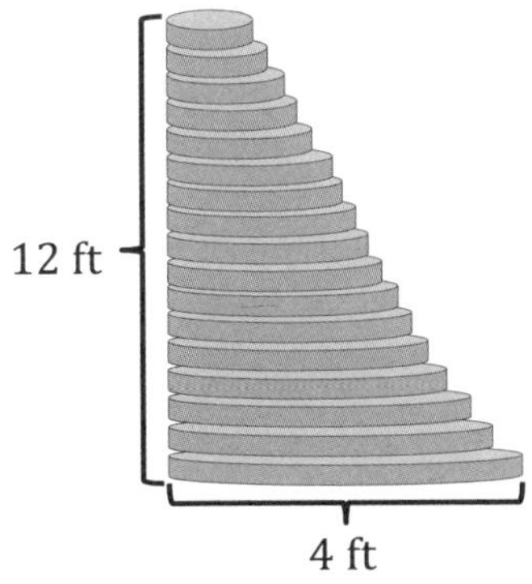

BEAT THE TEST!

1. Consider these two stacks of drink coasters.

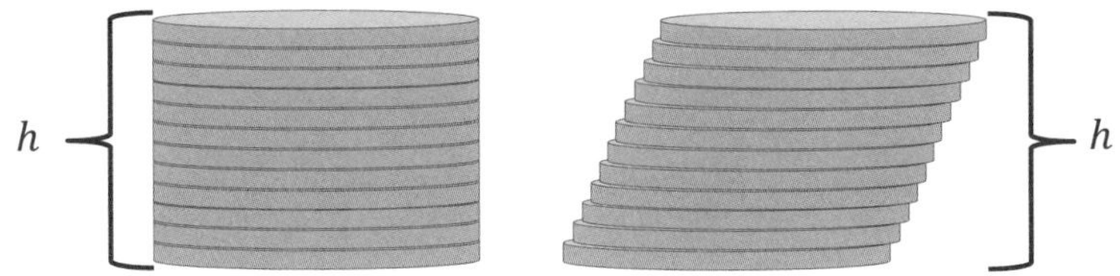

Which of the following statements is true?

Ⓐ By Cavalieri's principle, each cross section between the two stacks of drinking coasters is the same; therefore, the two volumes are equal.

Ⓑ By Cavalieri's principle, the heights of the two stacks of drinking coasters are the same; therefore, the two volumes are equal.

Ⓒ By Cavalieri's principle, each cross section between the two stacks of drinking coasters is the same and the heights of each solid are the same; therefore, the two volumes are equal.

Ⓓ By Cavalieri's principle, the heights of the two stack of drinking coasters are the same, but they are not arranged the same way; therefore, the two volumes are not equal.

2. Generally, a pair of clownfish will do well in tanks that are between 12 and 15 gallons. Miguel has an aquarium that is half of a 2-foot-diameter sphere for his two clownfish.

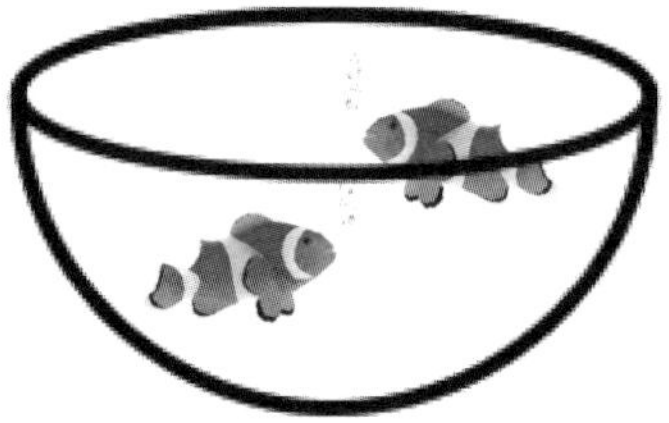

1 cubit foot = 7.48052 US liquid gallons.

Part A: Is Miguel's aquarium safe for his pair of clownfish? Justify your answer.

Part B: Write an equation to represent the area of the water's surface when filled to a height of h feet.

Part C: Miguel's mom bought him another aquarium with dimensions shown in the figure below.

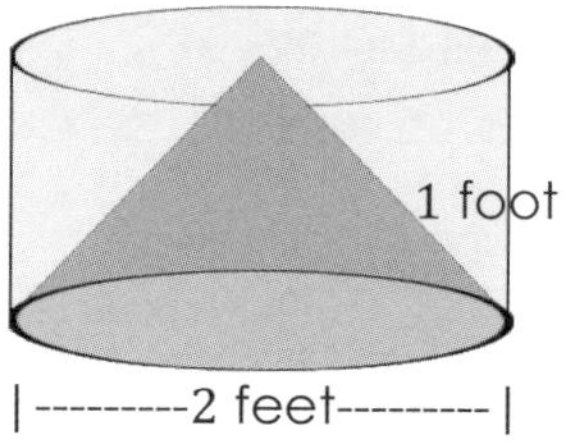

This new aquarium has the shape of a right cylinder with a diameter of two feet and a height of one foot, and it has an underwater one-foot tall right cone to put pictures and accessories.

Can Miguel transfer the water from his hemisphere aquarium to the new conic aquarium, or does he need to add/remove water? Justify your answer.

Section 11 – Topic 4
Cross Sections and Plane Rotations

Match each building represented in the table below with all of the geometric shapes that can be used to model it.

Building	Cone	Cylinder	Pyramid	Rectangular Prism
	☐	☐	☐	☐
	☐	☐	☐	☐
	☐	☐	☐	☐

What is a ***cross section***?

- A cross section is the shape we get when cutting straight through a solid with a ________________.
- In many cases, it is like a view into the _______________ of something after cutting through it.
- Cross sections are usually _____________ to the base like the figure below, but cross sections can be made in any direction.
- Cross sections can be _______________________, ______________________, or ______________________.

Consider the following cylinder with a horizontal plane cutting through it.

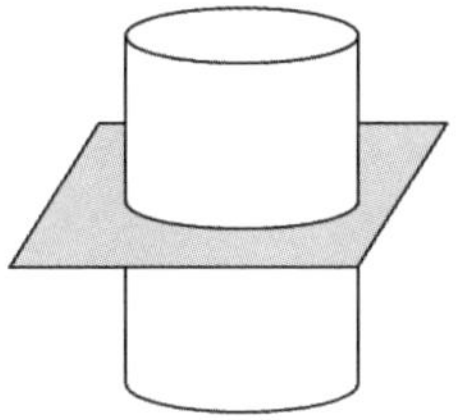

What is the shape that is projected on the gray plane? Draw it in the space provided below.

Consider the diagram below of triangular pyramid cut by a vertical plane.

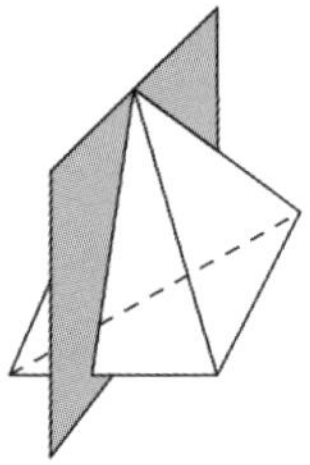

What is the shape that is projected on the intersecting plane? Draw it in the space provided below.

What is the cross section of the triangular pyramid here?

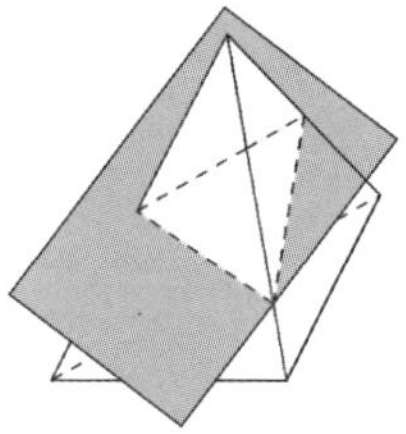

Let's Practice!

1. In the table below, describe the shape resulting from a vertical, angled, and horizontal cross section of each solid represented.

Solid	Cross Section
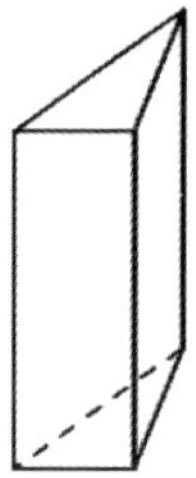	Vertical
	Angled
	Horizontal
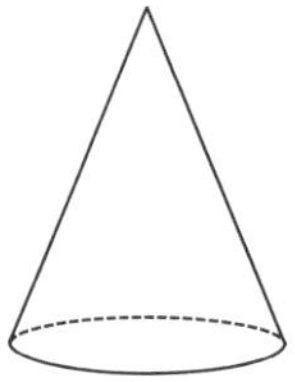	Vertical
	Angled
	Horizontal

2. Match the cross sections of each solid on the left with its corresponding shape on the right.

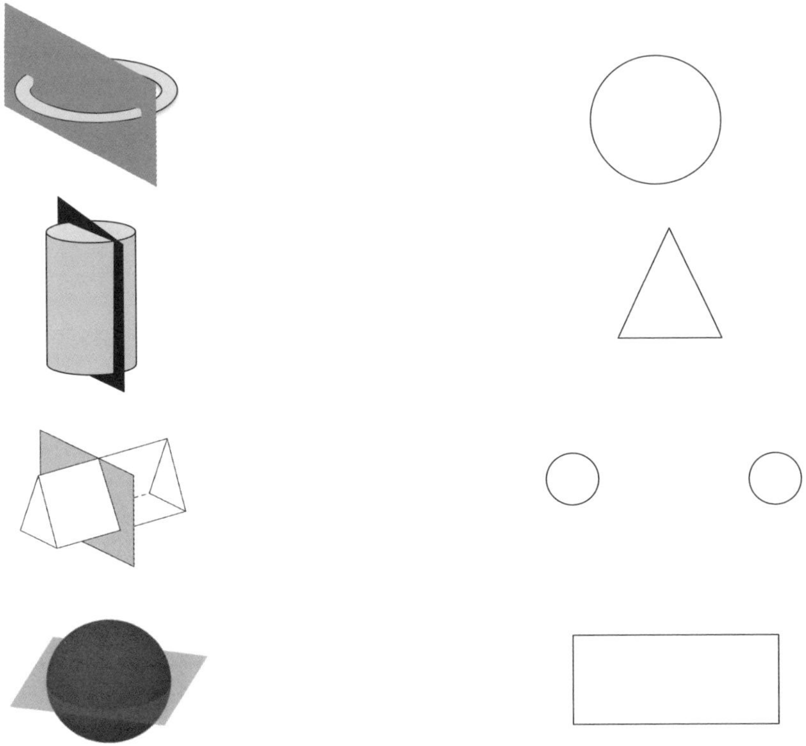

Try It!

3. Describe the shape of the cross section of each of the following objects.

   a. Right circular cone, cut by a plane through the vertex and perpendicular to the base

   b. Square pyramid, cut by a vertical plane that is parallel to an edge of the base and does not pass through the vertex

4. Describe the radius of the circular cross section created by a plane through the center of the sphere with radius r.

If we rotate the following polygons around a given line, what solid would we produce?

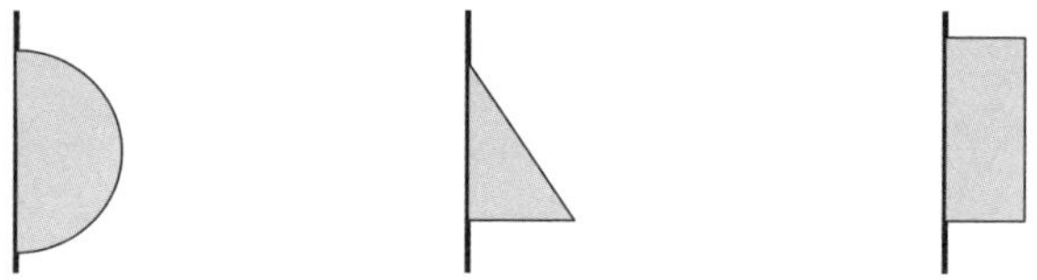

- A semicircle rotated about its diameter produces a __________.
- A right triangle rotated about one of its legs produces a __________.
- A rectangle rotated about its edge produces a ____________.
- These rotations are examples of ***plane rotations***.

Let's Practice!

5. Draw a rectangle rotated about a central axis (which must contain the midpoints of both of the sides that the axis intersects). What shape does the rotation produce?

Try It!

6. What is the surface area of the geometric solid produced by the triangle below when it is rotated $360°$ about the axis MN? Support your answer.

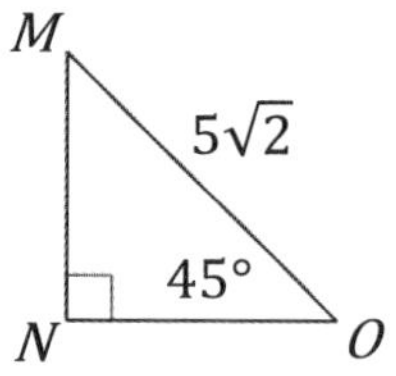

BEAT THE TEST!

1. Which of the following cross sections of an isosceles triangle being rotated about an axis of symmetry is NOT possible?

Ⓐ 

Ⓑ 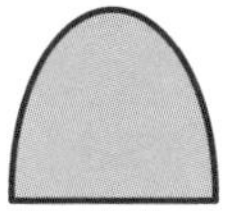

Ⓒ 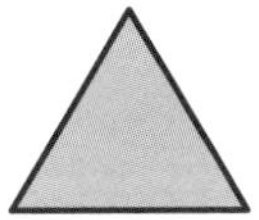

Ⓓ 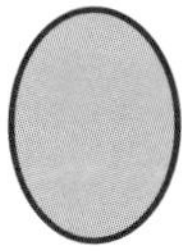

Section 11 – Topic 5
Volume of Prisms and Cylinders

A ***prism*** is a solid geometric figure with two polygonal bases that are congruent and parallel, with sides that are ________________________.

A ***cylinder*** is a solid geometric figure with two parallel and congruent ______________ bases and circular or oval cross sections that are congruent to the bases.

Identify each of the the following figures as prisms, cylinders, or neither.

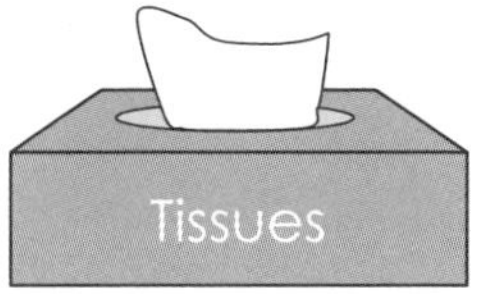

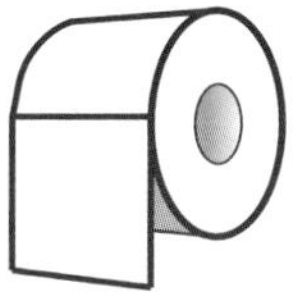

There are two different types of prisms.

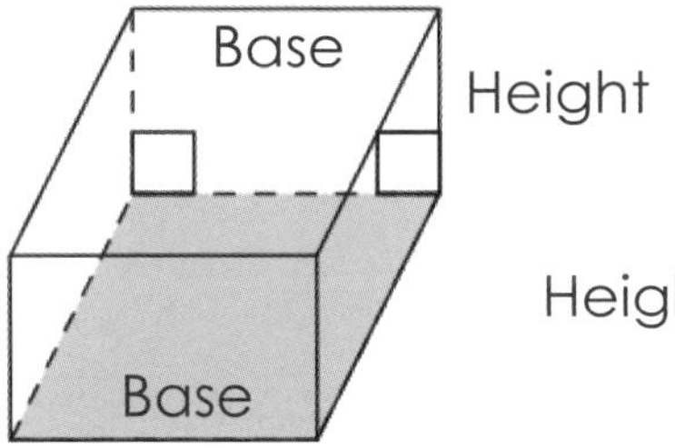

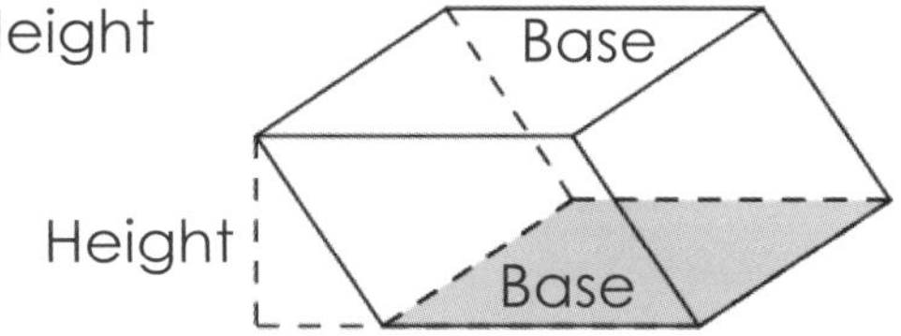

We have a stack of karate chopping boards.

What is the volume of one board that is 4 inches wide, 12 inches long, and 1 inch thick?

What is the total volume of space consumed by the stack of boards?

Derive the formula for the volume of a rectangular prism.

Describe the differences, if any, of the volume of a cylinder compared to the volume of a prism.

Consider the following roll of quarters.

The diameter of a quarter is 24.26 millimeters and the width is 1.75 millimeters. What is the approximate volume of the roll of quarters, to the nearest tenth?

Let's Practice!

1. Leo bought a fish tank that is 37 inches wide, 24 inches long and 15 inches high. One gallon of water fills 230.4 cubic inches of space.

   a. How many gallons of water (to the nearest tenth) will fill the fish tank?

   b. If the tank contains 4440 cubic inches of water, what percent of the fish tank is empty?

2. CadyCakes Cat Food Company needs to decide how to package their premium cat food. They've narrowed their choices down to two different containers. One container is a prism with a height of 5 inches and a 2-inch by 2-inch square base. Another container is a cylinder with a height of 5 inches and a diameter of 2 inches.

   Which container will hold the most premium cat food?

Try It!

3. Why do you think canned goods are usually packed in cylindrical containers?

4. The bakery *Delicias Culinarias* sells wedding cakes that are shaped like cylinders. The most popular cake in the bakery is available in two sizes that are labeled below with heights and diameters shown.

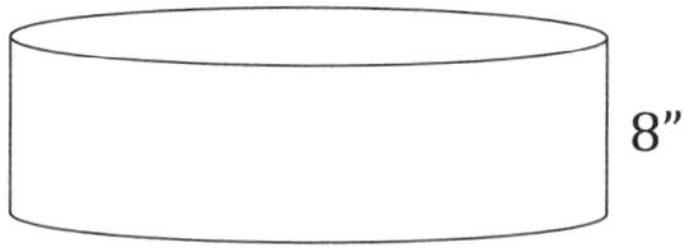

Small 10"

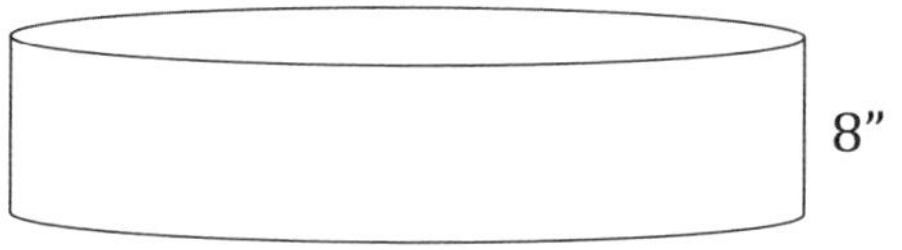

Large 14"

   The small cake is enough to feed 16 people. Will the large cake be enough to feed 20 people? What is the maximum number of people the large cake will feed? Justify your answers.

BEAT THE TEST!

1. Stephen works for an environmental protection agency responsible for toxic waste cleanup. Stephen has to remove the top 24" of contaminated soil in order to make sure the soil is not a health hazard. The soil covers a $1200' \times 1500'$ lot. How much soil must be removed?

   Ⓐ 3,600,000 ft^3
   Ⓑ 43,200,000 ft^3
   Ⓒ 259,200,000 ft^3
   Ⓓ 6,000,000,000 ft^3

2. Tito owns a cargo truck with a container measuring 7.5 feet by 15 feet by 7.50 feet.

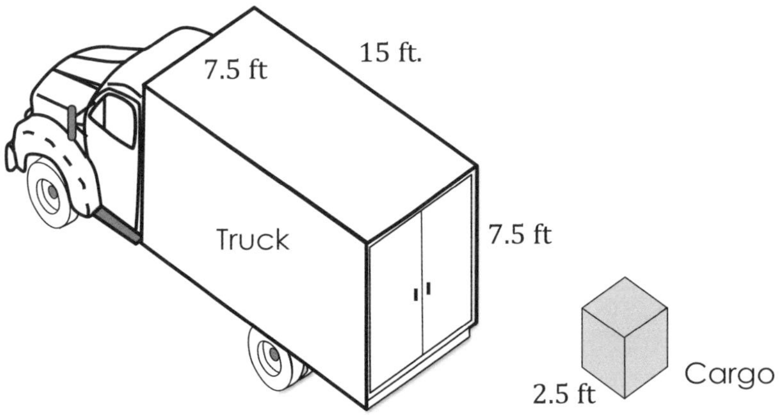

   Tito charges by the number of boxes he's able to transport.
   If the boxes measure 2.50 feet on each side, what is the maximum number of boxes he can fit in the truck? Justify your answer.

Section 11 – Topic 6
Surface Area of Prisms and Cylinders

The instructors in the dojo, or martial arts training room, have boxes containing karate chopping blocks.

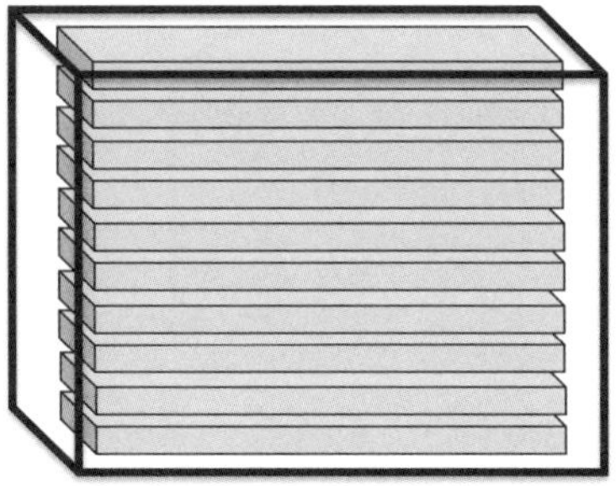

- The area of the box used to contain the chopping blocks is called the ______________ __________ of the box.

- Now imagine that there is a piece of paper that just wraps around the box. It doesn't cover the bottom or the top of the box. The area of the paper is called the ______________ _____________.

The surface area of a three-dimensional shape is the sum of all of the surface areas of each of the sides and the bases.

How would you calculate the lateral area?

How would you calculate the surface area?

Nets help you identify all the areas of a prism or a cylinder.

Consider the following diagram of a square prism.

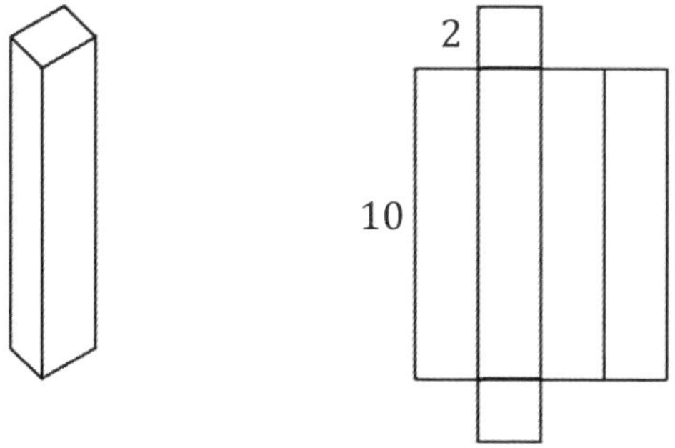

The above square prism was unfolded into a net with four rectangles 10 feet by 2 feet and two squares 2 feet by 2 feet.

Determine the lateral area of the square prism.

The formula for the lateral area of a square prism is

_____________________.

Determine the surface area of the square prism.

The formula for the surface area of a square prism is

_____________________.

Consider the following diagram of a cylinder and its net.

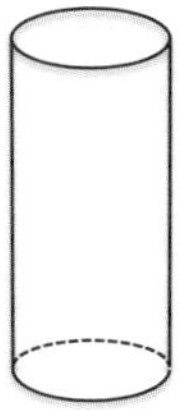

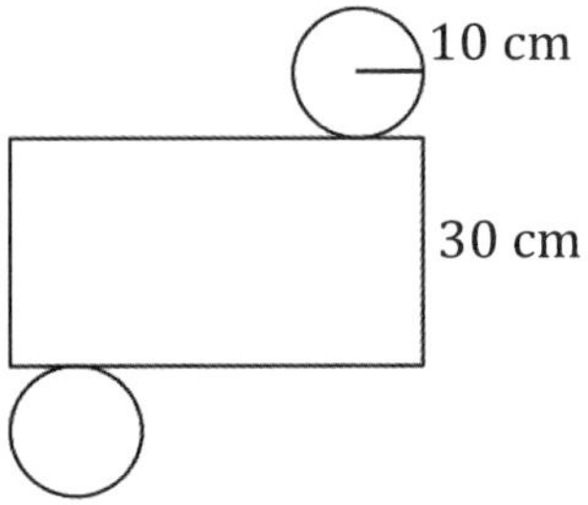

The cylinder was unfolded into a net with one rectangle that has a height of 30 centimeters and two circles with radius of 10 centimeters.

Determine the length of the rectangle.

Determine the lateral area of the cylinder.

Therefore, the formula for the lateral area of a cylinder is

______________________________.

Determine the surface area of the cylinder.

Thus, the formula for the surface area of a cylinder is

____________________.

Let's Practice!

1. Determine the lateral area of the isosceles trapezoidal prism with height of 6.3 m.

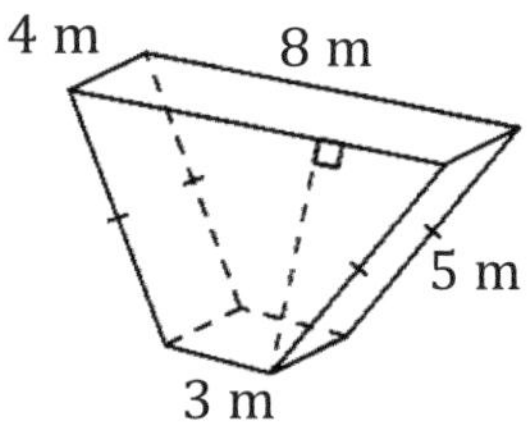

2. Determine the lateral area of the regular hexagonal prism with apothem of approximately 3.5 ft.

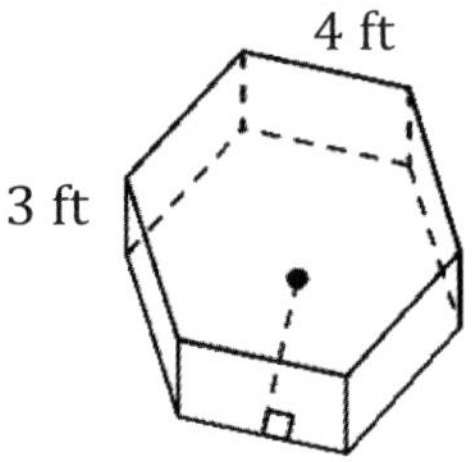

3. Is it possible to use the lateral area to find volume? Justify your answer.

Try It!

4. The bakery *Delicias Culinarias* sells wedding cakes that are shaped like cylinders with heights and diameters shown below. The most popular cake in the bakery is available in two sizes that are labeled below.

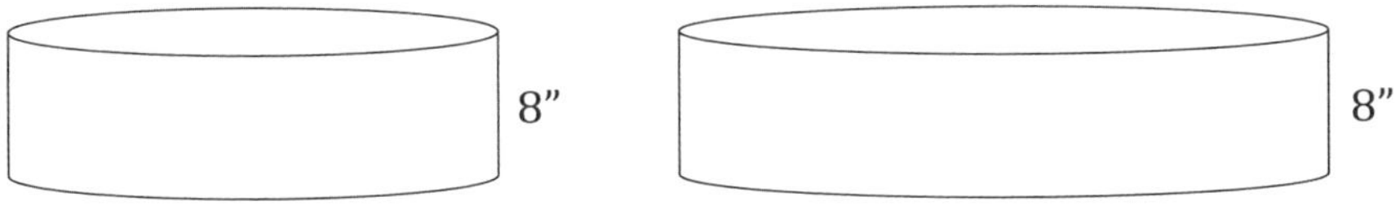

Small 10”   Large 14”

How much more area must the icing on the large cake cover compared to the small cake?

BEAT THE TEST!

1. *SmartPak* is a company that packs and labels different products for supermarkets. Cylindrical cans are sold by the dozen and may be packed in a rectangular container in four configurations: 2×6; 3×4; 2×3 in 2 layers; and 2×2 in 3 layers.

   A can of tomato sauce is 4 inches tall with a diameter of 3 inches. The company manager wants to use a package design that requires the least amount of boxing material. Which is the best package design?

   Ⓐ

   2×6 design

   Ⓑ

   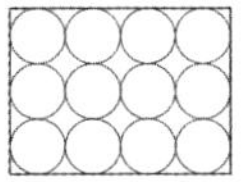

   3×4 design

   Ⓒ

   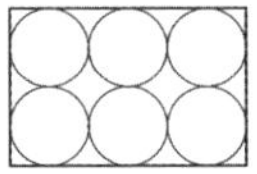

   2×3 design
   In 2 Layers

   Ⓓ

   2×2 design
   In 3 Layers

2. A local school has a gymnasium that is $48'$ long, $36'$ wide with an $18'$ ceiling. The school maintenance staff is painting the four walls. Each can of paint contains enough paint to cover 400 square feet. How many cans of paint are needed to cover the gym?

Ⓐ 4 cans
Ⓑ 7 cans
Ⓒ 8 cans
Ⓓ 12 cans

Section 11 – Topic 7
Volume of Pyramids and Cones

A ***pyramid*** is a solid formed by connecting a polygonal base and a point, called the _______________. Together, each base edge and apex form a triangle. The triangle is called a ***lateral face***.

A ***cone*** is a solid geometric figure that has a flat base (that is frequently, though not necessarily, a circle) that tapers to a point called the apex or vertex.

Name each type of pyramid below by observing the base of each figure.

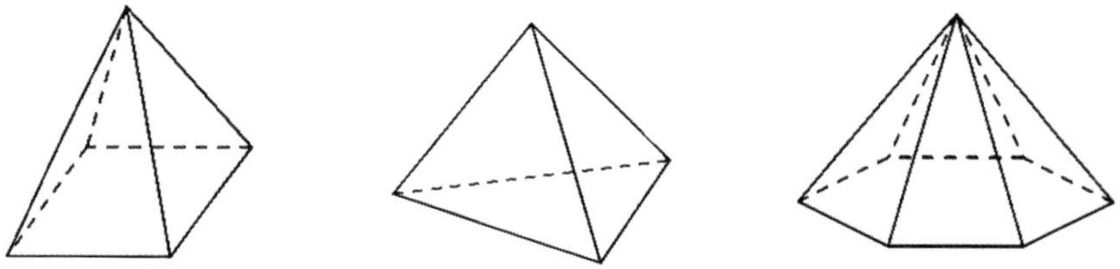

A.	B.	C.

Use the word bank below to label every part of the pyramid and cone.

Apex	Height	Slant Height
Radius	Base	Lateral Surface (Face)

Pyramid:

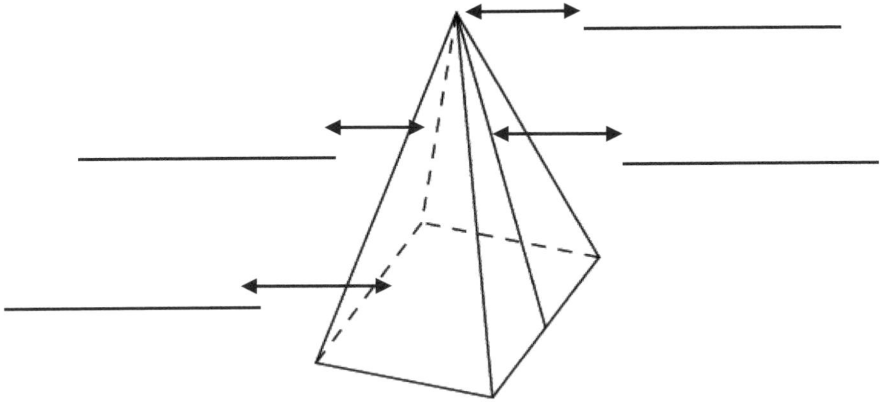

Cone:

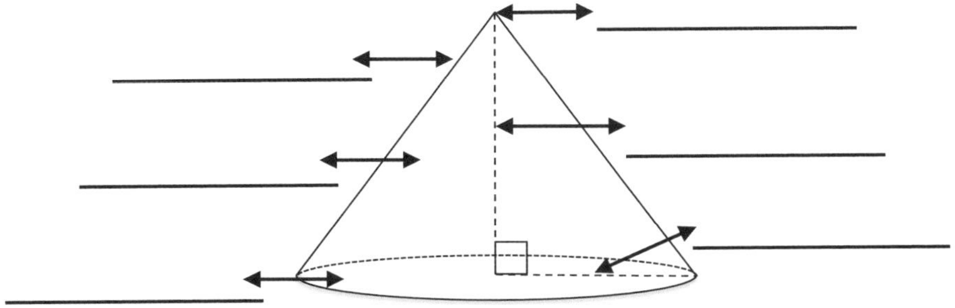

Consider the following pyramid and prism with equal side length and equal height.

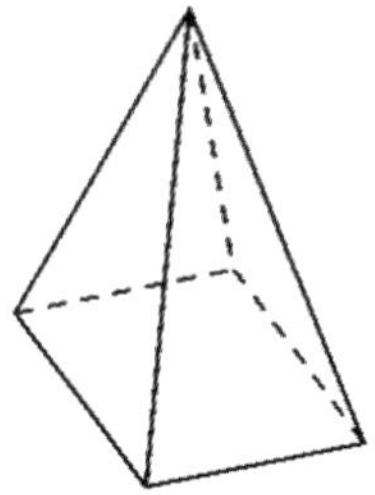

Volume = $266.\overline{6}\ cm^3$

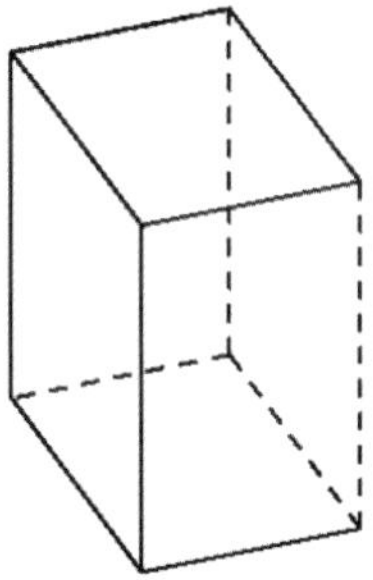

Volume = $800\ cm^3$

What is the ratio of the pyramid's volume to the prism's volume?

How many pyramids are required to fill the prism?

Consider the formula for the volume of a prism and derive the formula for the volume of the pyramid.

Consider the following cone and cylinder of equal diameter and equal height.

Volume = $(66.\bar{6}\pi)''$ Volume = $(200\pi)''$

What is the ratio of the cone to the cylinder based on volume?

How many cones does it take to fill the cylinder?

Consider the formula for the volume of a cylinder and derive the formula for the volume of the cone.

Let's Practice!

1. Caroline and Grant are building sandcastles in the annual Coney Island Sand Sculpting Contest. The diagram below represents their final products.

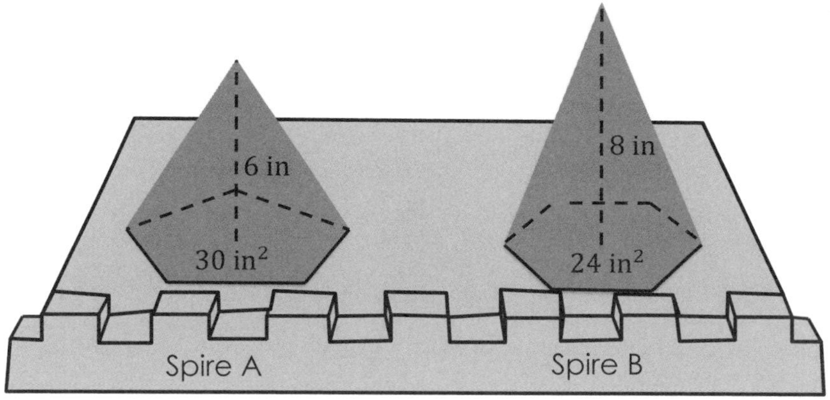

   a. Which sandcastle has a greater volume?

   b. How much more sand is required to make the spire with greater volume?

Try It!

2. Consider the diagram of the hourglass below.

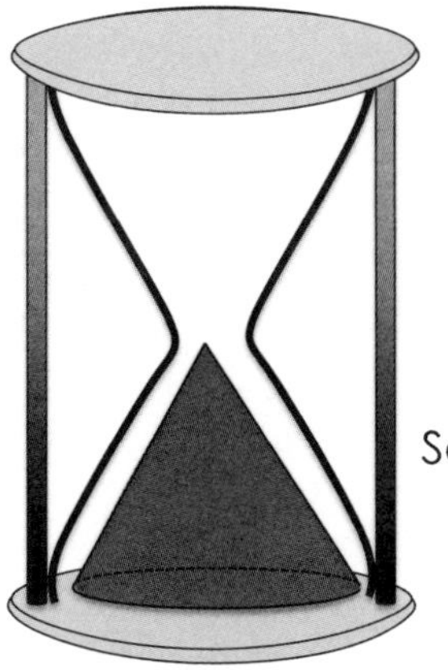

   a. Find the volume of the cone-shaped pile of sand above. Justify your answer.

   b. The sand falls through the opening at a rate of one cubic inch per minute. Is this hourglass a true "hour"-glass? Justify your answer. (1 hour = 60 minutes)

BEAT THE TEST!

1. The table below shows the approximate dimensions of the Luxor Pyramid in Las Vegas and the Great Pyramid of Khufu in Egypt. Both pyramids have square bases.

Pyramid	Height (feet)	Area of the Base (square feet)
Luxor	350	360,000
Khufu	455	570,025

Part A: The designer of the Luxor Pyramid has allocated 1000 ft^3 of space for each person. Approximately how many people is the hotel designed to hold, if it is filled to capacity?

Part B: The owners of the Luxor Pyramid want to build another hotel that features an innovative conical design with the same height and area of the base as the Great Pyramid of Khufu. What would be the diameter of the base of the new conical hotel?

Section 11 – Topic 8
Surface Area of Pyramids and Cones

Consider the following diagram of a pyramid with a square base and its net.

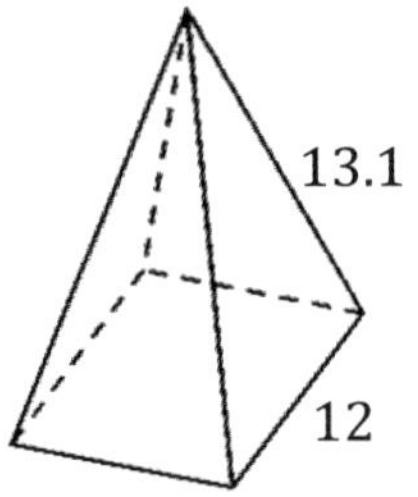

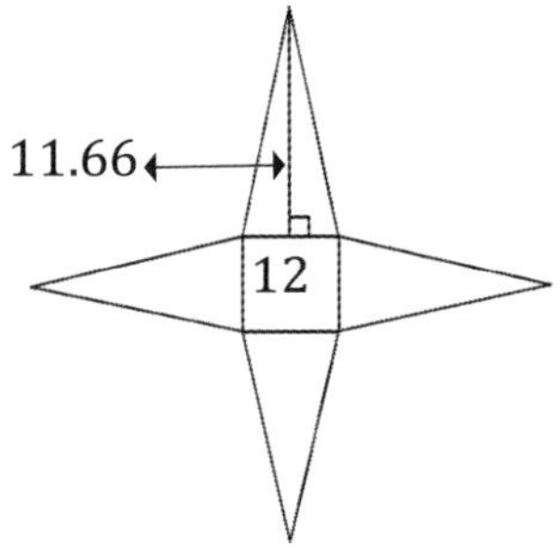

The pyramid was unfolded into a net with one square and four isosceles triangles.

Determine the lateral area of the square pyramid.

The formula for the lateral area of a square pyramid is

________________________.

Determine the surface area of the square pyramid above.

The formula for the surface area of a square pyramid is

________________________.

Consider the following diagram of a cone and its net.

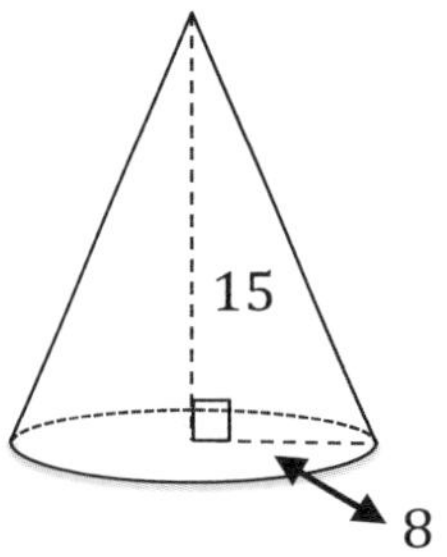

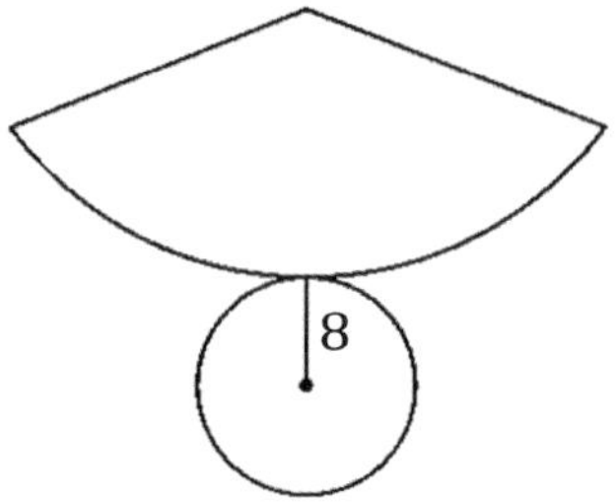

The cone was unfolded into a net as shown.

Determine the slant height of the cone.

Determine the lateral area of the cone.

The formula for the lateral area of a cone is

________________________.

Determine the surface area of the cone.

The formula for the surface area of a cone is

________________________.

Let's Practice!

1. Find the surface area of the regular pentagonal pyramid below.

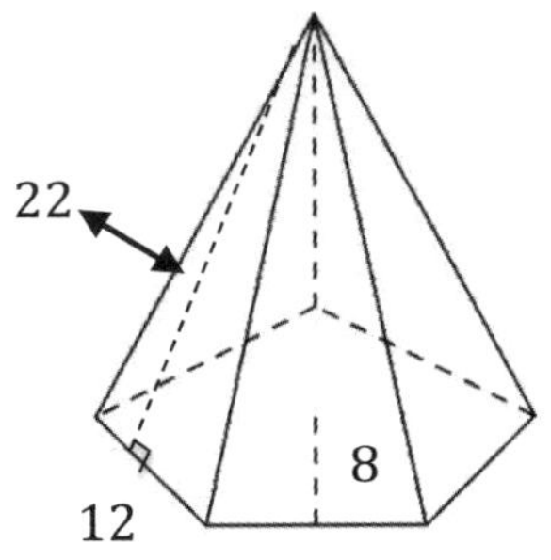

2. Determine the radius of a cone that has a lateral area of 70π and a total surface area of 120π.

Try It!

3. Copy the measurements given onto the net of the cone below and find the lateral and surface area of the cone.

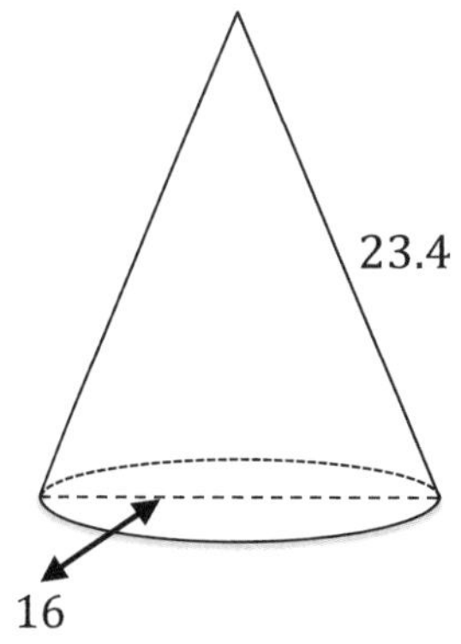

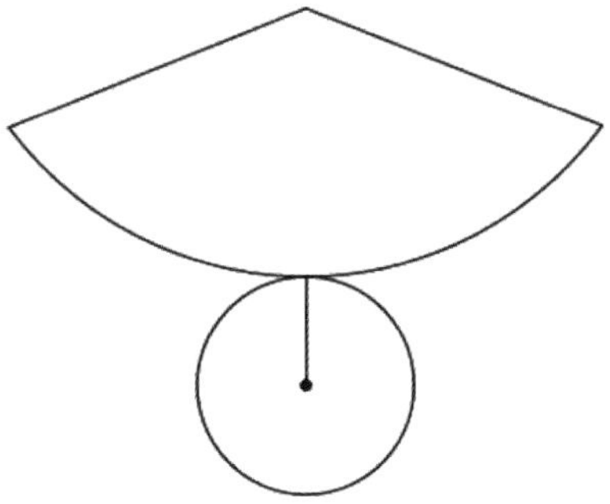

BEAT THE TEST!

1. Jordi's parents are throwing a huge birthday party for him. His parents asked Jordi to design the party hats. The following diagram shows Jordi's design.

Part A: Jordi attached a piece of elastic along the diameter. How long is the elastic on each hat? Round your answer to the nearest tenth.

[ ] inches

Part B: How much paper does Jordi need to make each hat?

Ⓐ Jordi needs a little over 8 square inches of paper to make each hat.

Ⓑ Jordi needs a little over 24 square inches of paper to make each hat.

Ⓒ Jordi needs a little over 27 square inches of paper to make each hat.

Ⓓ Jordi needs a little over 51 square inches of paper to make each hat.

2. Lourdes owns a house with a roof shaped like a square pyramid. The following diagram shows a model design of the house.

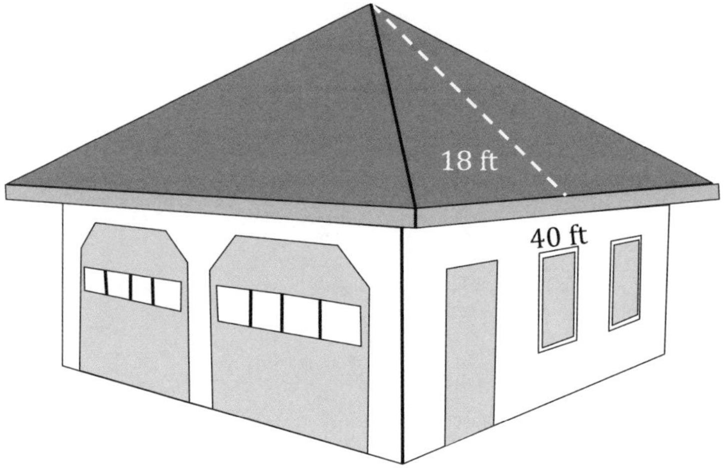

Lourdes is replacing the roof and installing shingles. In roofing terminology, a "square" is 100 square feet. Composition shingles come in bundles that cover 1/3 of a square. How many bundles should Lourdes buy to cover the roof? Justify your answer.

Section 11 – Topic 9
Spheres

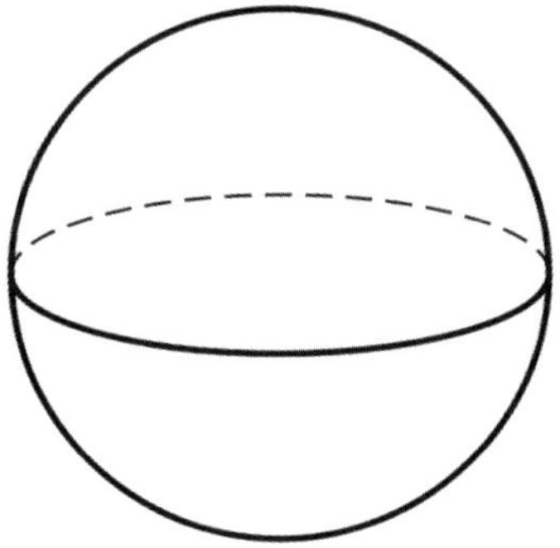

Fill in the blanks and make illustrations in the above sphere.

- A ***sphere*** is a set of points in _________ space equidistant from a point called the ____________ of the sphere.
- The distance from the center to the points on the sphere is called the ____________ of the sphere.
- Any segment whose endpoints are on the sphere is called the ____________________ of the sphere.
- Any chord that contains the center of the sphere is also the ___________________.
- One of the congruent halves of a sphere is called the ___________________.

The surface area of a sphere is exactly 4 times the area of a circle with the same radius.

Let's Practice!

1. Your grandmother buys 10 spherical grapefruits, each with a diameter of $3\frac{3}{4}$ inches. Your grandmother plans to juice the grapefruits and to save the peels to make candied citrus peels. She lays the peels out to dry on 9" × 13" rectangular pans. How many pans are required?

Try It!

2. Planet Earth has a diameter of 7,917.5 miles. What is the surface area of the Southern Hemisphere?

Consider the diagram below of a basketball and the container that the ball comes in. Based on this figure, complete each sentence below with the most appropriate answer.

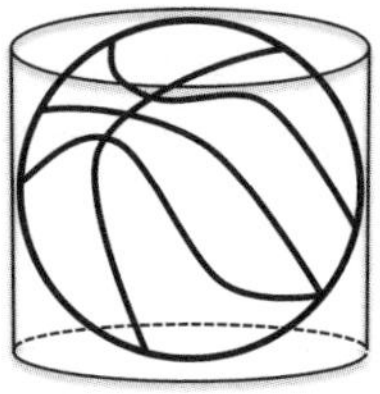

- Since the basketball can fit perfectly into the cylindrical box, the basketball has the __________ diameter of a cylinder.

- The cylinder would have a height (h) equal to the sphere's _________________.

- The diameter of the cylinder's bases would also be equal to the diameter of the _________________.

- The volume of a sphere is __________ the volume of a cylinder that has the same diameter and height as the sphere.

- The volume of a sphere is ________________________.

Let's Practice!

3. A cylindrical feed silo has a diameter of 45 feet and a height of 30 feet. What is the volume of the largest sphere that will fit into the cylinder?

Try It!

4. Compare and contrast the formulas for the volumes of a sphere, a cone, and a cylinder with equal height and radius. How are they related?

BEAT THE TEST!

1. Roger Federer bought a can of three tennis balls as a present for his nephew. The can is just large enough for the tennis balls to fit inside.

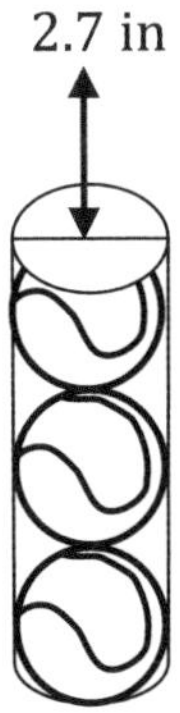

Part A: Find the total volume of the can.

[ ] in^3

Part B: Find the volume of empty space inside the can.

[ ] in^3

Part C: What percent of the can is occupied by the tennis balls?

Ⓐ $17\frac{1}{3}\%$

Ⓑ $33\frac{2}{3}\%$

Ⓒ $66\frac{2}{3}\%$

Ⓓ $83\frac{1}{3}\%$

2. Club Cool in Epcot offers free samples of Coke products distributed worldwide. Flavors include Fanta Pineapple, Fanta Melon, Inca Cola, VegitaBeta, and Sparberry. You can choose to have your sample served in either of the below containers:

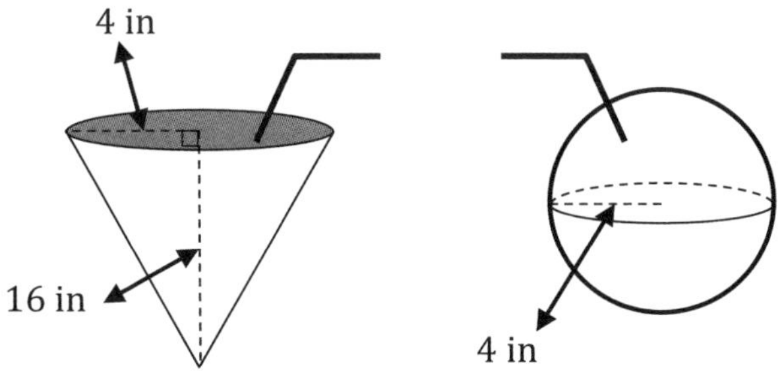

Select all the statements that are correct.

- ☐ Both containers hold the same amount of soda.
- ☐ The cone holds more soda.
- ☐ The sphere holds more soda.
- ☐ The volumes are the same because the height of the cone is 4 times its radius, and both containers have the same radius.
- ☐ The volume of the sphere is greater than the cone's, because $\frac{4}{3}\pi r^3$ is greater than $\frac{1}{3}\pi r^2$.
- ☐ The volume of the cone is greater than the sphere's, because the height is 4 times the radius of both containers.
- ☐ It cannot be determined which container holds more soda.

Section 11 – Topic 10
Area in Real-World Contexts

Use geometric shapes to describe these objects found in the real world.

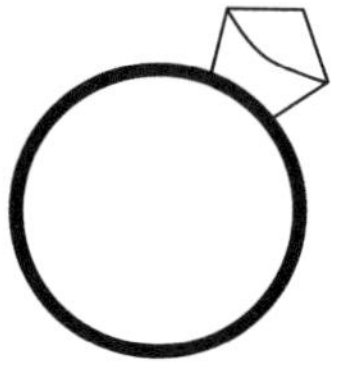

We can use measures of geometric shapes to find the area, volume, surface area, perimeter, or circumference of a shape found in the real world.

Let's Practice!

1. Four friends run at a circular track every evening after work. As shown below, the track has four lanes and each lane is 5 meters wide.

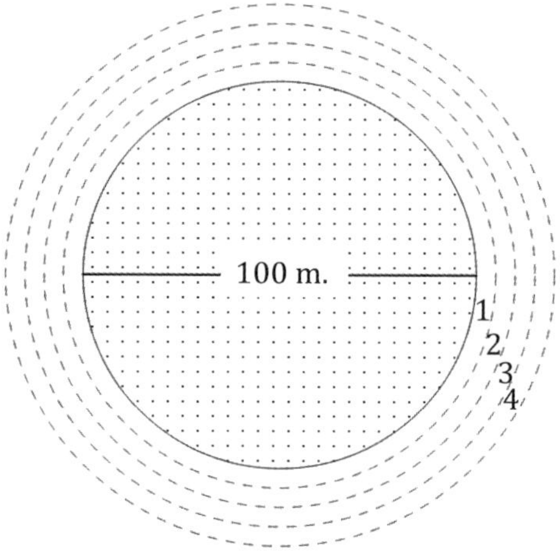

   a. How long is each lane?

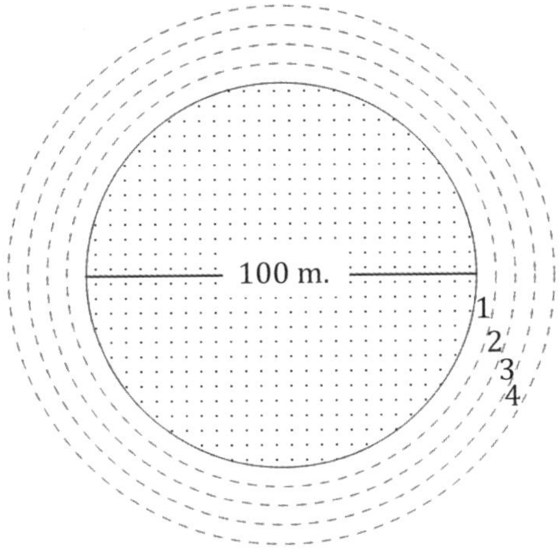

b. If the four friends want to race each other, then would the competition be fair for the runners on the outer lanes if they all started side by side? Why or why not?

c. How much longer would the race be for the runners in lanes $2, 3,$ and 4 than for the runner in lane 1?

Try It!

2. The new floor plan for the interior of a home is below. Marisa wants to cover various parts of the floors with carpet, tile, or wood.

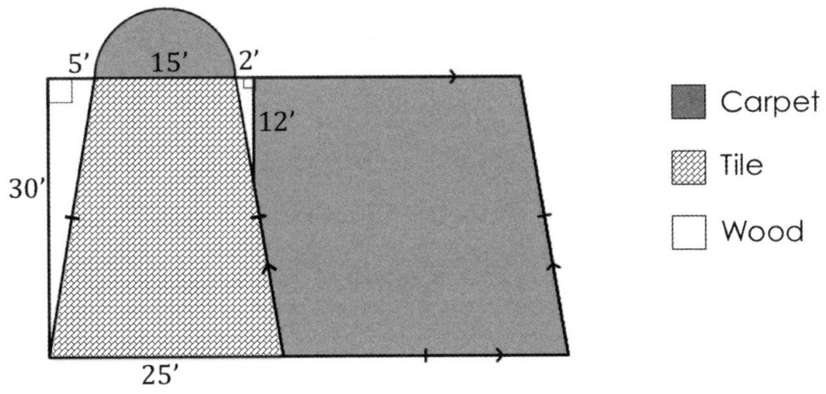

If carpet costs $\$1.14$ per square foot, tile costs $\$1.29$ per square foot, and wood flooring costs $\$1.99$ per square foot, then how much will this project cost?

BEAT THE TEST!

1. Your company, *Putting Around,* creates miniature golf courses. The diagram below shows the project design of one course.

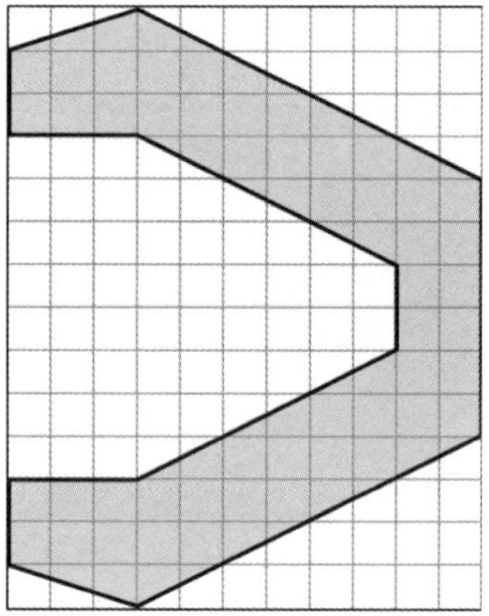

The diameter of the golf hole on a putting green is $4.25''$. The putting green will have 3 holes. How many square feet of turf will be needed to cover the putting green if one square represents 1.5 square feet? Justify your answer.

Section 11 – Topic 11
Geometric Design

A special case of geometry problems involves maximizing and minimizing.

For example:

- Maximizing or minimizing some dimensions, area, or volume
- Minimizing costs or maximizing profits

In what real world scenario do we need to maximize area or volume?

In what real world scenario do we need to minimize area or volume?

In what real world scenario do we need to minimize costs?

In what real world scenario do we need to maximize profits?

STUDY EDGE TIP

A quadratic function, $y = ax^2 + bx + c$, obtains it's maximum or minimum at $x = -\frac{b}{2a}$.

Let's Practice!

1. Coolmore Ashford Stud is a farm with one of the largest breeding operations of thoroughbred racehorses in the world. The director of operations of Coolmore Ashford needs to enclose a rectangular area for yearlings that have been purchased and are ready for pick-up.

   The director wants to find the largest possible area he can enclose with $2,400$ meters of fencing and he hires you to design the area.

   a. What is your equation for perimeter?

   b. What would be your area equation in terms of width?

   c. Once you have your area equation, how do you find the maximum area?

   d. What is the largest possible area that can be enclosed with $2,400$ meters of fencing?

   e. What are the dimensions of the enclosed rectangular pen that has the maximum possible area?

Try It!

2. It is little Alex's birthday party! Alex's parents plan to rent $1,600$ feet of fencing for a small petting zoo. They will form two paddocks with one shared fence running down the middle, one for donkeys and the other for goats. What is the maximum area that Alex's parents can obtain for the entire zoo? What are the dimensions of each paddock?

A ________________ __________ is a two-dimensional framework made up of a pattern of intersecting straight or curved lines.

This structure can be used to organize shapes in a logical manner.

The city of Oakland, California received a grant from the *Fédération Internationale de Football Association* (FIFA) to design and build a new soccer complex for local residents. A 700×400 feet rectangular tract of land is available in the city suburbs.

If each full-size soccer field measures 120×80 yards, then how many full-size soccer fields can fit in this site?

If each medium-size soccer field measures 60×40 yards, then how many medium size soccer fields can fit in this site?

Let's Practice!

3. The complex in Oakland, California, will contain two full-size soccer fields and a multipurpose building. The complex will meet the following specifications:

   - Each full-size soccer field must measure 120 by 80 yards.
   - Each field must be at least 60 feet from the boundaries of the tract.
   - At least 40 yards must separate each field.
   - The multipurpose building must be only one-story tall. It must be a trapezoid shape, and it must be at least 120 feet away from any of the fields.

   Sketch the design on the grid below, maximizing the size of the multipurpose building. The distance between gridlines is 60 feet.

BEAT THE TEST!

1. Using the following map, estimate the area of Lake Michigan. The distance between gridlines is 18 miles.

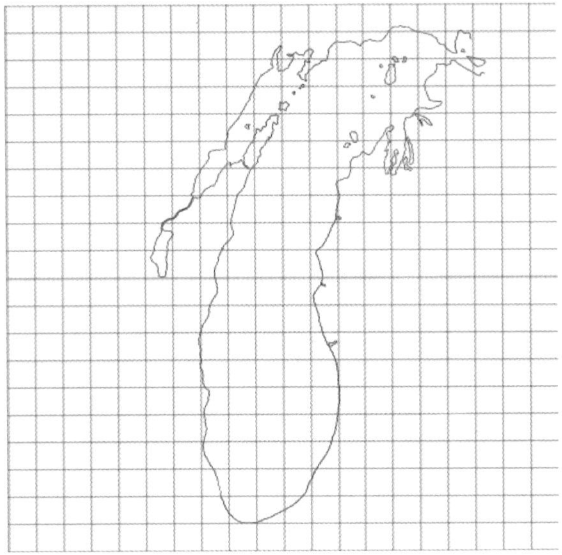

Which of the following is the *best* estimate of the area of the lake's surface?

Ⓐ $9{,}940 \text{ mi}^2$
Ⓑ $18{,}124 \text{ mi}^2$
Ⓒ $22{,}394 \text{ mi}^2$
Ⓓ $28{,}012 \text{ mi}^2$

2. The leaders of an afterschool program are creating a rectangular garden against the back of their building with a fence around it so that instructors can teach gardening principles to their students. They have only 120 feet of fencing available for the project.

What would the dimensions of the garden be if the builders attached one side of the fence to the building in order to make the area of the garden as large as possible?

Ⓐ 30×60 ft
Ⓑ 40×40 ft
Ⓒ 50×25 ft
Ⓓ 70×30 ft

Section 11 – Topic 12
Volume in Real-World Contexts

The company *SpaceY* is designing a commercial spherical spaceship and plans to start selling one-week trips to people who want to orbit around the Earth. *SpaceY* allocates 1,000 cubic feet per person, plus an additional 3,067.5 cubic feet for various necessary machinery. The diameter of the ship is 53.6 feet.

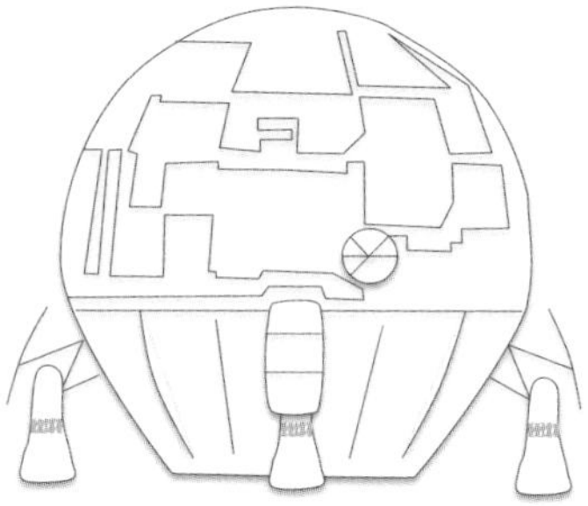

What is the maximum number of people who would be able to ride in the ship per trip?

A competitor, *Why Space?*, designs another spaceship, more accessible in terms of price, but smaller by a scale factor of $\frac{1}{3}$ with respect to the original dimensions.

What is the maximum number of people who would be able to ride in this ship?

Let's Practice!

1. At your local supermarket, there is a cylindrical sack full of rice with height of $20''$ and radius of $7''$.

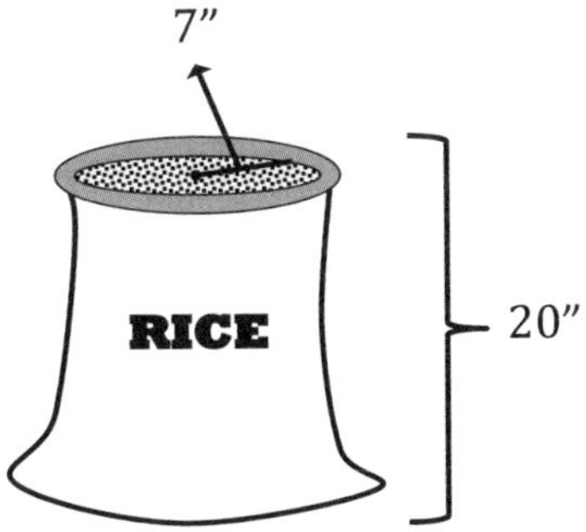

   a. If there are approximately 50 grains of rice in a cubic inch, then approximately how many grains of rice are in this sack?

   b. There is also a 2.5-kilogram bag of rice that is selling for the same price as the above cylindrical sack. If 64 grains of rice weigh 1 gram total, then is the cylinder sack or the bag of rice a better deal? Justify your answer.

Try It!

2. The local recreation center is building a new Olympic-size pool to be 164 feet long, 82 feet wide, and 12 feet deep.

   a. Approximately how much water will the pool hold?

   b. The excavated dirt for the pool described above will be hauled away by wheelbarrow and dumped into a truck. If the wheelbarrow holds 9 cubic feet of dirt, then how many wheelbarrows of dirt must be hauled away and dumped into the truck?

BEAT THE TEST!

1. Janitors at Strickland High School empty 25 full trash cans every day. The design of each trash can is shown below.

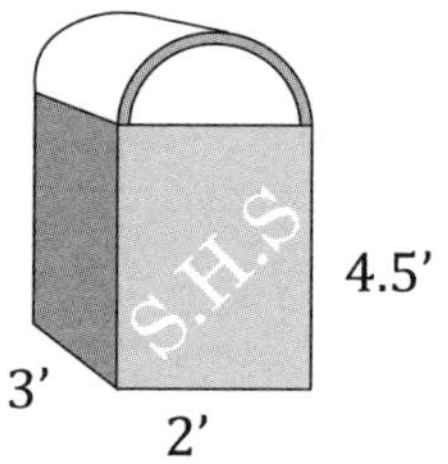

Based on the information and diagram above, what is the total volume of trash that the janitors empty every day?

[ ] ft^3

Section 11 – Topic 13
Density

What are some examples of density in the real-world?

Let's use geometry to understand density.

- Density is a ratio of two measurements of an object: __________ and ______________.
- The formula for density is ______________.

Density is used to calculate things like the mass and volume of metals, energy and British Thermal Units (BTUs), and food or liquids in different types of containers.

Let's Practice!

1. A group of friends are playing baseball with aluminum balls, each with a diameter of 7.26 centimeters. If aluminum has a density of 2.7 grams per cubic centimeters, what is the mass of each ball?

2. Homogenized milk has a density of $1.032\ \text{kg/L}$ and heavy cream has a density of $1.005\ \text{kg/L}$ at $10°\text{C}$. At $10°\text{C}$, a container holding 8 liters of liquid weighs 8.04 kilograms. Does the container hold homogenized milk or heavy cream? How do you know?

Try It!

3. An American Airlines policy states that carry-on luggage should not weigh more than 18.14 kilograms or have dimensions of more than $23 \times 36 \times 56$ centimeters, including handle and wheels. A passenger keeps track of the density of her bag, but she does not keep track of its mass. If the volume of her bag is $44{,}785$ cubic centimeters and density is 0.55 grams per cubic centimeter, then does her piece of luggage meet the criteria for American Airlines?

One of the most widely used density-related measures is the density of an area of land, such as a city.

This is determined by the ratio of the number of ____________ to area of land. This concept is called ____________________ __________________.

Let's Practice!

4. Use the table below to answer each of the following questions.

State	Population	Land Area (sq. mi.)
Florida	18,801,310	53,927
North Carolina	9,535,483	48,711
Georgia	9,687,653	57,906
Texas	25,145,561	261,797

a. Which state listed in the table has the greatest population density? Round your answer to the nearest person per square mile.

b. Explain why the population density of Georgia is lower than that of North Carolina despite Georgia's larger population and larger land area. How many more people does Georgia need in order to have a greater population density than North Carolina?

Try It!

5. The local theater has an area of 2,121 square feet. At the last banquet, the fire department surveyed the theater to make sure the event was not overcrowded. The fire department inspectors found the population density to be 0.1428 people per square foot. How many people attended the theater on that day? Justify your answer.

BEAT THE TEST!

1. Mr. De Leon's Geometry class has 34 students. After lunch everyone returns to the classroom. Within an hour, each person produces 800 BTUs of heat. The room is 25 feet by 32 feet by 12 feet. How many BTUs per cubic foot were produced?

   ☐ BTUs per cubic foot.

2. Consider the table below that lists some metals and their densities.

Metal	Density (g/cm^3)
Gold	19.32
Silver	10.50
Copper	8.96
Platinum	21.45
Bronze	9.87

A necklace found at a pawn shop is 192 grams and has a volume of 19.5 cubic centimeters. What metal is the necklace made of?

3. The density of gold is 19.32 grams per cubic centimeters. Jimmy Jackson built a pyramid made out of pure gold about 2.13 meters tall with a mass of 298.7 kilograms. If the base of the pyramid is a square, what are the dimensions of the base of the pyramid?

4. During an observational study, the same type of rabbit is raised in different zones. Zone A has a radius of 20 miles and has approximately $24{,}000$ rabbits after one year. Zone B has a radius of 36 miles and has approximately $75{,}000$ rabbits after one year. Determine and state which zone has the greater population density of rabbits at the end of the first year.

Section 11 – Topic 14
Similar Shapes

Consider the diagram of the two water bottles.

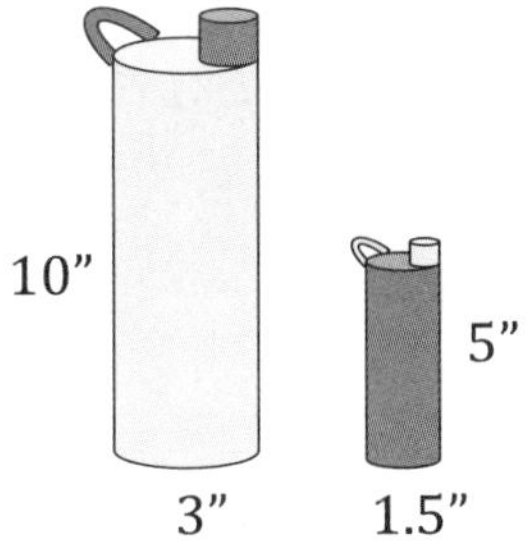

Are the two figures similar? How do you know?

What is the scale factor from the small bottle to the big bottle?

What is the ratio of the surface areas of the small bottle to the big bottle?

How does this ratio compare to the original scale factor?

What is the scale factor of the volumes from the small bottle to the big bottle?

How does this scale factor compare to the original scale factor?

When the dimensions of a solid increase by a factor of k, how does the surface area change? How does the volume change?

- Solids of the same type that have similar corresponding linear measures are ____________ solids.
- If two solids are similar, then the ratio of their surface areas is equal to the ________________ of the ratio of their corresponding linear measures.
- If two solids are similar, then the ratio of their volumes is equal to the _________ of the ratio of their corresponding linear measures.

Let's Practice!

1. Determine if a 14-inch wide square box is similar to a 19-inch long square box.

Try It!

2. The diagram below represents an NBA game basketball and a child's basketball.

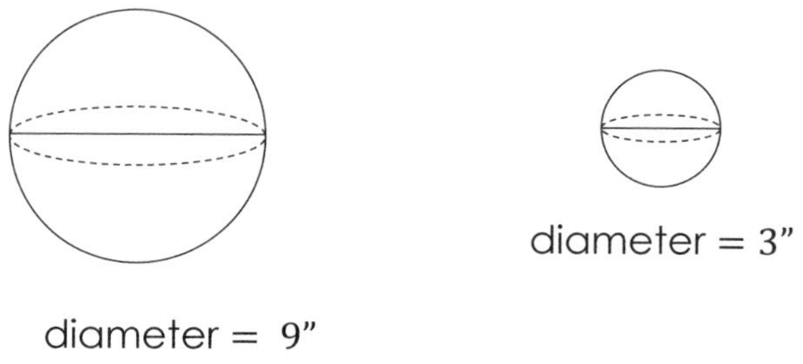

   a. Determine whether the basketballs above are similar.

   b. The volume of the NBA game ball is about how many times greater than the volume of the child's basketball?

Once we know two figures are similar in dimension with a ratio of similarity $\frac{a}{b}$, then we can use the measurements of one figure to determine the area and volume of another.

Let's Practice!

3. Consider the diagrams below. The surface area of Pyramid Y is $266.39\ \text{ft}^2$ and the two pyramids are similar. Determine the surface area of Pyramid X.

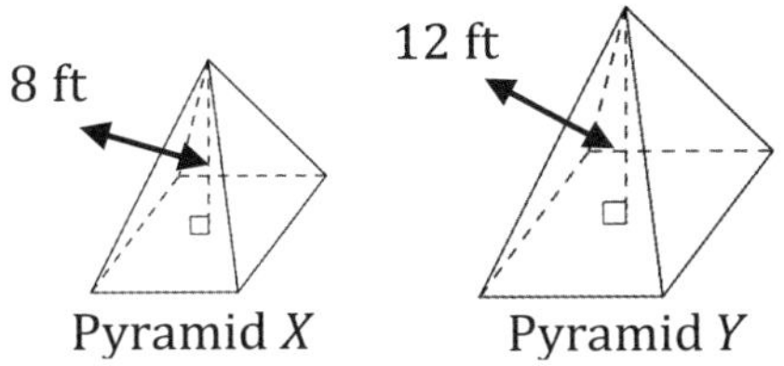

4. The boxes below are two similar solids. Find the value of the missing dimensions and support your answer.

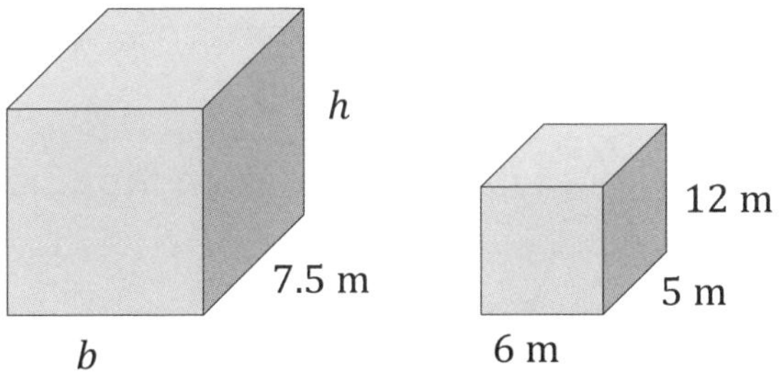

5. These are two similar packages. If the ratio of the areas is $25:36$, determine the height of the bigger package.

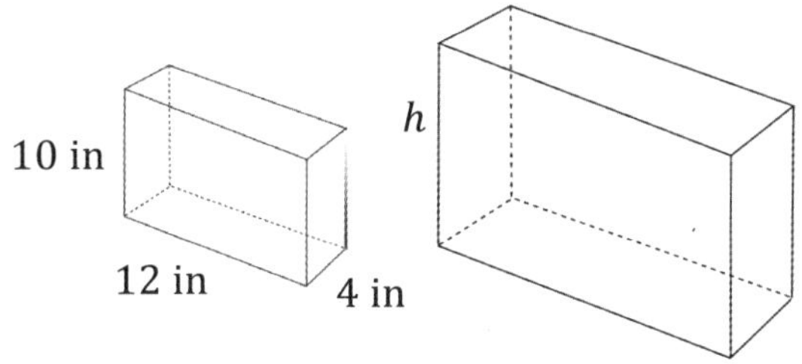

Try It!

6. Consider the diagrams below of two similar cones. Determine the volume of the smaller cone. Justify your answer.

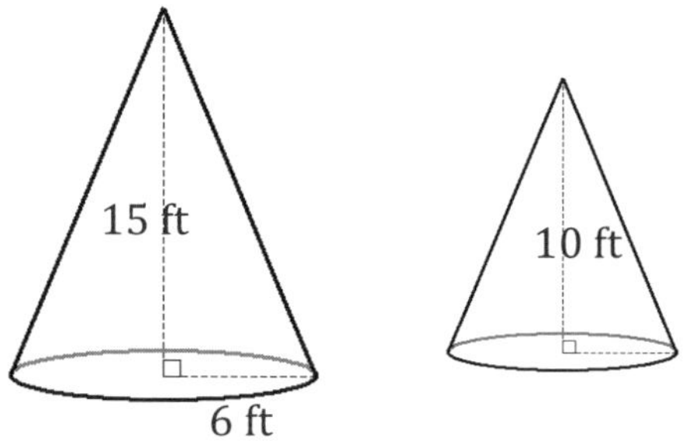

7. The ratio of the sides of two similar cubes is $4:3$. The smaller cube has a volume of 729 cubic inches. What is the volume of the larger cube?

BEAT THE TEST!

1. Sphere A and Sphere B are similar. The volumes of A and B are 17 and 136 cubic centimeters, respectively. The diameter of B is 6 centimeters. Determine the corresponding diameter of A.

   Ⓐ $\frac{1}{8}$

   Ⓑ $\frac{1}{2}$

   Ⓒ $\frac{2}{3}$

   Ⓓ 3

2. The ratio of the corresponding linear measures of two similar cans of beans is 4 to 7. If the smaller can has a surface area of 220 square centimeters, then determine the surface area of the larger can. Support your answer.

Test Yourself! Practice Tool

Great job! You have reached the end of this section. Now it's time to try the "Test Yourself! Practice Tool," where you can practice all the skills and concepts you learned in this section. Log in to Math Nation and try out the "Test Yourself! Practice Tool" so you can see how well you know these topics!

Index: Where Each Standard is Covered in Math Nation – Geometry

G-GPE.4:	Section 1 - Topic 10; Section 8 - Topics 2, 3, 11, and 12
G-GPE.5:	Section 1 - Topics 8 and 9; Section 6 - Topic 6
G-GPE.6:	Section 1 - Topics 4, 6, and 7
G-GPE.7:	Section 1 - Topics 5 and 10; Section 5 - Topic 3
G-MG.1:	Section 7 - Topic 12; Section 11 - Topics 2, 6, 8, 10, and 14
G-MG.2:	Section 11 - Topic 3
G-MG.3:	Section 11 - Topics 5, 9, 10, 11, and 12
G-SRT.1:	Section 4 – Topics 1, 2, and 3
G-SRT.2:	Section 4 - Topic 7; Section 6 - Topic 2
G-SRT.3:	Section 6 - Topic 1
G-SRT.4:	Section 5 - Topic 8; Section 7 - Topic 1
G-SRT.5:	Section 5 - Topics 4, 5, 6, 7, and 10; Section 6 - Topics 1 and 2; Section 7 - Topics 3, 6, and 7
G-SRT.6:	Section 7 - Topic 8
G-SRT.7:	Section 7 - Topics 8
G-SRT.8:	Section 7 - Topics 1, 2, 4, 5, 9, 10, and 11